PRINCETON ILLUSTRATED CHECKLISTS

Birds of Eastern Africa, by Ber van Perlo
Birds of Southern Africa, by Ber van Perlo
Birds of Southern South America and Antarctica, by Martín R. de la Peña and Maurice Rumboll
Birds of Western and Central Africa, by Ber van Perlo
Birds of Mexico and Central America, by Ber van Perlo
Birds of South America: Non-Passerines: Rheas to Woodpeckers, by Francisco Erize, Jorge R. Rodriguez Mata, and Maurice Rumboll

TO CEES

Published in the United States, Canada, and the Philippine Islands by
Princeton University Press
41 William Street, Princeton, New Jersey 08540

Originally published in English by HarperCollins Publishers Ltd under the title:

COLLINS FIELD GUIDE: BIRDS OF MEXICO AND CENTRAL AMERICA
Copyright © Ber van Perlo, 2006

Library of Congress Control Number 2004100190

ISBN-13: 978-0-691-12070-6
ISBN-10: 0-691-12070-6

This book has been composed in Goudy

nathist.princeton.edu

Color reproduction by Colourscan, Singapore
Printed and bound in Hong Kong by IMAGO

1 3 5 7 9 10 8 6 4 2

PRINCETON ILLUSTRATED CHECKLISTS

BIRDS

OF MEXICO AND CENTRAL AMERICA

Written and illustrated by
BER VAN PERLO

Princeton University Press
Princeton and Oxford

ACKNOWLEDGEMENTS

This book is made with the help of Cees, my brother, whose computer skills are indispensable for a work like this. I am also very grateful to Brian Gee, who supplied photos of museum specimens of hundreds of species and contributed the voice descriptions of over a hundred species. Special thanks are due to Paul Wood for his contributions to the distribution maps and useful suggestions for the text. In addition I am indebted to David E. Wolf for his comments on the text and maps.

Ber van Perlo
Rotterdam
The Netherlands

CONTENTS

Page

Introduction   8
Parts of a bird   19
The Plates   20

Plate

Seabirds: albatrosses, fulmars, petrel, shearwater   1
Seabirds: petrels   2
Seabirds: shearwaters, petrel   3
Seabirds: storm-petrels   4
Seabirds: tropicbirds, boobies, gannet, frigatebirds   5
Sea- and waterbirds: murrelets, puffins, loons, penguin   6
Grebes, gallinules, coots, sungrebe, sunbittern   7
Pelicans, cormorants, anhinga   8
Bitterns, egrets, herons   9
Egrets, herons, ibises, limpkin, spoonbill, jabiru, wood stork, flamingo, cranes   10
Swans, geese, mergansers, ducks   11
Ducks   12
Ducks   13
Vultures, osprey, eagle   14
Kites, hawks   15
Kites, harriers   16
Hawks   17
Eagle, hawks   18
Hawks, buzzard   19
Eagles, hawk eagles   20
Caracaras, forest falcons   21
Falcons   22
Chachalacas, guans, curassow, turkeys, rails   23
Rails, crakes, wood partridges   24
Quails, bobwhites, tinamous   25
Thicknee, plovers, oystercatchers, stilt, curlews, avocet, jacanas   26
Yellowlegs, willet, tattler, sandpipers, plovers   27
Godwits, sandpiper, ruff, dowitchers, snipes, phalaropes, turnstones, surfbird   28
Sandpipers   29
Jaegers, skuas, gulls   30
Gulls   31
Gulls   32
Terns   33
Terns, skimmer   34
Pigeons, quail doves   35
Doves, ground doves   36
Parakeets, parrotlets, parrots   37
Macaws, parrots   38
Cuckoos, roadrunners, anis   39
Owls   40
Owls   41

Potoos, oilbird, nightjar, nighthawks, pauraque, poorwills 42
Poorwills, nightjars 43
Swifts 44
Hummingbirds: hermits, sicklebill, sabrewings, jacobin, mangos 45
Hummingbirds: topaz, coquettes, thorntail, emeralds, lancebill 46
Hummingbirds: woodnymphs, hummingbirds, sapphires, snowcap 47
Hummingbirds: emeralds, hummingbirds 48
Hummingbirds: brilliant, violet-ears, mountain gems, plumeleteers, fairy, puffleg, starthroats 49
Hummingbirds: woodstars, sheartails, hummingbirds 50
Quetzals, trogons, jacamars 51
Motmots, kingfishers, puffbirds 52
Barbets, nunbird, nunlet, monklet, toucanets, toucans, woodpeckers 53
Woodpeckers 54
Woodpeckers 55
Woodpeckers: flickers, sapsuckers, woodpeckers 56
Woodcreepers 57
Woodcreepers, piculet, xenops, tuftedcheek, treehunter, treerunners, leaftossers 58
Spinetails, foliage gleaners, greytail, antvireos, tapaculos 59
Antshrikes, antwrens 60
Antbirds, antthrushes, antpittas 61
Flycatchers: kiskadees, flycatchers, kingbirds, cattle tyrant 62
Flycatchers: pewees, flycatchers, attila 63
Flycatchers: tyrranulets, flycatchers 64
Flycatchers: elaenias, pygmy tyrants, flycatcher, bentbills, tody flycatchers, spadebills 65
Flycatchers 66
Flycatchers: phoebes, tyrants, flatbills, kingbirds, twistwing, tyrannulet 67
Schiffornis, piha, mourners, sapayoa, piprites, manakins 68
Becards, cotingas, tityras, fruitcrow, umbrellabird, bellbird 69
Swallows, martins 70
Jays 71
Jays, nutcracker, crows, raven 72
Chickadees, tits, nuthatches, creeper, lark, wagtails, pipits 73
Wrens 74
Wrens 75
Wrens, silky-flycatchers, waxwing, peppershrike, shrikes, donacobius, starling, dipper 76
Warblers, kinglets, gnatwrens, gnatcatchers, greenlets, shrike vireos 77
Vireos 78
Catbirds, mockingbirds, thrashers 79
Solitaires, thrushes 80
Wheatear, bluebirds, thrushes 81
Wood warblers 82
Wood warblers 83
Wood warblers, whitestarts, redstart 84
Wood warblers, wrenthrush, ovenbird, waterthrushes 85
Bananaquit, conebill, dacnises, honeycreepers, tanagers 86
Chlorophonias, euphonias, tanagers 87

Tanagers   88
Tanagers   89
Saltators, grosbeaks, pyrrhuloxia, cardinal, bunting   90
Buntings, dicksissel, finches, brushfinches, ground sparrows   91
Sparrows, towhees, seedeaters, seedfinches, grassquit   92
Finches, grassquit, flowerpiercers, sparrows   93
Sparrows   94
Grass finch, bunting, sparrows, juncos, longspurs   95
Meadowlarks, blackbirds, grackles, cowbirds, oropendolas   96
Orioles, caciques   97
Bobolink, blackbirds, finches, siskins, grosbeaks, goldfinches, crossbill,
house sparrow   98

Page

Distribution maps   231
Bibliography and list of further reading   308
Indexes of scientific, Spanish and English names   309

INTRODUCTION

AREA AND SPECIES COVERED

This list is compiled to the best of my knowledge and based on as many sources as possible, including the American Ornithologists' Union (AOU) *Check-list of North American Birds*, checked and updated by the lists given on the website **www.bsc-eoc.org/links/checklist** and other websites, the available field guides for the area, and data up to the spring of 2003 in *Cotinga*, which is the magazine of the Neotropical Bird Club.

This book mentions all bird species in Mexico, Belize, Guatemala, Honduras, El Salvador, Nicaragua, Costa Rica, Panama and the adjacent parts of the Gulf of Mexico, the Caribbean Sea and the Pacific Ocean. See political map (opposite). It gives illustrations, keynotes for identification, basic information about habitat, distribution maps for all species and vocalisations for many.

SEQUENCE OF FAMILIES AND SPECIES

The sequence of families and species followed in this book is generally the traditional order as in most other bird books. In many cases, however, birds of similar habitats (sea birds), size (small quails and crakes) or visual similarity (e.g. grey kingbirds and other greyish birds on plate 67) are grouped together, which might make it harder for some people, familiar with the correct systematic sequence, to find them. See also, for instance, plate 7 where the swimming moorhen and coot (who systematically are rails, plates 23 and 24) are placed together with the grebes.

NOMENCLATURE

The scientific and English names in this guide follow the AOU (1998 *Check-list* and subsequent updates). Spanish names are those used in other field guides for the region. Species on each plate have their own number, caption and map; races that are distinguishable in the field are treated in the caption of the species they belong to and are indicated by letters (a, b, c, etc.) on the plates and maps. However, there are a few races, especially among the hummingbirds, that are treated as full species in Howell and Webb (see Bibliography), but not so by the AOU; these have their own number, map and place on the plates, but keep their names as determined by the AOU. See, for instance, 45.4 (*Phaethornis longirostris*, comprising a group of races) and 45.5 (*Phaethornis l. mexicanus*).

Sometimes the species' or subspecies' status is still uncertain. In such cases there is an entry in the text as (?/3), indicating that the bird might be a subspecies of the species treated under 3 on that plate. In this guide the term 'race' is used for 'subspecies' for its shortness.

The scientific name of a species is composed of two parts: the first refers to the genus, in which similar species are placed together, and the second part defines the specific species.

For example, there is a group of birds called yellowthroats belonging to the genus *Geothlypis*. The addition *trichas* (together *Geothlypis trichas*) refers to the 'Common Yellowthroat', as seen in the field. After it became clear that this species has different races, the first race ever described was given a name composed of three parts, *Geothlypis trichas trichas*. This is the 'nominate' form, abbreviated in this book to 'Nom'. Other races are the yellow-crowned *Geothlypis trichas chapalensis* and the yellow-bellied *Geothlypis trichas chryseola* (see plate 84).

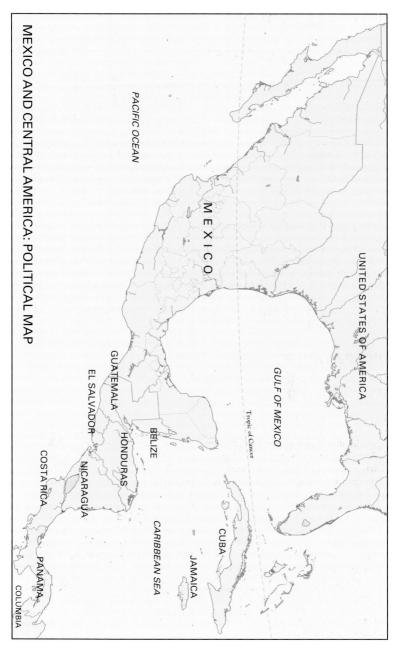

MEXICO AND CENTRAL AMERICA: POLITICAL MAP

PACIFIC OCEAN

M E X I C O

UNITED STATES OF AMERICA

GUATEMALA

EL SALVADOR

BELIZE

HONDURAS

COSTA RICA

NICARAGUA

PANAMA

COLUMBIA

GULF OF MEXICO

Tropic of Cancer

CARIBBEAN SEA

CUBA

JAMAICA

9

However, no such generally accepted system exists for English names. In this book the English names used are those that are most frequent in the consulted literature. Where there are differences, I follow the preference of the Neotropical Bird Club by using the name in Sibley and Monroe (1990 and 1993; see Bibliography). This name is given in bold capitals. Alternative names are added in lower case between brackets. In the names hyphens are used sparingly (mainly between adjectives and their modifiers, e.g. 'black-collared').

In most cases preference is given to accepted American names; for instance 'Hawk' is used for most members of the genus *Buteo* (called 'Buzzards' in the Old World), 'Jaeger' (not 'Skua') for the genus *Stercorarius* and 'Loon' (not 'Diver') for the genus *Gavia*. Sometimes, however, Old World names have been applied, such as 'Thrush' for members of the genus *Turdus*, instead of 'Robin' (except the well-known 'American Robin'). In very few cases an alternative is introduced, based on a proposal found in the literature: for instance the redstarts 84.16, 17 and 18 are named 'whitestarts' after the colour in their tails ('start' or rather 'staart' means 'tail' in Dutch).

SPANISH NAMES

There are many different (local) Spanish names in use. This book tries to give those mainly used in Mexico and Costa Rica. In many cases alternative Spanish names, found on websites or elsewhere, are added.

As in English, but in reverse order, most Spanish names consist of two words: the first is a general group name (e.g. Albatros), the second a specifying adjective (e.g. Patinegro, Black-footed). In the text the Spanish names are put between brackets. If group name and adjective used in Mexico and Costa Rica are different, both full names are given, separated by a semicolon (e.g. Anhinga Americana; Pato Aguja); if group name or adjective differs, they are separated by a slash (e.g. Gallineta/Gallareta Morada or Pardela Gris/Sombría). In the Spanish index all variants can be found.

IDENTIFICATION

Identification of a bird is based upon how it looks (jizz, appearance), together with what it does (habits), where we see it (habitat), the chance or probability that we see it there (occurrence) and the sounds it makes (voice).

JIZZ

What birders call 'jizz' is a difficult-to-define combination of size, relative proportions and body carriage of a bird. Part of a bird's jizz can be its stance (the angle of its body to the flat earth or to a horizontal perch).

APPEARANCE

Each species is illustrated as an adult male in breeding plumage. Other plumages are added when different, in which case the female is normally shown behind the male, in a more horizontal position. The symbols, abbreviations and other indications used in the text and on the plates are as follows:

SYMBOL	EXPLANATION
♂	male
♀	female
Ad	adult
Imm	immature
br	breeding plumage
n-br	non-breeding (or winter) plumage

Many species have a breeding and a non-breeding plumage, most of which are shown.

Every bird that has not attained full adult plumage is called an 'immature' (abbreviated to 'Imm' in this book). In a few cases, however, it was necessary to differentiate further, as follows:

ABBREVIATION	EXPLANATION
Imm	any bird that has not yet attained full adult plumage
Juv	an immature in its first plumage following the natal down
1stW or 1stS	an immature in the first winter or summer after hatching
2dW or 2dS	an immature in the second winter or summer after hatching
sub-adult	an immature in its last plumage before moulting to full adult plumage

Some species have similar-looking races, as well as one or more that is more distinct. Only races that are recognisable in the field are illustrated and marked (as a, b, c, etc.) on the plates, mentioned in the text and indicated on the maps.

A 'colour form' is not a race, but a variation of the normal plumage. These forms are represented on the plates when there is a chance of seeing them, for instance where at least 5–15% of the total population of a species is coloured differently in some way.

The text opposite the plates gives information about size, main characteristics and differences between similar species. Size is given in centimetres. For most species, this is the total length from tip of bill to end of tail (L); extra length for tail streamers is in most cases added in brackets, e.g. L 12 (+5) cm. For raptors/seabirds the size is given as wingspan (W).

Because measuring birds is difficult, size data in the literature are not uniform. For this reason sizes above 20 cm are often given in multiples of 5 cm. This enables the user to compare the size of a bird he/she wants to identify with the size of other birds.

Full descriptions of feathering and bare parts are not given because the plates contain sufficient information on these areas. Only when these are the most essential features or when they are not visible on the plate are they mentioned.

HABITS

Information about habits – though an important identification tool – is relatively sparse in order to keep the book at an optimal size.

HABITAT

Geography

The earth's crust is divided into about 13 plates of different sizes; they move slowly in relation to each other, separating, rubbing along or overrunning each other. Mexico and Central America occupy an area where these processes are very active.

From ridges in the ocean floor, where the plates are formed, they float in the direction of the landmasses; in our area the lighter oceanic Cocos Plate dives under the North American and Caribbean Plates. In doing so the top layer of the oceanic plate is stripped from the bottom layer and rubbed up on top of the continental plates as the mountain chains that run through the area. The combined weight of the plates exercises so much pressure that the magma in the interior of the earth seeks to escape via cracks and vents to the surface. A long row of active volcanoes through the area is the result.

The rubbing of plates along (but also over) each other is not a smooth process; like the teeth of saws they grip each other until the mounting pressure gets too high; then with a sudden movement they shoot along each other. This process is very evident along the west coast of North America, but also in Central America, where the resulting earthquakes are an all too well-known phenomenon.

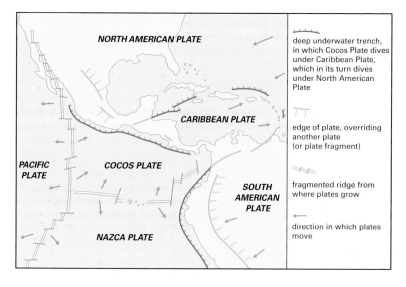

Altitude

The landscape of Mexico and Central America is dominated by a system of sierras (mountain ranges) running through the centre and separating two coastal plains (Pacific and Caribbean) of varying width. At some points these ranges are so low that the wildlife of both coastal plains is in touch with each other. Normally the mountains are so high that there is a noticeable difference between the bird faunas of the plains on each side. The mountain chain in Mexico is split into a Pacific and a Caribbean branch, encircling some high plateaus. Especially in Central America three altitudinal zones can be distinguished: (1) Tierre caliente, the hot zone with banana plantations, from sea level ('sl' in the text) to 900 m; (2) Tierra templada, the agreeable zone, where it is still warm enough to grow coffee, from 900 m to 1800 m, (3) Tierra fría, the cool zone, where it might even snow occasionally, above 2000–3000 m. The whole system of sierras, plateaus and planes is the base for different habitats, and each of these has its own wildlife, often with its own endemic species (see 'Endemism', page 17).

Vegetation

The vegetation is the result of the interaction between soil, water supply, altitude and climate. The prevailing wind in the area (part of the system of tradewinds) comes from the northeast. Between the Tropics the sun directly overhead warms the earth's surface; the air on top is heated and on rising takes moisture from the sea surface into the atmosphere. As a result of the earth's rotation, this moist air moves west or – more specifically – southwest on the northern side of the equator (and northwest to the south of it). Above land the moisture condenses in the form of rain and thunderstorms. The mountain chains through the middle block this rain for much of the year, so that it rains less in the Pacific lowlands. Only occasionally, especially in September–October under the influence of tropical low-pressure areas in the Caribbean region, can moist air from the Pacific Ocean come in, falling as rain on the western flanks.

In Central America the dry period between November and April is called verano (summer), while the wet period from April until November is called invierno (winter). In this book, however, 'winter' refers to the northern period October–March.

In Mexico the climate is greatly influenced by the cold California Ocean Current. The low evaporation from this current, combined with the size of the great inland landmasses and the height of the mountain chains (which prevent moisture from penetrating from the Gulf of Mexico), results in the semi-desert conditions of northwest Mexico.

Outside these semi-desert conditions most of Mexico and Central America was once covered by forest. Human occupation and cultivation transformed the parts of the landscape that were not too steep or too wet into a small-scale mosaic of fields, meadows, hedges and forest remains. Recent development has introduced large-scale plantations (e.g. bananas and pineapples) and the area of ranchland has been extended to areas where it was not found before. The forest is driven back, especially to the steeper slopes and to the hot, wet areas, where agriculture (still) is not possible. Many types of forest, however, still exist, from the rain forests with their lianas, epiphytes and – in the understorey – palms, in the hottest lowest places between sea level and 1000 m (depending on the amount and frequency of rain) to the montane oak forests (mixed with pine in Mexico) at elevations between 2000 and 3000 m. In between there is a wide range of other forest types; depending on the amount of rain and its distribution through the seasons, deciduous forest with a dense tangled understorey grows on drier slopes between sea level (Pacific coast) and 2000 m, while on wetter slopes a type of forest grows which is often described as 'cloud forest'. This forest, characterised by a rich growth of moss, epiphytes and tree ferns, is found at elevations where ascending hot moist air condenses, forming fog almost every day. At higher altitudes, where ever-present strong winds reduce the height to which trees can grow to about 5 m, cloud forest becomes 'Elfin Forest'.

Gallery forest, not indicated on the vegetation map (overleaf), is forest growing along streams and rivers in otherwise open, often dry country. The habitats at the Pacific and Caribbean sea sides are generally very different; the Caribbean Sea is warmer and does not have tides of any significance; coral reefs and mangrove are more abundant here.

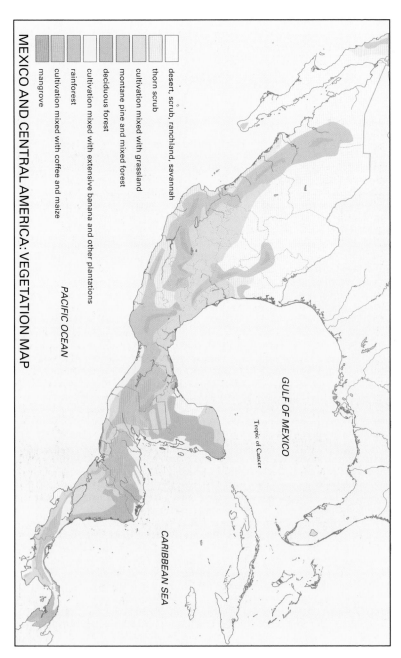

MEXICO AND CENTRAL AMERICA: VEGETATION MAP

desert, scrub, ranchland, savannah

thorn scrub

cultivation mixed with grassland

montane pine and mixed forest

deciduous forest

cultivation mixed with extensive banana and other plantations

rainforest

cultivation mixed with coffee and maize

mangrove

PACIFIC OCEAN

GULF OF MEXICO

Tropic of Cancer

CARIBBEAN SEA

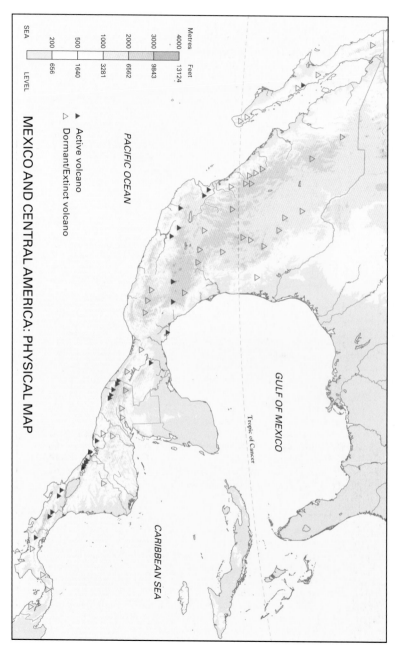

MEXICO AND CENTRAL AMERICA: PHYSICAL MAP

Metres	Feet
4000	13124
3000	9843
2000	6562
1000	3281
500	1640
200	656
SEA	LEVEL

▲ Active volcano
△ Dormant/Extinct volcano

PACIFIC OCEAN

GULF OF MEXICO

Tropic of Cancer

CARIBBEAN SEA

OCCURRENCE

Range, status and season determine the possibility of seeing a species in a certain area. This information can be found on the Distribution maps (after the plates). The shaded areas are an indication of the range of a species. The presence of most migrants depends on the northern seasons, but beware that individual birds may stay behind when all other members of that species return to their breeding grounds, for instance in North America.

Range

The maps give the range of the species. However, the very small scale of the maps and the differences in accuracy of the available information about distribution make it possible only to give an indication of where a certain species might be seen. In the text, basic information about the range of a species is given by adding the following abbreviations to the caption:

Thr   throughout the area

WSpr widespread, occurring in at least 7 countries in the area, including Mexico

Pac   Pacific Ocean

Car   Caribbean Sea

Me   occurring only in Mexico: NMe, SMe, YMe (North, South, Yucatan Mexico)

CAm occurring in at least 3 countries of Central America:
       Be (Belize), Gu (Guatemala), Sa (El Salvador), Ho (Honduras), Ni (Nicaragua),
       CR(Costa Rica), Pa (Panama)

Status

Each map also contains information about the status of a species. However, due to the scale of the maps, it was not possible to differentiate very much, so that local occurrence might deviate from the indication on the maps. See also the introduction to the maps, directly following plate 98. In the main text information about status is given (when appropriate) as:

U (uncommon to rare),

V (vagrant) and

Hyp (hypothetical: presence/sighting not sufficiently substantiated).

A species is uncommon when its range is very restricted or its total population very small. A vagrant lives in other parts of the world, reaches the region only by accident and hence has been seen less than about five times. A question mark (?) in the text and on the maps means that occurrence of the species in the area is insufficiently substantiated. In a few cases the symbol (I) is used for introduced species.

Season

The presence of a species in its indicated range depends in many cases on the seasonal rhythm in the Americas. Roughly speaking, birds can be divided into 'residents' and 'migrants'. In this book residents are species that are present in a certain area the whole year through; part of the year, however, there are also species present which only come to breed, and disperse to other areas outside the breeding season, or which breed elsewhere but come in to escape from temporarily unfavourable conditions (winter or drought) in their breeding quarters. Often birds, especially first-summer individuals, may stay behind and can be encountered in summer time in their winter quarters, when the main body of the species has returned to its breeding grounds.

Endemism

This is a fascinating phenomenon. An endemic is a species that occurs only in an area with well-defined boundaries like a continent, a country, an island or a habitat. Mexico and Central America have many bird species, perhaps more than a third of the total, endemic to the region. In this book the endemic birds of countries are marked E at the end of the relevant caption.

Bird waves

Especially in forest and woodland it pays to look around for 'bird waves'. Suddenly you see one or two birds and, waiting patiently, you discover more and more birds of several, sometimes many species, who wander together through all layers of the vegetation.

VOICE

Information about calls and/or song is given for many birds. Note, however, that the whole vocabulary could not be given and that voice examples could not be found for every species. The reason for this has been that the main sources for 'voice' have been tapes and CDs with bird vocalisations; no use has been made of annotations written down by other authors, who may hear and describe bird calls and songs differently. There is one exception, in the case of the voice descriptions of about hundred species indicated by an asterisk after 'voice*' (see Acknowledgements).

When in the vocalisations a distinction has been made between calls and song, the annotations are separated by a semicolon. Many migrants (e.g. most wood warblers) do not sing in their winter quarters and in these cases normally only the call is indicated. The most striking sound has been given as a transcription in italics. This is a hazardous endeavour because these transcriptions may well look confusing and even funny; reading them to each other when relaxing in your hotel or lodge can contribute to the merriment. However, if the reader can overcome his/her embarrassment and tries to pronounce the transcriptions in the given speed and pitch, he/she might have found another tool to confirm an identification, which is the only reason they are included.

Attention has been paid to pitch, loudness, sound quality, length and structure. General pitch has been given on a rough subjective scale:

DESCRIPTION	EXPLANATION
Ultra low	As low as you can imagine (e.g. American Bittern)
Very low	(e.g. Feral Pigeon)
Low	Pitch of an average man's voice (e.g. Great Horned Owl)
High	Pitch of an average woman's voice (e.g. Oystercatcher)
Very high	(e.g. Meadowlark)
Ultra high	So high that the sound is just within human hearing range (ear-reach) (e.g. Golden-crowned Kinglet or Blackpoll Warbler)

LOUDNESS is generally indicated by general terms such as soft, loud and crescendo.

SOUND QUALITY has been described in terms like shrieking, thin, liquid, etc. Often songs and calls are compared to those of other birds like magpies or canaries or to the mewing of a domestic cat.

LENGTH: if a transcription ends on '--' or '- -'the call or song goes on with at least three similar notes, syllables or phrases; (3s) means that the full strophe takes 3 seconds, (3/5s) that the phrases or syllables are repeated 3 times per 5 seconds and (5 x) that the sound is repeated 5 times.

STRUCTURE: the way in which notes follow each other is described in terms like accelerated, staccato and unstructured, and by the way the parts of a transcription are connected. For instance, in '*treet treet treet*' each syllable is well separated, '*treet-treet-treet*' sounds as one 'word' and '*treettreettreet*' as almost a trill.

The stressed (often higher-pitched) syllables in a phrase are indicated by an accent on the vowel.

A strophe is a recognisable complete part of a bird's repertoire that can be dissected successively into phrases, syllables and notes. Strophes can, however, be as short as one note.

A special feature of the song and/or call of many bird species is that it is given in duet. This means that two birds (normally a female and a male) produce sounds that might follow each other so closely or are interwoven so harmoniously that the resulting song or call sounds as though it is from a single bird.

ABBREVIATIONS:

U	Uncommon to rare	sl	Sea level
V	Vagrant	Thr	Throughout the area
Hyp	Hypothetical	WSpr	Widespread, occurring in at least
E	Endemic		7 countries in the area, including
I	Introduced		Mexico
♂	Male	Pac	Pacific Ocean
♀	Female	Car	Caribbean Sea
Ad	Adult	Me	Mexico
Imm	Immature	NMe	North Mexico
Juv	Juvenile	SMe	South Mexico
br	Breeding	YMe	Yucatan (Mexico)
n-br	Non-breeding	CAm	Central America occurring in at least
L	Length		3 countries
W	Wingspan/Northern Winter	Be	Belize
S	Northern Summer	Gu	Guatemala
1stW	First Winter (plumage)	Sa	El Salvador
2dW	Second Winter (plumage)	Ho	Honduras
1stS	First Summer (plumage)	Ni	Nicaragua
2dS	Second Summer (plumage)	CR	Costa Rica
Nom	Nominate	Pa	Panama

PARTS OF A BIRD

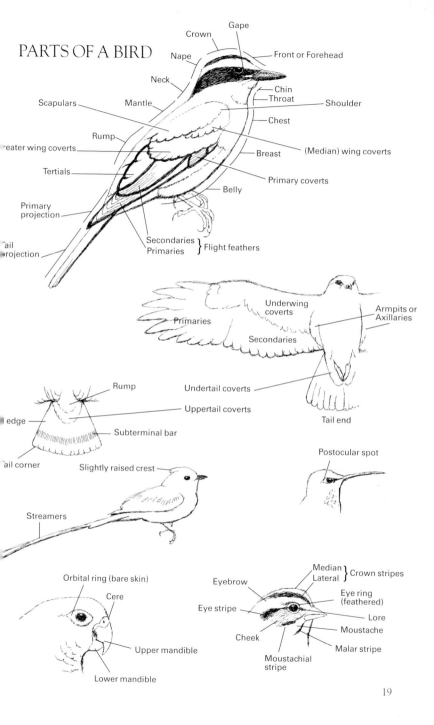

Crown
Gape
Nape
Front or Forehead
Neck
Chin
Throat
Shoulder
Scapulars
Mantle
Chest
Rump
(Median) wing coverts
eater wing coverts
Breast
Tertials
Primary coverts
Primary projection
Belly
ail rojection
Secondaries
Primaries
Flight feathers

Underwing coverts
Armpits or Axillaries
Primaries
Secondaries

Rump
Undertail coverts
Uppertail coverts
edge
Subterminal bar
ail corner
Tail end

Postocular spot

Slightly raised crest

Streamers

Orbital ring (bare skin)
Cere
Upper mandible
Lower mandible

Median
Lateral
Crown stripes
Eyebrow
Eye ring (feathered)
Eye stripe
Lore
Moustache
Cheek
Malar stripe
Moustachial stripe

19

Plate 1

1   SHORT-TAILED ALBATROSS *Diomedea albatrus* (Albatros Rabón)   W 225 cm. Note pink bill, pink feet and black tail. Habitat: offshore. V,Pac.

2   BLACK-FOOTED ALBATROSS *Diomedea nigripes* (Albatros Patinegro)   W 200 cm. Note pale brown rump, black feet, blackish tip to bill. Habitat: offshore. Pac.

3   WANDERING ALBATROSS *Diomedea exulans* (Albatros Viajero)   W 330 cm. Very large; full-grown adult with white tail. Habitat: offshore. V,Pa.

4   WAVED ALBATROSS *Diomedea irrorata* (Albatros de las Galápagos)   W 235 cm. Note white head with yellow bill. Habitat: offshore. V,Pa.

5   GREY-HEADED ALBATROSS *Diomedea chrysostema* (Albatros Cabecigrís)   W 200 cm. Note grey head and black sides to yellow bill. Habitat: offshore. Hyp,Pa.

6   LAYSAN ALBATROSS *Diomedea immutabilis* (Albatros de Laysan)   W 200 cm. Combination of dark brown upperwings with pink feet and bill diagnostic. Habitat: offshore, except near breeding sides. U,Pac.

7   NORTHERN FULMAR *Fulmarus glacialis* (Fulmar Norteño)   W 110 cm. Dark (a) and pale (b) forms shown. Stocky build. From 8 by grey tail. Note white patch on inner primaries. Habitat: offshore.

8   SOUTHERN FULMAR *Fulmarus glacialoides* (Fulmar Austral)   W 115 cm. Similar to 7, but with white tail. Habitat: offshore. Hyp,Pac.

9   BLACK (or Parkinson's) PETREL *Procellaria parkinsoni* (Petrel de Parkinson)   W 115 cm. All black, including chin. Habitat: offshore. U,Pac.

10   CORY'S SHEARWATER *Calonectris diomedea* (Pardela de Cory)   W 115 cm. Note yellowish, dark-ringed bill and clean white underwing, From 3.3 by uniform-coloured crown, neck and back. Habitat: offshore. V,Car.

Plate 1

Plate 2

1   **JUAN FERNANDEZ PETREL** *Pterodroma externa* (Petrel de Juan Fernandez)   W 95 cm. Note M mark across upperparts; from smaller 8–12 by white underwings and white bar across lower rump. (?/2) Habitat: offshore. Pac.

2   **WHITE-NECKED PETREL** *Pterodroma cervicalis* (Petrel Cuelliblanco)   W 100 cm. From 1 by white collar. Habitat: offshore. Hyp,Pac.

3   **DARK-RUMPED PETREL** *Pterodroma phaeopygia* (Petrel de Galápagos/Lomioscuro)   W 90 cm. Note dark sides of neck, forming a semi-collar. Underwing as 13, but with all-dark upperparts. Habitat: offshore. U,Pac.

4   **KERMADEC PETREL** *Pterodroma neglecta* (Petrel de Kermadec)   W 90 cm. Dark (a) and pale (b) forms shown. Much individual variation between dark and pale forms. White primary shafts (visible at close range) diagnostic. Habitat: offshore. U,Pac.

5   **HERALD PETREL** *Pterodroma arminjoniana* (Petrel Heráldico)   W 95 cm. Dark (a) and pale (b) forms shown. From very similar 4 by less white primary shafts. Habitat: offshore. U,Pac.

6   **MURPHY'S PETREL** *Pterodroma ultima* (Petrel de Murphy)   W 95 cm. As dark form of 5, but with whitish chin. Habitat: offshore. Hyp,Pac.

7   **TAHITI PETREL** *Pterodroma rostrata* (Petrel de Tahiti)   W 85 cm. Note contrasting white belly. Habitat: offshore. Pac.

8   **COOK'S PETREL** *Pterodroma cookii* (Petrel de Cook)   W 65 cm. Note uniform colouring from pale grey crown to mantle. Underside of wings inconspicuously marked. Habitat: offshore. Pac.

9   **BLACK-WINGED PETREL** *Pterodroma nigripennis* (Petrel Alinegro)   W 65 cm. Grey collar almost closed at throat. Strong underwing pattern but head concolorous with neck and mantle (unlike 11) and with white belly (unlike 10). Habitat: offshore. Hyp,Pac.

10   **MOTTLED PETREL** *Pterodroma inexpectata* (Petrel Moteado)   W 80 cm. Note grey belly and strong underwing pattern. Habitat: offshore. Hyp,Pac.

11   **STEJNEGER'S PETREL** *Pterodroma longirostris* (Petrel de Stejneger)   W 60 cm. Weak underwing pattern, crown darker than mantle. Habitat: offshore. V,Pac.

12   **WHITE-WINGED PETREL** *Pterodroma leucoptera* (Petrel de Gould)   W 70 cm. Crown contrasting with mantle; note conspicuous dark bar and margins to underwings. Habitat: offshore. Hyp,Pac.

13   **BLACK-CAPPED PETREL** *Pterodroma hasitata* (Petrel Gorrinegro)   W 95 cm. Note white collar and uppertail coverts. Habitat: offshore. V,Car.

14   **BULWER'S PETREL** *Bulweria bulwerii* (Petrel de Bulwer)   W 65 cm. Note long, narrow tail, small head, pale wing bar. Habitat: offshore. Hyp,Pac.

Plate 2

Plate 3

1 **PINK-FOOTED SHEARWATER** *Puffinus creatopus* (Pardela Patirrosada/Blanca Común)
W 110 cm. Pale underparts with pink legs and bill. Habitat: offshore, occasionally inshore. Pac.

2 **FLESH-FOOTED SHEARWATER** *Puffinus carneipes* (Pardela Patipalida) W 105 cm. All dark
with pink legs and black-tipped bill. Habitat: offshore, occasionally inshore. U,Pac.

3 **GREAT**(er) **SHEARWATER** *Puffinus gravis* (Pardela Mayor) W 110 cm. Note large body with
small head and black bill, dark undertail coverts and dark smudge on abdomen. Habitat: offshore.
V,Car.

4 **WEDGE-TAILED SHEARWATER** *Puffinus pacificus* (Pardela Colicuña) W 100 cm. Pale and
uncommon dark form shown. Note slender build, thin grey-brown bill and long pointed tail.
Habitat: offshore. U,Pac.

5 **BULLER'S SHEARWATER** *Puffinus bulleri* (Pardela de Buller) W 100 cm. Note black and grey
upperwing pattern. Habitat: offshore. U,Pac.

6 **SOOTY SHEARWATER** *Puffinus griseus* (Pardela Gris/Sombría) W 100 cm. Slender with
silvery underwings. Habitat: offshore, occasionally inshore. Pac(Car).

7 **SHORT-TAILED SHEARWATER** *Puffinus tenuirostris* (Pardela Colicorta) W 100 cm. From 6
by smaller bill and more rounded head. Habitat: offshore. U,Pac.

8 **CHRISTMAS SHEARWATER** *Puffinus nativitatus* (Pardela Pardo) W 75 cm. Overall very
dark, but underwings may show white reflections. Longer-billed and longer-tailed than other all-
dark sea birds. Habitat: offshore. U,Pac.

9 **BLACK-VENTED SHEARWATER** *Puffinus opisthomelas* (Pardela Mexicana) W 80 cm. As 1,
but smaller and less soaring, flying fast, close to the surface. Habitat: offshore and inshore. Pac.

10 **MANX SHEARWATER** *Puffinus puffinus* (Pardela Manx) W 80 cm. From 12 by different rump
pattern. Flies with rapid flutters interspersed with longer glides than 11 and 13. Habitat: offshore.
V,Car.

11 **LITTLE SHEARWATER** *Puffinus assimilis* (Pardela Chica) W 60 cm. Small with white
underwings. Habitat: offshore. Hyp,Car.

12 **TOWNSEND'S SHEARWATER** *Puffinus auricularis* (Pardela de Townsend) W 80 cm. Note
white sides on rump. Habitat: offshore, except near breeding sides. Pac.

13 **AUDUBON'S SHEARWATER** *Puffinus lherminieri* (Pardela de Audubon) W 70 cm. As 10,
but smaller with rounder wings. Underwings less extensive white than 11. Habitat: offshore,
except near breeding sides. PacCar.

14 **CAPE PETREL** *Daption capense* (Petrel Damero) W 85 cm. Unmistakable. Follows trawlers.
Habitat: offshore. Hyp,Pac.

Plate 3

Plate 4

1 WILSON'S STORM-PETREL *Oceanites oceanicus* (Paiño de Wilson) L 17 cm. Note wings held straight out. Yellow-webbed feet project beyond tail. Habitat: offshore. U,PacCar.

2 WHITE-VENTED STORM-PETREL *Oceanites gracilis* (Paiño de Elliot) L 16 cm. Only storm-petrel with white belly. Habitat: offshore. Hyp,Pac.

3 FORK-TAILED STORM-PETREL *Oceanodroma furcata* (Paiño Rabihorcado) L 20 cm. Unmistakable (in good light). Not yet recorded from the area. Habitat: offshore. Hyp,Pac.

4 LEACH'S STORM-PETREL *Oceanodroma leucorhoa* (Paiño de Leach) L 20 cm. Flight as 5–7 with angled wings, forming flattened M, but carpals more pressed up than other *Oceanodroma* species. Range overlaps those of 2 (not near coast of mainland), 5 (extinct), 6 (only seen near Revillagigedo Islands) and 7 (with more extensive white rump). Guadalupe form (not shown) with grey rump, other forms have white (a) or dark (b, from Mexican Pacific coast southwards) rump. Habitat: offshore, occasionally inshore. Pac(Car).

5 GUADALUPE STORM-PETREL *Oceanodroma macrodactyla* (Paiño de Guadelupe) L 20 cm. Note grey underwing and mottled rump. E,Guadalupe, probably extinct.

6 BAND-RUMPED (or Harcourt's, or Madeiran) **STORM-PETREL** *Oceanodroma castro* (Paiño de Harcourt/Rabifajeado) L 20 cm. Pale wing bar less pronounced than 4. No dark line down white rump patch. Rather steady flight with rapid wing beats, interspersed with short glides. Habitat: offshore. U,PacCar.

7 WEDGE-RUMPED (or Galápagos) **STORM-PETREL** *Oceanodroma tethys* (Paiño de Galápagos/Danzarín) L 19 cm. Note long white rump patch. Habitat: offshore, occasionally inshore. Pac.

8 ASHY STORM-PETREL *Oceanodroma homochroa* (Paiño Cenizo) L 20 cm. Less dark than other storm-petrels. Note pale underwing. Habitat: offshore. Pac.

9 BLACK STORM-PETREL *Oceanodroma melania* (Paiño Negro) L 25 cm. Overall dark including wing bar, which does not reach carpal joint. Note more languid flight, as 10. Habitat: offshore, except near breeding sites. Pac.

10 MARKHAM'S STORM-PETREL *Oceanodroma markhami* (Paiño de Markham) L 25 cm. Pale upperwing bar reaches carpal joint. Habitat: offshore. U,Pac.

11 LEAST STORM-PETREL *Oceanodroma microsoma* (Paiño Minimo/Menudo) L 14 cm. Note wedge-shaped tail and tiny size. Habitat: inshore. Pac.

12 WHITE-FACED STORM-PETREL *Pelagodroma marina* (Paiño Pechialbo) L 20 cm. Note white eyebrow and grey rump. Habitat: offshore. V,Pac.

Plate 4

Plate 5

1   **WHITE-TAILED TROPICBIRD** *Phaethon lepturus* (Rabijunco Coliblanco)   W 95 cm. Some adults have overall apricot wash. Imm from imms 2 and 3 by partly yellow bill, short eye stripe and from imm 3 by more black on outer primaries. Habitat: offshore and inshore. V,PacCar.

2   **RED-BILLED TROPICBIRD** *Phaethon aethereus* (Rabijunco Piquirrojo)   W 100 cm. Race *mesonauta* shown. Adult from 3 by black outer wings, from 1 and 3 by barred mantle and rump pattern. Imm as adult with large black area on outer wings, buff-orange dark-tipped bill and eye stripes connected over neck. Habitat: offshore and inshore. Pac(Car).

3   **RED-TAILED TROPICBIRD** *Phaethon rubricauda* (Paiño Colirrojo)   W 110 cm. Race *rothschildi* shown. Some adults have rosy tinge. Imm with rather coarse barring on upperparts and black bill, while all primaries are striped lengthwise without forming a black patch as imm 2. Habitat: more offshore than inshore. U,Pac.

4   **MASKED BOOBY** *Sula dactylatra* (Bobo Enmascarado/Blanco)   W 150 cm. Note red eyes, absence of yellow wash over head and black of trailing wing edge reaching body. Hypothetical breeder on San Benedicto and Clipperton Islands. Habitat: offshore, except at breeding sites. PacCar.

5   **BLUE-FOOTED BOOBY** *Sula nebouxii* (Bobo Patiazul)   W 150 cm. Blue feet diagnostic; note brown upperparts. Habitat: inshore. Pac(Car).

6   **BROWN BOOBY** *Sula leucogaster* (Bobo Vientre-blanco/Moreno)   W 140 cm. Note all-black upperparts. Habitat: offshore, but also inshore. PacCar.

7   **RED-FOOTED BOOBY** *Sula sula* (Bobo Patirrojo)   W 95 cm. Many colour forms, but red feet and red bill base diagnostic; dark (a) and pale (b) forms shown. Habitat: offshore. PacCar.

8   **PERUVIAN BOOBY** *Sula variegata* (Bobo Peruano)   W 70 cm. Small, otherwise rather nondescript; from 5 by yellowish bill. Habitat: normally offshore. V,Pa, during El Niño.

9   **NORTHERN GANNET** *Morus bassanus* (Bobo Norteño)   W 170 cm. White tail and black wing tips of adult diagnostic. From boobies by feathered chin. Habitat: normally offshore. U,Car.

10   **MAGNIFICENT FRIGATEBIRD** *Fregata magnificens* (Fragata Magnífica; Rabihorcado Magno) W 230 cm. From 11 by head colour (juv), colour pattern/feathering in armpit, bar over upperwing (♂). Habitat: coast and inshore. PacCar.

11   **GREAT FRIGATEBIRD** *Fregata minor* (Fragata Pelágica; Rabihorcado Grande) W 215 cm. Restricted range. Habitat: at offshore islands. Pac.

Plate 5

Plate 6

1   **COMMON MURRE** (or Guillemot) *Uria aalge* (Arao Común)   L 40 cm. Large (size as a small duck); slender bill and neck. Habitat: offshore, occasionally inshore. Pac.

2   **PIGEON GUILLEMOT** *Cepphus columba* (Arao Paloma)   L 35 cm. Unmistakable in full winter or summer plumage. Note wing pattern. Habitat: offshore. V,Pac.

3   **XANTUS'S MURRELET** *Synthliboramphus Hypoleucus* (Mérgulo de Xantus)   L 25 cm. Nom (a) and race *scrippsi* (b) shown. From 4 by heavier bill, paler underwings and smaller patches to sides of breast. Habitat: offshore, except at breeding sides. Pac.

4   **CRAVERI'S MURRELET** *Synthliboramphus craveri* (Mérgulo de Craveri)   L 20 cm. Black between eye and bill reaches slightly further down than 3. Note greyish (or dark) underwing. Habitat: offshore, except at breeding sides. Pac.

5   **ANCIENT MURRELET** *Synthliboramphus antiquus* (Mérgulo Antiguo)   L 25 cm. Note yellow tip to bill, and contrast between black head and grey upperparts. Habitat: offshore and inshore. V,Pac.

6   **CASSIN'S AUKLET** *Ptychoramphus aleuticus* (Alcita de Cassin)   L 25 cm. Chunky, dusky overall, with pronounced white bar on underwing. Note white crescent over eye, visible at close range. Habitat: offshore, except at breeding sides. Pac.

7   **CRESTED AUKLET** *Aethia cristatella* (Alcita Crestada)   L 19 cm. Dark plumage with red bill. Habitat: offshore. V,Pac.

8   **RHINOCEROS AUKLET** *Cerorhinca monocerata* (Alcita Rinoceronte)   L 35 cm. Note white belly, conspicuous pale eye and thick, yellowish bill. Habitat: offshore and inshore. Pac.

9   **PARAKEET AUKLET** *Cyclorrhynchus psittacula* (Mérgulo Lorito)   L 25 cm. From 8 by white breast and bill shape. Habitat: offshore. Hyp,Pac.

10   **TUFTED PUFFIN** *Fratercula cirrhata* (Frailecillo Coletudo)   L 40cm. Note rounded head, bill shape and red feet. Habitat: offshore. Pac.

11   **HORNED PUFFIN** *Fratercula corniculata* (Frailecillo Corniculado)   L 40 cm. Note sharply demarcated white underparts. Habitat: offshore. Hyp,Pac.

12   **RED-THROATED LOON** *Gavia stellata* (Colimbo Gorjirrojo)   L 60 cm. Winter plumage shows more white to sides of neck than similar plumage of 13. Note upturned bill. Habitat: offshore, bays, estuaries. U,Pac.

13   **PACIFIC LOON** *Gavia arctica* (Colimbo Artico)   L 65 cm. Note contrast and sharp demarcation between black and white at head and neck. Back appears uniform dark. Bill held horizontally. Habitat: offshore, bays. Pac.

14   **COMMON LOON** *Gavia immer* (Colimbo Común)   L 80 cm. Darker winter plumage than 15 with greyish bill. Habitat: offshore, bays, occasionally inland lakes. Pac(Car).

15   **YELLOW-BILLED LOON** *Gavia adamsii* (Colimbo Piquiamarillo)   L 85 cm. Note yellowish bill. In flight (as 14) with large feet and thick neck. Habitat: offshore, occasionally bays, estuaries. V,Pac.

Note: Loons are also known as Divers.

16   **GALAPAGOS PENGUIN** *Spheniscus mendiculus* (Pingüino de las Galápagos)   L 50 cm. Unmistakable. V (or escape?),Pac.

Plate 6

Plate 7

1   **LEAST GREBE** *Tachybaptus dominicus* (Zambullidor Menor/Enano) L 25 cm. Neat, small, compact; sharp, thin bill. Note yellow eye. Habitat: sheltered ponds, lake margins with floating vegetation, quiet rivers; sl–2500 m. Voice: high very rapid bickering and low *cheheheh--*. WSpr.

2   **PIED-BILLED GREBE** *Podilymbus podiceps* (Zambullidor Piquipinto) L 35 cm. Unmistakable. Note absence of dark bill ring in winter plumage. Pockets of breeding in Guatemala, Honduras and southern Mexico. Habitat: sheltered ponds, lakes with emergent and fringing vegetation, quiet rivers; sl–2500 m. Voice: very low *ow ow ow* with high bickering. Thr.

3   **ATITLAN GREBE** *Podilymbus gigas* (Zambullidor de Atitlán) L 45 cm. (?/2). Larger and darker than 2, with dark ring around bill in winter plumage. Possibly extinct. Status as species doubtful; at some time this form and 2 occurred at Lake Atitlan, but since birds varying in size are nowadays seen on this lake 3 might have merged with 2 by interbreeding. Habitat: Lake Atitlan. E,Gu.

4   **HORNED GREBE** *Podiceps auritus* (Zambullidor Cornudo) L 35 cm. From 5 in winter plumage by white cheeks and foreneck, from smaller 6 in winter plumage by cleaner cheeks, whitish bill tip and by peak behind, not over eye, giving flatter-headed appearance. Habitat: saline bays, estuaries. U,Pac.

5   **RED-NECKED GREBE** *Podiceps grisegena* (Zambullidor Cuellirroja) L 45 cm. Note long, fairly heavy bill, thick neck and difference from 4 in flight pattern. Habitat: vagrant from Europe; inshore, lakes. Hyp,NMe.

6   **EARED** (or Black-necked) **GREBE** *Podiceps nigricollis* (Zambullidor Orejudo/Mediano) L 30 cm. Note peaked crown. From 1 by slender build with long neck and red eye. Habitat: shallow ponds, lakes, estuaries with emergent vegetation; sl–3500 m. WSpr.

7   **WESTERN GREBE** *Aechmophorus occidentalis* (Achichilique Piquiamarillo) L 60 cm. From 8 by face pattern, bill colour, intensity of grey to body sides and extent of white in wings. Habitat: lakes with fringing reeds (summer); bays, estuaries (winter). Voice: ultra high rapid *pruprrrur*. Me.

8   **CLARK'S GREBE** *Aechmophorus clarki* (Achichilique Piquinaranja) L 60 cm. (?/7). See 7. Habitat: lakes with fringing vegetation, in winter less on saline waters than 7. Voice: very high irregular *pirrreweet*. Me.

9   **PURPLE GALLINULE** *Porphyrio martinica* (Gallineta/Gallareta Morada) L 30cm. Unmistakable. Note green mantle. Note also bright yellow legs, long wings and buff-brown neck sides of imm. Habitat: marshes, ponds, lagoons with emergent, floating and fringing vegetation. WSpr.

10 **PURPLE SWAMPHEN** *Porphyrio porphyrio* (Calamón Común) L 45 cm. Dark blue colouring, red frontal shield and large size make the species unmistakable. Habitat: marshes. Hyp,NMe.

11 **COMMON MOORHEN** *Gallinula chloropus* (Gallineta Común; Gallareta Frentirroja) L 35 cm. Unmistakable by its red frontal shield and white line along body sides. Habitat: ponds, marshes, floodplains with fringing and submergent vegetation. Voice: *tjúp tjip tjip prr*. Thr.

12 **AMERICAN COOT** *Fulica americana* (Gallareta/Focha Americana) L 40cm. Unmistakable. Red spots to bill and frontal shield missing in winter plumage. Habitat: open lakes, canals and other calm waters with submerged plants. Voice: sharp bouncing *bic* or *wruk wwurriet*. Thr.

13 **SUNGREBE** *Heliornis fulica* (Pájaro-cantil; Pato Cantil) L 30 cm. No similar bird in its habitat. Habitat: calm water with overhanging vegetation and branches in woodland, mangrove. Voice: grebe-like irregular barking descending *wek wek wek weh*. WSpr.

14 **SUNBITTERN** *Eurypyga helias* (Garza del Sol) L 45 cm. No similar bird in its habitat. Habitat: vegetation along rivers and streams in forest, also in swamps. Voice*: a high pure-whistled descending note (2–3s), sometimes with upwardly inflected disyllabic ending. Also a metallic rattle. (SMe)CAm.

Plate 7

Plate 8

1   **AMERICAN WHITE PELICAN** *Pelecanus erythrorhynchos* (Pelícano Blanco Americano) L 140 cm. Unmistakable by very large size, white colouring, contrasting wing pattern. Habitat: open, rather shallow fresh and coastal waters. WSpr.

2   **BROWN PELICAN** *Pelecanus occidentalis* (Pelícano Café/Pardo)   L 125 cm. Eastern race (a, *carolinensis*) and western race (b, *californicus*) shown, differing in bill colour of summer plumage. Habitat: coastal waters. WSpr.

3   **DOUBLE-CRESTED CORMORANT** *Phalacrocorax auritus* (Cormorán Bicrestado)   L 80 cm. From similar, but more slender yellow-chinned 5 by shorter tail. Habitat: any open fresh and coastal water. MeBe.

4   **GREAT CORMORANT** *Phalacrocorax carbo* (Cormorán Grande)   L 90 cm. Note large size, heavy bill, white cheeks. Shows white patches to thighs in br plumage. Habitat: basically at open coastal waters with rocky shores. Not recorded yet, but might invade from the USA. Hyp,YMe.

5   **NEOTROPIC** (or Olivaceous) **CORMORANT** *Phalacrocorax brasilianus* (Cormorán Neotropical)   L 65 cm. Race *olivaceus* shown. Note pointed, white border of gular skin, markedly long tail and slender build. Habitat: any coastal or inland water. Thr.

6   **BRANDT'S CORMORANT** *Phalacrocorax penicillatus* (Cormorán de Brandt) L 85 cm. Not in freshwater habitats. Note whitish throat patch. Habitat: rocky sea coast. Me.

7   **PELAGIC CORMORANT** *Phalacrocorax pelagicus* (Cormorán Pelágico)   L 70 cm. Race *resplendens* shown. Note long thin neck, thin bill and lack of yellow chin pouch. White thigh patch in br plumage. Habitat: rocky sea coast. U,NMe.

8   **GUANAY CORMORANT** *Phalacrocorax bougainvillea* (Cormorán Guano)   L 75 cm. Both adult and imm unmistakable by white underparts. Habitat: inshore. Hyp,Pa.

9   **ANHINGA** *Anhinga anhinga* (Anhinga Americana; Pato Abuja)   L 85 cm. Unmistakable in its habitat by large size, long neck and tail and by white feathering in back and wings. Habitat: any fresh and saline water with fringing and submergent vegetation in woodland. WSpr.

Plate 8

Plate 9

1 PINNATED (or South American) **BITTERN** *Botaurus pinnatus* (Aviator Neotropical) L 65 cm. Very secretive; from 2 by contrasting dark tail in flight, longer bill and different striping to sides of neck. Forneck not sharply demarcated from sides of neck as 4–6. Habitat: wet places with dense marshy vegetation. WSpr.

2 **AMERICAN BITTERN** *Botaurus lentiginosus* (Aviator Americano/Norteño) L 70 cm. Note striking neck pattern, including well-defined black stripe on side of neck, and rather uniform colouring of mantle and wing coverts. Habitat: dense marshy vegetation. Voice: ultra low mechanical *uhp-swádorwit*. WSpr.

3 **LEAST BITTERN** *Ixobrychus exilis* (Avetorito/illo Americano/Pantanero) L 30 cm. Note small size and bright buffy colour. In Central America isolated pockets of breeding. Habitat: high weeds in marshes. Voice: high rapid *whutwutwutit*. Thr.

4 **BARE-THROATED TIGER HERON** *Tigrisoma mexicanum* (Garza-tigre Gorjinuda/Cuellinuda) L 75 cm. From 5 by yellow chin, from smaller 6 by distinct black cap and stripe to sides of neck. Imm more finely barred than imms 5 and 6. Habitat: edges of open water in woodland. WSpr.

5 **RUFESCENT TIGER HERON** *Tigrisia lineate* (Garza-tigre de Silva) L 70 cm. No black cap, no yellow chin; rufous colouring diagnostic. Note: adult eyes may be black. Habitat: small ponds, streams, swamps in forest. U,CAm.

6 **FASCIATED TIGER HERON** *Tigrisoma fasciatum* (Garza-tigre de Río) L 65 cm. Very dark with short bill. Habitat: swift streams in hilly woodland. U,CRPa.

7 **SNOWY EGRET** *Egretta thula* (Garza Nivea; Garceta Nivosa) L 60 cm. Unmistakable by yellow naked parts (feet, lores, lower mandible), but see 11. Habitat: beaches, mudflats, swamps, lake edges. Thr.

8 **LITTLE BLUE HERON** *Egretta caerulea* (Garza/Garceta Azul) L 65 cm. Unmistakable; note green-yellow legs (not dark as imm 10) and bluish, black-tipped (not all-black) bill of imm. Habitat: any fresh and saline water with some fringing vegetation. WSpr.

9 **TRICOLOURED HERON** *Egretta tricolor* (Garza/Garceta Tricolor) L 65 cm. Unmistakable. Note white belly. Habitat: marshes. WSpr.

10 **REDDISH EGRET** *Egretta rufescens* (Garza/Garceta Rojiza) L 70 cm. Reddish (a) and less common white (b) forms shown. Pink base to bill diagnostic. Habitat: normally at coastal waters. WSpr.

11 **LITTLE EGRET** *Egretta garzetta* (Garceta Común) L 60 cm. Long br plumes of adult diagnostic. N-br from 7 by dark lores. More slender than 7. Habitat: marshes, swamps with some open water. Hyp,Me.

12 **CATTLE EGRET** *Bubulcus ibis* (Garza Ganadera; Garcilla Buyerera) L 50 cm. Jizz (short stocky build) differs from other egrets. Note greenish upperlegs of n-br. Habitat: ranchland with cattle near water. Thr.

13 **CHESTNUT-BELLIED** (or Agami) **HERON** *Agamia agami* (Garza Agami/Pechicastaña) L 70 cm. Unmistakable by white face sides. Imm from 9 by predominantly brownish colouring. Habitat: forest streams and swamps. U,SMeCAm.

14 **GREEN HERON** *Butorides virescens* (Garza/Garcella Verde) L 40 cm. Jizz with retracted neck, making bird compact-looking, diagnostic. Not really secretive, but well camouflaged at or among vegetation. Habitat: dense vegetation at shallow waters. Thr. Note: now split into GREEN HERON (*Butorides virescens*, as shown), and STRIATED HERON (*Butorides stratus*, E,Pa), with much paler, tawny-rufous underparts (not shown).

15 **BLACK-CROWNED NIGHT HERON** *Nycticorax nycticorax* (Garza-nocturna/Martinete Coroninegra) L 60 cm. Adult unmistakable; imm from similar 16 by yellow bill base, larger white wing spots and shorter legs. Habitat: wooded edges of lakes, swamps, marshes. Voice: low frog- or Mallard-like irregular low or very low *wrk-wrak- -* or *wrèeh wrèeh*. Thr.

16 **YELLOW-CROWNED NIGHT HERON** *Nyctanassa violacea* (Garza-nocturna Coroniclara; Martinete Cabecipinto) L 60 cm. Unmistakable. Habitat: mainly at coastal waters, mangrove, occasionally at fresh rivers, ponds, water bodies. Voice*: low rhythmical echoing *Ciauww* (1/10s). WSpr.

17 **BOAT-BILLED HERON** *Cochlearius cochlearius* (Garza Cucharón; Pico-Cichura) L 50 cm. Grey colour of upperparts varies from almost white to dark grey as shown. Bill form makes it unmistakable. Habitat: rivers, ponds, marshes with wooded edges, mangrove. Thr.

18 **CAPPED HERON** *Pilherodius pileatus* (Garza Capirotada) L 55 cm. Unmistakable by black cap. Habitat: swamps, marshes, river banks. U,Pa.

Plate 9

Plate 10

1 **GREAT BLUE HERON** *Ardea herodias* (Garzón Cenizo/Azulado) L 120 cm. Normal (a) and white (b) forms shown. Normal form from 3 by white cap, purplish neck sides and rufous thighs and sides of body. Note all-yellow legs of white form (only seen in Yucatan). In Yucatan isolated pockets of breeding. Habitat: any type of fresh and saline water. Thr.

2 **GREAT EGRET** *Casmerodius albus* (Garza/Garceta Grande) L 95 cm. Large size and all-black legs diagnostic. Habitat: marsh, lake edges, river margins, estuaries, mudflats. Thr.

3 **COCOI** (or White-necked) **HERON** *Ardea cocoi* (Garza Cuca) L 110 cm. Black-white pattern diagnostic. Habitat: marsh, river edges. U,Pa.

4 **WHITE IBIS** *Eudocimus albus* (Ibis Blanco) L 65 cm. Adult unmistakable; note long, curved, pink bill. Imm not safely separable from imm 5. Habitat: wet inland and coastal places with soft mud. Voice*: low monotone nasal honking *aark aark aark - -* and deep squabbling calls. WSpr.

5 **SCARLET IBIS** *Eudocimus ruber* (Ibis Rojo) L 60 cm. Adult unmistakable. Habitat: normally at coastal mudflats. Voice: as 4, but even more silent. Hyp,Pa.

6 **GLOSSY IBIS** *Plegadis falcinellus* (Ibis Lustroso/Morito) L 55 cm. Slender and black-looking. Adult from 7 by grey, not pink, lores. Habitat: marsh, pond margins, wet grassland. Voice: normally silent. U,YMeCRPa.

7 **WHITE-FACED IBIS** *Plegadis chihi* (Ibis Cariblanco) L 55 cm. From 6 by different patterning around eye, also leg colour in adult, but not always safely separable. Habitat: marsh. Voice: normally silent. MeGuSa.

8 **GREEN IBIS** *Mesembrinibis cayennensis* (Ibis Verde) L 55 cm. Stocky build. Note rather short tail and legs. Habitat: marsh in forested areas. Voice: loud far-carrying descending *cluk-clóok-clook-clook-clook*. CAm.

9 **BUFF-NECKED IBIS** *Theristicus caudatus* (Ibis Común) L 75 cm. Unmistakable by black underparts. Habitat: savanna with wet places. Voice: low harsh crescendoing and decrescendoing *wekwek---wekwek* (5s) or high irregular *cretchcretch-cretch- -*. V,Pa.

10 **LIMPKIN** *Aramus guarauna* (Carao) L 65 cm. From ibises by less decurved bill. Habitat: wooded, scrubby marshes, thick vegetation at edges of lakes in woodland. Voice: high loud screaming crane-like *tikwéeeer*. SMeCAm.

11 **ROSEATE SPOONBILL** *Ajaia ajaja* (Espátula Rosada) L 80 cm. Unmistakable by bill form and pink colouring. Habitat: any type of salt and fresh water. Voice*: very low barking series *ak-ak-ak-ak- -* descending slightly. WSpr.

12 **JABIRU** *Jabiru mycteria* (Jabirú) L 130 cm. Unmistakable. Habitat: open woodland with wet places. U,SMeCAm.

13 **WOOD STORK** *Mycteria americana* (Cigüeña Americana; Cigüeñón) L 95 cm. Unmistakable by bare black head and neck. Note yellowish feet. Habitat: marsh, swamp, mangrove. U,WSpr.

14 **GREATER FLAMINGO** *Phoenicopterus ruber* (Flamenco Americano) L 130 cm. Nom (American Flamingo) shown. This is the only wild flamingo in the area. All other races and species seen here are escapees. Habitat: wide, saline, shallow water. YMeBe.

15 **WHOOPING CRANE** *Grus americana* (Grulla Americana) L 130 cm. Unmistakable; note black outer wings in flight. Habitat: any type of open, cultivated country and coastal marshes. Voice: high/very high loud triumphant *whook-whook*. V,NMe.

16 **SANDHILL CRANE** *Grus canadensis* (Grulla Canadiense) L 125 cm. Unmistakable; from 15 by grey colour and different wing pattern. Habitat: open country with wet places, and cultivated fields. Voice: high upturned rattle *urrr-rrrr*. Me.

Plate 10

Plate 11

1   **FULVOUS WHISTLING DUCK** *Dendrocygna bicolor* (Pijiji Canelo)   L 50 cm. Note white side lines, erect stance, white uppertail coverts. Habitat: open, shallow water, marsh. Voice: ultra high scratchy *pichíe*. Me(CAm).

2   **WHITE-FACED WHISTLING DUCK** *Dendrocygna viduata* (Pijiji Cariblanco)   L 45 cm. Note contrasting white face. Habitat: marsh, flooded plains. Voice: ultra high lashing rapid fluted *weehweeh-weeh*. U,CRPa.

3   **BLACK-BELLIED WHISTLING DUCK** *Dendrocygna autumnalis* (Pijiji Aliblanco/Común) L 50 cm. Note red bill and legs, and broad white stripe on upperwing. Habitat: open, shallow water, floodplains, marsh. Voice: very high fluted shivering *witwéetwitrrr*. WSpr.

4   **TUNDRA** (or Whistling) **SWAN** *Cygnus columbianus* (Cisne de Tundra)   L 135 cm. From larger 5 by yellow in front of eye (although sometimes lacking). Habitat: shallow fresh water in open country, rivers. Voice: high cooing *woocoo woocoo wootjuuh*. U,Me.

5   **TRUMPETER SWAN** *Cygnus buccinator* (Cisne Trompetero)   L 165 cm. Longer bill than 4. Habitat: lakes, ponds, rivers in open woodland. Voice: low *tootjootooer*. Hyp,NMe.

6   **GREATER WHITE-FRONTED GOOSE** *Anser albifrons* (Ganso Careto Mayor).   L 75 cm. Unmistakable by belly barring. Note white ring at base of pinkish bill. Habitat: open water, marsh with adjacent grassland. Voice: very high cackling. Me.

7   **SNOW GOOSE** *Anser caerulescens* (Ganso Blanco)   L 75 cm. White (a) and uncommon blue (b) forms shown. From smaller 8 by blackish 'grin'. Habitat: marsh, open field. Voice: very high cackling. Me(Gu).

8   **ROSS'S GOOSE** *Anser rossii* (Ganso de Ross)   L 60 cm. White (a) and very rare blue (b) forms shown. From 7 by small size and small bill. Habitat: as 7, but in separate groups. Voice: high hoarse cackling. Me.

9   **BRANT** (or Brent Goose) *Branta bernicla* (Branta)   L 60 cm. Race *nigricans*. From 10 by lack of brown colouring. Habitat: coastal waters, estuaries. Voice: rather low rolled cackling. Me.

10   **CANADA GOOSE** *Branta canadensis* (Ganso Canadiense)   L 55–100 cm. Races *minima* (a, 55 cm) and *moffiti* (b, 100 cm) shown. From 9 by white band across cheeks, not across throat. Habitat: grassland, lakes, marsh, fields. Voice: high yelped cackling. Me.

11   **COMB DUCK** *Sarkidiornis melanotos* (Pato Crestudo) L 70 cm (♂), 60 cm (♀). Unmistakable; belly clean-white. Habitat: marsh in open or wooded country. U,Pa.

12   **MUSCOVY DUCK** *Cairina moschata* (Pato Real) L 80 cm (♂), 65 cm (♀). Unmistakable; note white wing patch in flight. Note: domestic types widespread but usually with some irregular white in plumage. Habitat: any type of wooded water, streams in forest, wooded marsh. U,WSpr.

13   **HOODED MERGANSER** *Lophodytes cucullatus* (Mergo de Caperuza) L 45 cm. Small size and thin, elegant bill diagnostic. From 13.14 by different bill form. ♀, (shown in flight) has dark eyes. Note large, erectile crest. Habitat: wooded ponds and lakes. U,Me.

14   **COMMON MERGANSER** *Mergus merganser* (Mergo Mayor) L 60 cm. White chin diagnostic. Habitat: open, deep water. NMe.

15   **RED-BREASTED MERGANSER** *Mergus serrator* (Mergo Copetón) L 60 cm. Bill more slender than 14. Eyes red, not black as 13. Habitat: coastal, sheltered waters. Me.

Plate 11

Plate 12

1   **WOOD DUCK** *Aix sponsa* (Pato Arcoiris) L 45 cm. Note white lines to sides of ♂ face and white eye patch of ♀. Habitat: quiet, sheltered waters with fringing vegetation and trees, wooded swamp. Voice: ultra high gliding-up *wheeík*. U,Me.

2   **GREEN-WINGED** (or Common) **TEAL** *Anas crecca* (Cerceta Aliverde) L 40 cm. Note conspicuous buffy streak (black-bordered in ♂) at undertail coverts. Habitat: shallow water, ponds, marsh. Voice: toy-trumpet-like *eeeh-eh-eh*; very/ultra high short flute *peek peeh*. Me(CAm)

3   **MALLARD** *Anas platyrhynchos* (Pato de Collar/Cabeciverde) L 60 cm. ♂ is unmistakable. Note dark centre of pinkish bill. Habitat: ponds, marsh, fields. Voice: *wraak* (♂), *raáak rak-rak-rak* (♀). U,NMe.

4   **HAWAIIAN DUCK** *Anas wyvilliana* (Pato de Hawaii) L 55 cm. As ♀ mallard, but with dark cap. Habitat: marsh, fields, quiet or swift streams. Hyp,Me.

5   **MEXICAN DUCK** *Anas diazi* (Pato Mexicano) L 60 cm. (?/3). Darker than ♀ 3, more distinct eye stripe and streak over crow, and lacking whitish tail. ♂ has conspicuous yellow bill. Habitat: as 3. Me.

6   **MOTTLED DUCK** *Anas fulvigula* (Pato Tejano) L 55 cm. As 5 with buffy face sides. In flight with very narrow white lines along speculum. Habitat: saline marsh. Me.

7   **AMERICAN BLACK DUCK** *Anas rubripes* (Pato Sombrío) L 60 cm. Very dark, lacking white lines in wings. Slim, graceful profile. Rear end of n-br ♂ and ♀ finely speckled contrasting with flanks. Habitat: coastal waters. Voice: *wrak wrak* (as 3). Hyp,NMe.

8   **NORTHERN PINTAIL** *Anas acuta* (Pato Golondrino Norteño/Rabudo) L 60 cm. In every plumage, adult or imm, this species looks slender with long neck and pointed tail. Note plain head. Habitat: ponds, lakes, marsh, estuaries. Voice: very high croaking *wrrik-wrrik-wrik*. WSpr.

9   **BLUE-WINGED TEAL** *Anas discors* (Cerceta Aliazul) L 40 cm. Face markings of ♂ diagnostic. ♀ shows white mark at base of lower mandible. Striking wing pattern in flight. Habitat: ponds, marsh, floodplains. Voice: ultra high *tjip* (♂), yelping *wec* (♀). Thr.

10   **GARGANEY** *Anas querquedula* (Cerceta Cejiblanca) L 40 cm. White ♂ eyebrow diagnostic. ♀ has characteristic face pattern. Small with graceful profile. Habitat: shallow water, ponds, marsh. Voice: dry rattle *crrrruh* (♂) and high loud hoarse cackling (♀). V,Me.

11   **CINNAMON TEAL** *Anas cyanoptera* (Cerceta Castaña) L 40 cm. ♂ is unmistakable. Note long bill and unmarked face of ♀. Habitat: shallow water with emergent vegetation. Voice: low cackling as 3, also low grumbling. Me(CAm).

12   **NORTHERN SHOVELER** *Anas clypeata* (Pato Cucharón Norteño/Cuchara) L 50 cm. Unmistakable by bill form. Habitat: open shallow water. Voice: funny low *duckduck* (as with full cheeks). WSpr.

13   **GADWALL** *Anas strepera* (Pato Pinto) L 50 cm. Note slender bill; black-and-white pattern at ♂ rear end diagnostic. From other similar ♀ ducks (especially 3) by orange even stripe along length of bill and different wing pattern. Habitat: marsh, lakes, estuaries. Very low nasal *creck* (♂), low *quack* (♀). Me.

14   **EURASIAN WIGEON** *Anas penelope* (Pato Silbón) L 50 cm. Note narrow black line between head and body. Yellow ♂ front diagnostic. Habitat: marsh, lakes, estuaries. Voice: low *grr-grr*; very high up-and-down *weeéeew*. U,Me.

15   **AMERICAN WIGEON** *Anas americana* (Pato Chalcuán/Calvo) L 50 cm. ♀ and n-br ♂ from 14 by paler and greyer head, more rufous flanks and whiter armpits. Habitat: marsh, lakes, estuaries. Voice: growl; very high mellow whistles *whec whec*. WSpr.

16   **WHITE-CHEEKED PINTAIL** *Anas bahamensis* (Pato Gargantillo) L 45 cm. Unmistakable by pronounced white cheeks. Habitat: coastal waters, but also on fresh ponds, lakes. Voice*: low upwardly inflected quacks, wheezy *sweeoo* and low grating *crrr crrr* calls. V,Pa.

Plate 12

♂ n-br

♀

1 n-br

♀

2 n-br

♂

3 ♀

4

5

6

♀

♀

♀

7

8

♂ n-br

♂ n-br

♀

10

9 ♀

♀

♀

♀

11 ♀

12 ♀

13 ♂ n-br

14 ♀

♂ n-br

15 ♀

♂

16

Plate 13

1   **CANVASBACK** *Aythya valisineria* (Pato Coacoxtle)   L 55 cm. From 2 by flat forehead and long black bill. Habitat: shallow lakes, ponds, lagoons. Me(GuHo).

2   **REDHEAD** *Aythya americana* (Pato Cabecirrojo)   L 50 cm. ♀ is overall reddish brown. Habitat: sheltered bays, lakes, marsh. Voice: high *thérethérethérewhere* or Mallard-like *wehwehweh*. MeGu.

3   **RING-NECKED DUCK** *Aythya collaris* (Pato Piquianillado; Porrón Collarejo)   L 40 cm. From 4 by lack of crest, grey flanks, peaked head (♂) and white crescent at face sides (♀). White collar of ♂ interrupted in neck. Habitat: wooded ponds, lakes, lagoons. WSpr.

4   **TUFTED DUCK** *Aythya fuligula* (Pato-boludo Moñudo)   L 40 cm. Unmistakable by black back, white flanks and tuft of ♂; ♀ shows little or no white at base of bill. Habitat: sheltered ponds, lakes, lagoons. Hyp,NMe.

5   **GREATER SCAUP** *Aythya marila* (Pato-boludo/Porrón Mayor)   L 45 cm. From smaller 6 by flat head, ♀ with more white in wing. Habitat: inshore, coastal waters. U,MeCR.

6   **LESSER SCAUP** *Aythya affinis* (Pato-boludo/Porrón Menor)   L 45 cm. Head taller, more narrow; see 5. Habitat: coastal waters, also on inland waters. Thr.

7   **HARLEQUIN DUCK** *Histrionicus histrionicus* (Pato Arlequín)   L 45 cm. Note white spot on cheeks of winter ♂ and ♀. Habitat: rough coastal waters. V,NMe.

8   **LONG-TAILED DUCK** *Clangula hyemalis* (Pato Colilargo)   L 50 cm. Despite varied plumages, very distinctive with always some white around eye. Habitat: inshore, coastal waters. V,NMe.

9   **BLACK SCOTER** *Melanitta nigra* (Negreta Negra)   L 50 cm. Unmistakable; ♀ dark with white cheeks. Habitat: inshore, bays. U,NMe.

10 **SURF SCOTER** *Melanitta perspicillata* (Negreta de Marejada)   L 50 cm. Note white spots to face sides of ♀. Habitat: inshore, coastal waters, harbours. Me.

11 **WHITE-WINGED SCOTER** *Melanitta fusca* (Negreta Aliblanca)   L 55 cm. Note 'swollen' forehead and white line behind bill and eye. Note also wing pattern of ♂ and ♀ with white extending to forewing. Habitat: inshore, coastal waters. U,NMe.

12 **COMMON GOLDENEYE** *Bucephala clangula* (Ojodorado Común) L 50 cm. From 13 by head shape, bill size, different flank pattern and more white in wing. Habitat: coastal waters, inland lakes. NMe.

13 **BARROW'S GOLDENEYE** *Bucephala islandica* (Ojodorado Islándico)   L 45 cm. See 12. Habitat: coastal waters, inland lakes. Hyp,NMe.

14 **BUFFLEHEAD** *Bucephala albeola* (Pato Monja)   L 35 cm. Unmistakable, only comparable with 11.13. Habitat: coastal waters, lakes. Me.

15 **RUDDY DUCK** *Oxyura jamaicensis* (Pato Tepalcate)   L 40 cm. Note dark line, starting at gape of ♀. Habitat: open water of marsh, lakes. Me(GuSa).

16 **MASKED DUCK** *Oxyura dominica* (Pato Enmascarado)   L 35 cm. Note distinctive jizz, face pattern and unique wing pattern in flight. Habitat: secluded ponds, marsh, among vegetation. Voice*: mid-high hollow nasal rising and falling phrase of five elements, the first longer than the others *phrooo-phrew phrew phrew ph-raaa*. U,WSpr.

Plate 13

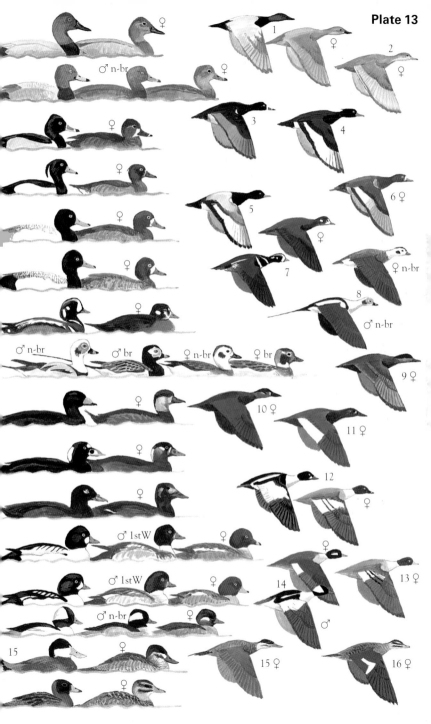

Plate 14

1 **BLACK VULTURE** *Coragyps atratus* (Zopilote Negro)   W 145 cm. From 2 and 3 by six white, dark-tipped primaries. Note short tail. Soars with flattened wings. Habitat: any place, including towns, refuse dumps, except true forest. Voice*: guttural, almost dog-like and various unpleasant 'reptilian' hissing and wheezing calls. Thr.

2 **TURKEY VULTURE** *Cathartes aura* (Aura/Zopilote Cabecirrojo)   W 190 cm. Red head diagnostic. Note black underwing coverts, contrasting with flight feathers and tail. Soars with wings held in a shallow V. Habitat: open country, woodland, rarely in forest. Voice*: high scratchy nasal rising and falling *krrreeeoww* in flight. Thr.

3 **LESSER YELLOW-HEADED** (or Savanna) **VULTURE** *Cathartes burrovianus* (Aura Sabanera; Zopilote Cabecigualdo)   W 160 cm. As 2, but with yellow head and, typically, white shafts visible in primaries on upperwing. Habitat: marsh, grassland, river margins in woodland. WSpr.

4 **KING VULTURE** *Sarcoramphus papa* (Zopilote Rey)   W 190 cm. Unmistakable, imm with stubby bill and black flight feathers. Habitat: forest, wet woodland. U,SMeCAm.

5 **CALIFORNIA CONDOR** *Gymnogyps californianus* (Cóndor Californiano)   W 270 cm. Huge; white underwing coverts reduced in imm. Voice*: low harsh, grating calls. (Extinct in the wild; no map).

6 **OSPREY** *Pandion haliaetus* (Gavilán/Aguila Pescador)   W 155 cm. In flight wings bent at wrist. Note long black eye stripe. Imm (not shown) with less defined eye stripe and more striped head and underparts. Habitat: at any type of clear, quiet, open water. Thr.

7 **BALD EAGLE** *Haliaeetus leucocephalus* (Aguila Cabeciblanca) W 200 cm. Note broad, straight-edged wings. Habitat: larger saline and freshwater bodies. U,NMe.

Plate 14

Plate 15

1   **GREY-HEADED KITE** *Leptodon cayanensis* (Milano/Gavilán Cabecigrís)   L 50 cm. Short, rounded wings. Dark (a) and pale (b) imms shown; pale imm from 20.4 by different tail pattern. Adult has black underwing coverts and barred flight feathers. Habitat: forest and adjacent areas, mangrove. Voice: rising crescendoing rapid *wekwek--* (14s). SMeCAm.

2   **HOOK-BILLED KITE** *Chondrohierax uncinatus* (Milano/Gavilán Piquiganchudo)   L 40 cm. Note broad wings, pinched in at the base. Clambers through trees, looking for its food: snails. ♂ may be all black. Habitat: forest and woodland with marsh, ponds, streams. Voice: short loud sharp *twitter witwítwitwitterr*. WSpr.

3   **SHARP-SHINNED HAWK** *Accipiter striatus* (Gavilán Pajarero)   L 30 cm. Takes prey by surprise, bursting from cover. Flies with quick flapping wings. Tail square at tip. Easily confused with other *Accipiter* hawks, especially Cooper's (5), which has relatively larger head and thicker legs. Habitat: woodland, second growth, cultivation; sl–1250(3000)m. Voice: very high slightly rising rapid *tjewtjew--* (4–8 x). Thr.

4   **WHITE-BREASTED HAWK** *Accipiter chionogaster* (Gavilán Pechiblanco)   L 30 cm. Similar to 3, but with mostly white underparts. Habitat: deciduous and pine woodland and forest; 500–3000 m. SMeCAm.

5   **COOPER'S HAWK** *Accipiter cooperii* (Gavilán de Cooper)   L 35 cm (♂), 45 cm (♀). As 3, but larger with relatively longer tail, rounded at tip, often with white nape and somewhat slower wing beat. Habitat: open woodland; 1000–3000 m. Voice: rising high *tjowtjow--* (12 x). WSpr.

6   **NORTHERN GOSHAWK** *Accipiter gentilis* (Gavilán Azor)   L 50 cm (♂), 65 cm (♀). Large, heavy, with rather pointed wings. Striking white undertail coverts. Habitat: forest with more or less pine; 1000–3000 m. Voice: sustained rising *wretwret--*. U,Me.

7   **BICOLOURED HAWK** *Accipiter bicolor* (Gavilán Bicolor)   L 30 cm (♂), 40 cm (♀). Dark (a) and pale (b) forms shown; rufous thighs diagnostic. Habitat: forest, tall second growth; sl–1750 m. Voice: low resounding *bucbuc--* (5s). U,WSpr.

8   **TINY HAWK** *Accipiter superciliosus* (Gavilán Enano)   L 25 cm (♂), 30 (♀). Note grey cheeks. Imms occur in different colour forms: rufous form (a) shown; grey form as adult but with yellow eyes and white-barred tail. Habitat: forest, tall second growth; sl–1250 m. Voice: low hoarse *aaah-áaah*. U,NiCRPa.

9   **CRANE HAWK** *Geranospiza caerulescens* (Gavilán Zancudo/Ranero)   L 50 cm. Slender, sluggish bird, specialised in extracting nestlings from hollow trees. Note long tail and white crescent across outer primaries. Habitat: open, swampy woodland, mangrove, forest edge; sl–1500 m. Voice*: mid-high mewing *sweeooo*, rising then falling and tapering off in *Buteo*-like call. Also hollow rattling *cuwokokokokoo*. WSpr.

Plate 15

Plate 16

1   **SWALLOW-TAILED KITE** *Elanoides forficatus* (Milano/Elanio Tijereta)   L 60 cm.
Unmistakable. Habitat: hilly forest, woodland; sl–2000(3000)m. Voice: very high thin running-up
weetweetweetweetwut. WSpr.

2   **WHITE-TAILED** (or Black-shouldered) **KITE** *Elanus leucurus* (Milano/Elanio Coliblanco)
L 40 cm. Note black shoulder and white tail. Habitat: open areas, marsh, savanna, fields;
sl–1500 m. Voice: ultra high *sweeét*. WSpr.

3   **MISSISSIPPI KITE** *Ictinia mississippiensis* (Milano de Misisipi; Elanio Colinegro)   L 35 cm.
Note black tail. Habitat: migratory over woodland. WSpr.

4   **PLUMBEOUS KITE** *Ictinia plumbea* (Milano/Elanio Plomizo)   L 35 cm. Rufous in wings
diagnostic. Habitat: open forest, woodland, mangrove; sl–1250 m. WSpr.

5   **PEARL KITE** *Gampsonyx swainsonii* (Elanio Enano) L 25 cm. Small, falcon-like. Habitat: open
woodland, savanna, wooded cultivation. Voice*: very high whistled begging-type call *kweeip
kweeip*, each strophe upwardly inflected. U,CAm.

6   **DOUBLE -TOOTHED KITE** *Harpagus bidentatus* (Milano Bidentado; Gavilán Gorgirrayado)
L 35 cm. Thickset jizz; black line down throat diagnostic. Sluggish, often perched in cover.
Superficially resembles an *Accipiter* hawk, especially 15.3. Habitat: forest, tall second growth.
Voice: ultra high *tjuh tjuh tjuh suwéeeeh*. WSpr.

7   **SNAIL KITE** *Rostrhamus sociabilis* (Milano/Elanio Caracolero)   L 40 cm. White tail with
subterminal black bar diagnostic. Habitat: open wooded marsh. Voice: low dry short rattle.
U,WSpr.

8   **SLENDER-BILLED KITE** *Rostrhamus hamatus* (Elanio Plomizo)   L 40 cm. Note yellow eyes and
unmarked tail. Habitat: swampy woodland and forest. Voice: very high toy-trumpet-like drawn-out
whi-èeeh. V,Pa.

9   **NORTHERN** (or Hen) **HARRIER** *Circus cyaneus* (Gavilán Rastrero; Aguilucho Norteño)
L 45 cm. Spends much time soaring gracefully, low over wetlands, with wings held in a shallow V.
Habitat: marsh, reed beds at lake margins. Thr.

10   **LONG-WINGED HARRIER** *Circus buffoni* (Aguilucho de Azara)   L 50 cm. Normal and black
(a) forms shown. Imm as ♀, but even more striped below. Large and very slender. Conspicuously
coloured black, grey and white. Perches mainly on the ground. Habitat: marsh, wet grassland.
Hyp,Pa.

Plate 16

Plate 17

1 **WHITE HAWK** *Leucopternis albicollis* (Aguililla Blanca; Gavilán Blanco)   L 50 cm.
Races *giesbreghti* (a) and *costaricensis* (b) shown. No similar bird in the area. Imm of (a) has black in
wings replaced by (barred) grey. Soars over canopy. Habitat: forest edge and clearings in hilly
country; sl–1500 m. Voice: high hoarse *sreeeh-Wéejer*. SMeCAm.

2 **SEMIPLUMBEOUS HAWK** *Leucopternis semiplumbea* (Gavilán Dorsiplomizo)   L 35 cm.
White underparts and black tail with single white bar diagnostic. Does not soar. Habitat: lower
storeys of forest and tall second growth. Voice: from high swept-up to ultra high *wuéuw*. U,CAm.

3 **PLUMBEOUS HAWK** *Leucopternis plumbea* (Gavilán Plomizo) L 35 cm. Note grey underparts,
white underwings, black tail with single black bar. Does not soar. Habitat: forest. Voice: drawn-up
falling-off *weeéeeeh*. U,Pa.

4 **BARRED** (or Black-chested) **HAWK** *Leucopternis princeps* (Gavilán Pechinegro)   L 55 cm.
No similar raptor in the area: all black above, finely barred below. Note striking difference between
pattern of uppertail (one white bar) and undertail (only distal third black). Habitat: montane
forest; 500–2500 m. Voice: very high fluting *Wíeuw*, accelerated to *wiewwiewwiew*. CRPa.

5 **BLACK-COLLARED HAWK** *Busarellus nigricollis* (Aguililla Canela; Gavilán de Ciénega)
L 45 cm. Adult unmistakable by general colour and black throat patch. Imm less distinct, but note
dark throat. Habitat: at clear, quiet waters in open or wooded country; <250 m. Voice: low dry
nasal *tetetjèeh*. WSpr.

6 **HARRIS'S** (or Bay-winged) **HAWK** *Parabuteo unicinctus* (Aguililla de Harris; Gavilán
Alicastaño)   L 50 cm. Beautiful and uniquely patterned. Resembles 18.1–4, but red shoulders
and underwing linings diagnostic. Habitat: dry areas with thorn scrub. Voice: magpie-like *wraah
wraah - -*. WSpr.

7 **WHITE-TAILED HAWK** *Buteo albicaudatus* (Aguililla/Gavilán Coliblanca/o)   L 55 cm.
Adult unmistakable by white underparts and tail and by red shoulders; imm not safely separable
from several other hawks, but note thickset jizz, white half-moon at base of tail, restricted white to
underside of primaries. Habitat: savanna, ranchland with some trees. Voice: very high nasal
prueéeeh, followed by curlew-like bouncing. WSpr.

Plate 17

Plate 18

1   **SOLITARY EAGLE** *Harpyhaliaetus solitarius* (Aguila Solitaria)   L 70 cm. Large, grey (not black) wing tip at or exceeding tail, yellow lore. Rarely looks crested. Note long eyebrow of imm. Habitat: hilly and montane forest; (<)500–2000 m. Voice: very high drawn-out *tjuuuwút* (as train whistle). U,WSpr.

2   **COMMON BLACK HAWK** *Buteogallus anthracinus* (Aguililla Negra Menor; Gavilán Cangrejero)   L 45 cm. Black wing tip almost reaches tail tip. Note dark beard stripe of imm. Habitat: mangrove, beach, forest edge at water. Voice: very/ultra high double-fluted *pweetpweetpweetwéetwéetwet*. WSpr.

3   **GREAT BLACK HAWK** *Buteogallus urubitinga* (Aguililla/Gavilán Negra Mayor)   L 60 cm. Note long tail and legs, double tail bars, grey lores. Imm rather pale below. Habitat: forest edge at water. Voice: very high shrill lonely *fjeeeehir fjuuuuuh*. WSpr.

4   **MANGROVE BLACK HAWK** *Buteogallus subtilis* (Gavilán del Pácifico)   L 45 cm. Probably race or short-winged form of 2. As 2, but with more extensive pale window in underwing, less black plumage. Normal imm plumage shown in flight; pale imm plumage (regularly occurring in Panama) shown in perched bird. Normally in different habitat. Does not soar. Habitat: mangrove, beach. Voice*: high ascending then descending laughing call. U,SMeCMa.

5   **ZONE-TAILED HAWK** *Buteo albonotatus* (Aguililla Aura; Gavilán Colifajeado)   L 50 cm. Long wings and tail. Double grey tail bar. Flight feathers below contrasting with black coverts. Habitat: dry woodland (summer); open areas often near marsh or streams (winter). Voice: very high plaintive *sueeeeeh* (or 'not-agáin'). Thr.

6   **SHORT-TAILED HAWK** *Buteo brachyurus* (Aguililla/Gavilán Colicorta/o)   L 45 cm. Normal (b) and rare all-black (a) forms shown. Normal form (b) may have rufous neck sides. Note white patch in front of eyes, dark tail, lack of yellow around eye. Habitat: forest, woodland, mangrove; sl–2000(3000)m. WSpr.

7   **GREY HAWK** *Asturina nitida* (Aguililla/Gavilán Gris)   L 40 cm. Adult unmistakable; imm with bold malar stripe, well-defined eyebrow and finely barred thighs. Habitat: open forest, savanna, often near streams. <1750 m. Voice: very high fluted *wéeeh dwéeew piuuuuew*. WSpr.

8   **ROADSIDE HAWK** *Buteo magnirostris* (Aguililla Caminera; Gavilán Chapulinero)   L 35 cm. Note yellow eyes, brown-rufous barring below, rufous base to primaries, seen in flight from above. Habitat: savanna, open woodland. Voice: very high nasal *Mjièeeh*. WSpr.

Plate 18

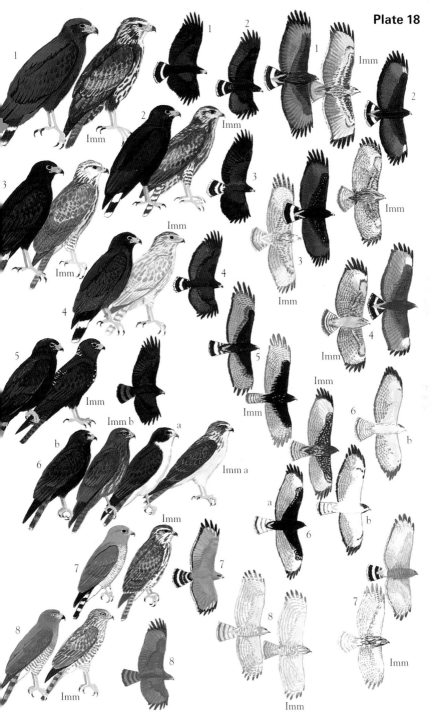

Plate 19

1 **SAVANNA HAWK** *Buteogallus meridionalis* (Gavilán Sabanero) L 55 cm. Slender, lanky jizz. Rufous appearance and single white tail bar (adult) diagnostic. Often walks on the ground. Habitat: open country. Voice: very high gull-like *tjeeejuw*. U,CRPa.

2 **RED-SHOULDERED HAWK** *Buteo lineatus* (Aguililla Pechirroja) L 50 cm. Nom (a) and race *elegans* (b, more solid red to head and breast) shown. Imm differs in intensity of red on underwings. Note strong barring of wings and tail. Habitat: woodland, often near streams. Voice: very high *tjí-er tjí-er tju-wuer* (each compressed). Me.

3 **BROAD-WINGED HAWK** *Buteo platypterus* (Aguililla/Gavilán Aluda/o) L 40 cm. Adult pale form (a) shown, coarsely barred dark rufous below, and dark form (b), both with distinct tail pattern. Habitat: open areas, forest edge, occasionally in forest; sl–2000 m. Voice: ultra high fluted *titjueeueeh*. WSpr.

4 **SWAINSON'S HAWK** *Buteo swainsoni* (Aguililla/Gavilán de Swainson) L 50 cm. Pale (a), dark (b) and intermediate (c, in flight) forms shown. Note diagnostic grey undertail and tawny undertail coverts, even in dark form. White underwing linings contrast with dark flight feathers. Habitat: over open country. Voice: very high fluted drawn-out *tfúuuuh wiNuuuh*. Thr.

5 **RED-TAILED HAWK** *Buteo jamaicensis* (Aguililla/Gavilán Colirroja/o) L 50 cm. Migrant and a widespread resident in interior Mexico. Pale (a, eastern) and dark (b, western) forms shown. Adult unmistakable, except Harlan's Hawk (c, race *harlani*), whose tail colour may vary, grey tail shown. Imm not safely separable from other *Buteo* hawks, but larger, except 6 and 7, which see. Habitat: pine forest, arid country (summer), sloping grassland, open woodland (winter); sl–3000 m. Voice: very high scratchy drawn-out *tscréeetch*. Thr.

6 **FERRUGINOUS HAWK** *Buteo regalis* (Aguililla Real) L 65 cm. Pale (a) and dark (b) forms shown. Very large with long-winged shape; jizz of 'long' head diagnostic. As 7 with feathered lower legs. Habitat: savanna, grassland with scattered trees; sl–2000 m. Voice: high *kheeeuww*. Me.

7 **ROUGH-LEGGED BUZZARD** (or Hawk) *Buteo lagopus* (Aguililla Artica) L 55 cm. Very variable; most common normal adult form and dark (a) and pale (b) imms shown; other adult forms (c, d, e) in flight. Compact, thickset. Feathered legs and whitish tail base diagnostic. Habitat: open country, marsh. U,NMe.

Plate 19

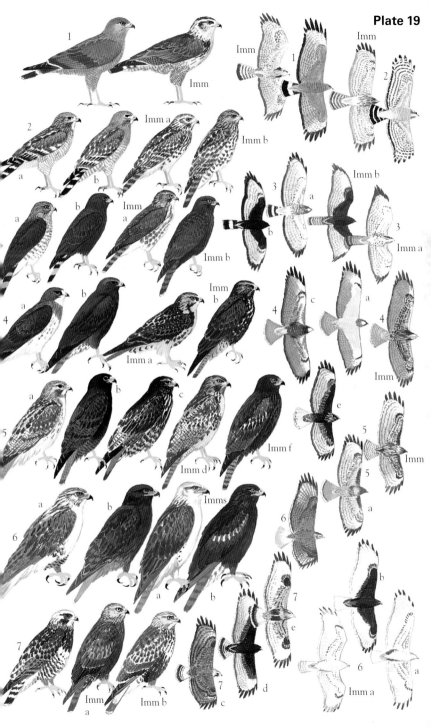

Plate 20

1 GOLDEN EAGLE *Aquila chrysaetos* (Aguila Real) W 210 cm. Shows 'golden' nape and undertail coverts. Note wing shape with bending-in of trailing edge near body. Imm shows diagnostic white windows in wings and tail. Habitat: dry montane areas. NMe.

2 CRESTED EAGLE *Morphnus guianensis* (Aguila Crestada) W 165 cm. Pale (a) and dark (b) forms shown. As 3–6 with short, rounded wings. Imm from similar 3 by less distinct tail bars. From 3 and 5 by fine barring below. Habitat: forest, tall second growth; <500 m. U,SMeCAm.

3 HARPY EAGLE *Harpia harpyja* (Aguila Arpía) W 190 cm. Large and very powerful looking with huge claws. Black breast band of adult diagnostic. Habitat: forest; <500 m. Voice: very high stressed *tjíuw*. U,CAm.

4 BLACK-AND-WHITE HAWK EAGLE *Spizaster melanoleucus* (Aguila Blanquinegra; Aquilillo Blanco y Negro) W 130 cm. Unmistakable in its habitat, but see 17.2 (with more restricted range). More *Buteo*-like than other eagles with, in flight, white leading edge to wings. Habitat: forest edge and clearings; 500–1500(2000)m. U,WSpr.

5 BLACK HAWK EAGLE *Spizaetus tyrannus* (Aguila Tirana; Aquilillo Negro) W 140 cm. Adult from very rare dark form of 2 by far less sharp demarcation between black breast and belly barring. Note also black underwing coverts. Habitat: forest edge and clearings; 500–1500 m. Voice: very high *pup-puphieiuw*. WSpr.

6 ORNATE HAWK EAGLE *Spizaetus ornatus* (Aguila Elegante; Aquilillo Penachudo) W 130 cm. Adult is unmistakable. Note white head of imm with contrasting black crest. Habitat: forest; sl–1500 m. Voice: very high fluted staccato *weet weet weetjr* or *pwu-pwu-pwípwípwípeh*. WSpr.

Plate 20

Plate 21

1   **RED-THROATED CARACARA** *Daptrius americanus* (Caracara Comecacao/Avispera)
L 55 cm. Normally in flocks of 3–10. Red head parts and white belly diagnostic. Habitat: forest
(edge) and adjacent areas; sl–1250 m. Voice: dry cackling macaw-like *tjáktjaktjaktják* or *tjak-tjaak*.
U,CRPa.

2   **CRESTED** (or Northern) **CARACARA** *Polyborus plancus* (Caracara Común/Cargahuesos)
L 55 cm. Unmistakable by black cap and red face. Habitat: open country, fields with scattered
trees, grassland, beaches. WSpr.

3   **YELLOW-HEADED CARACARA** *Milvago chimachima* (Caracara Cabecigualdo)   L 45 cm.
Solitary or in groups of up to 10. Unmistakable by combination of tawny head and body and dark
mantle and wings. Walks around on the ground or perches low on fences, poles and such. Habitat:
savanna, fields, ranchland; <500 m. Voice*: high piercing sibilant scream *sheeeargh*, sometimes run
into series. CRPa.

4   **LAUGHING FALCON** *Herpetotheres cachinnans* (Halcón Guaco)   L 50 cm. Unmistakable by
black mask. Note upright stance. Habitat: forest edge, forest remains, savanna. Voice: high *haa-
haah-hahhahhah* or high sustained *waak-waak- -* slowly rising in pitch. WSpr.

5   **BARRED FOREST FALCON** *Micrastur ruficollis* (Halcón-selvático Barrado; Halcón de Monte
Barreteado)   L 35 cm. Note yellow around large eyes. Imm with variable barring below, some
almost completely whitish; 18.7 in different (open) habitat. Habitat: forest; <1500 m. Voice: high
sweeping *wew*. WSpr.

6   **COLLARED FOREST FALCON** *Micrastur semitorquatus* (Halcón-selvático/Halcón de Monte
Collarejo)   L 50 cm. Despite colour variations (a), (b) and (c) unmistakable by large eyes, long,
white-barred tail, very short wings and habitat. Bird of understorey. Habitat: forest; <1750 m.
Voice: Peacock-like *áow*. WSpr.

7   **SLATY-BACKED FOREST FALCON** *Micrastur mirandollei* (Halcón de Monte Dorsigrís)
L 45 cm. Large, hazel eyes. No similar bird in its habitat, except maybe 17.2, which has much
shorter, differently patterned tail and red cere, gape and legs. Habitat: forest and adjacent areas;
<500 m. Voice: plaintive rising loud *waah-waah- -* (10 x). U,CRPa.

Plate 21

Plate 22

1   **AMERICAN KESTREL** *Falco sparverius* (Cernícalo Americano)   L 25 cm. Unmistakable. Hunts from perch, but also hovers frequently. Habitat: open woodland, savanna. Voice: ultra high dry *kleekleeklee-kleekleeklee- -*. Thr.

2   **APLOMADO FALCON** *Falco femoralis* (Halcón Aplomado)   L 40 cm. From 3 and 4 by white-buff eye stripe and very long tail. Habitat: savanna. U,WSpr.

3   **BAT FALCON** *Falco rufigularis* (Halcón Murcielaguero/Cuelliblanco)   L 25 cm. From larger 4 by solid dark grey breast. Note barred undertail coverts of imm. Habitat: forest edge, canopy and clearings, open woodland often near water; <1500 m. Voice: very high *turrit* or sharp hurried *twitwitwitwitweh*. WSpr.

4   **ORANGE-BREASTED FALCON** *Falco deiroleucus* (Halcón Pechirrufo)   L 35 cm. Similar to more common 3, which see. Habitat: forest and forest edge; sl–1750 m. WSpr.

5   **MERLIN** *Falco columbarius* (Esmerejón) L 30 cm. Races *suckleyi* (a) and *richardsoni* (b) shown. Small. Fast flyer, when stooping on and pursuing small birds, its prey. Note compact jizz, streaked underparts and banded tail. Habitat: open woodland. Thr.

6   **PEREGRINE FALCON** *Falco peregrinus* (Halcón Peregrino)   L 45 cm. Several races of which *anatum* (a, Peale's Falcon) and imm of smaller and paler race *tundrius* (b) are shown. Very fast, when stooping from high above on its prey, middle-sized birds. Distinctive, large 'tear' below eye. Note compact build, rather short wings and tail when perched, pointed wings in flight. Habitat: open woodland, savanna, rocky coasts. Thr.

7   **PRAIRIE FALCON** *Falco mexicanus* (Halcón Pradeño)   L 40 cm. From 5, 6 and 8 by white behind its eye. Note relatively long tail and dark armpits. Habitat: dry savanna and open woodland. Voice: very high sustained irregular *kekekekekekek--*. Me.

8   **GYRFALCON** *Falco rusticolus* (Halcón Gerifalte)   L 55 cm. Variable. Normal (a), white (b) and dark (c, imm) forms shown. Large and heavy with broad, rounded wings. Note weak moustache. Habitat: open country. Hyp,Me.

Plate 22

Plate 23

1   **PLAIN CHACHALACA** *Ortalis vetula* (Chachalaca Común/Olivácea)   L 55 cm. From similar 3 and 4 by darker, tawny underparts and range. Habitat: open forest with dense brush, woodland; sl–1750 m. Voice: high excited chattering *chatatáh-chátatah* in duet. WSpr.

2   **WAGLER'S** (or Rufous-bellied) **CHACHALACA** *Ortalis wagleri* (Chachalaca Vientre-castaña) L 65 cm. (?/3). Orange-rufous underparts and tail corners. Habitat: dry woodland, thorn bush; sl–2000 m. Voice: high hoarse *truterut-tút* in chorus. E,Me.

3   **WEST MEXICAN CHACHALACA** *Ortalis poliocephala* (Chachalaca Mexicana)   L 65 cm. From smaller 4 by tawny undertail coverts. Not in same range with 1. Habitat: dry woodland, thorn bush, montane forest; sl–2500 m. Voice*: low unpleasant pheasant-like nasal screeching in long rhythmic series. E,Me.

4   **WHITE-BELLIED CHACHALACA** *Ortalis leucogastra* (Chachalaca Vientre-blanco) L 45 cm. White belly and undertail coverts diagnostic. Habitat: woodland, forest edge; <750 m. Voice*: low harsh chicken-like *crat-crr-crarr* with last syllable ending in a trill. Repeated and running into a cacophonous duet. U,SMeCAm.

5   **GREY-HEADED CHACHALACA** *Ortalis cinereiceps* (Chachalaca Cabecigrís)   L 50 cm. Red in wing diagnostic. Habitat: forest edge, second growth. CRPa.

6   **HIGHLAND GUAN** (or Black Penelopina) *Penelopina nigra* (Pajuil)   L 60 cm. ♂ is unmistakable by black feathering and red chin wattle. ♀ from 1–5 by red legs and delicate dense barring. Arboreal as 1–5. Habitat: montane forest; 1000–3000 m. Voice: strange rising to very high *fueuuuuuuuuiii* (2 s) or descending *krrrrrrr*. U,SMeCAm.

7   **CRESTED GUAN** *Penelope purpurascens* (Pavo Cojolito; Pava Crestada)   L 80 cm. Large and slender; striped white below. Arboreal. Habitat: forest; sl–2500 m. Voice: goose-like falsetto *pfiuéet-pfiueet- -* or rising high sustained *pew-pew*. WSpr.

8   **HORNED GUAN** *Oreophasis derbianus* (Pavón Cornudo)   L 80 cm. Unmistakable. Habitat: montane forest. U,SMeGu.

9   **BLACK GUAN** *Chamaepetes unicolor* (Pava Negra)   L 65 cm. From 6 by different range and blue naked face parts. Arboreal. Habitat: montane forest. Voice: dry rattle *prr prrrrr* (2–3 s). U,CRPa.

10   **GREAT CURASSOW** *Crax rubra* (Hocofaisán; Pavón Grande)   L 90 cm. Two of several ♀ colour forms (a and b) shown. Normally on the ground. Unmistakable by forward curling crest and large size. Habitat: forest, mangrove; sl–1500 m. Voice: very low *hooó*; high *wick wick*. U,WSpr.

11   **WILD TURKEY** *Agriocharis gallopavo* (Guajalote Silvestre)   L 110 cm (♂), 90 cm (♀). Unmistakable. Habitat: open woodland. Voice: excited gobbling *wórkworkwork*. U,NMe.

12   **OCELLATED TURKEY** *Meleagris ocellata* (Guajalote Ocelado)   L 90 cm (♂), 70 cm (♀). Not unlike 11, but less black, more splendidly coloured green and blue, with white in wings, and in different habitat. Habitat: forest, woodland. Voice: hollow accelerated bickering. U,YMeBe.

13   **CHUKAR** *Alectoris chukar* (Perdiz Chucar)   L 35 cm. Introduced in the USA. Unmistakable. Habitat: rocky desert. Voice: high scratchy *wrutch wrutch*. Hyp,NMe.

14   **COMMON** (Ring-necked) **PHEASANT** *Phasianus colchicus* (Faisán Vulgar)   L 80 cm, incl. 35 cm tail (♂). Introduced; many colour forms exist, most common shown, all with red face wattle (♂). Long tail of ♀ diagnostic. Habitat: open woodland and cultivated areas. Voice: coarse *uuh-uuh*, followed by wing beating. Hyp,NMe.

15   **CLAPPER RAIL** *Rallus longirostris* (Rascón Picudo)   L 35 cm. Races *beldingi* (a) and *pallidus* (b) shown. Note long-necked, long-billed, narrow-bodied jizz. Secretive. Habitat: grassy, often brackish marsh. Voice: sharp dry mechanical *tjektjektjek--* or series of accelerated harsh shrieks. MeBe(CRPa).

16   **KING RAIL** *Rallus elegans* (Rascón Real)   L 45 cm. Normally more rufous than 15, especially on wings, with more pronounced barring to flanks. Habitat: freshwater marsh. Voice: grating calls; lowered and accelerated *tsehtsehtseh--* or *wehwehweh--*. Me.

17   **VIRGINIA RAIL** *Rallus limicola* (Rascón de Virginia)   L 25 cm. Smaller than 16 with less long-necked jizz and grey cheeks. Barring to flanks black. Habitat: marsh with high reeds. Voice: grating bouncing *tetjúh-tetjúh-tetjúh*. MeGu.

▶

Plate 23 continued

18   **GREY-NECKED WOOD RAIL** *Aramides cajanea* (Rascón Cuelligrís)   L 40 cm. Note grey neck with rufous cap. Habitat: swamp, mangrove, at water edges in forest and woodland. Voice: high dry *eh-hóc ehhóc - - chochochochoc.* WSpr.

19   **RUFOUS-NECKED WOOD RAIL** *Aramides axillaris* (Rascón Cuellirrufo)   L 30 cm. From larger 18 by rufous head. Habitat: mangrove, wet places in forest. Voice: high rhythmic *tjuw - -*, each slurred-down. WSpr.

20   **SPOTTED RAIL** *Pardirallus maculatus* (Rascón Pinto/Moteado) L 25 cm. Striped neck demarcated from barred belly. Red spot to bill base diagnostic. Imm variable, some like adult, others dark as shown. Habitat: dense marsh vegetation. Voice: grating *wreetwreetwreetwrit tjpprp.* WSpr.

Plate 24

1   **YELLOW RAIL** *Coturnicops noveboracensis* (Polluela Amarilla)   L 18 cm. Note striped appearance. From imm 7 by lack of white undertail coverts. Habitat: marsh with low vegetation. Extremely secretive; probably extinct in Mexico. Voice: irregular *tictictic--* as tapping on a stone. Hyp,Me.

2   **RUDDY CRAKE** *Laterallus ruber* (Polluela Rojiza/Colorada)   L 15 cm. Diagnostic coloured mainly red with black cap and grey face sides. Habitat: marsh, reed beds, wet grassland. Voice: very high shivering fast *srisrisri--.* WSpr.

3   **GREY-BREASTED CRAKE** *Laterallus exilis* (Polluela Pechigrís)   L 15 cm. Diagnostic red patch on nape. Habitat: tall grass in wet areas. Voice: very high *bic-bic- -* or shivering *srrrrr.* CAm.

4   **BLACK RAIL** *Laterallus jamaicensis* (Polluela Negra)   L 14 cm. Very dark; white spotting diagnostic. Habitat: marsh, wet grassland, floodplains. Voice: high dry *krauwkrauw--*; hurried *títítjuw.* U,Thr.

5   **WHITE-THROATED CRAKE** *Laterallus albigularis* (Polluela Gargantiblanca)   L 15 cm. Much smaller than 23.15 ,16 and 17. Note barring of undertail coverts and grey face sides. Habitat: thick vegetation in wet places. Voice: very high shrill fast *srrrrrr* or ultra high *sreeuw.* CAm.

6   **UNIFORM CRAKE** *Amaurolimnas concolor* (Polluela/Rascón Café)   L 20 cm. No similar bird in its habitat. Habitat: thick forest undergrowth. Voice: very high fluting *peuwhée - -* or *tjuuWeh.* SMeCAm.

7   **SORA** *Porzana carolina* (Polluela Sora)   L 20 cm. Note diagnostic black face mask in adult. Habitat: marsh. Voice: swept-up *oh what* or very high rather plaintive very fast *ohwhatagainthinbickering.* Thr.

8   **YELLOW-BREASTED CRAKE** *Porzana flaviventer* (Polluela Pechiamarilla)   L 13 cm. Diagnostic white eye stripe interrupted above eye. Habitat: marsh with high grass. Voice: grating *shruuk-shruuk.* U,WSpr.

9   **COLOMBIAN CRAKE** *Neocrex columbianus* (Polluela Colombiana)   L 19 cm. Very dark with tawny undertail coverts, no barring on flanks. Bill base red. Habitat: marsh. V,Pa.

10   **PAINT-BILLED CRAKE** *Neocrex erythrops* (Polluela Piquirroja)   L 19 cm. Belly and undertail coverts broadly barred black. Habitat: marsh, wet grassland, rice fields. Voice: croaking *wrrot-wrrot.* U,CRPa.

11   **OCELLATED CRAKE** *Micropygia schomburgkii* (Polluela Ocelada)   L 15 cm. Unbarred below. Habitat: dense grassland. Voice: ultra high shrieking *tsteertsjeer--* or *wihwih--.* V,CR.

12   **LONG-TAILED WOOD PARTRIDGE** *Dendrortyx macroura* (Gallina-de-monte Coluda)   L 30 cm. Head pattern and broad red breast striping diagnostic. Habitat: dense undergrowth of montane forest; 1250–1500 m. Voice: high sustained *uhjú-uhjú-uhjú* (in duet) or *tídderah - -.* E,Me. Note: 12, 13 and 14 live in forests, have long tails and red legs.

13   **BEARDED WOOD PARTRIDGE** *Dendrortyx barbatus* (Gallina-de-monte Veracruzana)   L 25 cm. Note head pattern. Habitat: dense undergrowth of montane forest; 1000–3250 m. Voice: very high shivering *wiwi--* (6 x); very high fluting *wuwuwuíuh - -.* E,Me.

▶

Plate 24

Plate 24 continued

14 **BUFFY-CROWNED WOOD PARTRIDGE** *Dendrortyx leucophrys* (Gallina-de-monte Centroamericana; Perdiz Montañera) L 35 cm. Greyer than 12 and 13; head pattern diagnostic. Habitat: dense undergrowth of montane forest; 500–3000 m. Voice: very high rising and crescendoing *úh úhw úhwe úhwec - -*. CAm. Note: 12, 13 and 14 are also called Tree Quails.

15 **SPOTTED WOOD QUAIL** *Odontophorus guttatus* (Codorniz Bolanchaco/Moteada) L 25 cm. From 16 and 17 by head pattern and by colouring of breast, with white streaks below. Habitat: dense forest undergrowth. Voice: high mellow fluted *witterohwitterohweeweeweet*. SMeCAm.

16 **BLACK-EARED WOOD QUAIL** *Odontophorus melanotis* (*erythrops*) (Codorniz Pechicastaña) L 25 cm. Note solid red breast. Habitat: forest; <1000 m. Voice: high wooden *tetjúuh tetjuuh* or very high *witwit wut*. U,CAm.

17 **MARBLED WOOD QUAIL** *Odontophorus gujanensis* (Codorniz Carirroja) L 25 cm. Uniform tawny below, bare reddish skin around eye. Habitat: undergrowth of forest, tall second growth; <1000 m. Voice: high excited *óhwhatnow-óhwhatnow- -* (duet). U,CRPa.

18 **BLACK-BREASTED WOOD QUAIL** *Odontophorus leucolaemus* (Codorniz Pechinegra) L 25 cm. Head and underparts distinctly patterned. Habitat: montane forest; 750–1500 m. Voice: *purrúp'pupuk--* (duet). U,CRPa.

19 **TACARCUNA WOOD QUAIL** *Odontophorus dialeucos* (Codorniz del Tacarcuna) L 25 cm. Dark body contrasting strongly with black-and-white head pattern. Habitat: montane forest. U,Pa.

Plate 25

1 **TAWNY-FACED QUAIL** *Rhynchortyx cinctus* (Codorniz Carirrufa) L 18 cm. ♂ from 2 by white chin and grey breast. Compact jizz and belly barring of ♀ diagnostic. Habitat: dense forest undergrowth; <750 m. Voice: very high descending fluted *pwuuuh* in chorus. U,CAm.

2 **SINGING QUAIL** *Dactylortyx thoracicus* (Codorniz Silbadora) L 20 cm. Head of ♂ and ♀ distinctly patterned. As 1, unobtrusive and shy forest dweller. Habitat: forest; 250–3000 m. Voice: very high crescendoing and rising *fjuut*; melodious fluted *weeterohwéetwit--*. WSpr.

3 **BANDED** (or Barred) **QUAIL** *Philortyx fasciatus* (Codorniz Barrada) L 20 cm. Unmistakable by belly barring. Habitat: dry thorn bush, scrub; sl–1500 m. Voice: very high wooden sustained *puwéeh puwéeh - -*. E,Me.

4 **SCALED QUAIL** *Callipepla squamata* (Codorniz Escamosa) L 25 cm. Tufted white crest and fine scalloping below diagnostic. Habitat: dry open bush; 1000–2000 m. Voice: very high squeaky *tsjieh*, low *tjouw-tjèh* or *ti-tjóuw*, or high *sreeuw*. U,Me.

5 **ELEGANT QUAIL** *Callipepla douglasii* (Codorniz Elegante) L 25 cm. Crest and finely striped head pattern diagnostic. Habitat: scrubby woodland; <1000 m. Voice: high *shruck*; *tut-twuéeh tut-twuéeh*. E,Me.

6 **GAMBEL'S QUAIL** *Callipepla gambelii* (Codorniz de Gambel) L 25 cm. Only comparable to 7, which see. Habitat: dry open scrub; sl–1500 m. Voice: Peacock-like *pwéew*; very high descending *swéar*. NMe.

7 **CALIFORNIA QUAIL** *Callipepla californica* (Codorniz Californiana) L 25 cm. Head pattern and scalloping below diagnostic. Habitat: dry scrub and woodland; sl–3000 m. Voice: *wut-wréet wet* or *weet-wit-wit*. NMe.

8 **MOUNTAIN QUAIL** *Oreortyx pictus* (Codorniz de Montaña) L 25 cm. Unmistakable. Habitat: dry woodland; 1000–3000 m. Voice: high loud *wuèeh*. U,NMe.

9 **MONTEZUMA QUAIL** *Cyrtonyx montezumae* (Codorniz de Moctezuma) L 20 cm. Unmistakable by black, white-spotted underparts. Habitat: savanna, dry woodland; 1000–3000 m. Voice: *wuk wuk wukkík*; very high sweet slightly descending *wreeeeh*. U,Me.

10 **OCELLATED QUAIL** *Cyrtonyx ocellatus* (Codorniz Ocelada) L 20 cm. (?/9). As 9 with same clownish head pattern, but with different colouring below and different range. Habitat: dry woodland; 1000–3000 m. U,SMeGuHo.

▶

Plate 25

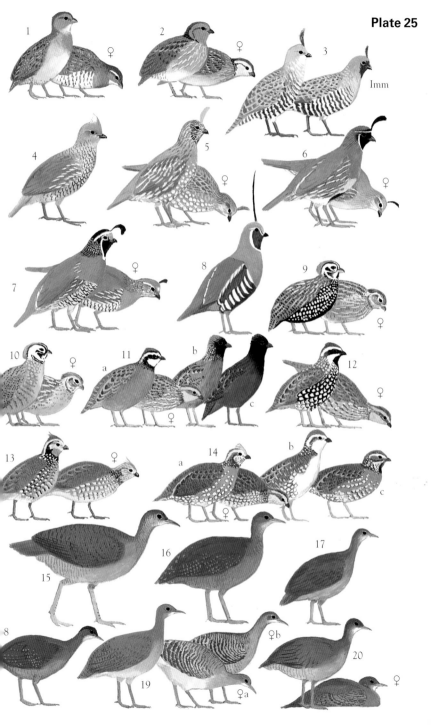

Plate 25 continued

11   **NORTHERN BOBWHITE** *Colinus virginianus* (Codorniz-cotui Norteña) L 20 cm. Of many races *graysoni* (a), *ridgwayi* (b) and *salvini* (c) shown, with solid buff-orange to dark chestnut underparts. Habitat: brushy woodland; sl–2500 m. Voice: very high resounding *lou-wup Whíte*. Me.

12   **BLACK-THROATED** (or Yucatan) **BOBWHITE** *Colinus nigrogularis* (Codorniz-cotui Yucateca) L 20 cm. Black-scaled underparts and black throat diagnostic. Habitat: brushy woodland; sl–250 m. Voice: ultra high *wup whieét*. YMeBe.

13   **CRESTED BOBWHITE** *Colinus cristatus* (Codorniz Crestada) L 20 cm. Rufous throat and white-spotted sides of neck diagnostic. Habitat: savanna, wet grassland. Voice: ultra high fluting *wuw wewwirríp*. CRPa.

14   **SPOT-BELLIED BOBWHITE** *Colinus leucopogon* (Codorniz-cotui Centroamericana; Codorniz Vientrimanchada) L 20 cm. Nom (a) and races *hypoleucus* (b) and *leylandi* (c) shown. (?/13). Greyish-cinnamon underparts with white spotting distinctive. Less strong head pattern than other bobwhites. Note distinctive eyebrow. Habitat: brushy woodland; sl–2000 m. Voice: very high running-up *tjup tjip tjip*. CAm.

15   **GREAT TINAMOU** *Tinamus major* (Tinamú Mayor/Grande) L 45 cm. Note large size, grey legs and fine barring of upperparts. Habitat: forest; sl–1250(1750)m. Voice: high resounding crescendoing *pjuuuh* (6 x). SMeCAm.

16   **HIGHLAND TINAMOU** *Nothocercus bonapartei* (Tinamú Serrano) L 40 cm. Characterised by grey cap, rufous underparts, pale spotted wings, grey legs. Habitat: montane forest; >1250(1500)m. Voice: high rhythmic sustained *wark wark - -*. U,CRPa.

17   **LITTLE TINAMOU** *Crypturellus soui* (Tinamú Menor/Chico) L 25 cm. Note plain upper- and underparts. Habitat: high weeds, dense humid scrub, forest edge; sl–1500 m. Voice: very high fluted *wieeéèh* or accelerated crescendoing rising *wuuuuh - -* (12 x). SMeCAm.

18   **CHOCO TINAMOU** *Crypturellus kerriae* (Tinamú del Chocó) L 25 cm. From 16 by red legs and white, not buff chin. Habitat: forest; <750 m. U,Pa.

19   **THICKET TINAMOU** *Crypturellus cinnamomeus* (Tinamú Canelo) L 30 cm. ♀♀ of races *occidentalis* (a) and *goldmani* (b) shown. ♂ rather grey with red legs. Habitat: dense scrub, second growth, forest edge; sl–1000 m. Voice: high level fluting *pjeeuw*. WSpr.

20   **SLATY-BREASTED TINAMOU** *Crypturellus boucardi* (Tinamú Jamuey/Pizarroso) L 30 cm. Note finely barred tawny underparts, dark grey neck and chest. ♀ with barred wings. Habitat: dense forest undergrowth; <750(1500)m. Voice: high drawn-out hollow almost level *huuuh-huuuuuuh* (6 s). WSpr.

Plate 26

1   **DOUBLE-STRIPED THICK-KNEE** *Burhinus bistriatus* (Alcaraván Americano) L 45 cm. Note large staring eye, long tail, bi-coloured bill. In flight long wings with distinctive white spots on black flight feathers. Crepuscular. Habitat: savanna, ranchland, open woodland. Voice: very high level chattering *wecwecwec--* in sort of duet. WSpr.

2   **SOUTHERN LAPWING** *Vanellus chilensis* (Avefría Sureña) L 35 cm. Unmistakable by long, thin crest. Habitat: short grass, swamps. Voice: very noisy, e.g. loud scolding metallic *keek-keek-keek- -*. V,Me;U,CAm.

3   **GREY** (or Black-bellied) **PLOVER** *Pluvialis squatarola* (Chorlo/Chorlito Gris) L 30 cm. Greyer than 4 and 5. Note diagnostic black armpit. Habitat: mainly coastal. Voice: very high plaintive drawn-up *puwéeeh - -*. WSpr.

4   **AMERICAN** (or Lesser) **GOLDEN PLOVER** *Pluvialis dominica* (Chorlo-dorado Americano; Chorlito Dorado Menor) L 25 cm. In br and n-br plumage with large darkish centres to all feathers, which makes this species look less bright than 5. Longer primary projection than 5, showing 4, not 3 primaries. Habitat: short grass, wet fields, lake shores. Voice: ultra high thin *puuèh*. WSpr.

5   **PACIFIC GOLDEN PLOVER** *Pluvialis fulva* (Chorlo-dorado Asiático) L 25 cm. W plumage from that of 3 by clean cheeks, more golden cast on plumage, long legs and heavier bill. Habitat: beach, short grass, wet fields, lake shores. Voice: very high *pjúit pjuít - -*. V,Me.

▶

Plate 26

Plate 26 continued

6   **AMERICAN OYSTERCATCHER** *Haematopus palliatus* (Ostrero Americano)   L 45 cm. Unmistakable. Habitat: sandy and rocky beaches. Voice: High sharp bouncing *wheet whit - - * suddenly accelerated to sort of trill. U,WSpr.

7   **BLACK OYSTERCATCHER** *Haematopus bachmani* (Ostrero Negro)   L 45 cm. Unmistakable. Habitat: rocky coast. NMe.

8   **BLACK-NECKED STILT** *Himantopus mexicanus* (Candelero Americano; Cigüeñuela Cuellinegro)   L 40 cm. Unmistakable. Habitat: shallow margins of inland and coastal waters. Voice: high dry sustained *wicwicwic--* (8–10 s). Thr.

9   **ESKIMO CURLEW** *Numenius borealis* (Zarapito Boreal)   L 30 cm. Small, rather short decurved bill, short legs. From Little Curlew (not yet seen, but which might turn up in the area) by wing tip exceeding tail tip and by more pronounced flank barring on buff underground. Habitat: basically coastal grasslands. Near to extinction. V,MeGu.

10   **WHIMBREL** *Numenius phaeopus* (Zarapito Trinador)   L 45 cm. Race *hudsonicus*. As 12, but head less 'clean' and flanks more barred. Habitat: mainly coastal. Voice: *bicbic--* (7 x). WSpr.

11   **LONG-BILLED CURLEW** *Numenius americanus* (Zarapito Piquilargo)   L 55 cm. Very long bill and clean cinnamon underwing diagnostic. Habitat: marsh, fields, margins of coastal waters. Voice: very high *curlèw* or mellow rolling *wutrrrrwit*. WSpr.

12   **BRISTLE-THIGHED CURLEW** *Numenius tahitiensis* (Zarapito del Pacífico)   L 40 cm. Stripe through eye more pronounced than 10. Habitat: marsh, wet grassland. Voice: very high yodelling *whooerwit*. Hyp,NMe.

13   **AMERICAN AVOCET** *Recurvirostra americana* (Avoceta Americana)   L 45 cm. Unmistakable by upturned bill. Habitat: coastal waters, lake margins, marsh. WSpr.

14   **NORTHERN JACANA** *Jacana spinosa* (Jacana Mesoamericana/Centroamericana)   L 20 cm. From 15 by yellow, not red shield and dusky legs. Habitat: floating vegetation at lake edges, marsh. Voice: hoarse *week-week-keek-week- -*. WSpr.

15   **WATTLED JACANA** *Jacana jacana* (Jacana Sureña)   L 25 cm. Frontal shield and wattles to gape red. More restricted range then 14. Habitat: floating vegetation at lake edges, marsh. Voice: very high sharp *week-week-week- -*, slightly changing in pitch and tempo. (CR)Pa.

Plate 27

1   **GREATER YELLOWLEGS** *Tringa melanoleuca* (Patamarilla/Patiamarillo Mayor)   L 30 cm. From 2 by longer, slightly upturned bill and shorter wings. Habitat: inland and coastal waters and marsh. Voice: very high rapid staccato descending *djîpdjipdjip*. Thr.

2   **LESSER YELLOWLEGS** *Tringa flavipes* (Patamarilla/Patiamarillo Menor).   L 25 cm. Straight bill as long as head. Looks more elegant than 1. Habitat: marsh, lake and pond edges, shallow water. Voice: very high staccato *yipyip yipyip-yip-yip-yip*. Thr.

3   **SOLITARY SANDPIPER** *Tringa solitaria* (Playero/Andarríos Solitario)   L 20 cm. Note dark rump, dark underwing and barred tail sides. Habitat: ponds and creeks with fringing vegetation. Voice: ultra high *swit swit swit*; very high fluted and rolling *triotriotriotrioh-ukwho-oh*. Thr.

4   **WILLET** *Catoptrophorus semipalmatus* (Playero Pihuihui; Pigüilo)   L 35 cm. Breeding plumage of western race *inornatus* (a) and smaller eastern race *semipalmatus* (b) shown; both races similar in n-br plumage. From 28.1–7 by thicker, greyish legs, grey-based bill and spectacular pattern in flight. Habitat: shallow margins of lakes, ponds, marsh, rocky shores. Voice: high melodious *uk-who-oh who-it-who-it- -*. WSpr.

5   **WANDERING TATTLER** *Heteroscelus incanus* (Playero Vagabundo; Correlimos Vagamundo) L 25 cm. Compact size, rather short yellow legs and uniform slate-grey upperparts diagnostic. Habitat: rocky shores. Voice: ultra high sharp loud trilling *wwwwwt*. WSpr.

6   **SPOTTED SANDPIPER** *Actitis macularia* (Playero Alzacolita; Andarríos Maculado)   L 19 cm. Note projecting tail and white patch in front of folded wing. Habitat: margins of lakes, ponds, rivers, lagoons. Voice: descending *weetweetweet*; hurried *prrrrWéetprrrWéet*. Thr.

▶

Plate 27

Plate 27 continued

7   **UPLAND SANDPIPER** *Bartramia longicauda* (Zarapito Ganga; Pradero)   L 30 cm. Long tail and long thin neck diagnostic. Habitat: dry, open grassland. Voice: slightly rising and falling bickering rrrrrrrrr. Thr.

8   **COLLARED PLOVER** *Charadrius collaris* (Chorlito/ejo Collarejo)   L 15 cm. No white between crown and mantle, diagnostic pink legs. Habitat: sandy beaches and coastal lagoons. Voice: very high staccato *peek-peek peek*. WSpr.

9   **SNOWY** (or Kentish) **PLOVER** *Charadrius alexandrinus* (Chorlito Nivéo; Chorlitejo Patinegro) L 16 cm. As pale as 12, but thin bill always black, darker cheeks and with different leg colour and tail pattern. Habitat: mainly coastal beaches, also at inland river margins. Voice: very high drawn-up *puriét puriét - -*. WSpr.

10   **WILSON'S PLOVER** *Charadrius wilsonia* (Chorlito Piquigrueso; Chorlitejo Picudo)   L 18 cm. Dark and with heavy bill. Habitat: sandy beaches, dry mudflats. Voice*: high *kwip-kwip-kwip- -*, repeated rapidly with variable spacing, each *kwip* upwardly inflected. WSpr.

11   **SEMIPALMATED PLOVER** *Charadrius semipalmatus* (Chorlito/Chorlitejo Semipalmado) L 18 cm. Note complete breast band, yellow legs and pink base to bill. Habitat: mudflats, sandy beaches, lake margins, marsh. Voice: high nasal *tjew-tjew- -*, slurred down to dry rattle. WSpr.

12   **PIPING PLOVER** *Charadrius melodus* (Chorlito Chiflador)   L 18 cm. Note short stubby bill and pale face sides. Habitat: mainly sandy beaches. Voice*: ultra/very high staccato *peep peep - -*. U,MeBe.

13   **KILLDEER** *Charadrius vociferus* (Chorlito/Chorlitejo Tildío)   L 25 cm. Note long partly rufous tail. Double breast band diagnostic. Habitat: open areas, grasslands, fields, marsh. Very/ultra high thin *thee-eeh*; descending *kilderdeedee*. Thr.

14   **MOUNTAIN PLOVER** *Charadrius montanus* (Chorlito Llanero)   L 25 cm. Large, plain overall, grey legs. Note protruding legs in flight. Habitat: open areas, away from water; sl–2000 m. Voice*: high quizzical upwardly inflected repeated *plewup - -*. U,NMe.

15   **EURASIAN DOTTEREL** *Charadrius morinellus* (Chorlito Carambolo)   L 20 cm. Plain wings in flight. Note faint white bar across darkish breast in 1stW plumage. Habitat: savanna, ranchland. Voice: very high fluted *puwéet-weet-weet*. V,NMe.

Plate 28

1   **HUDSONIAN GODWIT** *Limosa haemastica* (Picopando Ornemantado; Aguja Lomiblanca) L 40 cm. Black underwing coverts diagnostic. Note unmarked grey winter plumage, pink-based bill and white wing bar in flight. Habitat: coastal waters, marsh. Voice: ultra/very high hurried piping *whéetwítwit*. U,WSpr.

2   **BAR-TAILED GODWIT** *Limosa lapponica* (Picopando Colibarrado)   L 40 cm. From 1 by striped upperparts and neck and lack of wing bar. Tail barring diagnostic. Habitat: mainly coastal. Voice: high yelping *yapyap yapyepyap* or sustained *tetrútetrú--* or sandpiper-like hurried *wet wéetwut* . V,NMe.

3   **MARBLED GODWIT** *Limosa fedoa* (Picopando/Aguja Canelo/a)   L 45 cm. Upturned bill, buff-rufous colouring and cinnamon underwing lining diagnostic. Habitat: mainly coastal. Voice: high resounding cackling *tuwuucwuuc--*. WSpr.

4   **BUFF-BREASTED SANDPIPER** *Tryngites subruficollis* (Playero Pradero; Praderito Pechianteado)   L 19 cm. Note plump, short-billed, small-headed jizz. Habitat: short grass, wet places in savanna. U,WSpr.

5   **RUFF** *Philomachus pugnax* (Combatiente)   L 30 cm (♂), 25 cm (♀). White sides to tail diagnostic. White ring at base of bill (as if the bird is smoking a cigarette). Attains spectacular breeding plumages, some examples (a) shown. Habitat: shallow water, wet grassland, floodplains, savanna. V,CAm.

6   **SHORT-BILLED DOWITCHER** *Limnodromus griseus* (Costurero Piquicorto; Agujeta Común) L 25 cm. Shown is race *hendersoni* with (in breeding plumage) spotted, rather than barred neck sides; western race *griseus* indistinguishable from 7 except by call and by tail, which seems paler by thinner black barring. Habitat: shallow coastal waters, marsh, floodplains. Voice: high loud shivering *tjutjutju*. WSpr.

▶

Plate 28

Plate 28 continued

7   **LONG-BILLED DOWITCHER** *Limnodromus scolopaceus* (Costurero/Agujeta Piquilargo/a) L 30 cm. As 6 with yellow legs. Habitat: marsh, lake margins, floodplains, less in coastal habitats. Voice: very high sharp single note, *yip*. WSpr.

8   **WILSON'S SNIPE** *Gallinago delicata* (Agachona/Becacina Común) L 25 cm. Skulking. When flushed from among grass, zigzags away calling *critch* before dropping into cover within 200–300 m. Habitat: grassy marsh, wet grass, floodplains. Voice: low dry *critch*; e.g. very high sharp wooden *tretrúttetrút--*. Thr.

9   **AMERICAN WOODCOCK** *Scolopax minor* (Chocha Americana) L 30 cm. Secretive. When flushed escapes with 'twittering' wings. Habitat: damp woodland. Voice: silent outside breeding season. V,Me.

10   **WILSON'S PHALAROPE** *Steganopus tricolor* (Falárapo/Falaropo de Wilson) L 25 cm. Swims less and forages more on land than 11 and 12. Rather plump, yet graceful. In n-br plumage shows long thin bill, grey, not black eye patch, yellow legs (black in br plumage), no wing bar, diagnostic white rump without central stripe. Habitat: coastal waters. Thr.

11   **RED-NECKED PHALAROPE** *Phalaropus lobatus* (Falárapo Cuellirrojo; Falaropo Picofino) L 19 cm. From 10 and 12 by short, needle-like bill. In n-br plumage darker above than 12. May be blown inland by severe storms. Habitat: inshore, coastal waters. WSpr.

12   **RED** (or **Grey**) **PHALAROPE** *Phalaropus fulicarius* (Falárapo Piquigrueso; Falaropo Rojo) L 20 cm. From 11 by less slender jizz and stubbier bill. Habitat: offshore, occasionally inshore or coastal. WSpr.

13   **RUDDY TURNSTONE** *Arenaria interpres* (Vuelvepiedras Rojizo) L 25 cm. Hunched jizz and black crescents to sides of breast diagnostic. Habitat: rocky shores, beaches. Voice: very high staccato *ti tjeu tjew*, followed by some bickering. WSpr.

14   **BLACK TURNSTONE** *Arenaria melanocephala* (Vuelvepiedras Negro) L 25 cm. From 13 by less striking black crescents to sides of breast and less bright red legs. Habitat: rocky shores. Voice: high sustained shivering calls. NMe.

15   **SURFBIRD** *Aphriza virgata* (Playero de Marejada; Chorlito de Rompientes) L 25 cm. Short, stubby, bi-coloured bill diagnostic. Habitat: rocky coasts. Voice: high rather mewing slightly swept-up *kreékreékreé--*. WSpr.

Plate 29

1   **RED KNOT** *Calidris canutus* (Playero Gordo; Correlimos Grande) L 25 cm. Note large size, greenish legs, and finely barred flanks in n-br plumage. In flight shows seemingly grey rump and unmarked tail. From 10 by larger, heavier jizz and straight shorter bill. Habitat: beaches, mudflats. Voice: ultra high loud sharp *weetweet--*. U,WSpr.

2   **SANDERLING** *Calidris alba* (Playero Blanco/Arenero) L 20 cm. Winter plumage is very pale with darker shoulders. Striking wing bar in flight. Runs up and down the beach with each advancing and retreating wave. Habitat: sandy beaches. Voice: high *zupzupzup*. WSpr.

3   **SEMIPALMATED SANDPIPER** *Calidris pusilla* (Playerito/Correlimos Semipalmado) L 14 cm. Rather deep bill base. Greyer in br plumage than other stints. Short web between toes diagnostic. Habitat: beaches, coastal waters, lake edges. Voice: very high *tjerrup trrup jupjupjup*. WSpr.

4   **WESTERN SANDPIPER** *Calidris mauri* (Playerito/Correlimos Occidental) L 16 cm. Tends to have longer, more drooping bill than very similar 3. Br plumage with brighter scapulars. Habitat: beaches, coastal waters, lake edges. Voice: very high chattering *weeweeweet--* in chorus. WSpr.

5   **LEAST SANDPIPER** *Calidris minutilla* (Playerito Mínimo; Correlimos Menudo) L 14 cm. Note short, yellowish legs. Breast band often well defined. Tail as long as wings. Thin, decurved bill. Habitat: mainly freshwater mudflats with some low vegetation. Voice: ultra high thin *weet weetweet*. Thr.

6   **WHITE-RUMPED SANDPIPER** *Calidris fuscicollis* (Playerito Rabadilla-blanca; Correlimos Lomiblanco) L 17 cm. Red base to bill and white rump diagnostic. Habitat: shallow coastal waters, lakes. Voice*: very high quite musical passerine-like twittering calls and unstructured *trrreet-twip-twip* etc. WSpr.

▶

Plate 29

Plate 29 continued

7 **BAIRD'S SANDPIPER** *Calidris bairdii* (Playerito/Correlimos de Baird) L 16 cm. Note projecting wing tips and thin, straight bill. Habitat: dry mudflats, grassland, marsh. Voice: ultra high drawn-up *eeéeh-ih*. Thr.

8 **PECTORAL SANDPIPER** *Calidris melanotos* (Playero/Correlimos Pectoral) L 20 cm. Note sharply demarcated breast, long, flesh-based bill and yellow legs. No or faint wing bar. Habitat: mainly at edges of freshwater lakes, floodplains, marsh. Voice: rolling *trúttrút trut*. Thr.

9 **SHARP-TAILED SANDPIPER** *Calidris acuminata* (Correlimos Acuminado) L 20 cm. As 8, but breast more irregular than finely striped. Habitat: mudflats with some grass or weeds. Voice: very high *prrt-reet-reet*. Hyp,NMe.

10 **DUNLIN** *Calidris alpina* (Playero Dorsirrojo/Correlimos Pechinegro) L 20 cm. Note short neck and legs, combined with long, decurved bill. Habitat: beaches, coastal waters. Voice: tern-like hurried *sreeksreeksreek -*, immediately followed by very high sharp dry trill. WSpr.

11 **CURLEW SANDPIPER** *Calidris ferruginea* (Correlimos Zarapitín) L 20 cm. Longer wings, legs and neck than 10. Habitat: shallow fresh waters. Voice: coarse *tjirrup*. V,Me.

12 **ROCK SANDPIPER** *Calidris ptilocnemis* (Correlimos Roquero) L 20 cm. Stocky build, spotting below, bill colour and habitat diagnostic. Habitat: rocky coasts. Voice: mostly silent. Hyp, NMe.

13 **PURPLE SANDPIPER** *Calidris maritima* (Correlimos Oscuro) L 25 cm. From very similar 12 mainly by different range. Normally with some more yellow at base of bill. Habitat: rocky coasts. Voice: very high *kwit*. Hyp,NMe.

14 **STILT SANDPIPER** *Micropalama himantopus* (Playero Zancudo; Correlimos Patilargo) L 20 cm. Slender with long legs, white rump and decurved bill. Note lack of wing bar. Habitat: fresh and saline mudflats. Voice: thin *trrp*. WSpr.

Plate 30

1 **POMARINE JAEGER** *Stercorarius pomarinus* (Salteador/Págalo Pomarino) L 50 cm (incl. streamers). Normal (a) and dark (b) forms shown. Lengthened blunt twisted tail feathers diagnostic, but in worn plumage often missing. Black of underwings in pale form 'drips' over flanks; in n-br plumage head and breast densely barred brown. Note double concentric white on outer underwing in 2dS plumage. Habitat: offshore, occasionally inshore. PacCar.

2 **PARASITIC** (or Arctic) **JAEGER** *Stercorarius parasiticus* (Salteador/Págalo Parásito) L 45 cm. Pale (a) and dark (b) forms shown. Note pointed tail feathers. Imm more rufous-brown than imms 1 (brown) and 3 (cold-brown). Collar often less distinct than in 1. Habitat: offshore, occasionally inshore. U,PacCar.

3 **LONG-TAILED JAEGER** *Stercorarius longicaudus* (Salteador/Págalo Colilargo) L 50 cm. (incl. streamers). Chest band weak or absent. Note lack of white in wings. N-br as imm, but with underwing coverts unbarred. Black trailing edge to underwing in adult. Habitat: offshore. U,PacCar.

4 **GREAT SKUA** *Catharacta skua* (Págalo Grande) L 55 cm. Warmer-toned than 5. Note dark mask, strong striping on mantle. Habitat: offshore, occasionally inshore. V,Car.

5 **SOUTH POLAR SKUA** *Catharacta maccormicki* (Págalo Sureño; Salteador Polar) L 55 cm. Dark (a) and pale (b) forms shown. Bill rather small. Clean underparts. Habitat: offshore. U,Pac(Car).

6 **CHILEAN SKUA** *Catharacta chilensis* (Págalo Chileno) L 55 cm. Rufous-brown with distinct cap. Note distinctly bi-coloured bill. Habitat: offshore. Hyp,Pac.

7 **GREAT BLACK-BACKED GULL** *Larus marinus* (Gaviota Dorsinegra Mayor) L 70 cm. Adult from smaller 9 and 11 by pink legs and more white to wing tips. Note pale wing panel in 1st and 2dW plumage. Habitat: mainly beaches. Voice: low raucous *wraawraawraa--*. V,Car.

8 **LESSER BLACK-BACKED GULL** *Larus fuscus* (Gaviota Dorsinegra Menor) L 55 cm. Black wing tip of adult well demarcated from grey upperwing. Imm tail as imm 7, but black broader and more distinct. Habitat: coastal areas, including refuse sites. Voice: as 31.4. V,Car.

▶

Plate 30

Imm 1
a
a 2dS
b 2dS
b
Imm 2
a
a 2dS
Imm 3
n-br 3
2dS
b
b 2dS
Imm 4
Imm 5
a
b 5
4
b
6
7
6
Imm
br 8
n-br
7
1stW
2dW 7
n-br 9
8
1stW
9
Ad
br 10
n-br
9
1stS
2dS
br
n-br 11
12
12
Ad
12
2dS
1stS

Plate 30 continued

9 **KELP GULL** *Larus dominicanus* (Gaviota Dorsinegra Sureña) L 60 cm. Adult from 11 by leg colour. Imm tail as imm 8. Habitat: coastal waters. Voice*: typical gull screams *kiauw kiauw - -*. U,Me.

10 **OLROG'S GULL** *Larus atlanticus* (Gaviota Cangrejera) L 55 cm. As smaller 12, but black ring around bill more distinct. Habitat: coastal waters. Hyp,Ho.

11 **YELLOW-FOOTED GULL** *Larus livens* (Gaviota Patamarilla) L 65 cm. Yellow legs diagnostic in adult. Note all-black, sharply demarcated imm tail. Habitat: coastal waters, often at rocky beaches. Voice*: low long laughing series *ke-ke-ke-ke- -*. Me.

12 **BAND-TAILED** (or Belcher's) **GULL** *Larus belcheri* (Gaviota Colifajeada) L 50 cm. From larger 10 by more brown (not black) upperparts, more black to tail, shorter, less pointed wings. Habitat: coastal waters. V,Pa.

Plate 31

1 **BLACK-TAILED GULL** *Larus crassirostris* (Gaviota Colinegra) L 45 cm. Note faint grey cap of n-br plumage. Br plumage from 30.7, 9 and 11 by black bar across tail. Note white foreface of imm with sharp demarcation between lower breast and belly. Habitat: coastal waters. V,MeBe.

2 **SLATY-BACKED GULL** *Larus schistisagus* (Gaviota de Kamchatka) L 65 cm. From 30.8 and from 3 by thinner bill and different wing tip pattern. Juv with black bill, 1stW with yellow, black-tipped bill. Habitat: coastal waters, often with rocky shores. V,NMe.

3 **WESTERN GULL** *Larus occidentalis* (Gaviota Occidental) L 60 cm. Note heavy bill and general thickset jizz. From 30.8 by different range. Habitat: beaches, coast. Voice: very high shrieking *tjeew-tjeew-tjeew*, low barking *wowwow* or other low muttering. Me.

4 **HERRING GULL** *Larus argentatus* (Gaviota Plateada/Argéntea) L 60 cm. As 5, but less rounded head and with pink legs. Habitat: coastal areas, also at inland waters, refuse dumps. Voice: high typical gull-like *pjiauw pjiauw - -*, with changes in tempo and pitch. WSpr.

5 **CALIFORNIA GULL** *Larus californicus* (Gaviota Californiana) L 55 cm. Note rounded head, long bill, long wings. Yellow legs diagnostic in adult. Habitat: coastal and inland waters. Voice: low *tjaktjaktjak tsjaak* tsjaak or falsetto *shrieeow*. Me(Sa).

6 **GLAUCOUS-WINGED GULL** *Larus glaucescens* (Gaviota Aliglauca) L 65 cm. Normally relatively unpatterned; outerwing greyer than innerwing. Outer flight feathers greyer than remainder of wing. Habitat: coastal waters. Voice: ultra high *pjuwéeh*. U,NMe.

7 **GLAUCOUS GULL** *Larus hyperboreus* (Gaviota Blanca) L 70 cm. Almost all-white. Habitat: coastal waters, occasionally at inland lakes, rivers. U,NMe.

8 **THAYER'S GULL** *Larus thayeri* (Gaviota de Thayer) L 60 cm. Note wing tip pattern. Habitat: rocky coasts. U,NMe.

9 **GREY-HEADED** (or -hooded) **GULL** *Larus cirrocephalus* (Gaviota Cabecigrís) L 40 cm. Note drawn-out head profile, pale eye, red thin bill and legs. Habitat: coastal and inland waters. Voice: high hoarse *eorrh eorrh - -*. V,Pa.

10 **SWALLOW-TAILED GULL** *Creagrus furcatus* (Gaviota Tijereta) L 55 cm. Normally unmistakable by wing pattern and yellow-tipped black bill. Habitat: rocky coasts. Voice*: low guttural rattles with high strident *creeow* calls. V,Pa.

11 **GREY GULL** *Larus modestus* (Torero) L 45 cm. Note grey rump and tail. Grey body and white head diagnostic. Habitat: sandy beaches. Voice*: high trilling *rrrraargh* and soft mewing calls. Variable and not so harsh as most gull species. V,Pa.

Plate 31

Plate 32

1   HEERMANN'S GULL *Larus heermanni* (Gaviota de Heermann)   L 45 cm. From 31.11 by different bill colour and almost white uppertail coverts; from 30.4–6 by white edge to secondaries, different bill form and colour and absence of white window at base of primaries (beware, however: there is a rare colour form of this species with a white window as skuas). Habitat: coastal areas. Voice: low/high indignant *Uuhw Uuhw - -* or duck-like gobbling. Me(Gu).

2   MEW (or Common) GULL *Larus canus* (Gaviota Piquiamarilla)   L 45 cm. Smaller and more compact than 31.4–8 with thinner bill and finer, dark-tipped bill. Habitat: coastal and inland waters, fields, grassland, refuse dumps. Voice: high/ultra high *wèh-wèh sríew wehweh*. U,NMe.

3   RING-BILLED GULL *Larus delawarensis* (Gaviota Piquianillada)   L 50 cm. Black ring around bill and yellow legs diagnostic in adult; smaller, more elegant than 31.4. Habitat: coastal and inland waters, fields, grassland, refuse dumps. Voice: very high angry *píow píow - -* or high bleating *jweljweljwel*. WSpr.

4   BLACK-HEADED GULL *Larus ridibundus* (Gaviota Encapuchada)   L 40 cm. Wing pattern with white forewing diagnostic. Note 'ear phones' in winter plumage. Habitat: coastal and inland waters, fields, grassland, refuse dumps. Voice: high drawn-out *sreeuw sreeuw*. V,Me.

5   LAUGHING GULL *Larus atricilla* (Gaviota Reidora)   L 40 cm. Darker than 4 with all grey upperwing. Note colour of bill: black in n-br plumage, changing to dark red in br plumage. Habitat: coast. Voice: very high *mèew mèew mèew*. Thr.

6   FRANKLIN'S GULL *Larus pipixcan* (Gaviota de Franklin)   L 35 cm. Small and compact. Black in wing tip separated from grey in upperwing. Habitat: coastal and inland waters, marsh, fields, grassland, refuse dumps. Voice: very high sharp *wekwek--*. WSpr.

7   BLACK-LEGGED KITTIWAKE *Rissa tridactyla* (Gaviota Patinegra)   L 40 cm. Short legs and unmarked yellowish bill diagnostic. Note wing pattern. Habitat: offshore, occasionally inshore and at coastal waters. Voice: high barking toy trumpet-like *t-t-tjOoweh*. U,NMe.

8   BONAPARTE'S GULL *Larus philadelphia* (Gaviota de Bonaparte)   L 30 cm. From larger 4 by yellow-tipped (br) or all-black (n-br) bill. Habitat: coastal areas. Voice: low frog-like bickering. NMe(CAm).

9   SABINE'S GULL *Xema sabini* (Gaviota de Sabine)   L 30 cm. Wing pattern and forked tail diagnostic. Note dark grey, not reddish legs. Habitat: offshore and inshore. Voice*: high typical gull calls: *kekekekeke* or *krrep* or *kiaww kiaw kiaw* etc. WSpr.

10   LITTLE GULL *Larus minutus* (Gaviota Mínima)   L 25 cm. Lack of black to upperwing and black underwing of adult diagnostic. Strong black bar across imm upperwing. Habitat: coastal waters, occasionally inland. Voice: very high descending *tjow-tjowtjow- -*. V,Me.

Plate 32

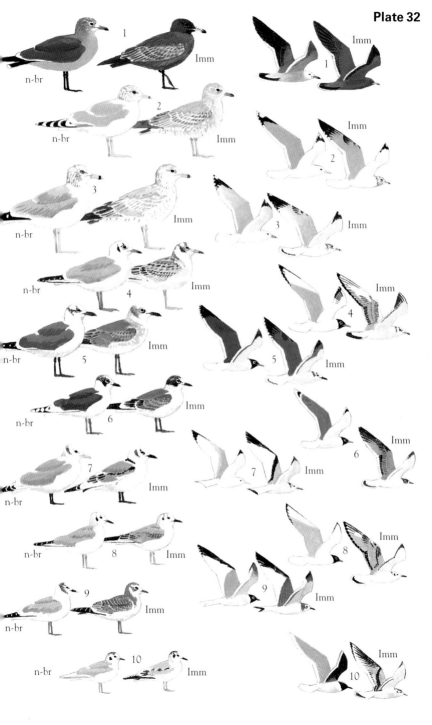

n-br   1   Imm

Imm   1

n-br   2   Imm

Imm   2

n-br   3   Imm

3   Imm

n-br   4   Imm

4   Imm

n-br   5   Imm

5   Imm

n-br   6   Imm

6   Imm

n-br   7   Imm

7   Imm

n-br   8   Imm

8   Imm

n-br   9   Imm

9   Imm

n-br   10   Imm

10   Imm

Plate 33

1   **CASPIAN TERN** *Sterna caspia* (Golondrina-marina Caspica; Pagaza Mayor) L 50 cm. Note heavy jizz, striking red bill, normally with subterminal black spot (often absent in br plumage), and bluish underwing tip. N-br adults and imm usually with densely spotted forehead. Bill relatively heavier and longer than 2. Imm less well marked on upperwings than other imm large terns. Habitat: coast, large lakes. Voice: low drawn-out scratchy *kraaá kraaáh*. WSpr.

2   **ROYAL TERN** *Sterna maxima* (Golondrina-marina/Pagaza Real) L 50 cm. From 1 by shorter, more orange bill and mostly white underwing tip. Note strongly patterned upperwing of imm. Habitat: estuaries, lagoons. Voice: very high *kéer kéer*. WSpr.

3   **ELEGANT TERN** *Sterna elegans* (Golondrina-marina/Pagaza Elegante) L 40 cm. Note slender, yellow bill with orange base. Little or no white around eye in n-br plumage. Habitat: beaches, estuaries. Voice*: high hoarse *kiaaarrgh*. U,WSpr.

4   **SANDWICH TERN** *Sterna sandvicensis* (Golondrina-marina de Sandwich; Pagaza Puntiamarilla) L 40 cm. Note black, yellow-tipped bill and flat crown. In flight, outer wing paler than inner wing. Imm shows all-black bill. Habitat: beaches, coral flats, estuaries. Voice: loud hoarse *kerrick*. WSpr.

5   **ROSEATE TERN** *Sterna dougallii* (Golondrina-marina Rosada) L 40 cm. From 6 by longer tail and paler upperwing. Bill only red for a few weeks in br plumage, otherwise black. Note dark scapulars of imm. Habitat: inshore and coastal waters. Voice: very high *weewee*. U,CAm.

6   **COMMON TERN** *Sterna hirundo* (Golondrina-marina/Charrán Común) L 35 cm. From 7 by heavier jizz, longer bill, longer legs. N-br adult often shows some red at base of bill. Note dark wedge between outer and inner primaries. Br adult from 5 by absence of pink wash below and shorter tail streamers. Imm often with bi-coloured bill and blackish bar. Habitat: in winter mainly coastal. Voice: very high drawn-out sharp *pRrrrriur*. WSpr.

7   **ARCTIC TERN** *Sterna paradisaea* (Golondrina-marina Artica) L 35 cm. Note short legs, short bill, long tail (often reaching wing tip), narrow dark trailing edge to primaries. Flight feathers 'translucent'. In br plumage greyer below than 6. Note all-red bill and white cheeks (br plumage) separated from grey underparts in flight. Habitat: inshore. Voice: high *eéeehr*. Pac.

8   **FORSTER'S TERN** *Sterna forsteri* (Golondrina-marina/Charrán de Forster) L 35 cm. Note pale upperwings (shown in flying bird) and dark smudge through eye of n-br bird. Habitat: shallow fresh waters. Voice: very high *tjeeuw-tjuwtjuwtjuw*. WSpr.

9   **LEAST TERN** *Sterna antillarum* (Golondrina-marina Mínima; Charrán Chico) L 25 cm. As 10, but with greyer rump and tail and with two, not three black primaries. Bill black in winter plumage. Habitat: waters close to the sea beach. Voice: very/ultra high drawn-up *wriít*. WSpr.

10 **YELLOW-BILLED TERN** *Sterna superciliaris* (Golondrina-marina Amazónica) L 25 cm. From 9 by larger, all-yellow bill (with small darkish point in winter plumage). Habitat: coastal waters. Voice: sharp *keek*. V,Pa.

Plate 33

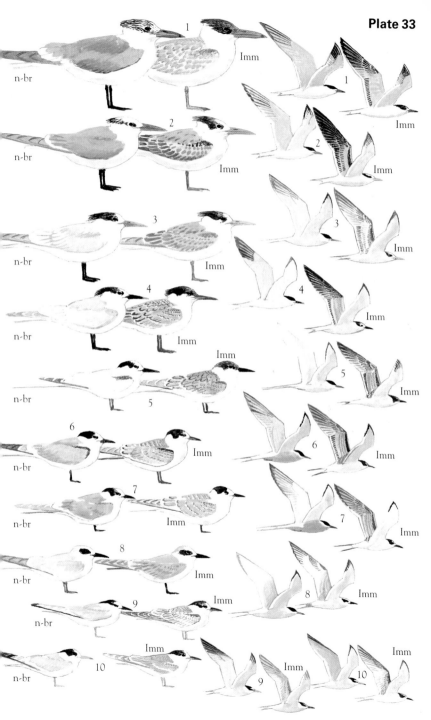

n-br 1 Imm 1 Imm

n-br 2 Imm 2 Imm

n-br 3 Imm 3 Imm

n-br 4 Imm 4 Imm

n-br 5 Imm 5 Imm

n-br 6 Imm 6 Imm

n-br 7 Imm 7 Imm

n-br 8 Imm 8 Imm

n-br 9 Imm Imm

n-br 10 Imm 9 Imm 10 Imm

Plate 34

1 **GULL-BILLED TERN** *Sterna nilotica* (Golondrina-marina Piquigruesa; Charrán Piquinegro) L 40 cm. Note short black bill, rounded head, long legs, all-grey very pale upperparts. Imm and n-br adult show little black behind eye. Flight straight, less buoyant than other terns. Habitat: often over marshes and dry land near coast. Voice: very high bickering *wecweckerwec* or *eeeh eeeh*. U,WSpr.

2 **BRIDLED TERN** *Sterna anaethetus* (Golondrina-marina/Charrán Embridada/o) L 35 cm. Black cap contrasts with grey upperparts. Note long tail, projecting beyond wing tip. White eyebrow extends behind eye. Habitat: mainly offshore. Voice*: high quizzical *quip quip quip - -*, like small dog's bark. Me(CAm).

3 **SOOTY TERN** *Sterna fuscata* (Golondrina-marina Oscura; Charrán Sombrío) L 40 cm. Cap and upperparts concolorous black. Note dark underparts of imm. Eyebrow short. Habitat: offshore and inshore. Voice: high *whydeeweeh*. PacCar.

4 **LARGE-BILLED TERN** *Phaetusa simplex* (Charrán Pecudo) L 40 cm. Unmistakable. Habitat: beaches, mangrove, estuaries. Voice: high nasal *pjwéet pjwéet*. U,Pa.

5 **BLACK TERN** *Chlidonias niger* (Golondrina-marina/Fumarel Negra/o) L 25 cm. Note black patch to sides of n-br plumage. In br plumage (probably not seen in the area) looks black with dark grey upperwing, white undertail coverts and underwings. Habitat: mainly coastal in winter. Voice: high scratchy *shrets shret - -*, accelerated to *--sretsretsret*. Thr.

6 **INCA TERN** *Larosterna inca* (Charrán Inca) L 40 cm. Unmistakable. Habitat: rocky coasts. Voice*: low guttural rattling, sometimes ending in trill *kekekekeke-krrr* and harsh *kar*. V,Pa during severe El Niño.

7 **BROWN NODDY** *Anous stolidus* (Golondrina-boba Café; Tiñosa Común) L 40 cm. From smaller 8 by paler-centred underwing and pale wing bar. Habitat: inshore and offshore. Voice: mostly silent. Me(CAm).

8 **BLACK NODDY** *Anous minutus* (Golondrina-boba/Tiñosa Negra/o) L 35 cm. More slender bill than 7. Habitat: inshore and offshore. Voice: mostly silent. U,YMeCAm.

9 (Common) **WHITE TERN** *Gygis alba* (Golondrina-boba/Charrán Blanco) L 30 cm. Unmistakable, no similar bird in its habitat. Habitat: coral islands. Voice*: harsh grating *krrp-kwip*. U,Pac.

10 **BLACK SKIMMER** *Rynchops niger* (Rayador Americano/Negro) L 45 cm. Unmistakable; very long-winged. Characterised by unique fishing method: ploughs with tip of lower mandible through water surface, until bills snaps shut when touching fish. Habitat: open coastal waters and rivers. Voice: low bouncing *wecwecwec* or *èck-èck-èckèck*. WSpr.

Plate 34

Plate 35

1   **FERAL PIGEON** *Columba livia* (Paloma Doméstica) L 35 cm. Shown is a form of the original wild Rock Dove. Feral pigeons live now in many cities in the world; they often show basic features like white rump, black wing bars and purple-green neck patches of their wild ancestors. Habitat: towns; occasionally at cliffs, away from settlement. Voice: well-known rolling cooing. No map.

2   **SCALED PIGEON** *Columba speciosa* (Paloma Escamosa) L 30 cm. Scaled neck and underparts diagnostic. Habitat: forest canopy, edge and clearings. Voice: high *wóook-kóokkukooh*. SMeCAm.

3   **PALE-VENTED PIGEON** *Columba cayennensis* (Paloma Vientre-claro/Colorada) L 25 cm. Note black bill, white belly and vent, reddish upperparts, absence of cheek markings. Habitat: mangrove, riverine belts, scattered tree stands, forest edge. Voice: very high *pooróopoóeh*. SMeCAm.

4   **PLUMBEOUS PIGEON** *Columba plumbea* (Paloma Plomiza) L 30 cm. Rather uniform coloured with pale eye. From 9 by more purple, not brown tinge. Restricted range. Habitat: forest, tall second growth. Voice: very high punctuated *wuk-wukwúk-wukwook*. V,Pa.

5   **WHITE-CROWNED PIGEON** *Columba leucocephala* (Paloma Coroniblanca) L 30 cm. Very dark with white crown. Habitat: forest, mangrove. YMeBe(HoCR).

6   **RED-BILLED PIGEON** *Columba flavirostris* (Paloma Morada/Piquirroja) L 35 cm. Overall dark with bi-coloured bill. Habitat: open forest and forest edge; <1750 m. Voice: high hollow drawn-out *wuuuh* or *wuúuh ukurriúh*. WSpr.

7   **BAND-TAILED PIGEON** *Columba fasciata* (Paloma Encinera/Collareja) L 40 cm. Note large size, grey upperparts, vinaceous underparts. Nom (shown) with narrower white collar; race *albilinea* (White-naped Pigeon CRPa, not shown) darker with more distinct white collar. Habitat: montane woodland, open forest; 1000–3000 m. Voice: high *hoooh hukk(e)rúh*. WSpr.

8   **SHORT-BILLED PIGEON** *Columba nigrirostris* (Paloma Piquinegra/Piquicorta) L 30 cm. Difficult to separate from next species but with different voice. Bill shorter and heavier. Habitat: forest; <1000 m. Voice: high *wóotrehhwóowuw* or *woot-wootwèwwew*. SMeCAm.

9   **RUDDY PIGEON** *Columba subvinacea* (Paloma Rojiza) L 30 cm. At higher elevations than 8. Habitat: montane forest; >(1000)1500 m. Voice: high cooing *wúk wukwúkooh*. SMeCAm.

10 **DUSKY PIGEON** *Columba goodsoni* (Paloma Oscura) L 25 cm. Note diagnostic grey head and neck. Habitat: forest. Voice: high wooden *wóooh-wukwuk* or slurred-up *urrrh*. V,Me.

11 **PURPLISH-BACKED QUAIL DOVE** *Geotrygon lawrencii* (Paloma-perdiz Morena/Sombría) L 25 cm. From 12 by pale tail corners and by range. Habitat: forest; <1500 m. Voice: very high descending *tju-íow*. U,NiCRPa.

12 **TUXTLA** (or Veracruz) **QUAIL DOVE** *Geotrygon carrikeri* (Paloma-perdiz de Veracruz) L 30 cm. No white in tail; restricted range. Habitat: montane forest; 350–2000 m. Voice*: very low *boom boom boom - -* in irregular series. Each strophe with downward inflection and slightly choked. E,Me.

13 **BUFF-FRONTED QUAIL DOVE** *Geotrygon costaricensis* (Paloma-perdiz Costarriqueña) L 25 cm. Note plump jizz, plain tail, dark eyes. Habitat: montane forest; 1000–3000 m. Voice*: low hooting series of between 6 and 9, each strophe with upward inflection *whoo whoo whoo - -*. U,CRPa.

14 **RUSSET-CROWNED QUAIL DOVE** *Geotrygon goldmani* (Paloma-perdiz de Goldman) L 30 cm. Note black malar stripe below pale rufous cheek and grey breast. Habitat: montane forest undergrowth; 750–1500 m. Voice: high hollow sharply descending *íooow*. U,Pa.

15 **RUFOUS-BREASTED** (or Chiriqui) **QUAIL DOVE** *Geotrygon chiriquensis* (Paloma-perdiz Pechicanela) L 30 cm. Uniform reddish-brown with grey crown. Habitat: undergrowth of montane forest; 500–3000 m. Voice: high hollow drawn-out *whuooow*. CRPa.

16 **OLIVE-BACKED QUAIL DOVE** *Geotrygon veraguensis* (Paloma-perdiz Bigotiblanca) L 25 cm. Note dark olive upperparts, rufous-tawny undertail coverts, well-marked face pattern. Habitat: ground level of dense forest; <500 m. Voice: U,NiCRPa.

17 **RUDDY QUAIL DOVE** *Geotrygon montana* (Paloma-perdiz Rojiza) L 25 cm. Distinctive head pattern. Habitat: forest; sl–1500 m. Voice: low drawn-out *uuh uuh uuh*. WSpr.

18 **VIOLACEOUS QUAIL DOVE** *Geotrygon violacea* (Paloma-perdiz Violácea) L 25 cm. Note violet neck, grey crown, reddish bill. Only quail dove in range to lack black malar stripe. Habitat: forest undergrowth, tall second growth, cacao plantations. Voice: very high hollow *wiuoh*, slightly descending. U,NiCRPa.

19 **WHITE-FACED QUAIL DOVE** *Geotrygon albifacies* (Paloma-perdiz Cariblanca) L 30 cm. Whitish throat and cheeks contrasting with grey crown and nape diagnostic. No malar stripe. Whitish striped neck sides. Habitat: montane forest; (250)1000–2750 m. Voice: high *wooh wooh - -*. WSpr.

Plate 35

Plate 36

1 **WHITE-WINGED DOVE** *Zenaida asiatica* (Paloma Aliblanca) L 30 cm. White wing bar diagnostic. Habitat: woodland, savanna, ranchland; sl–2500 m. Voice: high slow irregular *ehcooéh-coo cóoeh cóoeh* or *coocoo-coo-coo*. WSpr.

2 **ZENAIDA DOVE** *Zenaida aurita* (Paloma de Zenaida) L 30 cm. Note white trailing edge to secondaries. Habitat: coastal scrub, mangrove. Voice: high very slow *wuuuhuh wuhwuhwuh*. YMe.

3 **MOURNING DOVE** *Zenaida macroura* (Paloma Huilota/ Rabuda) L 30 cm. From 4 by grey, not rufous underwings and pointed tail. Habitat: open woodland, savanna, any area with scarce trees, hedges and scrub. Voice: high very slow pitiful *tehjóouw tjeh tjeh-tjeh*. Thr.

4 **SOCORRO** (or Grayson's) **DOVE** *Zenaida graysoni* (Paloma de Socorro) L 30 cm. Rufous-tawny below. Habitat: open forest. Voice: low hoarse slow *eeeehwúoow ooch ochoch*. Extinct in the wild.

5 **EARED DOVE** *Zenaida auriculata* (Paloma Torcaza) L 25 cm. Rich rufescent below except grey underwing, tail not pointed. Habitat: dry scrub, open woodland. Voice: low *wooUh wuuh-wuuh*. V,Pa.

6 **SPOTTED DOVE** *Streptopelia chinensis* (Tórtola Moteada) L 30 cm. Rather dark with diagnostic neck spots. Habitat: suburban regions. Voice: very high *prupróooh-pruh*. I,NMe.

7 **EURASIAN COLLARED DOVE** *Streptopelia decaocto* (Tórtola Turca) L 35 cm. Very pale with black, white-bordered collar. Habitat: suburban regions. Voice: high *cuk-cóoohcóooh-cuk-cooohcoooh--*. Hyp,MeBe.

8 **INCA DOVE** *Columbina inca* (Tórtola/ita Colilarga) L 20 cm. Adult unmistakable by scaly feathering above and below. Note absence of wing spots. Habitat: savanna, open cultivation. Voice: very high yelping *wehw-pwew* or *wehprew-prew*. WSpr.

9 **COMMON GROUND DOVE** *Columbina passerina* (Tórtola/ita Común) L 17 cm. From 10 by scaly breast and crown and by red-based bill. Habitat: open woodland, savanna, suburban areas. Voice: high plaintive slightly drawn-up or level repeated *uoóh - -*. WSpr.

10 **PLAIN-BREASTED GROUND DOVE** *Columbina minuta* (Tórtola/ita Pechilisa/Menuda) L 15 cm. Note all-black bill, absence of scaling, duller red in wing. Habitat: savanna. Voice: high *whep-whep- -* (10 x). WSpr.

11 **RUDDY GROUND DOVE** *Columbina talpacoti* (Tórtola/ita Rojiza) L 16 cm. ♂ unmistakable, ♀ from other ground doves by spots to scapulars. Habitat: open areas, suburbs. Voice: sustained *puwoh-puwoh-puwoh*. WSpr.

12 **BLUE GROUND DOVE** *Claravis pretiosa* (Tórtola/ita Azul/Azulada) L 20 cm. ♂ unmistakable; note rufous rump and tail of ♀. Habitat: forest interior, edge and clearings. Voice: high irregularly interspaced *hoop hoop hoop-hoop - -*. WSpr.

13 **MAROON-CHESTED GROUND DOVE** *Claravis mondetoura* (Tórtola/ita Pechimorada/Serranera) L 20 cm. ♂ unmistakable; ♀ from ♀ 12 by more rufous face sides, well demarcated from whitish chin and less rufous in pale-edged tail. Habitat: open forest, tall second growth, bamboo. Voice: high *tthooh tthooh tthooh - -*. U, SMeCAm.

14 **WHITE-TIPPED DOVE** *Leptotila verreauxi* (Paloma Arroyera/Coliblanca) L 25 cm. Pale-headed with rufous underwings. Large white tail corners. Habitat: forest undergrowth, second growth, woodland, cultivation. Voice: high slow hollow melancholic *fúfifjuuew*. WSpr.

15 **GREY-HEADED DOVE** *Leptotila plumbeiceps* (Paloma Cabecigrís/Coronigrís) L 25 cm. Dark brown upperparts except grey crown and neck. Note tail pattern. Habitat: forest undergrowth, second growth. Voice: low lowered *whuow*. WSpr.

16 **BROWN-BACKED DOVE** *Leptotila battyi* (Paloma Montaraz de Coiba) L 25 cm. From 15 mainly by rufous upperparts. Habitat: forest. U,Pa.

17 **CARIBBEAN** (or White-bellied) **DOVE** *Leptotila jamaicensis* (Paloma Caribeña) L 30 cm. From 15 by violet neck sides. Not in same range as greyer-breasted 18. In drier areas than 15 and 18. Habitat: dry woodland. Voice: high sad running-down *úptjooh-tutjow*. YMeBe.

18 **GREY-CHESTED DOVE** *Leptotila cassinii* (Paloma Pechigrís) L 25 cm. Note tail pattern and tawny-rufous nape. Habitat: second growth, plantations, forest undergrowth; <750(1250)m. Voice: low lowered sad *whuuow*. SMeCAm.

Plate 36

Plate 37

1   **GREEN PARAKEET** *Aratinga holochlora* (Perico Verde Mexicano) L 30 cm. From 2 by smaller, less deep bill and more orange to throat. Little overlap of ranges. Habitat: forest, plantations; sl–1750 m. WSpr.

2   **PACIFIC PARAKEET** *Aratinga strenua* (Perico Verde Centroamericano) L 30 cm. (?/1). See 1. Habitat: forest, woodland, plantations; sl–1500(2500 in Guatemala)m. SMeCAm.

3   **RED-THROATED PARAKEET** *Aratinga rubritorquis* (Perico Gorjirrojo) L 30 cm. (?/1). Orange throat diagnostic. Note purplish bare eye ring. Habitat: mixed pine and semi-deciduous forest; 500–2000 m. CAm.

4   **SOCORRO PARAKEET** *Aratinga brevipes* (Perico de Socorro) L 30 cm. (?/1). No other parakeets in its range. Habitat: forest; >500 m. U,Me.

5   **ORANGE-FRONTED PARAKEET** *Aratinga canicularis* (Perico Frentinaranja) L 25 cm. Of three races nom (a) and race *clarae* (b) shown. Note orange front, blue crown, blue in wings. Habitat: open forest, plantations; sl–1500 m. WSpr.

6   **CRIMSON-FRONTED PARAKEET** *Aratinga finschi* (Perico Frentirrojo) L 30 cm. Note red front and orange-yellow underwing pattern. Habitat: open woodland, ranchland, plantations. NiCRPa.

7   **OLIVE-THROATED** (or Aztec) **PARAKEET** *Aratinga nana* (Perico Pechisucio/Azteco) L 25 cm. Shows saffron wash over chest and throat. Habitat: dense woodland, open forest, cultivation; sl–1000 m. WSpr.

8   **BROWN-THROATED PARAKEET** *Aratinga pertinax* (Perico Pertinax) L 25 cm. Note saffron-olive cheeks and throat. Small overlap with range of 7. Habitat: savanna, woodland, mangrove; <1250 m. CRPa.

9   **SULPHUR-WINGED PARAKEET** *Pyrrhura hoffmannzi* (Perico Aliazufrado) L 25 cm. Head pattern and yellow in wings diagnostic. Note reddish tail. Habitat: montane forest; 750(1250)–3000 m. CRPa.

10   **PAINTED PARAKEET** *Pyrrhura picta* (Perico Pintada) L 20 cm. Distinctly patterned. Habitat: forest and forest remains. U,Pa.

11   **BARRED PARAKEET** *Bolborhynchus lineola* (Periquito Barrado/Listado) L 17 cm. Scaly appearance diagnostic. Paler below than above. Habitat: montane forest edge, tall second growth; attracted to seeding bamboo; 500–2500 m. U,SMeCAm.

12   **MEXICAN** (or Blue-rumped) **PARROTLET** *Forpus cyanopygius* (Periquito Mexicano) L 14 cm. Small, short-tailed, with bluish underwings. Habitat: forest, gallery forest, plantations; <1500 m. E,Me.

13   **SPECTACLED PARROTLET** *Forpus conspicillatus* (Periquito de Anteojos) L 13 cm. As 12, but not in same range. Habitat: forest, gallery forest, cultivation. U,Pa.

14   **ORANGE-CHINNED PARAKEET** *Brotogeris jugularis* (Periquito Barbinaranja) L 19 cm. Note white bill base, orange-olive chin and shoulders. Yellow underwings without red diagnostic. Habitat: savanna, open woodland, cultivation, suburban regions. SMeCAm.

15   **RED-FRONTED PARROTLET** *Touit costaricensis* (Periquito Alirroja) L 17 cm. Note red leading edge of wing. From 16 by head pattern. Habitat: montane forest; (sl)500–3000 m. U,CRPa.

16   **BLUE-FRONTED PARROTLET** *Touit dilectissima* (Periquito Cariazul) L 18 cm. Not in range of 15. Habitat: forest, tall second growth; <1000 m. U,Pa.

17   **WHITE-CROWNED PARROT** *Pionus senilis* (Loro Coroniblanco) L 25 cm. White crown diagnostic. Note blue underwings. Habitat: forest and forest edge; sl–1500 m. WSpr.

18   **BLUE-HEADED PARROT** *Pionus menstruus* (Loro Cabeciazul) L 25 cm. Blue head diagnostic. Habitat: open forest, woodland, plantations. CRPa.

Plate 37

Plate 38

1   **BLUE-AND-YELLOW MACAW** *Ara ararauna* (Guacamayo Azulamarillo)   L 85 cm.
Unmistakable. Habitat: swampy forest; <500 m. Pa.

2   **MILITARY MACAW** *Ara militaris* (Guacamaya Verde)   L 70 cm. Smaller than 4. Habitat: forest;
sl–2000 m. Me.

3   **SCARLET MACAW** *Ara macao* (Guacamaya/o Roja/o)   L 85 cm. Not in same range as 5.
Habitat: forest; <500(1000)m. U,SMeCAm.

4   **GREAT GREEN MACAW** *Ara ambigua* (Guacamaya/o Verde Mayor)   L 90 cm. From 2 by paler
head and back and with longer tail. Habitat: forest and forest remains. CAm.

5   **RED-AND-GREEN MACAW** *Ara chloroptera* (Guacamayo Aliverde)   L 95 cm. Green, not
yellow in wing. Habitat: forest, riverine belts. U,Pa.

6   **CHESTNUT-FRONTED MACAW** *Ara severa* (Guacamayo Severo)   L 50 cm. White bare skin
on head and red underwings diagnostic. Habitat: forest, tall second growth, often near swamp or
streams; <500 m. U,Pa.

7   **THICK-BILLED PARROT** *Rhynchopsitta pachyrhyncha* (Cotorra-serrana Occidental)   L 40 cm.
As 8 with black bill, but with red front and with different underwing pattern. Habitat: pine forest;
1500–3000 m. E,Me.

8   **MAROON-FRONTED PARROT** *Rhynchopsitta terrisi* (Cotorra-serrana Oriental)   L 40 cm.
Note black underwing with red leading edge. Habitat: pine forest; 2000–3000 m. E,Me.

9   **BROWN-HOODED PARROT** *Pionopsitta haematotis* (Loro Orejirrojo/Cabecipardo)   L 25 cm.
Dark chin and red armpits diagnostic. Habitat: forest, tall second growth; <1500 m. SMeCAm.

10   **SAFFRON-HEADED PARROT** *Pionopsitta pyrilia* (Loro Cabecigualdo)   L 25 cm. Distinctly
patterned. Habitat: forest, tall second growth; <1000 m. U,Pa.

Note: members of the following genus *Amazona* are often called 'Amazons'.

11   **WHITE-FRONTED PARROT** *Amazona albifrons* (Loro Frentiblanco)   L 30 cm. From 12 by
more red to greater wing coverts. Habitat: forest, open woodland, mangrove; sl–1750 m. WSpr.

12   **YELLOW-LORED** (or Yucatan) **PARROT** *Amazona xantholora* (Loro Yucateco)   L 30 cm.
Note blue-black ear patch and yellow lores. Habitat: forest and forest edge. YMeBe(Ho).

13   **RED-CROWNED PARROT** *Amazona viridigenalis* (Loro Tamaulipeco)   L 35 cm. As 14 but with
red, not lilac crown and not in same range. Habitat: forest, open woodland; <1000 m. U,NMe.

14   **LILAC-CROWNED PARROT** *Amazona finschi* (Loro Corona-violeta)   L 35 cm. See 13.
Habitat: woodland, mangrove; sl–2250 m. E,Me.

15   **RED-LORED** (or Yellow-cheeked) **PARROT** *Amazona autumnalis* (Loro Cachete-amarillo/
Frentirrojo) L 35 cm. Of several races nom (a) and race *salvini* (b) shown. From 13 by yellow face
sides (a) or less red on crown (b). Habitat: forest, open woodland; sl–750(1000) m. WSpr.

16   **YELLOW-CROWNED PARROT** *Amazona ochrocephala* (Loro Cabeciamarillo)   L 40 cm.
Many colour forms (or races) exist, of these *oratrix* (a), *parvipes* (b) and *auropalliata* (c, Yellow-
naped Parrot) shown. All have some red on shoulder. Habitat: woodland, tall bush, cultivation,
mangrove; <500 m. U,WSpr.

17   **MEALY PARROT** *Amazona farinosa* (Loro Verde)   L 40 cm. Nom (a) and race *guatemalae* (b)
shown. From 16 by absence of red on shoulder. Race b without yellow on head, but with bluish
nape. Habitat: forest; <500(1000) m. SMeCAm.

18   **YELLOW-HEADED PARROT** *Amazona oratrix* (Loro Cabeciamarillo)   L 40 cm. (?/16). All-
yellow head diagnostic. Habitat: open woodland, riverine belts, mangrove; <500 m. U,BeGuHo.

Plate 38

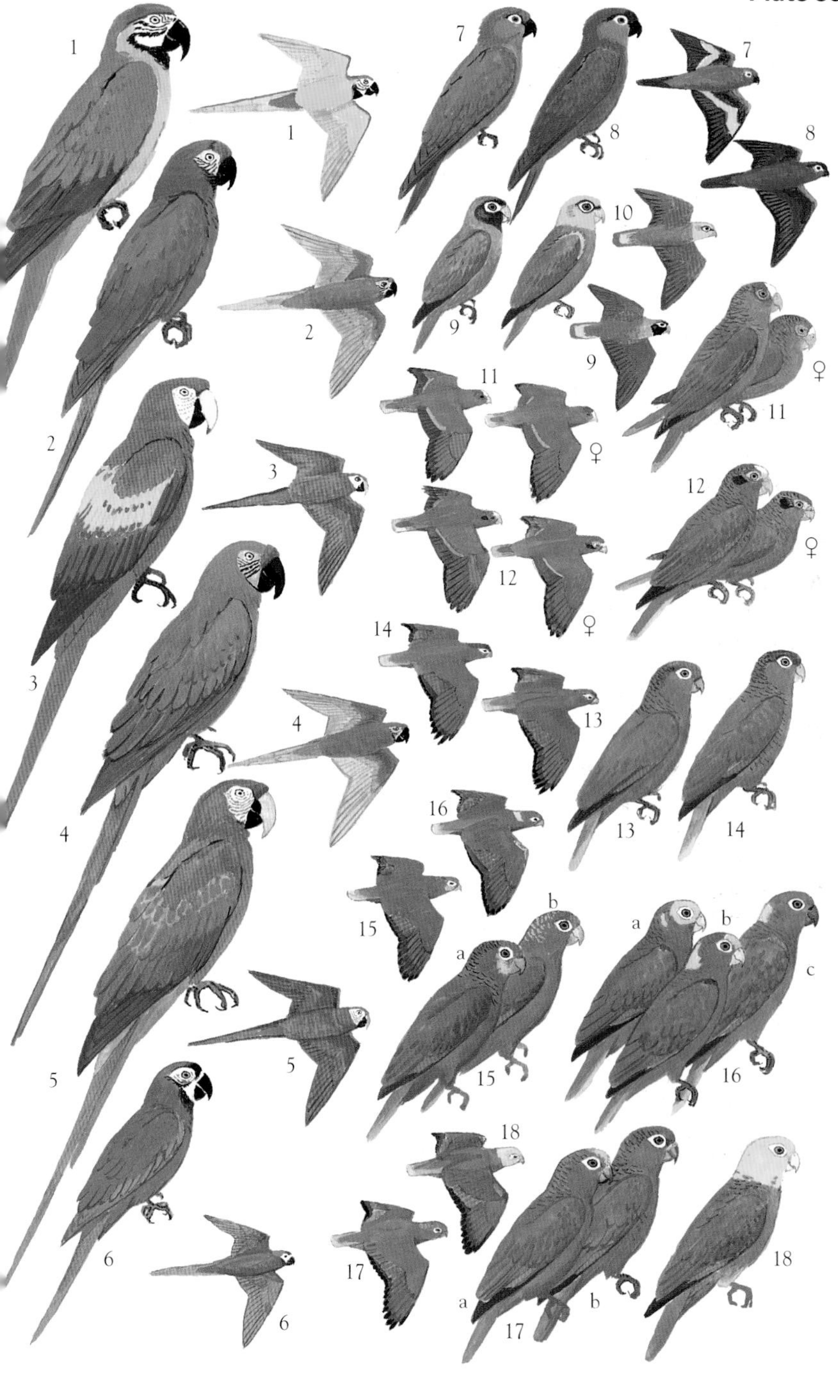
1
1
7
8
7
8
2
10
2
9
9
11
11
♀
11
2
♀
3
12
12
♀
12
♀
3
14
4
13
13
14
4
16
15
b
a
a
b
c
15
16
5
5
18
6
18
17
6
a
b
17

Plate 39

1   **DWARF CUCKOO** *Coccyzus pumilus* (Cuclillo Enano)   L 20 cm. Rufous chest and throat diagnostic. Note red eye and relatively short tail. Habitat: open woodland, cultivation, riverine belts, woodland, forest. Voice: very high House Sparrow-like *tjirp-tjirp-tjirp- -* (8–9 x). V,Pa.

2   **BLACK-BILLED CUCKOO** *Coccyzus erythropthalmus* (Cuco/Cuclillo Piquinegro)   L 30 cm. Lower mandible grey, not yellowish. Note tail pattern and red eyelids. Habitat: forest interior and edge; sl–3000 m. Voice: very high hurried *cuckcuckooh* or rapid *coocoh*. WSpr.

3   **YELLOW-BILLED CUCKOO** *Coccyzus americanus* (Cuco Piquiamarillo; Cuclillo Piquigualdo)   L 30 cm. Bi-coloured wings and white underparts diagnostic. Habitat: riverine belts, forest; sl–1500(2500)m. Voice: very high nasal *tjark-tjark- -* (8x) or bouncing *tjitjitji--*. WSpr.

4   **MANGROVE CUCKOO** *Coccyzus minor* (Cuco Manglero; Cuclillo de Antifaz)   L 35 cm. Note black mask and absence of rufous in wings. Habitat: mangrove and understorey of coastal woodland and forest. Voice: low croaking *crakrakrakcrowcrow*. WSpr.

5   **GREY-CAPPED CUCKOO** *Coccyzus lansbergi* (Cuclillo Cabecigrís)   L 25 cm. Contrast between grey crown and rufous upperparts diagnostic. Habitat: wooded marsh, forest. Voice: high rhythmic wooden rapid *jeWokokokokokokok*. U,Pa.

6   **COCOS CUCKOO** *Coccyzus ferrugineus* (Cuclillo de la Isla Coco)   L 30 cm. Only cuckoo in its range. Habitat: forest. E,CR.

7   **SQUIRREL CUCKOO** *Piaya cayana* (Cuco Ardilla)   L 45 cm. Races *mexicana* (a) and *thermophila* (b) shown. Unmistakable by rufous colouring and yellow bill. Habitat: forest, woodland, riverine belts, wooded savanna. Voice: very high well-separated yelping *wew wew wew - -* or low shrill *wietjer*. WSpr

8   **LITTLE CUCKOO** *Piaya minuta* (Cuco Menor)   L 25 cm. From much larger 7 by red orbital ring and less contrast between breast and further underparts. Habitat: dense undergrowth at forest edge, often near water; <500 m. Voice: *puuuw* (rising)-*kikikik* (very rapid). U,Pa.

9   **STRIPED CUCKOO** *Tapera naevia* (Cuco Rayado; Cuclillo Listado)   L 30 cm. Striped mantle diagnostic; from 10 by narrower tail. Habitat: open country, often near water; sl–1250 m. Voice: very high fluted slightly rising *fjut-fjeet(-fjeeteweet)* or drawn-up *fueeet*. WSpr.

10   **PHEASANT CUKOO** *Dromococcyx phasianellus* (Cuco/Cuclillo Faisán)   L 35 cm. Difficult to spot. Note small head, full tail. Habitat: ground and undergrowth of forest, woodland, plantations; sl–1500 m. Voice: high accentuated *heeeh* or low nasal *tjikurur* or high nasal *tu-ti tjurr*. WSpr.

11   **LESSER GROUND CUCKOO** *Morococcyx erythropygus* (Cuco-terrestre Menor; Cuclillo Sabanero)   L 25 cm. Note greenish wash and black-bordered, blue naked skin round eye. Evasive. Habitat: dry woodland and forest edge; sl–1500 m. Voice: very high nasal yet mellow fluted *preuww preuww - -*, drawn up to *djupdjupdjup*. WSpr.

12   **RUFOUS-VENTED GROUND CUCKOO** *Neomorphus geoffroyi* (Cuco Hormiguero)   L 50 cm. Jizz and movements as roadrunner, but in different habitat. Often at army-ant swarms. Note breast collar. Habitat: ground of dense forest undergrowth; <1000 m. Voice: explosive bill snaps. U,NiCRPa.

13   **LESSER ROADRUNNER** *Geococcyx velox* (Correcaminos Menor)   L 50 cm. Throat and breast unmarked, not striped as 14. Habitat: arid open woodland; sl–3000 m. Voice: low cooing descending *wooboo-wooboo- -*. WSpr.

14   **GREATER ROADRUNNER** *Geococcyx californianus* (Correcaminos Mayor)   L 55 cm. Striped throat and breast diagnostic. Habitat: open country, arid bush; sl–2500 m. Voice: cooing *woop-whoo-whoo-whoeoe*. Me.

15   **SMOOTH-BILLED ANI** *Crotophaga ani* (Garrapatero Piquiliso)   L 35 cm. From 16 mainly by smooth bill and voice. Habitat: open woodland, cultivation, marsh, cattle land; sl–2500 m. Voice: very high drawn-up slightly shivering shrieks or low mewing *wow-wow-wow*. (YMeBe)CRPa.

16   **GROOVE-BILLED ANI** *Crotophaga sulcirostris* (Garrapatero Asurcado)   L 30 cm. From 15 by grooved, less arched bill. Habitat: open woodland, cultivation, marsh, cattle land; sl–1750 m. Voice: very high staccato *tjirrúp tjirrúp - -*. WSpr.

17   **GREATER ANI** *Crotophaga major* (Garrapatero Mayor) L 45 cm. From smaller 15 and 16 by yellow eyes and stronger gloss. Habitat: forest, normally near water, riverine belts; <500 m. Voice: low mumbling croaking *whurroch whurroch - -* in chorus. Pa.

Plate 39

Plate 40

1 **BARN OWL** *Tyto alba* (Lechuza de Campanario/Ratonera)   L 35 cm. Unmistakable by very pale, almost white appearance. Habitat: open areas, cultivation, towns. Voice: harsh drawn-out screeches. Thr.

2 **CRESTED OWL** *Lophostrix cristata* (Búho Corniblanco/Penachudo)   L 40 cm. Unmistakable by large white ear tufts. Habitat: forest; sl–1750 m. Voice: very low drawn-up *wróng*. U,SMeCAm.

3 **SPECTACLED OWL** *Pulsatrix perspicillata* (Búho de Anteojos)   L 50 cm. Unmistakable by pied face pattern and contrasting upper- and underparts. Habitat: forest interior, edge and clearings; sl–1500 m. Voice: low rapid barking *wokwokwokwokwokwóhwokwok*. SMeCAm.

4 **GREAT HORNED OWL** *Bubo virginianus* (Búho Cornudo/Grande)   L 55 cm. Unmistakable by large size and thickset jizz. Habitat: any natural habitat, except true forest. Voice: low hooting *pooperoop poop poop*. WSpr.

5 **MOTTLED OWL** *Strix virgata* (Búho/Lechuza Café)   L 35 cm. Of several races *squamulata* (a) and dark form of nom (b) shown. Note round, 'friendly' face with white markings. Habitat: forest, open second growth; sl–1500(2500)m. Voice: very low *whów whów* or high mewing gliding up-and-down *miáol* or very high barking *wow-wow- -*. WSpr

6 **BLACK-AND-WHITE OWL** *Strix nigrolineata* (Búho Blanquinegro; Lechuza Blanco y Negro)   L 40 cm. Unmistakable by contrasting colouring with finely barred underparts. Habitat: forest and forest edge, plantations; sl–1250 m. Voice: mumbling *ruprupruprup* WUw. U,SMeCAm.

7 **SPOTTED OWL** *Strix occidentalis* (Búho Manchado)   L 45 cm. From 8 and 9 by rather barred, not striped underparts. Habitat: pine forest; >1000 m. Voice: low *hoot hoothoothoot*. U,Me.

8 **BARRED OWL** *Strix varia* (Búho Barrado)   L 50 cm. Not in same range as rather similar 9. Habitat: mixed pine forest; >1500 m. Voice: low rising *oh-oh-oh-oh -woow oohoe-oh-woew*. U,Me.

9 **FULVOUS OWL** *Strix fulvescens* (Búho Fulvo)   L 45 cm. From 8 by barred mantle. Habitat: forest; >1250 m. Voice: low barking *oh wow oh wow oh ooh-ooh*. MeGuSa.

10 **LONG-EARED OWL** *Asio otus* (Búho-cornudo Caricafé)   L 35 cm. More rufous-tinged than 11, especially in face. Also with more distinctly barred upperparts. Habitat: forest, in winter also in open woodland. Voice: high lonely *hoo hoo hoo*. Me.

11 **STYGIAN OWL** *Asio stygius* (Búho-cornudo Oscuro)   L 40 cm. From 10 by darker plumage and absence of rufous in wings. Habitat: pine forest; >1500 m. Voice: low hooting *woow woow - -* or well-separated *ooh ooh ooh*. WSpr.

12 **STRIPED OWL** *Asio clamator* (Búho-cornudo Cariblanco; Búho Listado)   L 35 cm. Unmistakable by white face and black eyes combined with ear tufts. Habitat: open woodland, savanna; <1000 m. Voice: low barking *whow* or very high slightly Peacock-like *weeuw*. U,WSpr.

13 **SHORT-EARED OWL** *Asio flammeus* (Búho Orejicorto; Lechuza Campestre)   L 35 cm. Note 'blazing' eyes, rufous in wings, short ear tufts. Terrestrial. Habitat: savanna, marsh; sl–3000 m. Voice: high sharp *mew-mew* or *sreeeeeh*. U,WSpr.

14 **NORTHERN SAW-WHET OWL** *Aegolius acadicus* (Tecolote-abetero Norteño)   L 19 cm. Note large head with small body. White spotting on upperparts diagnostic. Habitat: pine forest; 1750–3500 m. Voice: very high sustained hooting *woot-woot- -* (slightly rising). Me.

15 **UNSPOTTED SAW-WHET OWL** *Aegolius ridgwayi* (Tecolote-abetero Sureño; Lechucita Parda)   L 20 cm. Not in same range as 14. Habitat: mixed oak forest; 1500–3000 m. Voice: very high sustained hooting *woot-woot- -* (10-30 x). SMeCAm.

16 **BURROWING OWL** *Athene cunicularia* (Búho/Lechuza Llanero) L 20 cm. Unmistakable by posture (upright stance on ground) and habitat. Habitat: open country, dry savanna. Voice: (very) high lonely *tittereeh*. WSpr.

Plate 40

Plate 41

Note: owls on this plate are very variable in colour. Grey(-brown) and rufous forms shown of 8, 9a and 19.

1   **FLAMMULATED OWL** *Otus flammeolus* (Tecolote Flameado)   L 16 cm. Unmistakable by small size and black eyes. Habitat: pine forest; 1500–3000 m. Voice: very high irregular placed *ooh ooh ooh - -*. Me(Gu).

2   **EASTERN SCREECH OWL** *Otus asio* (Tecolote Oriental)   L 25 cm. Note greyish bill and coarse striping and barring below. Habitat: woodland; <1500 m. Voice: shivering descending *hihihihiererrr*. Me. Note: on the Pacific slope of Oaxaca (Me) there is a population of screech owls, resembling this species but with darker upperparts and more bristled than feathered toes, which might be a separate species: Oaxaca Screech Owl *Otus lambi*.

3   **WESTERN SCREECH OWL** *Otus kennicottii* (Tecolote Occidental)   L 25 cm. Finer barred below than 2; note black bill. Habitat: dry woodland; sl–2500 m. Voice: (very) high accelerated *ooh-ooh-ooh-oohohdear*. Me.

4   **TROPICAL SCREECH OWL** *Otus choliba* (Lechucita Neotropical)   L 25 cm. Shares range only with 8 and 9 (both forest species), separable only by voice and habitat. Habitat: open woodland, suburban areas; 500–1500 m. Voice: high loud hooted *prrrruowHów*. CRPa.

5   **BARE-SHANKED SCREECH OWL** *Otus clarkii* (Lechucita Serranera)   L 25 cm. Note weakly marked facial disk, absence of facial rim, rufous eyebrows. Habitat: montane forest interior, edge and clearings; >750(1250)m. Voice: high *poo-puuhpuuh* or *pooh-pooh-pooh-pooh*. NiCRPa.

6   **BALSAS SCREECH OWL** *Otus seductus* (Tecolote del Balsas)   L 25 cm. (?/3). Dark, but not black eyes. Habitat: tall thorn, high cactus, dry open country. Voice: high bouncing descending *ooh-ooh-ohohohrorr*. E,Me.

7   **PACIFIC SCREECH OWL** *Otus cooperi* (Tecolote de Cooper; Sabanera)   L 25 cm. (?/3). In range of 8 and 9, but not in the same habitat. Habitat: dry open woodland; >1000 m. Voice: high level loud *datdat--* or drawn-up *rrrorrororororor*. SMeCAm.

8   **WHISKERED** (or Spotted) **SCREECH OWL** *Otus trichopsis* (Tecolote Bigotudo)   L 18 cm. From 9 by coarse streaking below. Habitat: montane mixed oak forest; 750–2500 m. Voice: high hooted *hoothoot--(6–7 x)--hot*. WSpr.

9   **VERMICULATED** (or Guatemalan) **SCREECH OWL** *Otus guatemalae* (Tecolote/Lechucita Vermiculado/a) L 25 cm. Nom (a) shown and race *vermiculatus* (b, Middle American Screech Owl, probably a separate species). Naked toes diagnostic. Note inconspicuous ear tufts, little streaking below. Habitat: forest, scrubby woodland; <1500 m. Voice: very high trilling rising or level *drrr--* (6–7s). WSpr.

10   **BRIDLED** (or Bearded) **SCREECH OWL** *Otus barbarus* (Tecolote Barbudo)   L 18 cm. No ear tufts. From pygmy owls by different patterning of upperparts. Habitat: mixed pine forest; 1500–2500 m. Voice: very high rhythmic *how* (1/3s) or (accelerated) trill. U,SMeGu.

11   **MOUNTAIN PYGMY OWL** *Glaucidium gnoma* (Tecolotito Serrano)   L 16 cm. Nom (a) and race *cobanense* (b) shown. (?/12). In same range as 16 (which prefers lower altitudes), 17 (with more bi-coloured plumage and restricted range), 18 (grey-headed), 19 (with shorter and barred tail; lower elevations). Habitat: mixed forest; 1500–3500 m. Voice: very high slightly irregular hurried sustained *wegweg-wegweg- -*. MeGuHo. Note: all pygmy owls have a pseudo-face on the back of the head, see 13a and 19a.

12   **NORTHERN PYGMY OWL** *Glaucidium californicum* (Tecolotito Norteño)   L 17 cm. Could occur in range of 11 and 19; best distinguished by voice; 19 at lower elevations. Habitat: mixed pine forest; >2000 m. Voice: very high *ooh ooh* or barking *wew wew - -*. U,NMe.

13   **COSTA RICAN PYGMY OWL** *Glaucidium costaricanum* (Mochuelo Montañero)   L 15 cm. (?/11). Note diagnostic barring below. Habitat: montane, open forest and adjacent areas; 1000–3000 m. Voice: varied high hurried *weetweet--* or *weeetrurrurrrrr*. NiCRPa.

14   **CAPE PYGMY OWL** *Glaucidium hoskinsii* (Tecolotito del Cabo)   L 16 cm. (?/12). No other pygmy owl in its range. Habitat: pine forest; (500)1500–2000 m. Voice*: high long drawn-out irregularly spaced series of *phlew* notes (1/3s). Also a trilling *pooo-pu-pu-pu-pu-pu-pu-pu-pu-pu-pu* (4s). E,Me.

▶

Plate 41

Plate 41 continued

15 **LEAST PYGMY OWL** *Glaucidium minutissimum* (Mochuelo Enano) L 15 cm. Probably to be included in 18. As 18, but range from Panama southwards. Habitat: forest and adjacent areas; <750 m. Voice: very high regular or irregular *wood-hoot-hoot-* (10 x). U,NiCRPa.

16 **COLIMA PYGMY OWL** *Glaucidium palmarum* (Tecolotito Colimense) L 14 cm. (?/15). Scapular spots weak, rather short tail. Note finely spotted crown. Habitat: thorn forest; sl–1500 m. Voice high slightly descending *wook-wook-wok-wok-wok*. E,Me.

17 **TAMAULIPAS PYGMY OWL** *Glaucidium sanchezi* (Tecolotito Tamaulipeco) L 15 cm. (?/15). Restricted range; best distinguished from 11 by voice. Habitat: forest; 1000–2000 m. Voice: high plaintive hooting *fweet-fweet* or *oot-oot-oot*. E,Me.

18 **CENTRAL AMERICAN PYGMY OWL** *Glaucidium griseiceps* (Tecolotito Centroamericano) L 16 cm. (?/15). Head often greyer than unspotted mantle. Habitat: forest; sl–750(1250)m. Voice: high hooting slightly wooden or hurried *fjood-fjood-fjood*. U,SMeCAm.

19 **FERRUGINOUS PYGMY OWL** *Glaucidium brasilianum* (Tecolotito/Mochuelo Común) L 17 cm. Difficult to separate from 11, but crown streaked (not spotted), voice different and normally in different habitat. Habitat: forest, woodland, scrub, cultivation, plantations. Voice: very high barking sustained *wec-wec-wec- -*. WSpr.

20 **ELF OWL** *Micrathene whitneyi* (Tecolotito Enano) L 14 cm. Wings reach tail tip. Habitat: dry open woodland. Voice: high rapid *reprepripriprip* (1s) or mewing *wew wiw sreet*. Me.

Plate 42

Note: plumages of most species on this and following plate may vary between rufous and grey.

1 **GREAT POTOO** *Nyctibius grandis* (Biemparado/Nictibio Grande) L 50 cm. Variably coloured and patterned, but unmistakable by dark eyes. Habitat: forest; <500 m. Voice: loud spooky *WHOOUW*. SMeCAm.

2 **GREY** (or Common) **POTOO** *Nyctibius griseus* (Nictibio Urutaú) L 40 cm. Variable. Note large black spots around breast and mantle. Habitat: open woodland, savanna. Voice: very high calm descending to low wooden *fluu-flu-flu-fluh fluh*. U,CAm.

3 **NORTHERN POTOO** *Nyctibius jamaicensis* (Biemparado Norteño; Nictibio Común) L 40 cm. Variable. Not in range of 1 and 2, except in Costa Rica, where separated by mountains. Spots around mantle and breast smaller than 2. Habitat: savanna, open woodland, forest edge. Voice: high drawn-out croaking *crrrr-wahwah*. WSpr.

4 **OILBIRD** *Steatornis caripensis* (Guáchero) L 45 cm. Unmistakable. Habitat: forest. Sleeps and nests in caves. V,CRPa.

5 **SHORT-TAILED** (or Semi-collared) **NIGHTJAR** *Lurocalis semitorquatus* (Chotacabras/Añapero Colicorta/o) L 25 cm. Very dark without white in wings or tail. Note contrasting white throat. Habitat: forest; <500(1000) m. Voice: very high staccato fluted *piu piu - -* (6–12 x) or ultra high sweeping *tui tui - -* (5 x). U,SMeCAm.

6 **LESSER NIGHTHAWK** *Chordeiles acutipennis* (Chotacabras/Añapero Menor) L 20 cm. Note the characteristic long sharp-pointed wings of the nighthawks. Rather uniform grey with all flight feathers barred buff. Habitat: open woodland, savanna, marsh, cultivation; sl–2500 m. Voice: prolonged (5s) trills *rrrroh* or irritated *irrrrrr* or jabbering *jijiji--*. Thr.

7 **COMMON NIGHTHAWK** *Chordeiles minor* (Chotacabras Mayor; Añapero Zumbón) L 25 cm. Note bold markings on upperparts; flight feathers predominantly black. Habitat: dry open country, but also in forest; sl–2000 m. Voice: very high hoarse *sreeuw sreeuw - -*. Thr.

8 **ANTILLEAN NIGHTHAWK** *Chordeiles gundlachii* (Añapero Querequeté) L 20 cm. Not safely distinguishable from 7 except by voice. Habitat: dry open areas. Voice: ultra high hurried screeching *weetohweet*(*weetweet*). Hyp,YMe.

9 (Common) **PAURAQUE** *Nyctidromus albicollis* (Tapacaminos Picuyo/Común) L 25 cm. Note large white (buff in ♀) windows in wings and neat rows of black drops along scapulars. Habitat: forest, forest edge, riverine belts, plantations; <1750 m. Voice: very high *w-wéeeuw w-wíw* or very high *wuk wukweeeu* or ultra high *weeeuw*. WSpr.

▶

Plate 42

Plate 42 continued

10   OCELLATED POORWILL *Nyctiphrynus ocellatus* (Chotacabras Ocelado)   L 20 cm. Note 'bib', hiding large white throat patch of this and 11 and 12. Very uniform dark; from 43.10 by voice and at lower altitudes. Habitat: forest edge; <1350 m. Voice: high descending *wéeeeeeurw*. U,NiCRPa.

11   EARED POORWILL *Nyctiphrynus mcleodii* (Pachacua Prío)   L 20 cm. Note white wing spots and grey scapulars. Habitat: mixed forest, dry rocky woodland; 500–2500 m. Voice: very high sweeping *píuw píuw -*. E,Me.

12   YUCATAN POORWILL *Nyctiphrynus yucatanicus* (Pachacua Yucateca)   L 20 cm. Note large white tail corners (tail looks all-white below). Habitat: forest, scrub, woodland. Voice: very high rather mellow *whéeow wheeow*. YMeBe.

Plate 43

1   COMMON POORWILL *Phalaenoptilus nuttallii* (Pachacua Norteña)   L 20 cm. Short-tailed. Very large head, compared with rest of body. Habitat: dry, open country; sl–2500 m. Voice: very high *poorwittel-poorwittel- -* (4/5s). NMe.

2   (Northern) WHIP-POOR-WILL *Caprimulgus vociferus* (Tapacaminos Cuerprihuiu; Chotacabras Gritón)   L 25 cm. Very similar to 3, but with more white in tail. Ranges overlap marginally in winter. Note pale braces. Habitat: forest edge, open woodland, cultivation, suburbs. Voice: very high *wrup-wrrwèoh* or *whip-poor-wíll* (last part much higher). U,WSpr.

3   STEPHEN'S (or Mexican) WHIP-POOR-WILL *Caprimulgus arizonae* (Tapacaminos Cuerporruin)   L 25 cm. (?/2). See 2. Habitat: mixed forest; (500, winter) or 1250 (summer)–3000 m. Voice: as 2 but lower and slower. Me.

4   CHUCK-WILL'S-WIDOW *Caprimulgus carolinensis* (Tapacaminos Carolinense; Chotacabras de Paso)   L 30 cm. Overall rather rufous with characteristic tail pattern; 9, which is even more rufous, has different wing pattern in flight. Perches in trees. Habitat: forest, woodland with adjacent areas; sl–1500 m. Voice: very high fluting *tjúks-wills-wídow*. WSpr.

5   TAWNY-COLLARED NIGHTJAR *Caprimulgus salvini* (Tapacaminos Ti-cuer)   L 25 cm. No other nightjar with similar tail pattern in its range except 10 (in Panama), which is much darker rufous. Habitat: dry dense woodland; <500 m. Voice: very high fluting hurried sustained *pivrow-pivrow- -*. E,Me.

6   YUCATAN NIGHTJAR *Caprimulgus badius* (Tapacaminos Yucateco)   L 25 cm. (?/5). As 5, but with darker face, paler body, larger white tail corners and different range. Habitat: dense woodland. Voice: ultra high mellow fluted *muh-míouíow*. YMeGuHo.

7   BUFF-COLLARED NIGHTJAR *Caprimulgus ridgwayi* (Tapacaminos Préstame-tu-cuchillo)   L 25 cm. Overall grey with rufous cheeks and buff neck collar. Habitat: dry woodland; sl–1750 m. Voice: ultra high staccato sharp very fast running-up *tjiptjiptjipperíppip*. MeGuHo.

8   SPOT-TAILED NIGHTJAR *Caprimulgus maculicaudus* (Tapacaminos Colimanchado)   L 20 cm. Note white braces and rufous neck. Shows – apart from white tail corners – two rows of small white spots (difficult to see)across underside of tail. Habitat: savanna, marsh, open woodland; <500 m. Voice: very high sharp sizzled *putswéet*. SMe(Ho).

9   RUFOUS NIGHTJAR *Caprimulgus rufus* (Chotacabras Rojizo)   L 30 cm. Note pale braces, dark primaries with indication of a buff bar, characteristic tail pattern. Habitat: forest, forest edge, riverine belts; sl–1000 m. Voice: very high fluted *tjuk-wuksehwíow*. U,CRPa.

10   DUSKY NIGHTJAR *Caprimulgus saturatus* (Chotacabras Sombrío)   L 25 cm. Note very dark upperparts, rufous and buff breast and belly. Habitat: open montane forest and adjacent areas; >2000 m. Voice: very high *prruh-purríeh*. CRPa.

11   WHITE-TAILED NIGHTJAR *Caprimulgus cayannensis* (Chotacabras Coliblanco)   L 20 cm. Unmistakable by wing and tail pattern. Habitat: open areas; sl–750 m. Voice: ultra high sharp simple *pft-tsúiih*. CRPa.

Plate 43

Plate 44

1   BLACK SWIFT *Cypseloides niger* (Vencejo Negro)   L 18 cm. Very similar to 2, 3 and 4. Large, long-winged, black with slightly forked tail and with indication of white eyebrows. Habitat: montane skies. WSpr.

2   WHITE-CHINNED SWIFT *Cypseloides cryptus* (Vencejo Barbiblanco/Sombrío)   L 15 cm. As 1, 3 and 4 , but with slightly shorter and square tail. White chin difficult to see. Habitat: mainly over montane forest. CAm.

3   CHESTNUT-COLLARED SWIFT *Cypseloides rutilus* (Vencejo Cuellicastaño)   L 13 cm. Chestnut collar of ♂ distinctive, less so in ♀. Smaller, shorter-tailed than 1. Habitat: mainly over montane forest. WSpr.

4   SPOT-FRONTED SWIFT *Cypseloides cherriei* (Vencejo de Cherrie)   L 14 cm. White spots on head difficult to see. Habitat: montane skies. U,CR.

5   WHITE-FRONTED SWIFT *Cypseloides storeri* (Vencejo Frentiblanco)   L 14 cm. (?/2). As 2 but with paler forehead. Habitat: over forest. E,Me.

6   WHITE-COLLARED SWIFT *Streptoprocne zonaris* (Vencejo Cuelliblanco/Collarejo)   L 20 cm. Full collar diagnostic. Habitat: over forest. WSpr.

7   WHITE-NAPED SWIFT *Streptoprocne semicollaris* (Vencejo Nuquiblanco)   L 20 cm. Note white neck collar. As 6, heavy-looking. Habitat: mainly in montane skies. Me(Be).

8   CHIMNEY SWIFT *Chaetura pelagica* (Vencejo de Chimenea/de Paso)   L 13 cm. Rather uniform dark brown with paler throat and rump. Habitat: over forest edge; also over settlement. WSpr.

9   VAUX'S SWIFT *Chaetura vauxi* (Vencejo de Vaux/Común)   L 12 cm. On average with (slightly) paler throat and breast than larger 8. Habitat: over any type of country. Thr.

10   CHAPMAN'S SWIFT *Chaetura chapmani* (Vencejo de Chapman)   L 14 cm. Less capped appearance than 8 and 9. Rump and uppertail coverts slightly paler. Habitat: over lowland forest. U,Pa.

11   SHORT-TAILED SWIFT *Chaetura brachyura* (Vencejo Rabón)   L 10 cm. Black belly sharply demarcated from pale undertail coverts (black tail hidden by coverts). Note broad wings, short tail and bat-like flight. Habitat: mainly over lowland forest. U,Pa.

12   ASHY-TAILED SWIFT *Chaetura andrei* (Vencejo de Tormenta)   L 14 cm. Note pale saddle and throat. Habitat: over edges of lowland forest. V,Pa.

13   BAND-RUMPED SWIFT *Chaetura spinicauda* (Vencejo de Rabadilla Clara)   L 11 cm. Pale saddle sharply demarcated. Habitat: over any type of country. CRPa. Note: now split into two species; population in eastern Panama remains BAND-RUMPED SWIFT (*Chaetura spinicauda*, as shown), while population in western Panama plus eastern Costa Rica is now COSTA RICAN SWIFT (*Chaetura fumosa*, not illustrated), which has more extensive pale rump.

14   GREY-RUMPED SWIFT *Chaetura cinereiventris* (Vencejo Lomigrís)   L 10 cm. Note blue sheen on upperparts. Habitat: over lowland and montane forest. NiCRPa.

15   WHITE-THROATED SWIFT *Aeronautes saxatilis* (Vencejo Gorjiblanco)   L 17 cm. More white on breast and belly than 16 and 17. Habitat: near montane cliffs. WSpr.

16   LESSER SWALLOW-TAILED SWIFT *Panyptila cayennensis* (Vencejo-tijereta Menor)   L 13 cm. From 17 only by size. Habitat: mainly over lowland forest. U,SMeCAm.

17   GREAT SWALLOW-TAILED SWIFT *Panyptila sanctihieronymi* (Vencejo-tijereta Mayor)   L 19 cm. Little overlap of range with 16. Habitat: mainly over montane areas. U,SMeCAm.

Plate 44

Plate 45

1   **BRONZY HERMIT** *Glaucis aenea* (Ermitaño Bronceado)   L 10 cm. From larger 2 by range. Habitat: dense weedy vegetation at streams, in marsh, second growth; <250(500)m. CAm.

2   **RUFOUS-BREASTED HERMIT** *Glaucis hirsuta* (Ermitaño Hirsuto)   L 11 cm. Tail narrowly tipped white, rufous at base. Habitat: dense undergrowth; sl–1500 m. Pa.

3   **BAND-TAILED BARBTHROAT** *Threnetes ruckeri* (Ermitaño Barbudo)   L 11 cm. Bill shorter, straighter than in hermits. Note black chin. Striking black-and-white tail pattern. Habitat: forest understorey, dense second growth; <750 m. U,CAm.

4   **LONG-BILLED HERMIT** *Phaethornis longirostris* (Ermitaño Colilargo)   L 15 cm. As 5, but not in same range. Habitat: forest interior and edge; <1000 m. SMeCAm.

5   **MEXICAN** (or Western Long-tailed) **HERMIT** *Phaethornis l. mexicanus* (Ermitaño Mexicano) L 15 cm. Now treated as race of 4. Note whitish breast. Habitat: forest undergrowth and edge; 100–2000 m. E,Me.

6   **GREEN HERMIT** *Phaethornis guy* (Ermitaño Verde)   L 13 cm. From 8 by buff malar and throat stripes; also with longer tail and bill. Habitat: forest edge, tall second growth; 500–2000 m. CRPa.

7   **PALE-BELLIED HERMIT** *Phaethornis anthophilus* (Ermitaño Vientripálido)   L 13 cm. Unmistakable by whitish underparts. Habitat: thick edges of forest, woodland, riverine belts; sl–1500 m. U,Pa.

8   **WHITE-WHISKERED HERMIT** *Phaethornis yaruqui* (Ermitaño de Yaruqui)   L 13 cm. Bill rather straight; white stripe down throat and breast. Habitat: montane forest, dense secondary growth; <1250 m. V,Pa.

9   **STRIPE-THROATED HERMIT** *Phaethornis striigularis* (Ermitaño Chico/Enano)   L 9 cm. Mainly brown and rufous with green mantle. Habitat: undergrowth of forest, second growth, mangrove, wooded swamp; sl–1500 m. SMeCAm.

10   **WHITE-TIPPED SICKLEBILL** *Eutoxeres aquila* (Pico de Hoz)   L 13 cm. Unmistakable. Habitat: undergrowth of forest interior and edge; 250–750(1250) m. U,CRPa.

11   **TOOTH-BILLED HUMMINGBIRD** *Androdon aequatorialis* (Colibrí Piquidentado) L 14 cm. Unmistakable; ♂ has very small hook to tip of bill, ♀ has green neck. Habitat: forest understorey; >1000 m. U,Pa.

12   **WEDGE-TAILED SABREWING** *Campylopterus curvipennis* (Fandangero Colicuña)   L 12 cm. Note form and patterning of outer primaries of 12 – 16. As 13, but with shorter tail. Habitat: forest, woodland, gardens; <1500 m. MeBeGu(Ho).

13   **LONG-TAILED SABREWING** *Campylopterus excellens* (Fandangero Colilargo)   L 13 cm. See 12. Habitat: forest; sl–1250 m. E,Me.

14   **RUFOUS SABREWING** *Campylopterus rufus* (Fandangero Rufo)   L 13 cm. Note striking tail pattern with all-rufous outer feathers. Habitat: forest; (50)1000–2000 m. SMeGuSa.

15   **SCALY-BREASTED HUMMINGBIRD** *Phaeochroa cuvierii* (Fandangero Pechiescamoso; Colibrí Pechiescamado)   L 12 cm. Scaled green below with white tail corners. Habitat: forest, gardens, plantations; sl–500(1250) m. SMeCAm.

16   **VIOLET SABREWING** *Campylopterus hemileucurus* (Fandangero Morado; Ala de Sable Violácea)   L 14 cm. ♂ unmistakable. Note white tail corners and purple chin of ♀. Habitat: forest, second growth, forest remains, gardens; 100–1500(2500) m. SMeCAm.

17   **WHITE-NECKED JACOBIN** *Florisuga mellivora* (Jacobino Nuquiblanco)   L 12 cm. Unmistakable. Note chequered pattern of ♀ throat and breast. Habitat: forest, second growth; <500(750) m. SMeCAm.

18   **GREEN-BREASTED MANGO** *Anthracothorax prevostii* (Mango/Manguito Pechiverde) L 12 cm. See 19. Habitat: savanna, ranchland, gardens, forest edge; sl–1000 m. SMeCAm.

19   **BLACK-THROATED MANGO** *Anthracothorax nigricollis* (Mango Gorginegro)   L 12 cm. Black stripe further down breast than 18. Habitat: open areas with trees and scattered bush; <1000 m. Pa.

20   **VERAGUAS MANGO** *Anthracothorax veraguensis* (Mango de Veragua) L 12 cm. ♂ with little or no black on throat, ♀ not safely separable from ♀ 18. Habitat: open areas with trees and bush. Pa.

Plate 45

Plate 46

1 **RUBY TOPAZ** *Chrysolampis mosquitus* (Colibrí Rubí) L 9 cm. Unmistakable. Habitat: savanna, gardens. V,Pa.

2 **EMERALD-CHINNED HUMMINGBIRD** *Abeillia abeillei* (Colibrí Barbiesmeralda) L 7 cm. Note short black bill. Habitat: montane forest interiors. SMeCAm.

3 **VIOLET-HEADED HUMMINGBIRD** *Klais guimeti* (Colibrí Cabeciazul) L 8 cm. Note distinctive blue crown, narrow white tips to tail feathers and white eye spot. Habitat: canopy of forest, tall second growth, gardens; <1000 m. CAm.

4 **SHORT-CRESTED COQUETTE** *Lophornis brachylophus* (Coqueta Cresticorta) L 7 cm. (♀/6). Note distinctive tail pattern. Lower belly tawny. Habitat: forest; 1000–2000 m. E,Me.

5 **BLACK-CRESTED COQUETTE** *Lophornis helenae* (Coqueta Crestinegra) L 7 cm. Unmistakable. Habitat: canopy in open forest, forest edge, plantations; 100–1250 m. SMeCAm.

6 **RUFOUS-CRESTED COQUETTE** *Lophornis delattrei* (Coqueta Crestirrojiza) L 7 cm. Unmistakable. Note rufous whiskers of ♀. Habitat: forest edge and clearings; 500–2000 m. U,CRPa.

7 **WHITE-CRESTED COQUETTE** *Lophornis adorabilis* (Coqueta Crestiblanca) L 7 cm. Unmistakable. Habitat: normally in canopy of forest, second growth, plantations; 250–1250 m. U,CRPa.

8 **GREEN THORNTAIL** *Discosura conversii* (Colicerda Verde) L 7 (+ 3) cm. Unmistakable. Habitat: forest canopy; 750–1500 m. U,CRPa.

9 **CANIVET'S** (or Fork-tailed) **EMERALD** *Chlorostilbon canivetii* (Esmeralda de Canivet /Rabihorcada) L 8 cm. Bluish chin, rather short tail. Habitat: dry areas. MeGuBe. Note: 9, 10, 11, 12 and 13 might be races of South American Blue-tailed Hummingbird *Chlorostilbon mellisugus*.

10 **SALVIN'S EMERALD** *Chlorostilbon c. salvini* (Esmeralda de Salvin) L 8 cm. Now considered to be green-chinned race of 9. Habitat: dry areas. SMeCAm.

11 **GOLDEN-CROWNED EMERALD** *Chlorostilbon auriceps* (Esmeralda Mexicana) L 8 (+2) cm. (♀/9). Long, deeply forked tail. Golden wash on crown and mantle. Habitat: dry areas. Me.

12 **COZUMEL EMERALD** *Chlorostilbon forficatus* (Esmeralda de Cozumel) L 8 (+2) cm. As 11, but without golden wash. Habitat: woodland and edge. E,Me.

13 **GARDEN EMERALD** *Chlorostilbon assimilis* (Esmeralda Piquinegro) L 8 cm. Note all-black bill. Habitat: dry areas. CRPa.

14 **DUSKY HUMMINGBIRD** *Cynanthus sordidus* (Colibrí Prieto) L 10 cm. Note tail pattern and long postocular white stripe. Habitat: dry areas with some trees and scrub. E,Me.

15 **BROAD-BILLED HUMMINGBIRD** *Cynanthus latirostris* (Colibrí Piquiancho) L 10 cm. Nom (a) and race *lawrencei* (b) shown. Note striking red, broad bill. Habitat: dry scrub, woodland. Me.

16 **DOUBLEDAY'S HUMMINGBIRD** *Cynanthus l. doubledayi* (Colibrí de Doubleday) L 10 cm. Now treated as race of 15 with more bluish underparts; ranges overlap only slightly. Habitat: dry open woodland; <1000 m. E,Me.

17 **GREEN-FRONTED LANCEBILL** *Doryfera ludoviciae* (Pico de Lanza Frentiverde) L 12 cm. Unmistakable. Habitat: understorey of montane forest, especially near streams. U,CRPa.

Plate 46

Plate 47

1 MEXICAN WOODNYMPH *Thalurania ridgwayi* (Ninfa Mexicana)   L 10 cm. Note forked tail, blue crown, green gorget. Habitat: woodland. E,Me.

2 CROWNED WOODNYMPH *Thalurania colombica* (Ninfa Coronada/Violeta y Verde)   L 10 cm. Unmistakable by brilliant green and violet reflections. Note white throat, contrasting with greyish abdomen, and tail corners of ♀. Habitat: forest, often near streams; sl–750(1250)m. CAm. Note: now split into VIOLET-CROWNED WOODNYMPH (*Thalurania colombica*, most of Central America) and GREEN-CROWNED WOODNYMPH (*Thalurania fannyi*, eastern Panama, not shown), with greenish crown.

3 FIERY-THROATED HUMMINGBIRD *Panterpe insignis* (Colibrí Garganta de Fuego)   L 11 cm. Unmistakable by orange whiskers. Habitat: montane forest and edge; >1500 m. CRPa.

4 VIOLET-BELLIED HUMMINGBIRD *Damophila julie* (Colibrí de Julia)   L 9 cm. From 2 by all-green head, red-based lower mandible, rounded tail. Note tawny wash over underparts of ♀. Habitat: forest interior, edge and clearings; sl–1000 m. Pa.

5 SAPPHIRE-THROATED HUMMINGBIRD *Lepidopyga coeruleogularis* (Colibrí Garganta de Zafiro)   L 9 cm. Blue throat with forked tail diagnostic. ♀ is white below with green spotting to sides of breast; tail as ♂, but central pair green and pale tips to outer feathers. Habitat: woodland, scrub, mangrove. Pa.

6 BLUE-HEADED SAPPHIRE *Hylocharis grayi* (Zafiro Cabeciazul)   L 9 cm. From 5 by blue front and black-tipped bill. Habitat: forest edge, woodland, cultivation. V,Pa.

7 BLUE-THROATED GOLDENTAIL (or Sapphire) *Hylocharis eliciae* (Zafiro Gorjiazul; Colibrí Colidorado)   L 9 cm. Unmistakable by tail colouring. Habitat: forest edge, tall second growth, gardens, riverine belts; <1000 m. U,SMeCAm.

8 WHITE-EARED HUMMINGBIRD *Hylocharis leucotis* (Colibrí Orejiblanco)   L 10 cm. Unmistakable by mask and colouring of belly and tail. Habitat: clearings in mixed forests; 1250–3500 m. WSpr.

9 XANTHUS'S HUMMINGBIRD *Hylocharis xantusii* (Colibrí de Xantus)   L 9 cm. From 8 by tail and underparts colouring. Habitat: dry open woodland, gardens; sl–1500 m. E,Me.

10 VIOLET-CAPPED HUMMINGBIRD *Goldmania violiceps* (Colibrí de Goldman)   L 9 cm. From 48.5 by different range and pure green rump. Habitat: forest undergrowth; 500–1250 m. Pa.

11 STRIPE-TAILED HUMMINGBIRD *Eupherusa eximia* (Colibrí Colirrayado)   L 10 cm. Note tail pattern. Habitat: mainly in understorey of montane forest. SMeCAm.

12 WHITE-TAILED HUMMINGBIRD *Eupherusa poliocerca* (Colibrí Guerrerense)   L 11 cm. (?/11). Note tail pattern. Habitat: montane forest, woodland; plantations. E,Me.

13 BLACK-BELLIED HUMMINGBIRD *Eupherusa nigriventris* (Colibrí Pechinegro)   L 8 cm. Black face and belly diagnostic. Note all-white tail with green central feathers of ♀. Habitat: montane forest. U,CRPa.

14 BLUE-CAPPED HUMMINGBIRD *Eupherusa cyanophrys* (Colibrí Oaxaqueño)   L 11 cm. (?/11). Blue cap diagnostic. Habitat: montane forest; 750–1750 m. E,Me.

15 WHITE-TAILED EMERALD *Elvira chionura* (Esmeralda Coliblanca)   L 8 cm. From other green, white-bellied hummers by diagnostic tail pattern and absence of red in wing. Habitat: montane forest, gardens; 750–2000 m. CRPa.

16 COPPERY-HEADED EMERALD *Elvira cupreiceps* (Esmeralda de Coronilla Cobriza)   L 8 cm. Unmistakable by head, rump and tail feathering. Habitat: montane forest; 250–1500 m. E,CR.

17 RUFOUS-CHEEKED (or Pirre) HUMMINGBIRD *Goethalsia bella* (Colibrí del Pirre)   L 9 cm. Unmistakable, no other hummer with a sharply demarcated rufous tail. Habitat: forest interior and edge; mainly >1000 m. U,Pa.

18 SNOWCAP *Microchera albocoronata* (Copete de Nieve)   L 6 cm. Unmistakable; note tail colour of ♀. Habitat: forest canopy; 500–1650 m. U,CAm.

Plate 47

Plate 48

1 **WHITE-BELLIED EMERALD** *Amazilia candida* (Esmeralda Vientre-blanco; Amazilia Pechiblanca) L 10 cm. Note white underparts, including throat and chin, green tail with faint subterminal bar, long, bent, strong bill. Habitat: forest; sl–1500 m. WSpr.

2 **HONDURAN EMERALD** *Amazilia luciae* (Esmeralda Hondureña) L 10 cm. From 1 by bluish-green throat. Restricted range. Habitat: more or less open, dry woodland; <250 m. E,Ho.

3 **AZURE-CROWNED HUMMINGBIRD** *Amazilia cyanocephala* (Colibrí Coroniazul) L 11 cm. Only hummer with blue crown and all-white underparts. ♀ lacks coppery sheen on upperparts like 1. Habitat: forest edge, woodland; sl–2500 m. WSpr.

4 **MANGROVE HUMMINGBIRD** *Amazilia boucardi* (Amazilia Manglera) L 11 cm. No similar hummingbird in its range and habitat. Habitat: mangrove. E,CR.

5 **INDIGO-CAPPED HUMMINGBIRD** *Amazilia cyanifrons* (Amazilia Gorriazul) L 9 cm. See 47.10. Note blue-black colouring of tail. Habitat: forest, woodland, plantations, gardens. U,CR. Note: only specimen from the area (see question mark on distribution map) now considered to be a hybrid, which means that the species is considered not to occur in the area.

6 **STEELY-VENTED HUMMINGBIRD** *Amazilia saucerottei* (Amazilia Culiazul) L 10 cm. From 5 by green, not blue front and crown. Habitat: savanna, open woodland, gardens; sl–1500 m. NiCR.

7 **BLUE-TAILED HUMMINGBIRD** *Amazilia cyanura* (Colibrí/Amazilia Coliazul) L 10 cm. Nom. (a) shown and race *guatemalae* (b). As 9 with rufous in wings, but with steel-blue tail. Habitat: open forest, woodland, plantations; sl–1750 m. SMeCAm.

8 **SNOWY-BELLIED HUMMINGBIRD** *Amazilia edward* (Amazilia Vientriblanca) L 10 cm. Nom (a) and race *niveoventer* (b) shown. No rufous in wings; note difference in tail colouring between ♂ (rufous) and ♀ (blackish-blue). Habitat: variety of habitats, but not in forest. CRPa.

9 **BERYLLINE HUMMINGBIRD** *Amazilia beryllina* (Colibrí de Berilo) L 9 cm. Races *viola* (a) and *devillei* (b) shown. Unmistakable by tail and wing colouring. Habitat: forest, riverine belts, open woodland, gardens; <2000 m. MeGuNiSa.

10 **BLUE-CHESTED HUMMINGBIRD** *Amazilia amabilis* (Amazilia Pechiazul) L 9 cm. As 11 but green area on crown smaller. Habitat: forest edge, second growth, woodland, riverine belts, plantations; <500 m. NiCRPa.

11 **CHARMING** (or Beryl-crowned) **HUMMINGBIRD** *Amazilia decora* (Amazilia Corona de Berilo) L 10 cm. Note extension of green on head. As 10 with blue reflections to throat and rufous tail. Habitat: woodland, second growth, gardens; sl–1250 m. CRPa.

12 **RUFOUS-TAILED HUMMINGBIRD** *Amazilia tzacatl* (Colibrí Colirrufo; Amazilia Rabirrufa) L 10 cm. Striking rufous tail; green reflecting throat area ill-defined. Habitat: forest edge and clearings, plantations, cultivation; sl–1250 m. SMeCAm.

13 **BUFF-BELLIED HUMMINGBIRD** *Amazilia yucatanensis* (Colibrí Vientre-canelo) L 11 cm. Green 'upper half' and rufous 'lower half' diagnostic. Habitat: forest interior, edge and clearings; <1000 m. MeGuBe.

14 **CINNAMON HUMMINGBIRD** *Amazilia rutila* (Colibrí/Amazilia Canelo/a) L 10 cm. Predominantly rufous. Habitat: woodland, savanna, cultivation; sl–1500 m. WSpr.

15 **VIOLET-CROWNED HUMMINGBIRD** *Amazilia violiceps* (Colibrí Corona-violeta) L 10 cm. Brownish-green colouring and violet cap diagnostic. Habitat: dry scrubland, open pine forest, cultivation, suburban areas; sl–2500 m. Me.

16 **GREEN-FRONTED HUMMINGBIRD** *Amazilia viridifrons* (Colibrí Corona-verde) L 11 cm. Only hummer with all-white underparts and dull-rufous tail. Habitat: dry, open, mixed forest, riverine belts, suburban regions; 500–1500 m. MeGu.

17 **CINNAMON-SIDED HUMMINGBIRD** *Amazilia v. wagneri* (Colibrí Flanquicanelo) L 11 cm. Race of 16. From 16 by pale rufous margin to green. Habitat: dry woodland; <1000 m. E,Me.

Plate 48

Plate 49

1 **GREEN-CROWNED BRILLIANT** *Heliodoxa jacula* (Brillante Frentiverde) L 11 cm.
Brilliantly reflecting green all-over. Note long-headed jizz. ♀ chequered green below. Habitat:
forest interior and edge; 750–2000 m. U,CRPa.

2 **BROWN VIOLET-EAR** *Colibri delphinae* (Orejavioleta Café; Colibrí Orejivioláceo Pardo)
L 12 cm. Unmistakable. Habitat: forest canopy and edge, plantations; sl–1000(1500) m. U,CAm.

3 **GREEN VIOLET-EAR** *Colibri thalassinus* (Orejavioleta Verde; Colibrí Orejivioláceo Verde) L 11 cm.
Unmistakable by green ear tufts and tail pattern. Habitat: montane forest edge and clearings. WSpr.

4 **BRONZE-TAILED** (or Red-footed) **PLUMELETEER** *Chalybura urochrysia* (Colibrí Patirrojo)
L 11 cm. Race *melanorrhoa* (a, with black undertail coverts) and nom (b, with white undertail coverts)
shown. Red feet diagnostic. Note facial expression with unaccented lores and (in ♂) no white spot
behind ear. Habitat: edge of broken forest, tall second growth, adjacent areas; sl–750 m. U,CAm.

5 **WHITE-VENTED PLUMELETEER** *Chalybura buffoni* (Colibrí de Buffon) L 11 cm. No other
blue-chinned hummer with blue tail. Note absence of white spot behind eye in ♂. Habitat: forest
edge, open second growth; sl–2000 m. Pa.

6 **WHITE-BELLIED MOUNTAIN GEM** *Lampornis hemileucus* (Colibrí Montañés Vientriblanco)
L 11 cm. Note blue chin, white belly, tail pattern. Habitat: forest canopy; 750–1500 m. CRPa.

7 **GREY-TAILED MOUNTAIN GEM** *Lampornis c. cinereicauda* (Colibrí Montañés Coligrís)
L 11 cm. Race of 8. Chin white, belly green, tail pale grey. Note cinnamon-rufous underparts of
green-tailed ♀. Habitat: montane forest edge and clearings; >1750 m. E,CR.

8 **WHITE-THROATED MOUNTAIN** (or Blue-tailed) **GEM** *Lampornis castaneoventris* (Colibrí
Montañés Variable) L 11 cm. As 7, but with blackish tail and grey belly. ♀ as ♀ 7. Habitat:
undergrowth at forest edge and clearings; 1500 m. E,Pa.

9 **PURPLE-THROATED MOUNTAIN GEM** *Lampornis calolaema* (Colibrí Montañés Gorgimorado)
L 11 cm. Purple throat diagnostic. ♀ as ♀ 7. Habitat: canopy of montane forest. E,CR.

10 **GREEN-THROATED MOUNTAIN GEM** *Lampornis viridipallens* (Colibrí-serrano Gorjiverde)
L 11 cm. Note tail pattern. ♀ without throat spots. Habitat: montane forest edge and clearings;
1000–2750 m. SMeGuSaHo.

11 **GREEN-BREASTED MOUNTAIN GEM** *Lampornis sybillae* (Colibrí-serrano Pechiverde)
L 11 cm. From 10 by more extensive spotting to flanks and by blackish uppertail coverts.
Habitat: montane forest interior and edge; 1500-2250 m. HoNi.

12 **AMETHYST-THROATED HUMMINGBIRD** *Lampornis amethystinus* (Colibrí-serrano
Gorjiamatisto) L 11 cm. Unmistakable. Habitat: montane forest interior and edge; 1000–3000 m.
MeGuHo.

13 **BLUE-THROATED HUMMINGBIRD** *Lampornis clemenciae* (Colibrí-serrano Gorjiazul)
L 11 cm. Unmistakable. Note grey underparts and golden wash on rump. Habitat: open spaces in
montane woodland; 1750–3000 m. Me.

14 **GARNET-THROATED HUMMINGBIRD** *Lamprolaima rhami* (Colibrí Alicastaño) L 11 cm.
Unmistakable. Only hummingbird with all-rufous wings. Habitat: montane forest interior and
edge; 1250–3000 m. MeGuHo.

15 **MAGNIFICENT** (or Rivoli's) **HUMMINGBIRD** *Eugenes fulgens* (Colibrí Magnífico) L 11 cm.
Unmistakable. Note long, almost straight bill. Habitat: montane forest and edge, farmland;
1000–3000 m. WSpr.

16 **GREENISH PUFFLEG** *Haplophaedia aureliae* (Calzadito Verdoso Norteño) L 11 cm.
Unmistakable by white 'socks' and short bill. Habitat: undergrowth of montane forest. U,Pa.

17 **PURPLE-CROWNED FAIRY** *Heliothryx barroti* (Hada Coronimorada; Colibrí Picopunzón)
L 11 cm. Unmistakable by pure white underparts and jizz of peaked head. Habitat: forest interior
and edge; <500 m. U,SMeCAm.

18 **LONG-BILLED STARTHROAT** *Heliomaster longirostris* (Picolargo Coroniazul; Colibrí
Piquilargo) L 11 cm. Note pattern of rump. Habitat: forest edge and clearings; wooded country;
sl–1500 m. U,SMeCAm.

19 **PLAIN-CAPPPED STARTHROAT** *Heliomaster constantii* (Picolargo Coronioscuro; Colibrí
Pochotero) L 11 cm. From 18 by tail pattern and green crown. Spot behind eye more extensive.
Habitat: dry thorn bush, wooded dry country; sl–1500 m. WSpr.

Plate 49

Plate 50

1   SPARKLING-TAILED WOODSTAR *Tilmatura dupontii* (Colibrí Colipinto)   L 7 (+ 2) cm. Unmistakable by tail form and pattern. Note white tufts to rump sides of 1 – 3. Habitat: forest, open woodland; 500–2500 m. WSpr.

2   MAGENTA-THROATED WOODSTAR *Calliphlox bryantae* (Estrellita Gorgimorada)   L 7 (+ 2) cm. From 3 by rufous, shorter tail; ♀ similar. Habitat forest edge and clearings, open woodland, cultivation; 750–1750 m. U,CRPa.

3   PURPLE-THROATED WOODSTAR *Calliphlox mitchellii* (Estrellita de Mitchell)   L 7 (+ 4) cm. See 2; from 2 also by different range. Habitat: forest canopy; >1000 m. V,Pa.

4   MEXICAN SHEARTAIL *Doricha eliza* (Tijereta Yucateca)   L 9 (+ 2) cm. As 2, but underparts with more white, rounded tail tips, less rufous feathering; ♀ has white in tail. Habitat: low scrub, mangrove, gardens. E,Me.

5   SLENDER SHEARTAIL *Doricha enicura* (Tijereta Centroamericana)   L 9 (+ 3) cm. Long tail without rufous distinctive; note extent of rufous and tail pattern of ♀. Habitat: scrub, forest edge; 1000–2250 m. SMeGuHoSa.

6   LUCIFER HUMMINGBIRD *Calothorax lucifer* (Tijereta Norteña)   L 10 cm. Very much like 7, which see. Habitat: scrub, woodland, cultivation. Me. Note: 6 – 20 show a distinctive compact, almost stiff jizz.

7   BEAUTIFUL HUMMINGBIRD *Calothorax pulcher* (Tijereta Oaxaqueña)   L 9 cm. Very similar to 6, but with slightly shorter and straighter bill. Restricted range. Habitat: scrub, woodland, cultivation. E,Me.

8   RUBY-THROATED HUMMINGBIRD *Archilochus colubris* (Colibrí Gorjirrubí/Garganta de Rubí)   L 9 cm. ♂ is unmistakable; ♀ not safely separable from ♀ 9. Habitat: forest edge, woodland, cultivation. WSpr.

9   BLACK-CHINNED HUMMINGBIRD *Archilochus alexandri* (Colibrí Barbinegro)   L 10 cm. ♂ is unmistakable when chin reflections can be seen. Somewhat longer-tailed than 8. Habitat: dry country (summer); riverine belts, forest (winter). Me.

10   ANNA'S HUMMINGBIRD *Calypte anna* (Colibrí de Anna)   L 11 cm. Note crown colouring. Ruby whiskers rather short. ♀ normally with ruby spot to throat. Habitat: open woodland, savanna, suburban areas; sl–1750 m. NMe.

11   COSTA'S HUMMINGBIRD *Calypte costae* (Colibrí de Costa)   L 8 cm. Note long violet whiskers. Tail pattern of ♀ as ♀ 10, but note all-white throat. Habitat: desert, open dry scrubland, savanna; <1000 m. NMe.

12   CALLIOPE HUMMINGBIRD *Stellula calliope* (Colibrí de Caliope)   L 7 cm. Very small. Streaked throat separated from green cheeks by white line. ♀ from ♀ 13 (not in same range) by white, not buff eyebrow. Habitat: montane open forest, thorn bush, farmland. U,Me.

13   VOLCANO HUMMINGBIRD *Selasphorus flammula* (Chispita Volcanera)   L 8 cm. Different colour forms (a, b, c) shown with ruby, blue and green gorget. 12 has similar tail pattern. Habitat: open disturbed habitats; >1750 m. CRPa.

14   GLOW-THROATED HUMMINGBIRD *Selasphorus ardens* (Zumbador Ardiente)   L 7 cm. Both ♂ and ♀ with less rufous in tail than 15. Habitat: forest edge and clearings; 750–1750 m. E,Pa.

15   SCINTILLANT HUMMINGBIRD *Selasphorus scintilla* (Chispita Gorginaranja)   L 7 cm. Note extent of rufous in tail. See also ranges of 14 and 15. Habitat: scrubby areas, forest edge, cultivation; 750–2000 m. CRPa.

16   BROAD-TAILED HUMMINGBIRD *Selasphorus platycercus* (Zumbador Coliancho)   L 10 cm. Tail longer than similar species. Wings of perched birds often held crossed over tail. Habitat: pine forest. MeGu.

17   RUFOUS HUMMINGBIRD *Selasphorus rufus* (Zumbador Rufo)   L 8 cm. Amount of green on back variable, some without any. Habitat: forest interior, edge and clearings. Me.

18   ALLEN'S HUMMINGBIRD *Selasphorus sasin* (Zumbador de Allen)   L 9 cm. Extent of rufous on rump and back variable, some almost as 17, but feathers of spread tail narrower, even more pointed. Habitat: forest interior, edge and clearings. Me.

▶

Plate 50

Plate 50 continued

19 **BUMBLEBEE HUMMINGBIRD** *Selasphorus heloisa* (Zumbador Mexicano) L 7 cm. From 20 and from 13, 14 and 15 with similar tail pattern by range. Smaller and shorter-billed than 6 and 7. ♀ 12 has less rufous on flanks. Habitat: forest interior, edge and clearings. E,Me.

20 **WINE-THROATED HUMMINGBIRD** *Selasphorus ellioti* (Zumbador Centroamericano) L 7 cm. See 19. Habitat: forest interior, edge and clearings. U,SMeGuSaHo.

Plate 51

1 **BLACK-THROATED TROGON** *Trogon rufus* (Trogón Cabeciverde) L 25 cm. Note yellow bill, black-tipped in ♀. Habitat: dense undergrowth of forest, tall second growth; <1000 m. Voice: very high slow *piuw-piuw-piuw*. CAm.

2 **WHITE-TAILED TROGON** *Trogon viridis* (Trogón Coliblanco) L 25 cm. Note white undertail of ♂. From 5 by absence of white border to blue/brown breast. Habitat: forest canopy. Voice: very high *wewwew*-- (8–15 x). Pa.

3 **BLACK-HEADED TROGON** *Trogon melanocephalus* (Trogón Cabecinegro) L 25 cm. (?/4). From 4 by black eyes and blue uppertail. ♂ has undertail as ♀. Habitat: forest, tree stands, mangrove; <1000 m. Voice: very high shivering accelerated magpie-like chatter *wekwek--wekkering*. SMeCAm.

4 **CITREOLINE TROGON** *Trogon citreolus* (Trogón Citrino) L 25 cm. Yellow eyes diagnostic. Habitat: dry woodland, plantations, mangrove; <1000 m. Voice: high dry accelerated bickering. E,Me.

5 **VIOLACEOUS TROGON** *Trogon violaceus* (Trogón Violáceo) L 25 cm. Blue head and green tail diagnostic. Note also undertail pattern. Wing coverts pale grey. Habitat: forest edge, tall second growth, plantations; <1250 m. Voice: very high yelping *WefWefWef*-- (6–7 x) or *titjèhtjèh* --, slowing down and falling off to the end. WSpr.

6 **ORANGE-BELLIED TROGON** *Trogon aurantiiventris* (Trogón Vientrianaranjado) L 25 cm. Orange belly diagnostic. Note undertail pattern of ♀. Probably a colour form of 10. Habitat: lower storeys of montane forest. Voice: high *íuw íuw-íuw* or single *pruh*. U,CRPa.

7 **BLACK-TAILED TROGON** *Trogon melanurus* (Trogón Colinegro) L 30 cm. Black undertail diagnostic. ♀ similar to ♀ 12 but with yellow lower mandible. Habitat: forest, tall second growth, mangrove. Voice: very high *wéjwéjwéj*--. Pa.

8 **MOUNTAIN TROGON** *Trogon mexicanus* (Trogón Mexicano) L 30 cm. From 9 by different undertail pattern and by green, not brown central tail feathers. Habitat: montane mixed forest. Voice: very high well-spaced *tjieuw tjieuw - -* or rapid *tjuw-tjuw- -*. WSpr.

9 **ELEGANT TROGON** *Trogon elegans* (Trogón Elegante) L 30 cm. ♂ has undertail faintly spotted brown, distal half white. Habitat: canopy of forest in hilly country; <2400 m. Voice: croaking *oork-oork- -* (3–6 x). WSpr.

10 **COLLARED TROGON** *Trogon collaris* (Trogón Collarejo) L 25 cm. From 8 by tail pattern below. Note pink underparts of ♀. Habitat: lower storeys of montane forest. Voice: high plaintive *péewee-pée-* or *psweepeepee* or descending short trill *trrrreeh*. WSpr.

11 **BAIRD'S TROGON** *Trogon bairdii* (Trogón Vientribermejo) L 30 cm. Unmistakable by colour combination. Note dark wing coverts of ♀. Habitat: forest canopy; <1250 m. Voice: very high *wewwew*--rising to a bouncing trill. CRPa.

12 **SLATY-TAILED TROGON** *Trogon massena* (Trogón Colioscuro/Coliplomizo) L 30 cm. Green tail and pink bill diagnostic. Habitat: forest; <500 m. Voice: high barking rather staccato *uw-tjew-tjew wew- -* (3–6s). SMeCAm.

13 **LATTICE-TAILED TROGON** *Trogon clathratus* (Trogón Ojiblanco) L 25 cm. White eyes and undertail pattern diagnostic. Habitat: forest; <1000 m. Voice: high hurried *puhpuhuh*--(as hysterical laughter). U,CRPa.

14 **EARED QUETZAL** (or Trogon) *Euptilotis neoxenus* (Quetzal Mexicano) L 35 cm. Unmistakable. Note small-headed jizz. Habitat: upper storeys of mixed forest; 1750–3000 m. Voice: very/ultra high loud sharp *irriek-irriek- -* (3-4s) or *tjaktjak*. E,Me.

Plate 51

Plate 51 continued

15 **RESPLENDENT QUETZAL** *Pharomachrus mocinno* (Quetzal Centroamericano)
L 35 (+ 60) cm. Nom (a) and shorter-tailed race *costaricensis* (b) shown. Unmistakable. Habitat:
montane forest canopy and edge; 1500–3000 m. Voice: very high *kiauw kiauw kiauw* or magpie-like
ketjauw ketjauw. SMeCAm.

16 **GOLDEN-HEADED QUETZAL** *Pharomachrus auriceps* (Quetzal Cabecidorado)
L 35 (+ 10) cm. Unmistakable. Note pattern and colouring of wing coverts. Habitat: montane
forest; 1250–1500 m. Voice: very high fluted *weeweet-weeweet- -* (3–5s). U,Pa.

17 **DUSKY-BACKED JACAMAR** *Brachygalba salmoni* (Jacamar Dorsioscuro) L 18 cm. From
larger 18 by darker colouring and shorter tail. Habitat: at forest edge and clearings. Voice: very
high sustained *pseéhpseéhpseéh--*. U,Pa.

18 **RUFOUS-TAILED JACAMAR** *Galbula ruficauda* (Jacamar Colirrufo/Rabirrufo) L 25 cm.
Note long, straight bill and rufous outer tail feathers. Habitat: middle levels at forest edge and
clearings. Voice: high sustained *wéewt-wéewt- -*, often drawn-up and followed by yelled trills. SMeCAm.

19 **GREAT JACAMAR** *Jacamerops aurea* (Jacamar Grande) L 30 cm. Large with heavy, curved
bill. Habitat: middle and upper storeys of forest, tall second growth. Voice: very high lonely fluted
whéeeehmeeutjee. U,CRPa.

Plate 52

1 **TODY MOTMOT** *Hylomanes momotula* (Momoto Enano) L 17 cm. Small, rather short-tailed.
Note white whiskers. Habitat: forest understorey; sl–1500 m. Voice: (very) high owl-like *hooh-
hooh-hooh- -* (5–10 x). SMeCAm.

2 **BLUE-THROATED MOTMOT** *Aspatha gularis* (Momoto Gorjiazul) L 25 cm. Face pattern
diagnostic. Habitat: montane forest understorey; 1500–3000 m. SMeGuHo.

3 **RUSSET-CROWNED MOTMOT** *Momotus mexicanus* (Momoto Coronicafé) L 35 cm. Russet-
rufous crown, greenish throat and green tail diagnostic. Habitat: open woodland, thorn bush;
<1750 m. E,Me.

4 **BROAD-BILLED MOTMOT** *Electron platyrhynchum* (Momoto Piquiancho) L 30 cm. From
larger 5 by lack of blue in wing, greenish chin and less extensive rufous underparts. Habitat: middle
levels of open forest; <1500 m. Voice: high hoarse pushed-out *auw* (1/5 s). CAm.

5 **RUFOUS MOTMOT** *Baryphthengus martii* (Momoto Canelo Mayor) L 45 cm. Note blue
primaries and tail. Habitat: forest canopy to understorey; <1500 m. Voice: low wooden *wooteroot-
wóotwóot-wootwoot*. NiCRPa.

6 **KEEL-BILLED MOTMOT** *Electron carinatum* (Momoto Piquianillado/Pico Quilla) L 30 cm.
Frontal red spot diagnostic. Habitat: forest; <1500 m. U,SMeCAm.

7 **BLUE-CROWNED MOTMOT** *Momotus momota* (Momoto Coroniazul/Común) L 40 cm.
Races *coeruliceps* (a, with all blue crown) and *lessonii* (b, with black top of crown) shown. Red eyes
distinctive. Habitat: at forest edge and clearings, second growth, woodland. Voice: high dimmed
hooot-hoot. WSpr.

8 **TURQUOISE-BROWED MOTMOT** *Eumomota superciliosa* (Momoto Cejiturquesa/
Cejiceleste) L 35 cm. Races *bipartita* (a) and *australis* (b) shown. Striking pale blue wing and tail
pattern. Note long bare tail shafts. Habitat: dry forest, woodland, gardens; <1500 m. Voice: high
hoarse pushed-out *uhóooh*. SMeCAm.

9 **RINGED KINGFISHER** *Ceryle torquata* (Martin-pescador Collarejo) L 40 cm. Unmistakable
by large size, rufous underparts and dirty-yellow bill. Habitat: large inland and coastal waters,
marsh. Voice: sharp high chatter (3s). WSpr.

10 **BELTED KINGFISHER** *Ceryle alcyon* (Martin-pescador Norteño) L 30 cm. Smaller than 9 with
grey bill and different colouring below. Habitat: locations of clean, quiet water, inland and at
coast, rivers, streams, ponds, estuaries. Thr.

11 **GREEN-AND-RUFOUS KINGFISHER** *Chloroceryle inda* (Martin-pescador Vientrirrufo)
L 30 cm. Much larger than greyer-billed 14. Note whitish tip to bill. Habitat: fringing vegetation
at forest streams, mangrove. U,CAm.

▶

Plate 52

Plate 52 continued

12   **AMAZON KINGFISHER** *Chloroceryle amazona* (Martin-pescador Amazona/Amazónico) L 17 cm. Wings and tail uniform green, not barred and spotted white. Habitat: quiet spots at rivers, mainly in open landscape, lakes, lagoons, mangrove. WSpr.

13   **GREEN KINGFISHER** *Chloroceryle americana* (Martin-pescador Verde) L 18 cm. From 12 by white barring on tail and wings; note also differences in underparts. Habitat: quiet spots in all types of small streams and waters. Thr.

14   **AMERICAN PYGMY KINGFISHER** *Chloroceryle aenea* (Martin-pescador Enano) L 13 cm. Very small (smaller than House Sparrow) with white belly and undertail coverts. Habitat: fringing overhanging vegetation at streams, ponds in forest, swamp. SMeCAm.

15   **PIED PUFFBIRD** *Notharchus tectus* (Buco Pinto) L 15 cm. Small with white in wings and tail. Note long narrow white eye stripe. Habitat: forest canopy, tall second growth. Voice: ultra high descending fluted *whee whee wheeterrit wheeterrit territ-territ*. U,CRPa.

16   **WHITE-NECKED PUFFBIRD** *Notharchus macrorhynchos* (Buco Collarejo) L 25 cm. From 17 by face pattern. Habitat: forest canopy and edge, plantations. Voice: ultra high pressed-out descending *psssst*. U,SMeCAm.

17   **BLACK-BREASTED PUFFBIRD** *Notharchus pectoralis* (Buco Pechinegro) L 20 cm. Note black 'tears' running and spreading down. Habitat: forest canopy. Pa.

18   **WHITE-WHISKERED PUFFBIRD** *Malacoptila panamensis* (Buco Barbón) L 20 cm. Not barred, only with striped breast sides. Note red eyes and bi-coloured bill. Habitat: forest interior, edge and clearings; sl–750(1250)m. Voice: ultra high penetrating descending *ssiiiiiiiih*. SMeCAm.

19   **BARRED PUFFBIRD** *Nystalus radiatus* (Buco Barreteado) L 20 cm. Overall barring diagnostic. Habitat: forest interior and edge. U,Pa.

Plate 53

1   **SPOT-CROWNED BARBET** *Capito maculicoronatus* (Barbudo Coronipunteado) L 18 cm. Unmistakable. Habitat: forest edge; <1000 m. Voice*: low nasal scolding almost duck-like *krrk krrk krrk - -* with variable spacing and speed in long disjointed series. U,Pa.

2   **RED-HEADED BARBET** *Eubucco bourcierii* (Barbudo Cabecirroja) L 15 cm. Unmistakable. Habitat: forest and adjacent areas; 500–1750 m. Voice: high toneless *prrrrrrruh*. U,CRPa.

3   **PRONG-BILLED BARBET** *Semnornis frantzii* (Barbudo Cocora) L 17 cm. Unmistakable, but check 90.10. Habitat: montane forest and adjacent areas. Voice: low wooden cackling *wukwukwuk--* in chorus. CRPa.

4   **WHITE-FRONTED NUNBIRD** *Monasa morphoeus* (Monja Frentiblanca) L 30 cm. Unmistakable. Some birds might lack white chin feathering. Habitat: forest (canopy) and nearby areas; <750 m. Voice: excited rising cackling *wheetwheetwheet--* in chorus. CMa.

5   **LANCEOLATED MONKLET** *Micromonacha lanceolata* (Monjito Rayado) L 13 cm. Unmistakable. Small-sized and short-necked. Habitat: forest; <750 m.

6   **GREY-CHEEKED NUNLET** *Nonnula ruficapilla* (Nonula Carigrís) L 15 cm. Note contrasting grey face sides and sharp, slightly decurved bill. Habitat: lower forest storeys. Voice*: series of very high fluty notes averaging 25, rising slightly, then monotone *plip plip plip plip - -*. U,Pa.

7   **EMERALD TOUCANET** *Aulacorhynchus prasinus* (Tucaneta/Tucancillo Verde) L 30 cm. Of several races nom (a) and races *wagleri* (b) and *caeruleogularis* (c) shown. Unmistakable. Habitat: forest canopy and edge, plantations; 750(1250)–3000 m. Voice: high barking irregular hesitant *wah wah wah - -*. WSpr.

8   **YELLOW-EARED TOUCANET** *Selenidera spectabilis* (Tucancillo Orejiamarillo) L 35 cm. Unmistakable by black breast. Voice: *tch-trrr* (last part as a very short dry trill). Habitat: forest canopy; 250–1250 m. CMa.

9   **COLLARED ARACARI** *Pteroglossus torquatus* (Tucancillo Collarejo) L 40 cm. From 10 mainly by bill pattern. In east Panama without brown in neck and bill sides fully barred black. Habitat: forest, tall second growth, plantations; sl–1250 m. Voice: very high very sharp *sreewit*. SMeCAm.

▶

Plate 53

Plate 53 continued

10   **FIERY-BILLED ARACARI** *Pteroglossus frantzii* (Tucancillo Piquianaranjado) L 45 cm. Partly red bill sides diagnostic. Habitat: forest and clearings; <1500 m. Voice: high sustained *wreeet-wreeet- -*, each slightly drawn-up. CRPa.

11   **KEEL-BILLED TOUCAN** *Ramphastos sulfuratus* (Tucan Pico-multicolor/Pico Iris)   L 50 cm. Bill patterning diagnostic. From 12 and 13 by black, not dark brown body feathering. Habitat: forest canopy, tall second growth; descends for berries; sl–1000(1250) m. Voice: high frog-like sustained *prut-prut-prrut-pruit- -*. SMeCAm.

12   **CHESTNUT-MANDIBLED** (or Swainson's) **TOUCAN** *Ramphastos swainsonii* (Tucan de Swainson)   L 55 cm. See 13. Habitat: forest canopy and edge; <1500 m. Voice: toy-trumpet-like *tuwuweet-tuweet-wutwut- -*, in chorus. CAm.

13   **CHOCÓ TOUCAN** *Ramphostos brevis* (Tucan del Chocó)   L 50 cm. From 12 by partly black, not dark rufous bill and very different voice. Habitat: forest canopy and edge. V,Pa.

14   **PALE-BILLED WOODPECKER** *Campephilus guatemalensis* (Carpintero Piquiclaro/Picoplata) L 35 cm. White bill diagnostic. Probably not in range of 16. Habitat: forest, plantations, mangrove; sl–750(2000) m. Voice: doubletap, followed by very high irregular rapid *tudurrut tudder - -*. WSpr.

15   **CRIMSON-BELLIED WOODPECKER** *Campephilus haematogaster* (Carpintero Carminoso) L 35 cm. Unmistakable by red underparts. Habitat: forest interior. Voice: loud double-tap, first stroke much louder. U,Pa.

16   **CRIMSON-CRESTED WOODPECKER** *Campephilus melanoleucos* (Carpintero Crestirrojo) L 35 cm. From 14 by grey bill, spot on side of face (♂), white whiskers (♀); from 56.11 by different head pattern. Habitat: forest, woodland; <1000 m. Voice: very rapid whinnying *widurwit*. Pa.

17   **IMPERIAL WOODPECKER** *Campephilus imperialis* (Carpintero Imperial)   L 60 cm. Very large, all-black underparts, ♂ with red crest. Habitat: open, montane pine forest. Me, probably extinct.

Plate 54

1   **LEWIS'S WOODPECKER** *Melanerpes lewis* (Carpintero de Lewis)   L 25 cm. Unmistakable by red face and black back. Habitat: open woodland; sl–2000 m. Voice: dry clicking *tsjitsjiklak--*. U,NMe.

2   **ACORN WOODPECKER** *Melanerpes formicivorus* (Carpintero Arlequín/Careto)   L 25 cm. Unmistakable by white eyes and black back. Habitat: woodland; 500–3000 m. Voice: high short scratchy mewing chatter or rising and falling *chattoh-chattoh- -* (5s). WSpr.

3   **GOLDEN-NAPED WOODPECKER** *Melanerpes chrysauchen* (Carpintero Nuquidorado) L 18 cm. From 8 by golden nape and more white on mantle. Habitat: higher storeys of forest interior and edge, woodland. Voice*: high harsh *krrr krrr krrr - -*. U,CRPa.

4   **RED-HEADED WOODPECKER** *Melanerpes erythrogaster* (Carpintero Cabecirroja)   L 25 cm. Unmistakable. Habitat: open woodland, fields with scattered trees. Voice: high short *whráa*. Hyp,NMe.

5   **YUCATAN** (or Red-vented) **WOODPECKER** *Melanerpes pygmaeus* (Carpintero Yucatero) L 17 cm. Nom (a) and race *tysoni* (b) shown. Note yellow around bill base, small bill, small body. Habitat: forest interior and edge, coastal scrub. YMeBeHo.

6   **RED-BELLIED WOODPECKER** *Melanerpes carolinus* (Carpintero Vientrirrojo)   L 25 cm. Note speckled rump, central tail feathers spotted white. Habitat: woodland. Hyp,NMe.

7   **GILA WOODPECKER** *Melanerpes uropygialis* (Carpintero de Gila)   L 25 cm. No similar woodpecker in most of its range except 9 (different head pattern) and 12 (different neck colouring). Habitat: open woodland, savanna; sl–1500 m. Voice: high rapid whinnying *tdrruh*. NMe.

8   **BLACK-CHEEKED WOODPECKER** *Melanerpes pucherani* (Carpintero Cachetinegro/ Carinegro)   L 18 cm. Unmistakable. Note thin barring of upperparts. Habitat: forest, second growth, plantations; sl–1000 m. Voice: high rapid rattling chatters. SMeCAm.

9   **GOLDEN-CHEEKED WOODPECKER** *Melanerpes chrysogenys* (Carpintero Cachetidorado) L 20 cm. Diagnostic black around eye. Habitat: forest, broken forest, open woodland; sl–1500 m. Voice: very high short chatter *witwitwit*. E,Me

▶

Plate 54

Plate 54 continued

10 GREY-BREASTED WOODPECKER *Melanerpes hypopolius* (Carpintero Pechigrís) L 20 cm.
Note faint white eye ring. Habitat: dry, open areas with scarce tree stands and bush; 1000–1750 m. E,Me.

11 HOFFMANN'S WOODPECKER *Melanerpes hoffmannii* (Carpintero de Hoffmann) L 20 cm.
Note white rump and uppertail coverts. Extensive yellow on nape. Interbreeds with 12, resulting in
individuals with intermediate plumage. Habitat: dry, open areas with tree stands and bush;
<250 m. Voice: high bickering *titrrrrih*. NiCR.

12 GOLDEN-FRONTED WOODPECKER *Melanerpes aurifrons* (Carpintero Frentidorado)
L 25 cm. Races *leei* (a) and *polygrammus* (b) shown. From smaller 5 by barred uppertail coverts and
lack of yellow to chin. From smaller 11 (little overlap in ranges) by more orange on nape. Habitat:
dry open woodland, forest edge; sl–2500 m. Voice: high sharp short whinnying *trrruh*. WSpr.

13 RED-CROWNED WOODPECKER *Melanerpes rubricapillus* (Carpintero Nuquirrojo) L 17 cm.
No similar woodpecker in its range. Note orange nape. Habitat: broken forest, riverine belts,
second growth, mangrove; <1500 m. Voice*: high harsh strident *skrrr skrrr skrrr - -*, higher pitched
than 3, though similar. Also drumming in 3–4 second bursts. CRPa.

Plate 55

1 LADDER-BACKED WOODPECKER *Picoides scalaris* (Carpintero Listado) L 18 cm. From 2 by
absence of black crown (♂); note yellow wash over underparts. Black markings in face narrower, less
distinct than in 2. Habitat: dry open country with scattered trees and cacti; sl–3000 m. Voice: very
short rapid bickering *weetwitwit--* (2–3s). WSpr. Note: 1 – 6 lack the white oval ring in wing of 56.5 – 8.

2 NUTTALL'S WOODPECKER *Picoides nuttallii* (Carpintero de Nuttall) L 19 cm. See 1.
Restricted range. Habitat: dry open country, riverine belts; sl–1500 m. Voice: very/ultra high
toneless short trill *trrrrih*. U,NMe.

3 HAIRY WOODPECKER *Picoides villosus* (Carpintero-velloso Mayor; Carpintero Serranero)
L 19 cm. Several races, mainly in Mexico, differing in amount of white spots on mantle and wings,
intensity of buff wash over underparts and in size, but all with all-white outer tail feathers; race
sanctorum (a) shown; also Central American race *icastus* (b). Habitat: montane forest; 1250–
3500 m. Voice: very high whinnying *whit whitterwit whit*. WSpr.

4 DOWNY WOODPECKER *Picoides pubescens* (Carpintero Plumonado) L 16 cm. Note small bill
and black tips of tail feathers. Underparts may have a faint buff wash. Habitat: forest, woodland,
cultivation. Voice: ultra high descending thin *tsee-tsee-tsee tseetseeit*. Hyp,NMe.

5 STRICKLAND'S (or Brown-barred) WOODPECKER *Picoides stricklandi* (Carpintero de
Strickland) L 18 cm. From black 3 by speckled and barred underparts; 6 has plain back and is
paler. Habitat: pine woodland; 2500–4000 m. Voice*: very high variable unstructured jumble of
strident whipped-up and trilled calls, e.g. *tsip-scrrr-crrr sip sip sip skrrr-skrrr - -*. E,Me.

6 ARIZONA WOODPECKER *Picoides arizonae* (Carpintero de Arizona) L 20 cm. (?/5). Note
uniform colouring of back. Habitat: dry woodland; 1250–2500 m. Might be a race of 5. Me.

7 BRONZE-WINGED WOODPECKER *Piculus r. aeruginosus* (Carpintero Alibronceado) L 20
cm. Race of 8. From 8 by absence of red eyebrow. Habitat: forest interior and edge, plantations;
sl–2000 m. Voice*: very high series of 8–12 notes *phwip phwip phwip - -*. E,Me.

8 GOLDEN-OLIVE WOODPECKER *Piculus rubiginosus* (Carpintero Oliváceo/Verde Dorado)
L 20 cm. Note blackish stripe down crown. Habitat: forest, plantations; sl–2000 m. Voice: very
high *eeuw*; very high trill *trrrrrrih* (2s). SMeCAm.

9 GREY-CROWNED WOODPECKER *Piculus auricularis* (Carpintero Coronigrís) L 17 cm. Red
restricted to malars. Habitat: forest interior and edge; sl–2500 m. Voice: descending *tjeeuw*. E,Me.

10 RUFOUS-WINGED WOODPECKER *Piculus simplex* (Carpintero Alirrufo) L 18 cm. Pale eye
diagnostic. Habitat: forest; <750 m. U,CAm.

11 STRIPE-CHEEKED WOODPECKER *Piculus callopterus* (Carpintero Panameño) L 17 cm.
From larger 10 (not in same range) by black eyes and (for ♀) different head pattern. Habitat: forest
interior and edge; 250–1000 m. E,Pa.

▶

Plate 55

Plate 55 continued

12   GOLDEN-GREEN WOODPECKER *Piculus chrysochloros* (Carpintero Verdidorado)
L 20 cm. Mask through pale eye diagnostic. Note face pattern of ♀. Habitat: swampy forest.
Voice*: high harsh grating scream, like *krrraaargh*, descending at end. Also crow-like cawing. U,Pa.

13   SPOT-BREASTED WOODPECKER *Piculus punctigula* (Carpintero Pechipunteado)   L 20 cm.
Barring above and spotting/barring below distinctive. Habitat: open woodland, mangrove. Voice:
very high bouncing slightly descending *bicbicbicbicbicbic*. U,Pa.

Plate 56

1   NORTHERN (or Common) FLICKER *Colaptes auratus* (Carpintero Collarejo)   L 30 cm.
Of several races *mexicanoides* (a) and grey-headed *collaris* (b, shown on ground) shown. From 2 by
all-black tail. Habitat: forested and wooded dry country; >750 m. Voice: very high sharp rapid
bickering *witwitwit--* (4s) or *kiliaw kiliaw - -*. WSpr.

2   GILDED FLICKER *Colaptes chrysoides* (Carpintero de California)   L 30 cm. (?/1). From 1 by
grey extending to neck sides, spotted outer tail feathers, absence of golden moustache (♀).
Habitat: dry open woodland, often at streams; 250–1000 m. NMe.

3   SMOKY-BROWN WOODPECKER *Veniliornis fumigatus* (Carpintero Café/Pardo)   L 16 cm.
No similar woodpecker in the area. Habitat: forest interior and edge, tall second growth,
plantations; sl–1500 m. Voice: high *tjiawtjiawtjiaw*. WSpr.

4   RED-RUMPED WOODPECKER *Veniliornis kirkii* (Carpintero Lomirrojo)   L 16 cm. Red rump
diagnostic. Habitat: forest, mangrove. Voice: very high sandpiper-like *wreet wreet wreet - -*.
U,CRPa.

5   YELLOW-BELLIED SAPSUCKER *Sphyrapicus varius* (Chupasavia Vientre-amarillo; Carpintero
Bebedor)   L 20 cm. From 6 by absence of separate red nape. Yellow of belly not always obvious. Habitat:
forest and adjacent wooded country; 1000–3000 m. Voice: high *tsjeer*. WSpr.

6   RED-NAPED SAPSUCKER *Sphyrapicus nuchalis* (Chupasavia Nuquirroja)   L 20 cm. (?/5). Red
nape diagnostic. Habitat: forest interior and edge; sl–2500 m. Voice: hawk/buzzard-like *wjéew
wjéew*. Me.

7   RED-BREASTED SAPSUCKER *Sphyrapicus ruber* (Chupasavia Pechirroja)   L 20 cm. (?/5).
Distinctive by red head patterning. Habitat: pine forest; 500–3000 m. Voice: dry toneless shivering
srrrrrrr. U,NMe.

8   WILLIAMSON'S SAPSUCKER *Sphyrapicus thyroideus* (Chupasavia de Williamson)   L 20 cm.
Note uniform black neck and mantle of ♂; ♀ very different. Habitat: pine forest; 1000–3500 m.
Voice: high rapid churring *chut-chut-chut- -*. U,Me.

9   CINNAMON WOODPECKER *Celeus loricatus* (Carpintero Canelo) L 20 cm. Unmistakable by
large, bushy crest. Note also barred tail and underparts. Habitat: forest (canopy) and nearby
wooded areas; <750 m. Voice: ultra high *whéetwhéetwitwit*. U,NiCRPa.

10   CHESTNUT-COLOURED WOODPECKER *Celeus castaneus* (Carpintero Castaño)   L 25 cm.
From 9 by different crest shape, pale head, black tail and uniform basic colouring of body. Habitat:
dense forest interior and edge; <750 m. Voice: high nasal slurred-down *piuw*. SMeCAm.

11   LINEATED WOODPECKER *Dryocopus lineatus* (Carpintero Lineado)   L 35 cm. From 53.14
and 53.16 by different, less red head pattern. Note white stripes running parallel on back, not
coming together in a V-shape. Habitat: forest, woodland, areas with scattered tree stands;
sl–1500 m. Voice: high resounding *wuutwuutwuut--*, slightly descending. WSpr.

12   PILEATED WOODPECKER *Dryocopus pileatus* (Carpintero Cabecirroja)   L 45 cm. From
smaller 11 by black cheek, uniform black upperparts and black belly. Habitat: forest, tall trees in
second growth. Voice: very high sharp bickering *wutwut--* (4s). Hyp,NMe.

Plate 56

Plate 57

1 **TAWNY-WINGED WOODCREEPER** *Dendrocincla anabatina* (Trepatroncos Alileonado; Trepador Alirrubio) L 19 cm. No barring or streaking , pale eyebrow, short straight bill, tawny contrasting flight feathers. Habitat: forest, tall second growth, mangrove; sl–1250 m. Voice: very high *tjuuw*; very high sharp *tjutjutju--* (5–60s,), falling off at the end. SMeCAm.

2 **PLAIN-BROWN WOODCREEPER** *Dendrocincla fuliginosa* (Trepador Pardo) L 20 cm. Uniform coloured, dark moustache, grey cheek. Habitat: forest (lower levels) and adjacent areas; <750 m. Voice: ultra high *sweep*; very high fast *tititi--titututjitu*, lowered and decelerated at the end. CAm.

3 **RUDDY WOODCREEPER** *Dendrocincla homochroa* (Trepatroncos/Trepador Rojizo) L 20 cm. Uniform reddish brown with brighter crown, greyish eye ring. Habitat: woodland, dry forest; 500–1250 m. Voice: very high running-down trill (3s). SMeCAm.

4 **LONG-TAILED WOODCREEPER** *Deconychura longicauda* (Trepador Delgado) L 19 cm. Small and slender jizz, restricted striping below, short bill. Habitat: lower forest levels; 250–1250 m. Voice: *truetruetrue--*; very high sharp *feefeefeeweetjeetjee*. U,CAm.

5 **STRONG-BILLED WOODCREEPER** *Xiphocolaptes promeropirhynchus* (Trepatroncos/Trepador Gigante) L 30 cm. Large size, strong bill, dark moustache. Habitat: forests, including pine and mixed, but also lowland; sl–3500 m. Voice: sharply rising *yèèsss?*; *puhWéehWéeh--*. WSpr.

6 **BARRED WOODCREEPER** *Dendrocolaptes certhia* (Trepatroncos Barrado; Trepador Barreteado) L 30 cm. Only woodcreeper with overall barring. Note large size. Habitat: forest, open woodland; <500(1000)m. Voice: *ochgut*; *uuwéet-uuwéet-uwéetjutju*. WSpr.

7 **BLACK-BANDED WOODCREEPER** *Dendrocolaptes picumnus* (Trepatroncos Vientre-barrado; Trepador Vientribarreteado) L 25 cm. From larger 5 by relatively smaller bill, no malar stripe. Habitat: forest; 1500–3000 m. Voice: very high excited *werwerwerwer--* (5s), slightly lowered at the end. U,SMeCAm.

8 **STRAIGHT-BILLED WOODCREEPER** *Xiphorhynchus picus* (Trepatroncos Piquirrecto) L 20 cm. Note pale bill and plain mantle. Habitat: coastal wooded areas, mangrove. Voice: very high shivering *wuuwi--witjtji*, lowered by 4 notes at the end. U,Pa.

9 **COCOA WOODCREEPER** *Xiphorhynchus susurrans* (Trepatroncos Gorjipálido; Trepador Gorgianteado) L 20 cm. Throat unmarked, but with thin malar stripe. Striping to breast and mantle faintly demarcated. Habitat: forest interior and edge, plantations, mangrove; <500(1000)m. Voice: high *djuudjuu--* (8 x), gradually running down. CAm.

10 **IVORY-BILLED WOODCREEPER** *Xiphorhynchus flavigaster* (Trepatroncos/ Trepador Piquiclaro) L 25 cm. From smaller 8 by distinct striping on mantle. Habitat: forest edge and clearings; 250–1000(2500)m. Voice: high *tjouw*; very high sharp rapid rising and falling-off *tititi--titjutju*. WSpr.

11 **SPOTTED WOODCREEPER** *Xiphorhynchus erythropygius* (Trepatroncos/Trepador Manchado) L 25 cm. Mantle almost plain, but some races might have white spots. Note pale lower mandible, spotting on underparts and distinct eye ring. Habitat: forest; (100)500–(1750)2250 m. Voice: very high whinnying *whiwhiwhi--*. WSpr.

12 **BLACK-STRIPED WOODCREEPER** *Xiphorhynchus lachrymosus* (Trepador Pinto) L 25 cm. Note bold patterning. Habitat: forest interior and edge; <1200 m. Voice: long descending series of *tjew tjiw - -* (4s). NiCRPa.

13 **WHITE-STRIPED WOODCREEPER** *Lepidocolaptes leucogaster* (Trepatroncos Blanquirrayado) L 20 cm. More marked with white than other woodcreepers. Note thin, decurved bill. Habitat: pine and mixed forest; 750–3500 m. Voice: shrill descending trilling *trrr--iuuup*. E,Me.

14 **STREAK-HEADED WOODCREEPER** *Lepidocolaptes souleyetii* (Trepatroncos Corona-rayada; Trepador Cabecirrayado) L 19 cm. Note dense streaking of crown, neck and underparts, and thin, decurved bill. . Habitat: open woodland, plantations, gardens, forest edge, riverine belts, mangrove; sl–1500 m. Voice: very high very fast descending *titritri--triup*. SMeCAm.

15 **SPOT-CROWNED WOODCREEPER** *Lepidocolaptes affinis* (Trepatroncos Corona-punteada; Trepador Cabecipunteado) L 20 cm. Note white crown spots and red nape. Overall rather dark. Habitat: montane forest, adjacent areas. Voice: ultra high loud shrill descending very rapid *suseesusee--susee*. Thr.

Plate 57

Plate 57 continued

16   **RED-BILLED SCYTHEBILL** *Campylorhamphus trochilirostris* (Trepatroncos Piquirrojo) L 25 cm. Longer and paler bill than 17. Habitat: forest edge, woodland; <1000 m. Voice: high hurried fluting *wiweetwéetweetweet*. U,Pa.

17   **BROWN-BILLED SCYTHEBILL** *Campylorhamphus pusillus* (Trepador Pico de Hoz) L 25 cm. Bill darkish brown, striping deeper buff than 16. Note slight striping on mantle. Habitat: forest; 250–1750 m. Voice: very high fluting *tjuuk-tjuktjiek or wjuk wjuk wjuk wjuk*. U,CRPa.

Plate 58

1   **OLIVACEOUS PICULET** *Picumnus olivaceus* (Carpinterito Oliváceo) L 9 cm. Tiny, creeps about thin twigs, vines, rarely over trunks. Does not support itself on tail. Unmistakable. Often in mixed bird parties. Habitat: forest edge, woodland, plantations, gardens. CAm.

2   **PLAIN XENOPS** *Xenops minutus* (Picolezna Sencillo; Xenops Común) L 12 cm. From 3 by faint streaking of cheeks and throat. Habitat: forest; <1000 m. Voice: very high hurried *tjitjurrrr*. SMeCAm.

3   **STREAKED XENOPS** *Xenops rutilans* (Xenops Rayado) L 13 cm. Streaking and habits as 1, but supporting itself on tail. Streaking quite different from 2, which see. Restricted range. Habitat: forest and edge; 500–1750 m. Voice: *tjutju*; ultra high slightly descending *fjuhwéetwéetswát*. CRPa.

4   **SPOTTED BARBTAIL** *Premnoplex brunnescens* (Subepalo Moteado) L 14 cm. Darkish bird with distinctive markings below. Creeps along branches and over trunks, occasionally supported by its tail. Habitat: montane forest interior. Voice: ultra high shrill trill (2s). CRPa.

5   **WEDGE-BILLED WOODCREEPER** *Glyphorhynchus spirurus* (Trepatroncos Piquicuña; Trepadorcito Pico de Cuña) L 15 cm. Note bill form and pale panel in wing. Habitat: forest, often in undergrowth along streams; sl–1250 m. Voice: ultra high staccato *tjitjitjuw*; very high rising warbling crescendoing *wiwiwiwehwéhweh*. SMeCAm.

6   **OLIVACEOUS WOODCREEPER** *Sittasomus griseicapillus* (Trepatroncos Oliváceo; Trepadorcito Aceitunado) L 16 cm. Plain with greyish-olive head and underparts, except rufous undertail coverts. Bill very short. Habitat: forest interior and edge, plantations; <2000 m. WSpr.

7   **BUFFY TUFTEDCHEEK** *Pseudocolaptes lawrencii* (Trepamusgo Cachetón) L 29 cm. Unmistakable by tufted cheeks. Note long-headed jizz. Habitat: montane forest. U,CRPa.

8   **STREAK-BREASTED TREEHUNTER** *Thripadectes rufobrunneus* (Trepamusgo Cuellirojizo) L 20 cm. Note large size, heavy bill and rufous undertail coverts. Habitat: montane forest, tall second growth. Voice: hurried *tudrut* or hurried *tiederruut*. U,CRPa.

9   **BEAUTIFUL TREERUNNER** *Margarornis bellulus* (Subepalo Bello) L 15 cm. Distinctively marked. Habitat: mainly montane forest. U,Pa.

10   **RUDDY TREERUNNER** *Margarornis rubiginosus* (Subepalo Rojizo) L 16 cm. Note whitish eyebrow and throat. Habitat: montane forest and adjacent areas. Voice*: very high squeaking calls running into descending trill *kip kip krpkrpkrprprprprprrr*. CRPa.

11   **TAWNY-THROATED LEAFTOSSER** *Sclerurus mexicanus* (Tirahojas Pechirrufo) L 16 cm. From 12 and 13 by thinner bill, from wrens by unbarred plumage. Note distinctive rufous rump. Habitat: ground of lowland to foothill forest. Voice: ultra high *swéeeh-swéeeh-swéeh* (as Black Swift). WSpr.

12   **SCALY-THROATED LEAFTOSSER** *Sclerurus guatemalensis* (Tirahojas Barbiescamado) L 18 cm. Darkish below with uniform upperparts. Habitat: ground of lowland forest. Voice: ultra high meandering *sweetswitswitswit--*, starting high and wandering off. U,SMeCAm.

13   **GREY-THROATED LEAFTOSSER** *Sclerurus albigularis* (Tirahojas Gargantigrís) L 17 cm. Bill shorter than in 11 and 12. Note bright rump and rufous collar. Habitat: ground of montane forest. Voice: fluted *títítítjuwtjuw*, starting very high. U,CRPa.

14   **SHARP-TAILED STREAMCREEPER** *Lochmias nematura* (Riachuelero) L 15 cm. Conspicuous white spotting. Bird of undergrowth, often along streams. Habitat: ground storeys of forest. Voice: sustained sharp *titititi--*; ultra high short trill *srrrrrruw*. U,Pa.

Plate 58

Plate 59

1 **RUFOUS-BREASTED SPINETAIL** Synallaxis erythrothorax (Guitío Pechirrufo) L 16 cm. Note throat pattern and chequered throat. Habitat: marsh, dense scrub; <750 m. Voice: very high rising slightly shrieking *wrutuwit-wít-truw*. WSpr. Note: spinetails (1–3) forage alone or in pairs in dense undergrowth.

2 **SLATY SPINETAIL** Synallaxis brachyura (Arquitecto Plomizo) L 15 cm. Very dark with rufous cap and wings. Tail concolorous with body. Habitat: young second growth, dense scrub; 500–1250 m. Voice: very high very fast dry trill *tititjrrrr* (1/2s). CAm.

3 **PALE-BREASTED SPINETAIL** Synallaxis albescens (Arquitecto Güitío) L 14 cm. Resembling 2, but with pale face and underparts. Habitat: low scrub; savanna; <1250 m. Voice: very high scratchy *wéetjirr wéetjrr - -* (or *wéedzir*). CRPa.

4 **RED-FACED SPINETAIL** Cranioleuca erythrops (Colaespina Carirroja) L 15 cm. No other bird with similar red face. Habitat: lianas and small branches in forest and at forest edge; 750–2250 m. Voice: very high short sharp bickering *tjitjitjitutjijer*. CRPa.

5 **COIBA SPINETAIL** Cranioleuca dissita (Colaespina de Coiba) L 15 cm. No similar bird in its range. Habitat: lianas and small branches in forest and at forest edge. E,Pa.

6 **LINEATED FOLIAGE GLEANER** (or Woodhaunter) Syndactyla subalaris (Trepamusgo Lineado) L 19 cm. From 7 by shorter bill, brighter tail, pronounced eyebrow and eyering. Note pale, cinnamon throat of imm; imm from 58.8 by presence of narrow, pale eyebrow and lack of breast striping. Habitat: low forest storeys; >750 m. Voice: high nasal almost-trill *wit-witwit--wtwt* (6s). CRPa. Note: foliage gleaners forage alone, in pairs or in mixed bird flocks in the middle or lower forest storeys.

7 **STRIPED FOLIAGE GLEANER** Hyloctistes subulatus (Trepamusgo Rayado) L 18 cm. See 6. Habitat: understorey of forest, tall second growth; <500 m. Voice: high sharp shrieking *treeh - -* (2/5s) or *trseet-tseet-tseet*. U,NiCRPa.

8 **SCALY-THROATED** (or Spectacled) **FOLIAGE GLEANER** Anabacerthia variegaticeps (Trepamusgo de Anteojos) L 17 cm. Spectacles more striking than scales to throat and breast. Habitat: middle to upper storeys of forest; 500–2250 m. Voice: ultra high *tsjik*; high rusty staccato *wheetwheet--wit* (5–7s) or ultra high *sreet-sreet-sreet*. WSpr.

9 **SLATY-WINGED FOLIAGE GLEANER** Philydor fuscipennis (Trepamusgo Alipizarrosa) L 16 cm. Note eye stripe and dark wing. Habitat: middle to upper storeys of forest; <1000 m. Voice*: high unstructured phrases including descending trills and rattles, e.g. *tsip skrrrr swipskrrrr krrr*. U,Pa.

10 **BUFF-FRONTED FOLIAGE GLEANER** Philydor rufus (Trepamusgo Rojizo) L 19 cm. From 11 by buff front, greyish crown and mantle, distinctive rufous wings and arboreal habits. Habitat: forest edge; 1250–2000 m. Voice: ultra high bouncing descending *tittittit--titurit*. CRPa.

11 **BUFF-THROATED FOLIAGE GLEANER** Automolus ochrolaemus (Breñero Gorgipallido; Hojarrasquero Gorgianteado) L 18 cm. Lowland species; rather plain with eye ring, short eyebrow and rufous tail. Habitat: forest understorey; <1250 m. Voice: e.g. very high short descending shivering *wrrrrit* (2/5s). SMeCAm.

12 **RUDDY FOLIAGE GLEANER** Automolus rubiginosus (Breñero/Hojarrasquero Rojizo) L 20 cm. Unpatterned dark rufous. Habitat: forest undergrowth; 750–1350 m. Voice: high slightly mewing swept-up *truwéeh-truwéeh*. SMeCAm.

13 **DOUBLE-BANDED GREYTAIL** Xenerpestes minlosi (Colagrís Alibandeado) L 10 cm. Very warbler-like, but with different habits (creeps about dense foliage, often hanging upside down). Habitat: forest canopy, second growth. U,Pa.

14 **PLAIN ANTVIREO** Dysithamnus mentalis (Batarito Sencillo/Cabecigrís) L 12 cm. Note thickset, heavy-headed jizz , sluggish behaviour, wing bars. ♀ from 77.14 by olive, not green upperparts, presence of wing bars and dark eyes. Habitat: forest interior, lower storeys; <1250 m. Voice: high nasal *watje watjwatwaturururur*, sounding as rattle. SMeCAm.

15 **SPOT-CROWNED ANTVIREO** Dysithamnus puncticeps (Batarito Cabecipunteado) L 12 cm. Note irregular crown spotting and faint breast streaking. Habitat: forest undergrowth to middle storeys; <500 m. U,CRPa.

▶

Plate 59

Plate 59 continued

16 **STREAK-CROWNED ANTVIREO** *Dysithamnus striaticeps* (Batarito Pechirrayado)   L 11 cm. From 15 by more distinct breast striking; spots on crown arranged in rows. Habitat: understorey and middle levels of forest; <750 m. Voice: very high *wutwutwútwutwuterrrrrr*. HoNiCR.

17 **TACARCUNA** (or Pale-throated) **TAPACULO** *Scytalopus panamensis* (Tapacuelo de Tacarcuna)   L 11 cm. Secretive, as other tapaculos living close to the ground. From 18 by different range, from 19 by white eyebrow. Habitat: forest undergrowth; 1000–1500 m. Voice*: high trill accelerating into rattle *kepkepkepkepkepkrrrrrrrr*. U,Pa.

18 **SILVERY-FRONTED TAPACULO** *Scytalopus argentifrons* (Tapacuelo Frentiplateado)   L 11 cm. Not in range of 17. Note white forehead (however white may be missing, even in most or all of eyebrow). Habitat: forest, bamboo; 1000–3000 m. Voice: high scolding fast staccato *tutrittrittrittrit*. CRPa.

19 **NARIÑO TAPACULO** *Scytalopus vicinior* (Tapacuelo de Nariño)   L 12 cm. Not in range of 18. Habitat: forest undergrowth; 750–1500 m. Voice: high penetrating staccato *wrbicbicbic* (4s). U,Pa.

Plate 60

1 **GREAT ANTSHRIKE** *Taraba major* (Batará Mayor/Grande)   L 20 cm. Unmistakable by large size, bill and black-and-white pattern. ♀ rufous and white. Habitat: dense weedy vegetation at forest edge, young second growth, bamboo tangle at streams; <1000 m. Voice: high accelerated bouncing *wuut-wuut-wuutwuut wtwrwtwr - -* (6s), ending in upturned -*wick*. U,SMeCAm.

2 **BARRED ANTSHRIKE** *Thamnophilus doliatus* (Batará Barrada/Barreteado)   L 17 cm. Note yellow eyes and crest. ♀ unbarred and rufous. Habitat: dry forest, scrub, thick weedy vegetation, thickets; <1500 m. Voice: low drawn-out *jwaarrr* in duet; low *puppippirririririt* (3s), bouncing up and down. WSpr.

3 **FASCIATED ANTSHRIKE** *Cymbilaimus lineatus* (Batará Lineado)   L 18 cm. From 2 by red eyes, finer barring. Face barred, not striped. Habitat: forest canopy and edge, tall second growth; <1250 m. Voice: high plaintive *pjiuúpjuúpjuúpjuh*. U,CAm.

4 **SPECKLED ANTSHRIKE** *Xenornis setifrons* (Batará Moteado)   L 16 cm. Two-toned appearance diagnostic. ♀ uniform brown, speckled paler. Habitat: forest interior; mainly <500 m. U,Pa.

5 **BLACK ANTSHRIKE** *Thamnophilus nigriceps* (Batará Negro)   L 15 cm. White underwing coverts of ♂ diagnostic. ♀ with distinctly striped head and breast. Habitat: dense second growth, woodland. U,Pa.

6 **BLACK-HOODED ANTSHRIKE** *Thamnophilus bridgesi* (Batará Negruzco)   L 17 cm. Unmistakable when sparse wing spotting can be seen. ♀ as 5, but with olive upperparts. Habitat: thickets at forest edge, in woodland, also in mangrove; <1000 m. Voice: high wooden *wekwekwekkerwikkerwek*, varied in speed and length. U,CRPa.

7 **RUSSET ANTSHRIKE** *Thamnistes anabatinus* (Batará Café)   L 15 cm. Note especially its stocky jizz and heavy bill. From 59.10 by shorter tail and lack of buff front. Habitat: upper forest strata; 250–1000 m. Voice: very high accelerated *tjúuw-tjuuwtjuuwtjuw*. U,SMeCAm.

8 **SLATY ANTSHRIKE** *Thamnophilus atrinucha* (Batará/Apizarrada Plomizo)   L 14 cm. Note heavy bill, wing bars, peaked head. Habitat: forest undergrowth, second growth; <1000 m. Voice: high rattling *wekwekwek--wéh*. CAm.

9 **SLATY ANTWREN** *Myrmotherula schisticolor* (Hormiguerito Apizarrado/Pizarroso)   12 cm. Note black throat and stripe down breast, contrasting more or less with flanks and upperparts. Face sides of ♀ same colour as underparts. Habitat: sl–1250 m. Voice*: high squeaky kitten-like *myaaar* with whining quality. Also rattling calls. U,SMeCAm.

10 **CHECKER-THROATED ANTWREN** *Myrmotherula fulviventris* (Hormiguerito Café)   L 10 cm. Note pale eyes. Habitat: forest understorey; <750 m. Voice: ultra high sweeping *swit-swit-swit- -*. U,CAm.

11 **WHITE-FLANKED ANTWREN** *Myrmotherula axillaris* (Hormiguerito Flanquiblanco)   L 9 cm. Note white tufts along scapulars. ♀ from ♀ 10 by dark eyes. Habitat: forest understorey; <1000 m. Voice: running-down *peew-peew- - pew* (8 x), starting ultra high. CAm.

▶

Plate 60

Plate 60 continued

12 **DOT-WINGED ANTWREN** *Microrhopias quixensis* (Hormiguerito Alipunteado)   L 11 cm.
From 11 by white sides to tail, all-black underparts, more white in wing. Habitat: forest edge;
<1000 m. very/ultra high *tweeut-tweeet- -* running down to *- -twitweeh*. SMeCAm.

13 **STREAKED ANTWREN** *Myrmotherula surinamensis* (Hormiguerito Rayado)   L 9 cm.
Unmistakable. ♀ from ♂ by tawny, faintly dark streaked crown, nape and neck. Habitat: dense
vegetation at forest edge, in clearings, woodland; <500 m. Voice: very high dry trill *prurrrr* (3–4s)
or high *pwutwéetwéetwutwut*. Pa.

14 **PYGMY ANTWREN** *Myrmotherula brachyura* (Hormiguerito Pigmeo)   L 7 cm. Note unstreaked
yellow underparts. Habitat: upper forest storeys, tall second growth; <500 m. Voice*: very high
descending accelerating trill of 2.5 seconds, typical of genus, *swip swip sipsipsipsipprrrt*. U,Pa.

15 **WHITE-FRINGED ANTWREN** *Formicivora grisea* (Hormiguerito Blancibordado)   L 12 cm. ♂
unmistakable; note white tail tips, dark brown flight feathers and faint striping on throat of ♀.
Habitat: shrubby woodland. Voice*: very high disyllabic *plew-tip* calls and fluty piping trill
plewplewplewplew-- (4s). U,Pa.

16 **RUFOUS-WINGED ANTWREN** *Herpsilochmus rufimarginatus* (Hormiguerito Alirrufo)
L 11 cm. Rufous in wing and white tail sides diagnostic; note rufous crown of ♀. Habitat: forest
canopy; <1000 m. Voice*: high accelerating trill with harsh descending end, like *pipiprrrreough* and
harsh *kaw* notes when foraging. Pa.

17 **RUFOUS-RUMPED ANTWREN** *Terenura callinota* (Hormiguerito Lomirrufo)   L 12 cm. Note
rufous rump and yellow wing bend. Habitat: middle storeys of forest; 750–1000 m. Voice: ultra high
tsit; very high *tsitsjtrrrrrr*. CRPa.

OCHRE-BREASTED ANTPITTA *Grallaricula flavirostris* (Tororoi Piquigualdo) L 10 cm.
Unmistakable by small size. Habitat: forest understorey; <1250(1750)m. Voice: very high *piuw
piuw*. U,CRPa.

FULVOUS-BELLIED ANTPITTA *Hylopezus fulviventris* (Tororoi Pechicanelo) L 13 cm. Note
grey crown and buff lower belly. Habitat: dense undergrowth at forest edge, second growth;
<1000 m. Voice: e.g. very high running-up hurried *tututu--* (3s). U,CAm.

SCALED ANTPITTA *Grallaria guatimalensis* (Hormiguero-cholino Escamoso; Tororoi
Dorsiescamado)   L 19 cm. Unmistakable by large size, scaled upperparts and by throat pattern.
Habitat: forest floor, especially near water; 500–3000 m. Voice: low hollow turned-up *rrurrurúr*
(3s). U,WSpr.

BLACK-CROWNED ANTPITTA *Pittasoma michleri* (Tororoi Pechiescamoso)   L 19 cm.
Unmistakable by striking patterning. Habitat: forest floor; 250–1000 m. Voice: sharp rattle; very
high very rapid loud *wicwic--wic wic* (30–70s), at the end slowed down and running up. U,CRPa.

Plate 61

1   **DUSKY ANTBIRD** *Cercomacra tyrannina* (Hormiguero Negruzco)   L 14 cm. From larger 60.8 by slender shape, relatively smaller bill, grey crown and less white in wing. Habitat: thickets at forest edge, second-growth bamboo; <750(1250)m. Voice: chirping *tjurrrp*; very high loud bickering *wirdripdripdrip--wirdripdripdrip--*. SMeCAm.

2   **JET ANTBIRD** *Cercomacra nigricans* (Hormiguero Azabache)   L 14 cm. Note undertail pattern. Habitat: woodland, second growth. Voice: high wooden chattering *tetjúhtetjúhtetjuk*. U,Pa.

3   **BARE-CROWNED ANTBIRD** *Gymnocichla nudiceps* (Hormiguero Calvo)   L 16 cm. From larger 4 by white in wings. Habitat: forest interior and edge, second growth; <250 m. Voice: ultra high accelerated *pieuw-peeuw--peepee*. U,CAm.

4   **IMMACULATE ANTBIRD** *Myrmeciza immaculata* (Hormiguero Immaculado)   L 20 cm. Unmistakable by large size and blue orbital ring. Habitat: forest understorey; 250–1750 m. Voice: very high loud *sreeet - - (8 x)* or high *sruuh*. CAm.

5   **CHESTNUT-BACKED ANTBIRD** *Myrmeciza exsul* (Hormiguero Dorsicastaño)   L 14 cm. Nom (a, ♂) and race *cassini* (b, ♀, with white wing spots) shown. From 6 by blue orbital ring. Habitat: forest undergrowth; <1000 m. Voice: high fluted resounding *fjut fjuut*. CAm.

6   **DULL-MANTLED ANTBIRD** *Myrmeciza laemosticta* (Hormiguero Alimaculado)   L 14 cm. Note narrow wing bars; ♀ shows fine white spotting on chin. Habitat: forest undergrowth, often near streams. Voice: *dzing dzing*; ultra high loud *fjeet-fjeetuhfjeetfjeetfjeetweet*. U,CRPa.

7   **WHITE-BELLIED ANTBIRD** *Myrmeciza longipes* (Hormiguerito Vientriblanco)   L 15 cm. Note grey rim at black throat. White belly distinctive. Habitat: forest undergrowth, riverine belts, dense scrub; <500 m. Voice: *tjúuw tjúuw*; running-down rapid *tjitji--tjiw (4s)*. Pa.

8   **BICOLOURED ANTBIRD** *Gymnopithys leucaspis* (Hormiguero Bicolor)   L 15 cm. Unmistakable; note black cheeks. Habitat: forest undergrowth; <1750 m. Voice: raucous *wrouw*; ultra high *sweepsweep--pijèh*. CAm.

9   **WING-BANDED ANTBIRD** *Myrmornis torquata* (Hormiguerito Alifranjeado)   L 15 cm. Note pattern to sides of face and throat. From other terrestrial birds by wing bands. Habitat: forest undergrowth; sl–1250 m. U,NiPa.

10   **SPOTTED ANTBIRD** *Hylophylax naevioides* (Hormiguero Moteado)   L 12 cm. Not unlike 9, but with different jizz and patterning. Habitat: forest undergrowth; <1000 m. Voice: very high sharp-fluted up-and-down *puweet-puweet- - (10 x)*, slightly descending. CAm.

11   **OCELLATED ANTBIRD** *Phaenostictus mcleannani* (Hormiguero Ocelado)   L 20 cm. Unmistakable by large bare area around eye and bold spotting. Habitat: forest undergrowth; sl–1250 m. Voice: very high *weet-weet- -* accelerated to trill just before *- -titjuh*. U,CAm.

12   **BLACK-HEADED ANTTHRUSH** *Formicarius nigricapillus* (Gallito Hormiguero Cabecinegro)   L 18 cm. Unmistakable when properly seen. Habitat: forest floor; 500–1500 m. Voice: high accelerated and decelerating running-up *wukwukwuk-- (5s)*, CRPa. Note: antthrushes do not hop, but walk; in general are much more easily heard than seen.

13   **MEXICAN ANTTHRUSH** *Formicarius moniliger* (Hormiguero-gallito Mexicano)   L 19 cm. Note grey underparts. Habitat: forest floor; sl–1750 m. Voice: rapid series of slightly descending rich fluted notes. MeBeGuHo. Note: might be a race of 14 (AOU), but treated here as full species by different voice and range.

14   **BLACK-FACED ANTTHRUSH** *Formicarius analis* (Gallito Hormiguero Carinegro)   L 17 cm. From 13 also by voice. Habitat: forest floor; <1000 m. Voice: fluting *puweet*; very high resounding slow hesitating meandering *feeh fufuh-week week week*. CAm.

15   **RUFOUS-BREASTED ANTTHRUSH** *Formicarius rufipectus* (Gallito Hormiguero Pechicastaño)   L 19 cm. Breast rufous, not grey. Habitat: montane forest floor. Voice: very high *peeppéep* or *fuut fuut fuuh*. U,CRPa.

16   **SPECTACLED ANTPITTA** *Hylopezus perspicillatus* (Tororoi Pechilistado)   L 13 cm. Note distinctive breast streaking and buff spotting and buff-spotted wing bars. Habitat: forest floor; <1250 m. Voice: very high slow slowly going-up-and-down *fuuh-fuuh-fúuhfuuh- - (4s)*. U,CAm. Note: all antpittas, like this species, hop, not walk and are secretive floor dwellers.

◀

Plate 61

Plate 62

1 **GREAT KISKADEE** *Pitangus sulphuratus* (Luis/Bienteveo Grande) L 25 cm. Note rufous edges to flight feathers. Heavier-billed than smaller 2. Habitat: marsh, woodland, open areas with trees and hedges, savanna, gardens; sl–1750 m. Voice: e.g. high loud sharp *chéck today*. WSpr.

2 **LESSER KISKADEE** *Philohydor lictor* (Bienteveo Menor) L 16 cm. Note long, slender bill; less along open rivers than 1. From 1 and 4 by call. Habitat: wooded marsh, tree stands along slow streams. Voice: very high slurred-up hoarse *tjweeh*. Pa.

3 **BOAT-BILLED FLYCATCHER** *Megarynchus pitangua* (Luis Piquigrueso; Mosquerón Picudo) L 25 cm. Note heavy bill; from 1 by absence of rufous in wings and rump. Habitat: forest canopy and edge, plantations, open woodland; sl–1500 m. Voice: high canary-like twitter or *weeh weeh weeh* or chattering slightly nasal *pirruhweck* or hurried *purpurpurrewèh*. WSpr.

4 **SOCIAL FLYCATCHER** *Myiozetetes similis* (Luis Gregario; Mosquero Cejiblanco) L 17 cm. Note short, stubby bill. More olive above, less brown than 5 and 6; pale feather edges suggest wing bars. Habitat: open woodland, cultivation, forest edge; <1750 m. Voice: burst of ultra high squeaking in chorus. WSpr.

5 **RUSTY-MARGINED FLYCATCHER** *Myiozetetes cayanensis* (Mosquero Alicastaño) L 16 cm. Restricted yellow in crown, rufous edges to primaries. From 4 by voice. Habitat: scrubland and clearings near water. Voice: very/ultra high squeaky *tjeeweetwee tjuwertjuwer*. Pa.

6 **WHITE-RINGED FLYCATCHER** *Conopias albovittata* (Mosquero Cabecianillado) L 16 cm. Note black cap isolated by white eye stripes meeting at nape. Longer bill than 4 and 5. Habitat: forest canopy and edge; <500 m. Voice: high *wíerrrr* or very high fast sharp *rirírirí--*. CAm.

7 **GOLDEN-BELLIED FLYCATCHER** *Myiodynastes hemichrysus* (Mosquero Vientridorado) L 20 cm. Note malar stripe, olive-green mantle, buff- yellow edges to flight feathers. Habitat: forest edge and clearings; 750–1750(2250)m. Voice: very high sustained rather nasal *piuh piuh - -*. U,CRPa.

8 **GOLDEN-CROWNED FLYCATCHER** *Myiodynastes chrysocephalus* (Mosquero Coronidorado) L 20 cm. From 7 by buff throat and more distinct striping on breast. Habitat: forest canopy and edge; >1000 m. Voice: ultra high strong *tssjuw tssjuw*. U,Pa.

9 **STREAKED FLYCATCHER** *Myiodynastes maculatus* (Papamoscas Rayado; Mosquero Listado) L 20 cm. From very similar rufous-tailed 10 by whiter belly, white chin; streaking on flanks and belly further down; black malar does not extend on to chin. Habitat: forest interior, edge and clearings, plantations; sl–1750 m. Voice: high sustained *wit-wit-wit- -*. WSpr.

10 **SULPHUR-BELLIED FLYCATCHER** *Myiodynastes luteiventris* (Papamoscas Vientre-amarillo; Mosquero Vientriazufrado) L 20 cm. See 9. Note thick black malar extending to chin. Habitat: forest canopy, edge and clearings, plantations, woodland; sl–1750(2000)m. Voice: ultra high rapid repeated *féetjeweeh - -*. Thr.

11 **PIRATIC FLYCATCHER** *Legatus leucophaius* (Papamoscas/Mosquero Pirata) L 16 cm. As larger 9 and 10, but tail olive-brown, not rufous, with stubby bill. Habitat: open areas, woodland, forest canopy and edge; sl–1000(1500)m. Voice: very high *wéeeh* or rapid *wutwutwut tsjeeeh*. WSpr.

12 **GREY-CAPPED FLYCATCHER** *Myiozetetes granadensis* (Mosquero Cabecigrís) L 17 cm. Note pale eye, very short eyebrow and modest bill. Habitat: cultivation, open woodland, forest edge; <1650 m. Voice: e.g. high *djup-djup sréeeh*. CAm.

13 **TROPICAL KINGBIRD** *Tyrannus melancholicus* (Tirano Tropical) L 20 cm. Very similar to 14, but with slightly longer bill; 13 and 14 from other yellow-bellied kingbirds by pale grey crown, extensive bright yellow underparts and forked tail. Habitat: open landscape with scattered trees; sl–2000(2500)m. Voice: ultra high bickering fast *witrtrtrtr* or *purreeeh*. WSpr.

14 **COUCH'S KINGBIRD** *Tyrannus couchii* (Tirano de Couch) L 20 cm. (?/13). From 13 also by voice. Habitat: open woodland, forest edge, plantations. Voice: very high cautious *puweeh puweeh wieeh puREeeh wiWjiew wiWjieew* and fast twittering. MeBeGu.

15 **CASSIN'S KINGBIRD** *Tyrannus vociferans* (Tirano de Cassin) L 20 cm. Darker than 13 and 14 with short stubby bill and slightly rounded, pale-tipped tail. Habitat: areas with scattered trees and scrub; sl–2500 m. Voice: very high mewing *fuuwéeh*. WSpr.

16 **THICK-BILLED KINGBIRD** *Tyrannus crassirostris* (Tirano Piquigrueso) L 25 cm. More olive-brown than 67.5 and different range. Habitat: dry areas with scattered trees and scrub, woodland; sl–2000 m. Voice: very high *truweeh*. Me.

▶

Plate 62

Plate 62 continued

17 **WESTERN KINGBIRD** *Tyrannus verticalis* (Tirano Occidental) L 20 cm. Distinguished by white sides to square black tail. Habitat: areas with scattered trees and scrub, ranchland, woodland; sl–2500 m. Voice: very high musical partly harsh unstructured twittering *wutwuturrwut--*. Me(Gu). Note: for Eastern and Grey Kingbird see 67.5–6.

18 **CATTLE TYRANT** *Machetornis rixosus* (Atrapamoscas Jinete) L 20 cm. Kingbird-like, but feeding on the ground, often among cattle. Habitat: ranchland. Voice: ultra high tinkling *tritwitwit-trit-sreewit- piurrr-tritswit- -*. V,Pa.

Plate 63

1 **OLIVE-SIDED FLYCATCHER** (or Boreal Pewee) *Contopus borealis* (Pibí Boreal) L 17 cm. Note contrasting white belly and throat with olive flanks. Habitat: pine, mixed and other forest, mostly at edge; 250–2500 m. Voice: high *pip-pip-pip*. Thr.

2 **DARK PEWEE** *Contopus lugubris* (Pibí Sombrío) L 17 cm. Uniform dark coloured with peaked crest. Habitat: montane forest edge. Voice: high loud sharp *bic-bic-bic-bic bic-tic*. U,CRPa.

3 **WESTERN WOOD PEWEE** *Contopus sordidulus* (Pibí Occidental) L 14 cm. Note long primary projection, faint blotching of undertail coverts. Habitat: forest, woodland, open areas with trees and hedges; 750–3000 m. Voice: very/ultra high fluted sharp *pueeeh sréeeh tjktjktjk*. Thr.

4 **EASTERN WOOD PEWEE** *Contopus virens* (Pibí Oriental) L 14 cm. Lower mandible less extensively dark than 2, but safely separable only by voice. Habitat: forest, woodland, open areas with scattered trees and hedges; sl–1500(2750)m. Voice: very high *puwéeeh puwééh*. WSpr.

5 **GREATER PEWEE** *Contopus pertinax* (Pibí Mayor) L 18 cm. Note large size, long bi-coloured bill, unstriped flanks, clean undertail coverts. Habitat: forest interior, edge and clearings. Voice: very high sharp loud *peederée-peederée fujwééh - -*. WSpr.

6 **TROPICAL PEWEE** *Contopus cinereus* (Pibí Tropical) L 14 cm. From larger 3 and 4 by shorter primary projection, clean undertail coverts and white lores. Perches lower than both. Habitat: (semi-)open areas with tree stands, hedges, some bush; sl–1250 m. Voice: very high trill *trirrrr--* (1–2s). SMeCAm.

7 **OCHRACEOUS PEWEE** *Contopus ochraceus* (Pibí Ocráceo) L 17 cm. Note yellow underparts, tinged ochraceous. From 64.18 by pale, not cinnamon throat. Habitat: canopy at forest edge and clearings; 2000–3000 m. U,Ni(CR).

8 **PANAMA FLYCATCHER** *Myiarchus panamensis* (Copetón Colipardo) L 19 cm. From kingbirds 62.13–18 by olive-brown, not grey crown, from 9 – 15 by lack of rufous in wings. Habitat: open forest, (semi-) open areas with tree stands, hedges, some bush, mangrove. CRPa.

9 **DUSKY-CAPPED** (or Olivaceous) **FLYCATCHER** *Myiarchus tuberculifer* (Copetón Triste/Crestioscuro) L 17 cm. Races *olivascens* (a) and *lawrencei* (b) shown. No or little rufous on underside of tail. Note thin bill. Habitat: open forest, woodland, (semi-)open areas with trees, hedges, some bush; sl–2000(2750)m. Voice: very high sharp *whéuw* or trill or swept-up *whip*. Thr.

10 **YUCATAN FLYCATCHER** *Myiarchus yucatanensis* (Copetón Yucateco) L 19 cm. Wing bars indistinct, slightly peaked crown, white edges to tertials. Habitat: forest interior and edge, woodland. Voice: very high *whueet whuéeet*, partly pressed-out. YMeBeGu.

11 **ASH-THROATED FLYCATCHER** *Myiarchus cinerascens* (Copetón Gorjicenizo/Garganticeniza) L 19 cm. Pale below, red in wings contrasting with white edges to secondaries and tertials, dark tips to tail feathers below. Habitat: open areas with some scrub, riverine belts; sl–2500 m. Voice: very high compact loud *wtwt tji wrwr tjirwir - -*. WSpr

12 **NUTTING'S FLYCATCHER** *Myiarchus nuttigi* (Copetón de Nutting) L 18 cm. As 14, but with yellow inside of mouth and different voice. Habitat: forest interior, edge and clearings, dry woodland, open areas with some trees and scrub; sl–1250(1750)m. U,WSpr.

13 **GREAT CRESTED FLYCATCHER** *Myiarchus crinitus* (Copetón Viajero) L 20 cm. Note large size, heavy bill and bright yellow belly. Underside of tail extensively rufous. Habitat: forest interior, edge and clearings, wooded areas; sl–1000(1750)m. Voice: very high sharp loud well-separated *Wéetwit tjutju Wéew*. WSpr.

▶

Plate 63

Plate 63 continued

14   **BROWN-CRESTED FLYCATCHER** *Myiarchus tyrannulus* (Copetón Tirano/Crestipardo)
L 19 cm. Races *brachyurus* (a) and larger-billed *magister* (b) shown. Long, heavy bill. Very difficult
to separate from 13 (with whiter margins to wing coverts and tertials) and 11 (with dark-tipped
tail). Habitat: open areas with scattered trees, bush, mangrove; <1000 m. Voice: very high
sustained decisive *writ - -* or *wreet wreet - -* or *Wútoweet*. WSpr.

15   **FLAMMULATED FLYCATCHER** *Deltarhynchus flammulatus* (Copetón Piquiplano)   L 16 cm.
Thickset with broad bill. Note cinnamon edges to wing coverts. Habitat: dry scrubby woodland;
sl–1500 m. Voice: very high slightly descending drawn-out *tjúuuuuuh* (1s). E,Me.

16   **SCRUB FLYCATCHER** *Sublegatus arenarum* (Mosquero Gorgigrís)   L 14 cm. Note stubby bill
and contrast between white breast and yellowish lower underparts. Habitat: mangrove, open
woodland scrub and edges. Voice: very high irregular *tjuwtjuw wuutwuutwiwitwit*. U,CRPa.

17   **TAWNY-BREASTED FLYCATCHER** *Myiobius villosus* (Mosquerito Pechileonado)   L 14 cm.
Tawny colouring runs down over flanks. At higher elevations than 18. Habitat: montane forest.
V,Pa.

18   **SULPHUR-RUMPED FLYCATCHER** *Myiobius barbatus* (Rabadilla-amarilla/Lomiamarillo)
L 12 cm. Note bright tawny breast. Habitat: forest undergrowth; <1000 m. Voice: ultra high
sweeping *twéet*. SMeCAm.

19   **BLACK-TAILED FLYCATCHER** *Myiobius atricaudus* (Mosquero/ito Colinegro)   L 12 cm.
From 17 and 18 by pale and dull-brownish breast and paler yellow abdomen. Habitat: undergrowth
at forest and mangrove edge, second growth; <1000 m. U,CRPa.

20   **BRIGHT-RUMPED ATTILA** *Attila spadiceus* (Atila Rabadilla-brillante/Lomiamarilla)
L 19 cm. Note upright stance, hooked bill. Plumage variable but all share diagnostic yellow rump
(difficult to see). Habitat: forest interior, edge and clearings, woodland; <1500 m. Voice: ultra high
wiwit or very high loud sharp crescendoing fluted running-up and -down *weetwut-weetwut weetwut
wéetwurruut weetwurruut - -*. WSpr.

Plate 64 continued

TAWNY-CHESTED FLYCATCHER *Aphanotriccus capitalis* (Mosquero Pechileonado)
L 12 cm. From 63.7 by white lore and chin. Habitat: at forest streams and edges; <1000 m.
Voice: very high rapid *tututut Uureh*. U,NiCRPa.

TUFTED FLYCATCHER *Mitrephanes phaeocercus* (Mosquero/ito Penachudo/Moñudo) L 12 cm.
Races *vividus* (a) and nom (b) shown. As 63.7, but with saffron, not yellowish chin. Crest more
shaggy. Habitat: forest interior, edge and clearings, tree stands; 450(750)–2000(3000)m. Voice:
ultra high sharp *sreeeet* or scolding *wheet-cheetweetweet*. WSpr.

BELTED FLYCATCHER *Xenotriccus callizonus* (Mosquero Fajado)   L 12 cm. Ochraceous breast
band sharply demarcated from yellow belly. Lore more distinct than 63.7. Habitat: dry, scrubby
woodland; 1250–2000 m. Voice: ultra high rather hoarse *priuw* or bickering *tut-tutwrueet*.
U,SMeGuNi.

PILEATED FLYCATCHER *Xenotriccus mexicanus* (Mosquero del Balsas) L 14 cm. Note olive
breast. Eye ring more distinct than other small flycatchers with crests. Habitat: scrubby forest;
1250–3000 m. Voice: high *tsjip - -* (1/4s); Whimbrel-like sounds included in song. E,Me.

Plate 64

1   **WHITE-FRONTED** (or Zeledon's) **TYRANNULET** *Phyllomyias zeledoni* (Mosquerito Frentiblanco) L 12 cm. Note grey head; pale lower mandible diagnostic. Habitat: forest canopy, edge and clearings; 1250–2250m. Voice: series of ultra high sharp *sheeet sheeet - -*. U,CRPa.

2   **SOOTY-HEADED TYRANNULET** *Phyllomyias griseiceps* (Mosquerito Coronitiznado) L 10 cm. Note stubby bill, grey-olive crown, olive mantle, faint wing bars. Habitat: forest canopy, edge and clearings. Voice: very high rapid fluted *pir weetweettujr*. U,Pa.

3   **PALTRY** (or Mistletoe) **TYRANNULET** *Zimmerius vilissimus* (Mosquerito Cejiblanco/Cejigrís) L 11 cm. Greyish yellow below, prominent yellow edging to wing feathers. Habitat: forest edge and clearings, plantations, areas with scattered trees; 500–2500m. Voice: very/ultra high sustained *swee swee - -* (20–30s). SMeCAm.

4   **YELLOW-BELLIED TYRANNULET** *Ornithion semiflavum* (Mosquerito Vientre-amarillo/Cejiblanco) L 9 cm. Note grey cap, short tail and indistinct greenish edging to wing feathers. Habitat: forest canopy, tall second growth; <500(1500)m. Voice: very high slightly running-down *peeuw peepeuwuohwút*. SMeCAm.

5   **BROWN-CAPPED TYRANNULET** *Ornithion brunneicapillum* (Mosquerito Gorricafé) L 8 cm. From 4 by brown, not grey cap. Habitat: forest canopy, tall second growth; <750m. Voice*: very high thin *sweep-sweep* at same pitch, then 5–6 descending notes with final note ascending. CRPa.

6   **NORTHERN BEARDLESS TYRANNULET** *Camptostoma imberbe* (Mosquerito Lampino Norteño/Chillón) L 10 cm. Grey-olive overall, with slight yellow wash below. Note bushy crest. Habitat: broken forest, dry open woodland, semi-open areas; sl–2000m. Voice: ultra high thin *fjeet-fjeet fjeetwit*. WSpr.

7   **SOUTHERN BEARDLESS TYRANNULET** *Camptostoma obsoletum* (Mosquerito Silbador) L 10 cm. As 6, but brighter. Habitat: open woodland, savanna; <750m. Voice: very high pinched *fjéeh-tjee-tjeeprr*. CRPa.

8   **MOUSE-COLOURED TYRANNULET** *Phaeomyias murina* (Mosquerito Murino) L 12 cm. Note flesh-based lower mandible and pronounced eyebrow; brownish tone to upperparts. Habitat: cultivation with scattered trees, savanna. Voice: very high accelerated rising *wit-witwitwitwttr*. U,CRPa.

9   **YELLOW-CROWNED TYRANNULET** *Tyrannulus elatus* (Mosquerito Coroniamarillo) L 10 cm. Note very small, stubby bill. Habitat: woodland, forest edge, gardens. Voice: high wooden *pjutjew*. CRPa.

10   **YELLOW TYRANNULET** *Capsiempis flaveola* (Mosquerito Amarillo) L 11 cm. Yellow colouring distinctive. Habitat: open areas with scrub, trees, hedges, often near water; <500(1250)m. Voice: very high loud scolding *wurriwurriWecWicWic*. CAm.

11   **YELLOW-GREEN TYRANNULET** *Phylloscartes flavovirens* (Mosquerito Amarillo-verdoso) L 11 cm. Note distinctive eye ring and wing bars and long tail. Habitat: forest and woodland canopy. E,Pa.

12   **RUFOUS-BROWED TYRANNULET** *Phylloscartes superciliaris* (Mosquerito Cejirrufo) L 11 cm. Unmistakable. Habitat: forest canopy; <1250m. Voice: ultra high thin *pseeet*. U,CRPa.

13   **BRAN-COLOURED FLYCATCHER** *Myiophobus fasciatus* (Mosquero/ito Pechirrayado) L 12 cm. Note general colouring and breast streaking. Habitat: scrubland, neglected fields and pastures; 750–1250m. Voice: very high *wikjrrrrrr*. U,CRPa.

14   **YELLOW-OLIVE FLYCATCHER** *Tolmomyias sulphurescens* (Picoplano Ojiblanco; Piquiplano Azufrado) L 13 cm. Races *flavoolivaceus* (a) and *cinereiceps* (b) shown. No other similar-looking flycatcher with yellow eyes. Note olive crown and white lores of imm. Habitat: forest, plantations, woodland, gardens, tree stands; sl–1500m. Voice: ultra high inhaled thin *tsee tsee tsee*. SMeCAm.

15   **YELLOW-MARGINED FLYCATCHER** *Tolmomyias assimilis* (Piquiplano Aliamarillo) L 13 cm. Note dark eye and white panel in primaries, also broad 'flat' bill in this and 14. Habitat: higher levels of forest, tall second growth; <1000m. Voice: very high *prrrrt* or ultra high *tseet-tseet - -* (4 x). (Ni)CRPa.

16   **BLACK-BILLED FLYCATCHER** *Aphanotriccus audax* (Mosquero Piquinegro) L 13 cm. All-black bill diagnostic. Note white supraloral stripe, greenish belly with broad olive breast band. Habitat: forest undergrowth. U,Pa.

◀

Plate 64

Plate 65

1 **GREENISH ELAENIA** *Myiopagis viridicata* (Elenia; Elainia Verdosa) L 14 cm. Faint eyebrow, faint wing bars, slender bill, long tail. Habitat: higher levels of forest, woodland, plantations; <1500m. Voice: very high slurred-down thin *tseeeeech* or *tseewéh*. WSpr.

2 **FOREST ELAENIA** *Myiopagis gaimardii* (Elainia Selvática) L 13 cm. From 1 by distinct wing bars. Note: as other elaenias normally with concealed crest. Habitat: forest canopy, tall second growth. Voice*: high thin ascending *tsweeeup* slightly disyllabic. Pa.

3 **GREY ELAENIA** *Myiopagis caniceps* (Elainia Gris) L 13 cm. ♂ is greyest of the small flycatchers; ♀ with grey restricted mainly to neck and crown. Habitat: forest canopy, tall second growth; <500m. Voice*: high *seewip-seeoo* then rising and falling slurred trill *tsetsetsetsetse*. U,Pa.

4 **CARIBBEAN ELAENIA** *Elaenia martinica* (Elenia Caribeña) L 14 cm. Dark with flesh-based lower mandible. Habitat: woodland, scrub. Voice*: very high single note *pseeeeoo*. YMeBe.

5 **YELLOW-BELLIED ELAENIA** *Elaenia flavogaster* (Elenia Viente-amarillo; Elainia Copetona) L 16 cm. Note shaggy crest, often looking split down the middle. From 63.8 by olive chin and chest. Habitat: woodland, open areas with trees, scrub, hedges; sl–2000m. Voice: very high penetrating *shreek sréeeeh*. SMeCAm.

6 **MOUNTAIN ELAENIA** *Elaenia frantzii* (Elenia Serrana; Elainia Montañera) L 14 cm. Note thin eye ring and lack of crest. Habitat: cultivation with scattered trees, hedges, forest patches; 1250–2500m. Voice: very high *pieeeew*, gliding down. CAm.

7 **LESSER ELAENIA** *Elaenia chiriquensis* (Elainia Sabanera) L 14 cm. Overall less yellow than other elaenias. Habitat: scrubby marsh, plantations, cultivation with scattered trees, hedges, forest patches; sl–1500(1750)m. Voice: very high *wéejw weéjw*. CRPa.

8 **SCALE-CRESTED PYGMY TYRANT** *Lophotriccus pileatus* (Mosquerito de Yelmo) L 9 cm. Unmistakable by crest and red-rimmed pale eye. Habitat: upper storeys of montane forest. Voice*: high monotone series of 4–6 short slurred *plip plip plip plip* notes, typical of genus. CRPa.

9 **PALE-EYED PYGMY TYRANT** *Atalotriccus pilaris* (Mosquerito Ojiblanco) L 9 cm. As 8, but without crest and with less distinct striping below. Habitat: low woodland scrub. Voice: very high excited bouncing-up and tailing-off *wrrrrrtruw*. U,Pa.

10 **BLACK-CAPPED PYGMY TYRANT** *Myiornis atricapillus* (Mosquerito Colicorto) L 7 cm. Unmistakable. Note absence of yellow on belly. Habitat: forest canopy, tall second growth; <750m. Voice: very high *psit psit - -*. U,CRPa.

11 **BRONZE-OLIVE PYGMY TYRANT** *Pseudotriccus pelzelni* (Mosquerito Bronceado) L 11 cm. Distinct red eye and rufous wing feather edges. Habitat: forest undergrowth; 1250–1500m. Voice: dry voiceless very short rattle or ultra high short trill *psrrr*. U,Pa.

12 **RUDDY-TAILED FLYCATCHER** *Terenotriccus erythrurus* (Mosquerito Colirrufo) L 10 cm. Habitat: forest undergrowth and middle storeys; <500m. Voice: very high *(tuu)wét*. SMeCAm.

13 **NORTHERN BENTBILL** *Oncostoma cinereigulare* (Picocurvo/Piquitorcido Norteño) L 10 cm. Unmistakable by pale eye and bill shape. Habitat: scrubby open woodland, undergrowth at forest edge; sl–1500m. Voice: toy-trumpet-like *Trurrrr*. SMeCAm.

14 **SOUTHERN BENTBILL** *Oncostoma olivaceum* (Piquitorcido Sureño) L 9 cm. As 13, but grey restricted to lores. Habitat: woodland and forest undergrowth. Voice*: a high fluty trilling tody-flycatcher-like *prrrp prrrp prrrp - -*. Pa.

15 **SLATE-HEADED TODY FLYCATCHER** *Todirostrum sylvia* (Espatulilla Cabecigrís) L 9 cm. Note grey head, long flat bill, striking wing bars and clean underparts. Habitat: forest edge, dense scrubby growth; <1000m. Voice*: very high slurred fluty *sip-prrrru*, sometimes followed by further descending *prrrru* calls. SMeCAm.

16 **COMMON TODY FLYCATCHER** *Todirostrum cinereum* (Espatulilla Común) L 10 cm. Note yellow chin and eye. Habitat: stays low in areas with scattered trees, scrub, hedges, mangrove. Voice: ultra high trilling *wiedewiet wiedewiet*. SMeCAm.

17 **BLACK-HEADED TODY FLYCATCHER** *Todirostrum nigriceps* (Espatulilla Cabecinegra) L 8 cm. From 16 by white chin, dark eye and shorter, all-black tail. Habitat: forest canopy and edge; <1000m. Voice: ultra high *fjit-fjit-fjit*. CRPa.

▶

Plate 65

Plate 65 continued

18   **STUB-TAILED SPADEBILL** *Platyrinchus cancrominus* (Picochato Rabón; Piquichato Norteño) L 9 cm. (?/19). As 19, but with paler breast and smaller yellow crown patch. Habitat: forest understorey; sl–1500m. Voice: sharp nasal hurried *gifitme*. SMeCAm.

19   **WHITE-THROATED SPADEBILL** *Platyrinchus mystaceus* (Piquichato Gargantiblanco) L 10 cm. Note breast band separating white throat from belly. Habitat: montane forest understorey. Voice: ultra high soft *sih* or song round *basic -wic-*. CRPa.

20   **GOLDEN-CROWNED SPADEBILL** *Platyrinchus coronatus* (Piquichato Coronirrufo) L 9 cm. As 18 and 19 with broad bill base. Golden crown distinctive. Habitat: forest understorey; <1250m. Voice: ultra high cicada-like buzz *srrrrirrrrr* (2s). CAm.

Plate 66

1   **COCOS FLYCATCHER** *Nesotriccus ridgwayi* (Mosquero de la Isla del Coco) L 13 cm. Only flycatcher on Cocos Island. Note long bill. Habitat: swampy forest, second growth. E ,CR.

2   **YELLOW-BELLIED FLYCATCHER** *Empidonax flaviventris* (Mosquero/ito Vientre-amarillo) L 12 cm. Note yellow wash over throat. Habitat: forest interior, edge and clearings, plantations, woodland; <1500m. Voice: very high feeble *wéewuh* or very high *sweep*. WSpr.

3   **ACADIAN FLYCATCHER** *Empidonax virescens* (Mosquero/ito Verdoso) L 14 cm. Very difficult to separate from 2, 4 and 5, slightly more yellow-tinged overall with largest bill; in autumn yellowish below and then not safely separable from slightly smaller 2. Habitat: forest, woodland, scrub; sl–2500m. Voice*: high insistent disyllabic *tsweéolit*, sometimes followed by *sip-sip-sip-sip-sip-sip* and *whip*, lashed upwards. WSpr.

4   **ALDER FLYCATCHER** *Empidonax alnorum* (Mosquero Ailero; Mosquerito de Charral) L 13 cm. From 5 also by call. Habitat: open woodland, marshy areas, neglected cultivation; sl–2000(2500)m. Voice: very high *swept*. WSpr.

5   **WILLOW** (or Traill's) **FLYCATCHER** *Empidonax traillii* (Mosquero Saucero; Mosquerito de Traill) L 13 cm. From very similar 4 by indistinct eye ring, slightly whiter throat and slightly longer bill. Habitat: areas with tree stands, bush, hedges, marsh; sl–2000m. Voice: swept-up *writ*. Thr.

6   **WHITE-THROATED FLYCATCHER** *Empidonax albigularis* (Mosquero Gorjiblanco; Mosquerito Gargantiblanco) L 13 cm. Brownish with buff wing bars. Habitat: swampy areas with trees and scrub; 1250–3000m. Voice: low hoarse *tetrúit*. WSpr.

7   **LEAST FLYCATCHER** *Empidonax mimimus* (Mosquero Mínimo; Mosquerito Chebec) L 12 cm. Small, yellow, with dark-tipped lower mandible, distinct eye ring. Habitat: forest interior, edge and clearings, tall second growth; sl–1250(2500)m. Voice: very high *tjet tjet tjet*. Thr.

8   **HAMMOND'S FLYCATCHER** *Empidonax hammondii* (Mosquero de Hammond) L 13 cm. Rather short-tailed; long primary projection. Small dark bill; underparts rather grey. Habitat: forest interior, edge and clearings; (250)1000–3000m. Voice: high *pijèh*. WSpr.

9   **DUSKY FLYCATCHER** *Empidonax oberholseri* (Mosquero Oscuro) L 14 cm. Rounded head, not slightly peaked as 8; slender and long-tailed; short primary projection. Habitat: dry scrub, open woodland, forest edge; sl–3000m. Voice: thin *wit*. Me(Gu?).

10   **GREY FLYCATCHER** *Empidonax wrightii* (Mosquero Gris) L 14 cm. Grey plumage and long slender bill distinctive. Habitat: dry areas with scattered trees and scrub; sl–2500m. Voice: very high *sreet*. Me.

11   **PINE FLYCATCHER** *Empidonax affinis* (Mosquero Pinero) L 14 cm. As 12 and 13 but with longer primary projection. Habitat: open woodland, montane forest; 1500–3500m. MeGu.

12   **PACIFIC SLOPE FLYCATCHER** *Empidonax difficilis* (Mosquero Occidental) L 13 cm. Broader bill than 11 and with shorter primary projection. Habitat: forest, dry woodland; sl(1000)–1500 (3500)m. Voice: ultra high drawn-up *puwéet*. Me.

13   **CORDILLERAN FLYCATCHER** *Empidonax occidentalis* (Mosquero Barranqueño) L 13 cm. From 12 only by voice and even then difficult to separate. Habitat: forest, woodland; 500(1000)–1500(3500)m. Voice: *wujéet* or ultra high *tiet tiet*. Me.

▶

Plate 66

Plate 66 continued

14 BUFF-BREASTED FLYCATCHER *Empidonax fulvifrons* (Mosquero Pechicanelo) L 12 cm.
Rather bright buff-cinnamon. No crest. Habitat: woodland, cultivation; sl(500)–2500(3500)m.
Voice: very high rather irregular *tuweeh-tweeh-tuweeh-tuwee- -*. WSpr.

15 OCHRE-BELLIED FLYCATCHER *Mionectes oleagineus* (Mosquero Vientre-ocre/Aceitunado)
L 13 cm. Distinctively coloured. Habitat: forest interior, edge and clearings, adjacent areas;
<1000(1250)m. Voice: very high *weet*; high *wut-wut-wut- -* or *priet pupriet - -*. WSpr.

16 YELLOWISH FLYCATCHER *Empidonax flavescens* (Mosquero/ito Amarillento) L 13 cm. Rich
yellow below. Habitat: damp montane forest; 100(750)–3000m. Voice: very high *seeéh*. SMeCAm.

17 BLACK-CAPPED FLYCATCHER *Empidonax atriceps* (Mosquero/ito Cabecinegro) L 12 cm.
Unmistakable by black cap. Habitat: montane forest and edge. Voice: very high *wit*. CRPa.

18 OLIVE-STRIPED FLYCATCHER *Mionectes olivaceus* (Mosquerito Colicorto/Ojimanchado)
L 13 cm. Note spot behind eye and striping on underparts. Habitat: forest, second growth;
750–2250m. Voice: ultra high *tsstsstss*. CRPa.

19 SLATY-CAPPED FLYCATCHER *Leptopogon superciliaris* (Mosquerito Orejinegro) L 13 cm.
Note dusky ear patch and slaty crown. Habitat: middle forest levels; 500–1500m. Voice: very high
tjeet-tsjeet tsjeewrrrrr tsjeet tojeefuhwrrrrr. U,CRPa.

20 SEPIA-CAPPED FLYCATCHER *Leptopogon amaurocephalus* (Mosquero Gorripardo;
Mosquerito Cabecipardo) L 13 cm. Sepia cap distinctive. Habitat: forest understorey, tall second
growth, plantations; sl–1300m. Voice: very high angry bickering slurred-down *tutrrrrrriit*. WSpr.

Plate 67

1 BLACK PHOEBE *Sayornis nigricans* (Mosquero Negro/de Agua) L 16 cm. Unmistakable. Perches
low. Dips tail. Habitat: in open areas at streams and lakes; sl–3000m. Voice: very high *fibée*. Thr.

2 EASTERN PHOEBE *Sayornis phoebe* (Mosquero Fibí) L 17 cm. Jizz and habits as 1. Large-
headed. Habitat: open areas with scattered trees and hedges, often near water; sl–2500m. Voice:
very/ultra high *tsjip*. Me.

3 SAY'S PHOEBE *Sayornis saya* (Mosquero Llanero) L 18 cm. No similar-coloured flycatcher.
Habitat: dry open country with scattered trees, scrub, hedges; sl–2500m. Voice: high loud fluted
tidjuuw tidjuh. Me.

4 VERMILION FLYCATCHER *Pyrocephalus rubinus* (Mosquero Cardenal) L 15 cm.
Unmistakable. Note belly colouring of ♀ and imm. Habitat: open areas with scattered trees and
hedges, often near water; sl–2500m. Voice: ultra high thin *tittiitthrrEe-it* or *seeh seeh*. MeBeGu.

5 GREY KINGBIRD *Tyrannus dominicensis* (Tirano Gris) L 20 cm. Pure grey and white. Habitat:
open areas with scattered trees, scrub and hedges. Voice*: high trilling phrases ending in a short
liquid trill like *pseeoprrt pseeoprrt - -*. U,YMeBe.

6 EASTERN KINGBIRD *Tyrannus tyrannus* (Tirano Viajero/Norteño) L 20 cm. Distinctively
patterned and coloured. Note small bill. Habitat: open woodland, forest margins. Voice: ultra high
thin rhythmic varied *ttsréewit--*. WSpr.

7 GIANT KINGBIRD *Tyrannus cubebsis* (Tirano Real) L 25 cm. From smaller 6 by very heavy
bill. Habitat: at water in forest, woodland. Hyp,YMe.

8 SIRYSTES *Sirystes sibilator* (Atrapamoscas de Rabadilla Blanca) L 19 cm. Unmistakable by wing
pattern. Habitat: forest canopy; <1000m. Voice: high *bic-bic-bic- -*. U,Pa.

9 FORK-TAILED FLYCATCHER *Tyrannus savana* (Tirano-tijereta Sabanero; Tijereta Sabanera)
L 18 (+ 20) cm. Unmistakable. Habitat: savanna with scattered bush; sl–1500m. Voice: ultra high
very short rattling *cratch-cratch-cratch- -*. WSpr.

10 SCISSOR-TAILED FLYCATCHER *Tyrannus forficatus* (Tirano-tijereta Rosado; Tijereta
Rosada) L 20 (+ 15) cm. Unmistakable. Habitat: dry open country with scattered bush and trees;
sl–1500m. Voice: very high sweet twittering *wit-wéetwit-wit-weetwrit*. WSpr.

▶

Plate 67

Plate 67 continued

11   **LONG-TAILED TYRANT** *Colonia colonus* (Mosquero Coludo) L 13 (+ 10) cm. Unmistakable. Habitat: forest edge and clearings; <1000m. Voice: very high swept-up strong *whiéh*. CAm.

12   **EYE-RINGED FLATBILL** *Rhynchocyclus brevirostris* (Picoplano/Piquiplano de Anteojos) L 16 cm. Robust with striking white eye ring. As 13 with very broad, flat bill. Habitat: middle storeys of forest; sl–2000m. Voice: ultra high inhaled *hiss*. WSpr.

13   **OLIVACEOUS FLATBILL** *Rhynchocyclus olivaceus* (Piquiplano Oliváceo) L 15 cm. From 12 by weaker eye ring, paler breast; wing linings rufous-tinged. Habitat: forest; <500m. Voice: high short trill *srrrih*. U,Pa.

14   **ROYAL FLYCATCHER** *Onychorhynchus coronatus* (Mosquero Real) L 17 cm. Unmistakable, especially when showing (transverse deployed) crest. Habitat: lower storeys at forest edge, often near streams; sl–1250m. Voice: high disyllabic *píoh* (1/5s). WSpr.

15   **BROWNISH TWISTWING** *Cnipodectes subbrunneus* (Alitorcedo Pardo) L 17 cm. Note bright-coloured tail. Shows characteristic wing stretching, one at a time. Habitat: forest undergrowth, tall second growth. U,Pa.

16   **PIED WATER TYRANT** *Fluvicola pica* (Tirano de Agua Pinto) L 13 cm. Unmistakable in its habitat. Habitat: scrub at marshes and ponds. Voice: dry nasal *pjièh*. U,Pa.

17   **TORRENT TYRANNULET** *Serpophaga cinerea* (Mosquerito Guardarríos) L 10 cm. Unmistakable in its habitat; perches on stones in streams or low hanging twigs. Habitat: swift montane streams; 250–2000m. Voice: ultra high *pTséek*. CRPa.

18   **SHARPBILL** *Oxyruncus cristatus* (Picoagudo) L 16 cm. Unmistakable by face pattern and sharp bill. Habitat: foothill forest canopy and middle storeys. Voice: very high strange cicada-like slurred-down *tiuuuuu--* (3s). U,CRPa.

Plate 68

1   **THRUSHLIKE SCHIFFORNIS** (Mourner or Manakin) *Schiffornis turdinus* (Llorón Café; Tordo-saltarín) L 16 cm. Several races, of which *dumicola* (a) and *veraepacis* (b, less rufous except in wing) shown. Note staring eye and pale eye ring. Difficult to see in forest undergrowth. Habitat: forest understorey; <1750m. Voice: e.g. very high fluted penetrating *piuuuuh-wít(wet)*. SMeCAm.

2   **RUFOUS PIHA** *Lipaugus unirufus* (Piha Rufa/Rojiza) L 25 cm. Difficult to separate from 3, except by voice and size. Habitat: upper forest levels; <1250m. Voice: croaking *krrrrich*; high explosive resounding *piuWéeah* or *piuWaeh* (onomatopoeic). SMeCAm.

3   **RUFOUS MOURNER** *Rhytipterna holerythra* (Llorón/Plañidera Rojizo/a) L 25 cm. Difficult to separate from larger 2 except by voice. Habitat: upper forest levels; <750m. Voice: high plaintive *wuéeh-jíeeh*. SMeCAm.

4   **SPECKLED MOURNER** *Laniocera rufescens* (Llorón/Plañidera Moteado/a) L 20 cm. Note wing bars, pale tips to flight feathers and tertials. Shows faint barring below. Habitat: mid forest levels at streams, wooded swamps; <750m. U,SMeCAm.

5   **BROAD-BILLED SAPAYOA** (or Manakin) *Sapayoa aenigma* (Sapayoa) L 16 cm. Coloured olive-green, paler below with broad bill and concealed yellow crown spot. Habitat: forest understorey. U,Pa.

6   **GREY-HEADED PIPRITES** (or Manakin) *Piprites griseiceps* (Saltarín Cabecigrís) L 12 cm. Note distinctive eye ring in grey head. Habitat: middle storeys of forest, tall second growth; <750m. Voice: very high *wut-wut wut*. U,CAm.

7   **GOLDEN-COLLARED MANAKIN** *Manacus vitellinus* (Saltarín Cuellidorada) L 11 cm. ♂ is unmistakable. ♀ not safely separable from similar red-legged 8 (but different range), 9 (slightly more yellowish below), 11 (bill paler). Habitat: undergrowth at forest edge, second growth. Voice*: high short descending *krreow* repeated, various *prrt-prrt* calls and short descending trills. Pa.

Note: ♂♂ manakins congregate at so-called leks, where they perform collective ballets, while uttering pistol-like *tic*'s and wing whirrs. Visiting ♀♀ choose the best performer to mate.

▶

Plate 68

Plate 68 continued

8 **WHITE-COLLARED MANAKIN** *Manacus candei* (Saltarín Cuelliblanco) L 11 cm.
Unmistakable, ♀ see 7. Habitat: undergrowth at forest edge, plantations, tall second growth, often
at streams; <750m. Voice: pistol-like *tíc tictic* or rasping explosive dry rattles in chorus. SMeCAm.

9 **ORANGE-COLLARED MANAKIN** *Manacus aurantiacus* (Saltarín Cuellinaranja) L 10 cm.
♂ from 7 by orange, not yellow collar, ♀ see 7. Habitat: undergrowth at forest edge, plantations,
gardens; <1000m. Voice: pistol-like *tíc* or rattling *trric* and *PafPafPaf--* in chorus. CRPa.

10 **GREEN MANAKIN** *Chloropipo holochlora* (Saltarín Verde) L 12 cm. Larger than other
manakins with longer tail. Habitat: understorey of forest interior. U,Pa.

11 **GOLDEN-HEADED MANAKIN** *Pipra erythrocephala* (Saltarín Capuchidorado) L 9 cm.
Unmistakable, ♀ see 7. Habitat: forest, tall second growth. Voice: very high *tjeouw-tujrr.* U,Pa.

12 **RED-CAPPED MANAKIN** *Pipra mentalis* (Saltarín Cabecirrojo) L 10 cm. ♂ unmistakable, ♀
difficult to separate from similar grey-legged 10 (longer-tailed and different range), 13 (shows
whitish chin), 16 (greyish head), 17 (deeper green). Habitat: forest interior and edge; <1000m.
Voice: very high explosive *tsjit tsjittitertsjit* or *prutpritprut* or slow wooden rattle. SMeCAm.

13 **WHITE-RUFFED MANAKIN** *Corapipo leucorrhoa* (Saltarín Gorgiblanco) L 10 cm.
Unmistakable, ♀ see 12. Habitat: lower levels of forest interior, at edge and clearings;
500–1000(1500)m. Voice: very high *ssssrrrrih*. NiCRPa.

14 **LONG-TAILED MANAKIN** *Chiroxiphia linearis* (Saltarín Colilargo/Toledo) L 11 (+ 10) cm.
♂ deeper black than 16, ♀ with long reddish middle tail feathers. Habitat: forest undergrowth,
riverine belts, mangrove; <1500m. Voice: very high shrill *sueet* or mellow fluted *towheedo*.
SMeCAm.

15 **LANCE-TAILED MANAKIN** *Chiroxiphia lanceolata* (Saltarín Coludo) L 13 (+ 1) cm.
Note greenish gloss of ♂. ♀ with elongated green middle tail feathers. Habitat: middle storeys of
dry forest; stands of tall trees; 1000–1500m. Voice: *mjèw* or high mellow *pjiupurr.* CRPa.

16 **WHITE-CROWNED MANAKIN** *Pipra pipra* (Saltarín Coroniblanco) L 10 cm. Unmistakable,
♀ see 12. Habitat: forest undergrowth; 500–1500m. Voice: very high loud *sriéw.* U,CRPa.

17 **BLUE-CROWNED MANAKIN** *Pipra coronata* (Saltarín Coroniceleste) L 9 cm.
Unmistakable, ♀ see 12. Habitat: forest undergrowth, tall second growth; <1350m. Voice:
jumping-up *prupréeh* or shivering *pipipi--pir.* CRPa.

Plate 69 continued

8 **BARE-NECKED UMBRELLABIRD** *Cephalopterus glabricollis* (Pájara-sombrilla Cuellinudo)
L 40 cm. Unmistakable. Habitat: middle storeys of forest; 100–2000m. Voice: ultra low *Wuhh*
(2/5s). U, CRPa.

9 **THREE-WATTLED BELLBIRD** *Procnias tricarunculata* (Campanero Tricarunculado)   L 30 cm.
Unmistakable. Habitat: forest; tall trees elsewhere; 1000–3000m. Voice: resounding *prOingg* as
closing of an iron gate. CAm.

Plate 69

1 **ONE-COLOURED BECARD** *Pachyramphus homochrous* (Cabezón Unicolor) L 16 cm. ♂ is uniform dark slate. Note rufous tail of ♀, absence of pale lore. Habitat: forest canopy, tall second growth. U,Pa.

2 **ROSE-THROATED BECARD** *Pachyramphus aglaiae* (Llorón Degollado/Plomizo) L 17 cm. Races *albiventris* (a) and *latirostris* (b, darker without rose spot) shown. Note that nape is paler than crown. Habitat: canopy of forest edge, riverine belts; <250m. Voice: very high whistled *píweeeh* or unstructured excited twittering. Thr.

3 **GREY-COLLARED BECARD** *Pachyramphus major* (Cabezón Cuelligrís) L 15 cm. From 5 – 8 by tail pattern. Note rufous ♀ upperparts. Habitat: forest interior and edge, plantations; sl–2500m. Voice: high wooden *pip-pipppijüeh*. U,WSpr.

4 **CINNAMON BECARD** *Pachyramphus cinnamomeus* (Cabezón Canelo) L 14 cm. Note red tail, pale lore. Habitat: forest edge and clearings, open woodland, mangrove; <2750m. Voice: ultra high sharp whistled *tjeet-tjeettittit*, slightly running down. SMeCAm.

5 **WHITE-WINGED BECARD** *Pachyramphus polychopterus* (Cabezón Aliblanco) L 15 cm. Not in same range as 3; no supraloral pale stripe. ♀ with olive upperparts and greyish crown. Habitat: semi-open woodland, riverine belts, mangrove; <1250m. Voice: very high strong rattle *tjut-tjirrrrrr* or *tjuu-tjuw-tjuw*. CAm.

6 **BLACK-AND-WHITE BECARD** *Pachyramphus albogriseus* (Cabezón Cejiblanco) L 14 cm. Not in range of 3. Note lack of white border to mantle. ♀ distinctive. Habitat: forest interior and edge, tall second growth; 750–1750m. Voice: ultra high *tjak wéetje-wéetje-wéetje- -*, rising. U,CRPa.

7 **BARRED BECARD** *Pachyramphus versicolor* (Cabezón Ondeado) L 12 cm. Barring below and tail pattern diagnostic. Note rufous shoulders and wing edging of ♀. Habitat: higher levels of mountain forest; 1500–2500(3000)m. Voice: very high rising *wit-weetweetwitrrrr*. U,CRPa.

8 **CINEREOUS BECARD** *Pachyramphus rufus* (Cabezón Rufo) L 14 cm. Mantle grey without white border. From 6 by narrow pale edges to all tail feathers (not tipped white). ♀ very red, contrasting with white underparts. Habitat: forest canopy; 750–1500m. Voice: ultra high *juwéeh*; very high accelerated rising *wreetweetwéettrrrrr*. U,Pa.

9 **LOVELY COTINGA** *Cotinga amabilis* (Cotinga Azuleja/Linda) L 19 cm. ♂ without eye ring, ♀ not tawny below as 10; spotted above, not uniform as 11. Check range. Habitat: forest canopy and edge; sl–1500(1750)m. U,SMeCAm.

10 **TURQUOISE COTINGA** *Cotinga ridgwayi* (Cotinga Turquesa) L 18 cm. ♂ from 11 by black neck spots. Check range. Habitat: forest canopy, tall second growth; sl–1750m. U,CRPa.

11 **BLUE COTINGA** *Cotinga nattererii* (Cotinga Azul) L 19 cm. More black in wing coverts and scapulars than 10. Check range. Habitat: forest canopy, tall second growth. Voice: croaking toneless *wretwretwret--wiet wiet*. U,Pa.

12 **MASKED TITYRA** *Tityra semifasciata* (Tityra Enmascarada/Carirroja) L 20 cm. Unmistakable. Habitat: forest canopy, tall trees elsewhere; sl–1500(1750)m. Voice: croaking *ráspberry-ráspberry-terryterry* in chorus. WSpr.

13 **BLACK-CROWNED TITYRA** *Tityra inquisitor* (Tityra Piquinegra/Coroninegra) L 19 cm. Unmistakable. Note black cap. Habitat: forest canopy, tall trees elsewhere; sl–1000(1250)m. WSpr.

14 **SNOWY COTINGA** *Carpodectes nitidus* (Cotinga Nivosa) L 20 cm. From 16 by black bill. Habitat: forest canopy, tall trees elsewhere; sl–750m. U,CAm

15 **BLACK-TIPPED COTINGA** *Carpodectes hopkei* (Cotinga Blanca) L 20 cm. Note pale eyes. Habitat: forest canopy; <1000m. U,Pa.

16 **YELLOW-BILLED COTINGA** *Carpodectes antoniae* (Cotinga Piquiamarillo) L 20 cm. Yellow bill diagnostic. Habitat: forest, mangrove. U,CRPa.

17 **PURPLE-THROATED FRUITCROW** *Querula purpurata* (Quérula Gorgimorada) L 30 cm. ♂ unmistakable. Note silvery bill of ♀. Habitat: forest canopy; <500m. Voice: very high Scops Owl-like *piupiupiu uuh* in chorus. NiCRPa.

◀

Plate 69

Plate 70

1   **BROWN-CHESTED MARTIN** *Phaeoprogne tapera* (Martín de Ríos)   L 18 cm. Note white chin, brown stripe down breast and large size. Habitat: open areas. U,CRPa.

2   **PURPLE MARTIN** *Progne subis* (Martín Azul/Purpúrea)   L 17 cm. No other all-blue martin in area except vagrant 6. ♀ with restricted blue to head and grey half-collar. Habitat: open areas, towns. Voice: high mellow *prutprut*. Thr.

3   **GREY-BREASTED MARTIN** *Progne chalybea* (Martín Pechigrís)   L 17 cm. Not safely separable from uncommon ♀ 4 (preferring higher elevations) or from vagrant ♀ 5. Habitat: towns, open areas, forest edge and clearings. Voice: high rough *trrrt-trrrt*. WSpr.

4   **SINALOA MARTIN** *Progne sinaloae* (Martín Sinaloense)   L 18 cm. Note broad white stripe on belly and up breast. Habitat: forests, woodland. U,MeGu.

5   **CARIBBEAN MARTIN** *Progne dominicensis* (Martín Grande)   L 17 cm. Vagrant, not in range of 4. Habitat: open areas near water, cliffs, towns. Hyp,YMe.

6   **SOUTHERN MARTIN** *Progne modesta* (Martín Sureño) L 19 cm. Race *elegans* (shown). ♂ not separable from smaller 2, ♀ all-dusky below. Habitat: open areas in forested country, near cliffs, towns, coast. V,Pa.

7   **TREE SWALLOW** *Tachycineta bicolor* (Golondrina Arbolera/Bicolor)   L 14 cm. From 8 and 9 by broader green/dark grey band through rump. Habitat: open areas near water. Voice: very high scratchy sharp *tjirp-tjirp-tjirp*. Thr.

8   **MANGROVE SWALLOW** *Tachycineta albilinea* (Golondrina Manglera/Lomiblanca)   L 12 cm. Note white-and-green rump and white edges to tertials. Habitat: mangrove, coastal waters, marsh. WSpr.

9   **VIOLET-GREEN SWALLOW** *Tachycineta thalassina* (Golondrina Cariblanca/Verde Violácea) L 13 cm. Note white sides to purple rump. Habitat: open desert, woodland. Voice: very high rapid *tjittjittjit--tutjit-witwit*. WSpr.

10   **WHITE-WINGED SWALLOW** *Tachycineta albiventer* (Golondrina Aliblanca)   L 14 cm. Extensive white in wing. Habitat: open spots in mangrove, over beaches, along rivers. Voice: very high rasping repeated *screetch - -*. U,Pa.

11   **BLUE-AND-WHITE SWALLOW** *Notiochelidon cyanoleuca* (Golondrina Azuliblanca) L 12 cm. Unmistakable. Habitat: montane areas near towns and villages. Voice*: very high slightly mournful drawn-out *psweet psweet*, tailing off. (MeGu)CAm.

12   **BLACK-CAPPED SWALLOW** *Notiochelidon pileata* (Golondrina Gorrinegra)   L 13 cm. As 11. Note blue restricted to forehead, brown spotting to throat sides and brown flanks. Habitat: woodland, towns, villages. SMeGuHoSa.

13   **WHITE-THIGHED SWALLOW** *Neochelidon tibialis* (Golondrina Musliblanca)   L 12 cm. Dark uniform brown distinctive. White thighs difficult to see. Habitat: forest edge and clearings, often at rivers. U,Pa.

14   **BANK SWALLOW** (or Sand Martin) *Riparia riparia* (Golondrina Ribereña)   L 12 cm. From larger 1 by more well-defined collar. Habitat: open areas, often near water. Voice: high nasal *tjitjitjisreesreetzitzi*. U,Thr.

15   **RIDGWAY'S ROUGH-WINGED SWALLOW** *Stelgidopteryx ridgwayi* (Golondrina-aliserrada Yucateca)   L 13 cm. Darker overall than 16. White spots between eye and bill diagnostic. Not in range of 17. Habitat: mainly forest edge and clearings. SMeBeGu. Note: not recognised as full species by AOU.

16   **NORTHERN ROUGH-WINGED SWALLOW** *Stelgidopteryx serripennis* (Golondrina-aliserrada Norteña)   L 13 cm. From 17 by darker rump and pale greyish throat. Habitat: open areas. Voice: very high *wrahurah wraah*. Thr.

17   **SOUTHERN ROUGH-WINGED SWALLOW** *Stelgidopteryx ruficollis* (Golondrina-alirrasposa Sureña)   L 12 cm. Pale rump and buff chin diagnostic. Habitat: open areas. Voice: high swept-up *wrrr wreh-wreh-wreh*. CAm.

18   **CAVE SWALLOW** *Hirundo fulva* (Golondrina Pueblera)   L 13 cm. Races *pallida* (a) and darker-coloured *citata* (b) shown. From 19 mainly by pale orange throat. Habitat: open areas, towns. Voice: high nasal *witwit wit cheek - -*. Me(CAm).

▶

Plate 70

Plate 70 continued

19 **CLIFF SWALLOW** *Hirundo pyrrhonota* (Golondrina Risquera) L 14 cm. Races *tachina* (a) and *melanogaster* (b, with red front) shown. Habitat: open areas, towns, cliffs. Voice: high mewing *tjawtjaw tjaw* or low dry trills. Thr.

20 **BARN SWALLOW** *Hirundo rustica* (Golondrina Ranchera/Tijereta) L 16 cm. No similar swallow in the area. Habitat: anywhere, except in true forest. Voice: incessant twittering including inhaled *sreeeh*. Thr.

Plate 71

1 **STELLER'S JAY** *Cyanocitta stelleri* (Chara de Steller) L 30 cm. Races *diodemata* (a) and *suavis* (b, with smaller crest) shown. Crest and wing barring diagnostic. Habitat: pine and mixed montane forest; 1000–3500m. Voice: *shráak; tjaktjaktjaktjiktjak* and other varied shrieks. WSpr.

2 **BLUE JAY** *Cyanocitta cristata* (Chara Crestada) L 30 cm. Distinctive face pattern. White in wings diagnostic. Habitat: forest, town parks and other areas with oaks. Voice: short bursts of varying pitch and melody, most reminiscent of badly oiled wheels. Hyp,Me.

3 **PINYON JAY** *Gymnorhinus cyanocephalus* (Chara Piñonera) L 25 cm. Note almost uniform pale blue colouring. Habitat: dry pine forest; 1500–3000m. Voice: very high mewing *wèhwèhwèh*. U,NMe.

4 **SCRUB JAY** *Aphelocoma californica* (Chara Azuleja) L 30 cm. Note distinctive bib. From 5 by white eyebrow. Several races, of which *remota* shown. Habitat: dry open areas with some scrub, hedges, tree stands; sl–2750m. Voice: very high dry shriek *srieeh srieeh* or rapid *wekwekwek*. Me.

5 **MEXICAN** (or Grey-breasted) **JAY** *Aphelocoma ultramarina* (Chara Pechigrís) L 30 cm. Rather pale overall, lacking any eyebrow. Habitat: dry woodland; 1000–3500m. Voice: very high swept-up *wheeet*. Me.

6 **AZURE-HOODED JAY** *Cyanolyca cucullata* (Chara Gorriazul; Urraca de Toca Celeste) L 30 cm. Hood diagnostic. Habitat: montane forest; 1000–2000m. Voice: very varied, e.g. low *verdríet-verdríet* or high *shreek shreek* or high dry rapid ticking. WSpr.

7 **BLACK-THROATED JAY** *Cyanolyca pumilo* (Chara de Niebla) L 25 cm. Distinctive head pattern. Habitat: montane forest; 1500–3000m. Voice: high dry *rèèk-rèèk* or *rupreprep*. SMeGuHoSa.

8 **DWARF JAY** *Cyanolyca nana* (Chara Enana) L 25 cm. From 9 and 10 by blue crown. Habitat: montane forest; 1500–3000m. Voice: very high swept-up *iréet-iréet*. E,Me.

9 **WHITE-THROATED** (or Omiltemi) **JAY** *Cyanolyca mirabilis* (Chara de Omiltemi) L 25 cm. Paler than 10 with cheek bordered white all around. Habitat: montane forest; 1750–3000m. Voice: very high shrill warbling *srieoh-srieoh*. E,Me.

10 **SILVERY-THROATED JAY** *Cyanolyca argentigula* (Urraca Gorgiplateada) L 25 cm. Very dark azure-blue. Habitat: montane forest. Voice: high *wehwehwehweh*. U,CRPa.

11 **BUSHY-CRESTED JAY** *Cyanocorax melanocyaneus* (Chara Centroamericana) L 30 cm. Nom (a) and race *chavezi* (b) shown. From 12, 13 and 14 by black legs, more distinct crest and different range. Note black belly of nom. Habitat: open woodland; >750m. Voice: very high *sraksraksraksrak--*. CAm.

12 **SAN BLAS JAY** *Cyanocorax sanblasianus* (Chara de San Blas) L 30 cm. Note yellowish legs. From 13 and 14 by different range. Habitat: dry woodland, plantations; sl–1250m. Voice: very high scratchy *shriiik-shriiik-shriiiik*. E,Me.

13 **YUCATAN JAY** *Cyanocorax yucatanicus* (Chara Yucateca) L 30 cm. Note yellow eyelids of imm. Juv is white, changing to black after first moult. Habitat: forest, second growth, plantations; <250m. Voice: varied, e.g. high rapid dry chatters of varying length. YMe.

14 **PURPLISH-BACKED JAY** *Cyanocorax beecheii* (Chara de Beechy) L 35 cm. Dark purplish-blue above. Legs brighter yellow than 12, glossy colour of upperparts more violet. Habitat: dry woodland; <500m. Voice: high hurried *shrèèk-shrèèk-shrèèk*. E,Me.

Plate 71

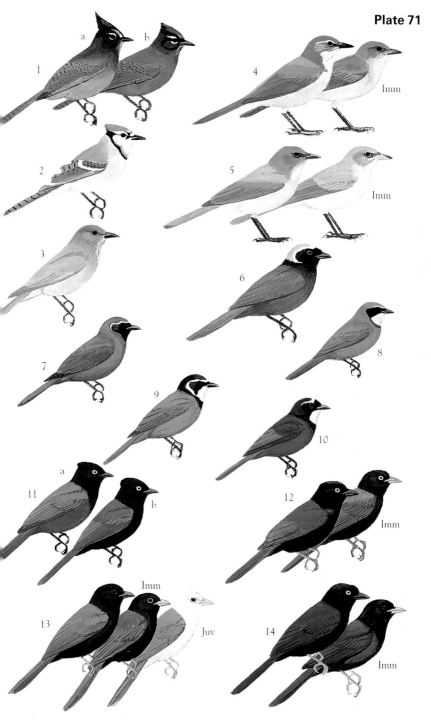

Plate 72

1 BLACK-CHESTED JAY *Cyanocorax affinis* (Urraca Pechinegra) L 30 cm. Black head and whitish belly diagnostic. Habitat: tall second growth in upper levels of forest, woodland, riverine belts, plantations; <1250m. Voice: high staccato rapid *tjeowtjeow(tjeow)*. U,CRPa.

2 GREEN JAY *Cyanocorax yncas* (Chara Verde) L 30 cm. Of several races *luxuosus* (a) and *maya* (b) shown. Unmistakable. Note yellow wing feathers in flight. Habitat: forest interior and edge, woodland, plantations; sl–2000m. Voice: harsh dry clicks and shrieks of varied pitch and quality. WSpr.

3 UNICOLOURED JAY *Aphelocoma unicolor* (Chara Unicolor) L 35 cm. Rich blue overall, much darker than 71.3, which not in the same range. Habitat: forest interior and edge; 1500–3000m. Voice: very high sweeping rapid *wheetwheet*. MeGuHo.

4 BROWN JAY *Cyanocorax morio* (Chara Papán; Urraca Parda) L 40 cm. Nom (a) and race *fuliginosus* (b, with white-tipped tail) shown. Note long-necked jizz. Habitat: open forest and forest remains, areas with scattered trees and hedges; sl–1500m. Voice: high loud *tuéeer*. WSpr.

5 BLACK-THROATED MAGPIE JAY *Calocitta colliei* (Urraca-hermosa Carinegra) L 70 cm. Colour forms a and b shown. From 6 by longer tail and black, not white, front and lores. Habitat: dry woodland, areas with scattered tree stands; sl–1750m. Voice: very high mellow yelping *wow wew-wew - -* and other sounds like mewing *weeeeéh*. E,Me.

6 WHITE-THROATED MAGPIE JAY *Calocitta formosa* (Urraca-hermosa Cariblanca/Copetona) L 50 cm. Note white around eyes. Habitat: dry woodland, areas with scattered tree stands, cultivation; sl–1500m. Voice: e.g. high shrill rasping *shreer-shreer* or sharp *trreeer*. WSpr.

7 TUFTED JAY *Cyanocorax dickeyi* (Chara Pinta) L 35 cm. No similar jay in (restricted) range. Habitat: mixed montane forest; 1500–2000m. Voice: (very) high loud *tjatatat* and other low – very high pitched chatters. E,Me.

8 CLARK'S NUTCRACKER *Nucifraga columbiana* (Cascanueces Americano) L 30 cm. Unmistakable. Note (partly) white secondaries. Habitat: interior and clearings of pine forest; 2500–3750m. Voice: very high dry almost rattling *wrrrekkrrk-krrrek* (like winding of a clock). U,NMe.

9 AMERICAN CROW *Corvus brachyrhynchos* (Cuervo Americano) L 50 cm. Note cut-off tail, small nose bristles, pointed bill. Habitat: open woodland, areas with scattered tree stands and hedges. Voice: high well-known *wraah wraah-wraah*. U,NMe.

10 TAMAULIPAS (or Mexican) **CROW** *Corvus imparatus* (Cuervo Tamaulipeco) L 40 cm. Not in range of 11. Voice distinctive. From 12 by size, bill, gloss, tail form, flight jizz. Habitat: areas with scattered tree stands and hedges, settlement, cultivation, towns; <750m. Voice: very low croaking *wèhih-wèhih-wèhwèh*. NMe.

11 SINALOA CROW *Corvus sinaloae* (Cuervo Sinaloense) L 35 cm. From 9 by call, size, gloss. Habitat: areas with scattered tree stands and hedges, settlement, cultivation, towns; <1000m. Voice: very high mewing *tjouw tjouw-tjouw*. E,Me.

12 CHIHUAHUAN (or White-necked) **CROW** *Corvus cryptoleucus* (Cuervo Llanero) L 50 cm. From 9 by larger, cut-off bill with larger nose bristles. Note rounded tail. Habitat: open country with fields, tree stands, hedges; sl–2500m. Voice: low dry *roh-roh*. NMe.

13 COMMON (or Northern) **RAVEN** *Corvus corax* (Cuervo Grande) L 65 cm. Note throat hackles, wedge-shaped tail. Maybe best feature is voice. Habitat: dry areas, rocky country, fields; sl–3500m. Voice: dry deep *sraa sraa*. WSpr.

14 HOUSE CROW *Corvus splendens* (Cuervo Domestico) L 45 cm. Unmistakable by slender long bill and brown neck and underparts; not yet seen in the area, but has already spread (ship-assisted) from Asia to Africa and Europe. Habitat: towns and settlement. Voice: high *kwah kwah*. Hyp.

Plate 72

Plate 73

1   **MEXICAN CHICKADEE** *Parus sclateri* (Paro Mexicano) L 12 cm. Unmistakable by black cap and bib and greyish sides. Habitat: pine and mixed forest; 1500–3000m. Voice: *tjektjektjek*; high fast *tjerreWrée-tjerreWrée*. Me.

2   **MOUNTAIN CHICKADEE** *Parus gambeli* (Paro Cejiblanco) L 13 cm. Unmistakable; not in range of 1. Habitat: pine and mixed forest; 1500–3000m. Voice: rapid *fitidjèhdjèh*; ultra high sharp *tjeehtjeehtjeeh* or *fjéejee*. U,NMe.

3   **BRIDLED TITMOUSE** *Parus wollweberi* (Paro Embridado) L 13 cm. Unmistakable by facial pattern and crest. Habitat: pine and mixed forest; 1000–3000m. Voice: varied fast rattles. Me.

4   **BLACK-CRESTED TITMOUSE** *Parus atricristatus* (Paro Crestinegro) L 13 cm. Unmistakable. Note buff forehead and flanks. Habitat: forest, woodland, areas with scattered tree stands and hedges; sl–2250m. Voice: high fast loud *pjerpjer--fjer* or higher *péterpéterpéter* or *sresresresreh*. Me.

5   **PLAIN TITMOUSE** *Parus inornatus* (Paro Sencillo) L 15 cm. Unmistakable by plain plumage, small crest. From imm 4 by absence of buff on flanks. Habitat: dry woodland; 500–2500m. Voice: ultra high *fititjow-tow* or short strong rattle or *djrdjrdjrdjerre*. U,NMe. Note: now split into, OAK TITMOUSE (*Parus inornatus*, a) and greyer JUNIPER TITMOUSE (*Parus ridgwayi*, b).

6   **VERDIN** *Auriparus flaviceps* (Baloncillo) L 10 cm. May show in normally concealed red shoulder patch. From other small drab birds by thin sharp bill. Habitat: dry open country with some trees and scrub; sl–2000m. Voice: very high rather sharp *was-it-so-good?* or *tjerr*. NMe.

7   **BUSHTIT** *Psaltriparus minimus* (Sastrecillo) L 11 cm. Several races, which can be arranged in different groups. Races *minimus* (from Plain Bushtit group) and race *personatus* (from Black-eared Bushtit group) shown. Distinctive (small, long-tailed, gregarious). Note pale ♀ eye. Habitat: dry scrub, woodland, forest edge; sl–3500m. Voice: very high dry *tjp*; ultra high thin unstructured twittering in chorus. MeGu.

8   **WRENTIT** *Chamaea fasciata* (Camea) L 16 cm. Secretive. Note angry-looking face; often with raised tail. Habitat: dry scrub; sl–2500m. Voice: high descending *tjet-tjet--* ending in fast rattle. NMe.

9   **RED-BREASTED NUTHATCH** *Sitta canadensis* (Saltapalos Canadiense) L 12 cm. Unmistakable by eyebrow and colour of underparts. Habitat: pine and mixed forest; 1000–2750m. Voice: nasal *wèèèh-wèèèh-wèèèh-wikwik- -*. V,NMe.

10   **WHITE-BREASTED NUTHATCH** *Sitta carolensis* (Saltapalos Pechiblanco) L 14 cm. No stripe through eye. Note pattern of undertail coverts. Habitat: dry woodland; 1500–3500m. Voice: low mewing wooden *kewkewkew* or *whitwhitwhitwhit*. Me.

11   **PYGMY NUTHATCH** *Sitta pygmaea* (Saltapalos Enano) L 11 cm. Note dark eyeline. Habitat: pine forest; 2000–3500m. Voice: very/ultra high plover-like *piweet-piweet- -*. Me.

12   **BROWN CREEPER** *Certhia americana* (Trepador Americano) L 13 cm. Unmistakable. Unlike 9 – 11 supports itself on tail. Habitat: pine and mixed forest, woodland; 1500–3500m. Voice: ultra high *tseetsee*; ultra high *pféet-tjur-wéetwéet*. WSpr.

13   **HORNED LARK** *Eremophila alpestris* (Alondra Cornuda) L 18 cm. Unmistakable by head pattern. Habitat: dry open grassland, bare fields; sl–3500m. Voice: very high unstructured sharp twittering. Me.

14   **WHITE WAGTAIL** *Motacilla alba* (Lavandera Blanca) L 18 cm. From 16 by grey mantle and more black in wings. Habitat: at water in open areas. Voice: very high *tjírruk* or ultra high *tsissik*. V,Me.

15   **YELLOW WAGTAIL** *Motacilla flava* (Lavandera Amarilla) L 17 cm. Unmistakable; terrestrial, seen on the ground or barbed wire; 1stW birds from pipits by unstriped plumage. Habitat: open, wet, grassy areas. Voice: very high *zweep*. V,Me.

16   **BLACK-BACKED WAGTAIL** *Motacilla lugens* (Lavandera Dorsinegra) L 18 cm. Black back and white wing coverts distinctive. Habitat: open areas, shores, fields. Hyp,NMe.

17   **RED-THROATED PIPIT** *Anthus cervinus* (Bisbita Gorrirufa) L 16 cm. Winter plumage from 19 and 20 by white mantle stripe and streaked flanks. Habitat: mainly in coastal open areas. Voice: very high *tíuktíuktíuk*. V,Me.

18   **AMERICAN PIPIT** *Anthus rubescens* (Bisbita Americana) L 16 cm. Summer plumage distinctive. Note barely striped mantle of winter bird. Habitat: open areas, mainly near water, bare fields, short grass. Voice: ultra high *jit jirrit jit*. Me(GuHoSa).

▶

Plate 73

Plate 73 continued

19   **SPRAGUE'S PIPIT** *Anthus spragueii* (Bisbita de Sprague)   L 16 cm. From smaller 20 by range. Habitat: open grassland; 1000–2500m. Voice: ultra high *sweep*. Me.

20   **YELLOWISH PIPIT** *Anthus lutescens* (Bisbita Caminero)   L 13 cm. Compact and small. Habitat: open grassland near water; <1250m. Voice*: high and distinctive: two rapid *tzip* notes, then a long descending buzzing note, slowing towards end: *tzip-tzip sweeeeooooo*. Pa.

21   **OLIVE-BACKED PIPIT** *Anthus hodgsoni* (Bisbita Dorsiolivo)   L 16 cm. Heavily striped below, faintly striped above, isolated white ear mark behind eye. Habitat: open woodland. Hyp, no map provided.

Plate 74

1   **STRIPE-BREASTED WREN** *Thryothorus thoracicus* (Soterrey Pechirrayado)   L 13 cm. Striped breast diagnostic. Note barred wings. Habitat: forest interior and edge, damp second growth; <1000m. Voice: very high mellow fluted *wéetweettjuwéhweet* or *here weáreagáin*. CAm.

2   **SPOT-BREASTED WREN** *Thryothorus maculipectus* (Saltapared Pechimanchado; Soterrey Pechimoteado)   L 13 cm. Warm brown back and spotted breast diagnostic. Habitat: dense vegetation at forest edge, plantations and rivers; <1250m. Voice: very high *weetweetweetuwwéet* or buzzing two-part trill, second drawn-up. WSpr.

3   **HAPPY WREN** *Thryothorus felix* (Saltapared Feliz)   L 13 cm. Distinctive facial pattern with white throat, rest of plumage not or faintly marked. May have almost white underparts. Habitat: dry forest interior and edge, second growth, plantations; sl–2000m. Voice: very high rapid fluted *tsjuwéeh wupwupwup*. E,Me.

4   **RUFOUS-AND-WHITE WREN** *Thryothorus rufalbus* (Saltapared/Soterrey Rufiblanco)   L 15 cm. From 3 by weaker cheek pattern and brown ear mark. From smaller 5 by different range. Habitat: forest edge, open woodland, riverine belts, mangrove; <1000m. Voice: high hollow rapid meandering flutes, often as human whistling. SMeCAm.

5   **SINALOA** (or Bar-vented) **WREN** *Thryothorus sinaloa* (Saltapared Sinaloense)   L 13 cm. From warmer-coloured 3 in same range by weaker face pattern. Habitat: dry forest interior and edge, second growth, plantations; sl–2000m. Voice: very high short warbles with small rattles. E,Me.

6   **BANDED WREN** *Thryothorus pleurostictus* (Saltapared Vientre-barrado; Soterrey de Costillas Barreteadas)   L 14 cm. Pattern of flanks, neck and face distinctive. Not in range of 13 (which has distinctly marked tail). Habitat: dry forest and edge; sl–1500m. Voice: hurried tickling or series of hurried ultra high rattles. WSpr.

7   **CAROLINA WREN** *Thryothorus ludovicianus* (Saltapared de Carolina)   L 13 cm. Several races, differing in intensity of barring to flanks. Note mottled neck sides, striped undertail coverts, two-toned wings, wing spots. Habitat: forest interior and edge; sl–2000m. Voice: very high short fluted hurried almost-rattles like *weetjeweet - -* (4 x). Me(GuNi).

8   **PLAIN WREN** *Thryothorus modestus* (Saltapared Sencillo; Soterrey Chinchirigüí)   L 13 cm. Unmistakable in its range. Prominent eye stripe, buff underparts, unbarred undertail coverts. Habitat: forest edge, scrubby woodland, weedy vegetation, neglected fields and grassland; sl–2000m. Voice: very high *tjuptjupprrrrrrrréer* or ultra high drawn-up *treehwéewitwitwit*. SMeCAm.

9   **SOOTY-HEADED WREN** *Thryothorus spadix* (Soterrey Cabecisombrio)   L 14 cm. From 14 by white undertail coverts and face pattern. Habitat: forest undergrowth, weedy vegetation at forest edge; 500–1250m. Voice: high melodious *wéet-wúttuttwéetutut*. U,Pa.

10   **BLACK-THROATED WREN** *Thryothorus atrogularis* (Soterrey Gorginegro)   L 15 cm. Very dark with uniform underparts. Habitat: thickets in forested areas, often at streams. Voice: varied high fluted strong *wuhwéeh-wuh wuw wirwir*. CAm.

11   **BLACK-BELLIED WREN** *Thryothorus fasciatoventris* (Soterrey Vientrinegro)   L 15 cm. Breast sharply demarcated from barred belly. From 12 by facial pattern. Habitat: forest interior and edge; <500m. Voice: high *achfúuh-bubblebub*. CRPa.

12   **BAY WREN** *Thryothorus nigricapillus* (Soterrey Castaño)   L 15 cm. Only wren with black cap (except otherwise very different 75.17) and nape. Habitat: thickets at streams in forested country; <1000m. Voice: short sharp dry rattle; very high *tjee-tjee-wikwikwik*. CAm.

▶

Plate 74

Plate 74 continued

13   **RIVERSIDE WREN** *Thryothorus semibadius* (Soterrey Pechibarreteado)   L 13 cm. No other all-barred wren with unmarked crown and mantle. Habitat: forest edge, dense vegetation near streams; <1250m. Voice: very high hurried low sustained *sweet sweet - -*. CRPa.

14   **STRIPE-THROATED WREN** *Thryothorus leucopogon* (Soterrey Golirrayado)   L 12 cm. Only wren with pale eyes. Habitat: middle levels of forest interior and edge. Voice: very high staccato dry fluted *tuutjútuut*. Pa.

15   **RUFOUS-BREASTED WREN** *Thryothorus rutilus* (Soterrey Carimoteado)   L 13 cm. Facial pattern with densely marked throat distinctive. Note strong tail barring. Habitat: dense vegetation at forest edge, woodland; 250–1250m. Voice: very high rapid fluted partly staccato *tjéefeetwiúwwuw wwwwwwur*. CRPa.

16   **BUFF-BREASTED WREN** *Thryothorus leucotis* (Soterrey Pechianteado)   L 13 cm. As 8, but wings and tail more distinctly barred and with different song. Habitat: dense woodland undergrowth, often at water; <500m. Voice: high fast short repeated *weetwéetweetTReet*. Pa.

17   **CANYON WREN** *Catherpes mexicanus* (Saltapared Barranquero)   L 13 cm. Note distinctive long-billed jizz. Reddish underparts, contrasting with white breast diagnostic. Habitat: rocky spots, buildings in dry open country; sl–3000m. Voice: long decelerating fluted warble, starting very high. Me.

18   **NAVA'S WREN** *Catherpes navai* (Cuevero de Nava)   L 16 cm. (?/19). Terrestrial bird, not in range of 19. Habitat: rocky spots in forest; <750m. Voice: very high fluted unhurried *teeteeteetjuw* or *téetuttéeturwéewéeh*. E,Me.

19   **SLENDER-BILLED** (or Sumichrast's) **WREN** *Catherpes sumichrasti* (Cuevero de Sumichrast) L 16 cm. From 18 by white breast and by range. Habitat: rocky spots in forest; <1000m. Voice: short decelerating loud warble or loud sharp *sweeep*. E,Me.

Plate 75

1   **WHITE-BELLIED WREN** *Uropsila leucogastra* (Saltapared Cantarino)   L 10 cm. Note faint barring to wings, tail and undertail coverts. Habitat: understorey of dry forest, woodland; <500m. Voice: very high short rapid warble *dibliyou*. SMeBeGuNi.

2   **BEWICK'S WREN** *Thryomanes bewickii* (Saltapared de Bewick)   L 13 cm. Distinguishable by long, barred tail, barred undertail coverts, distinctive eyebrow. Habitat: dry open areas with scattered tree stands, scrub, bush, gardens; sl–3000m. Voice: ultra high *sree-sree-triurrrrr*. Me.

3   **HOUSE WREN** *Troglodytes aedon* (Saltapared-continental Norteño; Soterrey Cucarachero) L 12 cm. Races *parkmanii* (a, Northern House Wren), *brunneicollis* (b, Brown-throated Wren) and *musculus* (c, Southern House Wren) shown. From 2 by weak eyebrow, from 4 by longer tail, from 5, 6 and 7 by range. Habitat: open woodland, cultivation, gardens; sl–2500m. Voice: very high hurried rattling *drieohdrieweewutwutwut*. Thr.

4   **OCHRACEUS WREN** *Troglodytes ochraceus* (Soterrey Ocroso)   L 10 cm. From 3 by short tail and rich buff eye stripe. Habitat: montane forest, tall second growth, adjacent areas; sl–3000m. Voice: ultra high hurried sharp descending warble (3s). CRPa.

5   **COZUMEL WREN** *Troglodytes beani* (Saltapared de Cozumel)   L 12 cm. (?/3). Only wren on Cozumel. Habitat: open, scrubby woodland. E,Me.

6   **CLARION WREN** *Troglodytes tanneri* (Saltapared de Clarión)   L 13 cm. Only wren on Clarion. Habitat: dry open areas with some scrub. Voice: high chattering *wekekekekrrwek*. E,Me.

7   **SOCORRO WREN** *Troglodytes sissonii* (Saltapared de Socorro)   L 12 cm. Only wren on Socorro. Habitat: dry open areas with some scrub and trees. Voice: ultra high sharp chattering hurried *wuutwutwéetwéetohwéet*. E,Me.

8   **WINTER WREN** *Troglodytes troglodytes* (Saltapared Invernal)   L 10 cm. Dark, very small with short, cocked tail. Not in range of 9. Habitat: forest and woodland undergrowth, often at streams; sl–2000m. Voice: ultra high resounding *sreesreesreeohsreewitwitwitwit*. U,Me.

9   **RUFOUS-BROWED WREN** *Troglodytes rufociliatus* (Saltapared Cejirrufo)   L 11 cm. No similar wren in its range and habitat. Habitat: lower levels of pine and mixed forest; 1750–3000m. Voice: ultra high shrill hurried *swéetsreeweetohwéet*. SMeCAm.

▶

Plate 75

Plate 75 continued

10   **MARSH WREN** *Cistothorus palustris* (Saltapared Pantanero)   L 12 cm. Note striking eyebrow and distinct mantle striping and wing pattern. Habitat: reedy marshes; 1000–2500m. Voice: ultra high staccato rattles. Me.

11   **SEDGE** (or Grass) **WREN** *Cistothorus platensis* (Saltapared/Soterrey Sabanero)   L 11 cm. Unmarked below with distinct brown-and-white mantle barring, crown finely streaked. Habitat: marsh and damp grass; 500–3000m. Voice: very varied, e.g. phrases of inhaled *sreeeh* alternated with staccato *tjitjitjit*. WSpr.

12   **TIMBERLINE WREN** *Thryorchilus browni* (Soterrey del Bambú)   L 10 cm. Distinct eyebrow. Note white in wings. Habitat: bamboo and scrub at montane forest edge; >2250m. Voice: ultra high sustained *tehsreehweeh--*. CRPa.

13   **WHITE-BREASTED WOOD WREN** *Henicorhina leucosticta* (Saltapared-selvatico/Soterrey de Selva Pechiblanco)   L 11 cm. Contrasting dark above and white below. Habitat: forest undergrowth; 250–1000(1750)m. Voice: very high sharp fluted loud *tsjiep-tjurrup* or ultra high descending *feetfeetfeet*. WSpr.

14   **GREY-BREASTED WOOD WREN** *Henicorhina leucophrys* (Saltapared-selvatico/Soterrey de Selva Pechigrís)   L 11 cm. Less contrastingly marked than 13 with grey breast. Habitat: forest; 500– 1000(3000)m. Voice: *tuttrrrrréet*; high fluting *wiedewéet*. WSpr.

15   **NORTHERN NIGHTINGALE WREN** *Microcerculus philomela* (Saltapared/Soterrey Ruiseñor)   L 11 cm. Almost black with long bill. Habitat: forest undergrowth; sl–1500m. Voice: high meandering fluted well-separated *wuh wuh uuweeh tuwee-wuh*, like human whistling. SMeCAm.

16   **SOUTHERN NIGHTINGALE** (Song or Whistling) **WREN** *Microcerculus marginatus* (Soterrey Cholincillo)   L 11 cm. Unmistakable; not in range of 15. Habitat: forest undergrowth. Voice: high fluted *tjuuuh - -* or sustained *tjuhtjuh--*. CRPa.

17   **SONG WREN** *Cyphorhinus phaeocephalus* (Soterrey Canoro)   L 12 cm. Black cap and blue orbital ring diagnostic. Could be confused with some antbirds (see plate 61). Habitat: forest undergrowth; <1000m. Voice: series of high flutes and short cackles. NiCRPa.

18   **ROCK WREN** *Salpinctes obsoletus* (Saltapared /Soterrey Roquero)   L 14 cm. Unmistakable by pale colouring, jizz and habitat. Habitat: dry, open rocky areas, grassy montane slopes; sl–3000m. Voice: ultra high staccato *weeetweeetweeet* or very high rhythmic *yellyellyell--*. WSpr.

Plate 76 continued

BLACK-CAPPED DONACOBIUS *Donacobius atricapillus* (Donacobio)   L 20 cm. Unmistakable by yellow iris. Habitat: marsh, damp weedy places. Voice: high sharp disyllabic *weetweetweet*. U,Pa.

EUROPEAN STARLING *Sturnus vulgaris* (Estornino Europeo)   L 20 cm. Unmistakable. Breeding plumage blacker (narrower pale feather margins) with more gloss. Note sharp pointed bill. Delta-shaped in flight. Habitat: cultivation, villages, towns. Voice: very varied, e.g. *wisreet-wisreet- -* mixed with dry toneless twittering. Me.

AMERICAN DIPPER *Cinclus mexicanus* (Mirlo-acuático Americano/Plomizo)   L 16 cm. Unmistakable in its habitat. Habitat: swift, rocky, montane streams. Voice: series of short repeated strophes *weetweet-rrrrr-tjertjer-swirswir- -*. U,WSpr.

Plate 76

1 WHITE-HEADED WREN *Campylorhynchus albobrunneus* (Soterrey Cabeciblanco) L 19 cm. No similar white-headed bird in the area. Habitat: mid-levels at forest edge. Voice: harsh rapid castanet-like chattering. Pa.

2 GIANT WREN *Campylorhynchus chiapensis* (Matraca Chiapaneca) L 20 cm. Distinctive tail pattern. Restricted range. Habitat: open areas with tree stands, hedges, scrub, gardens, cultivation; <250m. Voice: very high mewing *peeohweeoh--*. E,Me.

3 RUFOUS-NAPED WREN *Campylorhynchus rufinucha* (Matraca/Soterrey Nuquirrufa/o) L 17 cm. Races *capistratus* (a), *humilis* (b) and nom (c) shown. Note white underparts; from 6 by absence of flank barring. Habitat: forest edge, open woodland, riverine belt, savanna, cultivation; sl–750(1250)m. Voice: high croaking *wefwuf* or staccato *wic* or *weoh - -*. WSpr.

4 BAND-BACKED WREN *Campylorhynchus zonatus* (Matraca-barrada Tropical; Soterrey Matraquero) L 18 cm. From similar wrens by buff belly. Habitat: forest edge, broken forest, riverine belts, woodland, gardens; sl–1750(3000)m. Voice: very high sharp chattering *tsjirp-tsjirp- -*. WSpr.

5 GREY-BARRED WREN *Campylorhynchus megalopterus* (Matraca-barrada Serrana) L 18 cm. From 8 by barred mantle, spotted breast, different range. Habitat: montane forest interior and edge; 2000–3000m. Voice: very high magpie-like *sreetsreet--*. E,Me.

6 SPOTTED WREN *Campylorhynchus gularis* (Matraca Manchada) L 17 cm. Rufous cap and barred, buff flanks diagnostic. Habitat: scrubby woodland, open areas with scattered bush, cacti; 750–2500m. Voice: chicken-like *whec* or *erc* or *chatchatchatchat*. E,Me.

7 BOUCARD'S WREN *Campylorhynchus jocosus* (Matraca del Balsas) L 18 cm. Not in range of 6, 8 or 9. Habitat: dry areas with scrub and cacti; 750–2500m. Voice: high rather rasping *uwrEetit - -* or *uhwéet*. E,Me.

8 YUCATAN WREN *Campylorhynchus yucatanicus* (Matraca Yucateca) L 18 cm. No similar wren in range. Habitat: dry scrub, gardens. Voice: mewing *ewktjic - -*. E,Me.

9 CACTUS WREN *Campylorhynchus brunneicapillus* (Matraca Desértica) L 18 cm. Races *affinis* (a) and *couesi* (b) shown. Note rufous cap and heavily marked throat. Habitat: dry scrubby areas with cacti; sl–2000m. Voice: very high *sreeusreeu--*. Me.

10 CEDAR WAXWING *Bombycilla cedrorum* (Ampelis Americano) L 18 cm. Unmistakable. Habitat: forest edge, open woodland, areas with scattered tree stands and hedges, gardens; sl–(2000)3000m. Voice: ultra high thin irregular *feeeh feeehfeeeh feeh*. WSpr.

11 GREY SILKY-FLYCATCHER *Ptilogonys cinereus* (Capulinero Gris) L 20 cm. From 12 by nape and crest colouring and by range. Habitat: pine and mixed forest canopy and edge; 500–3000m. Voice: high *wekwek* or meandering twittering round basic *èh*. MeGu.

12 LONG-TAILED SILKY-FLYCATCHER *Ptilogonys caudatus* (Capulinero Colilargo) L 19 cm. Unmistakable in its range. Habitat: canopy of montane forest and adjacent areas. Voice: very high *tjirp tjirp tjirp*. CRPa.

13 PHAINOPEPLA *Phainopepla nitens* (Capulinero Negro) L 19 cm. Unmistakable; shows white wing windows in flight. Note red iris. Habitat: dry open country with some trees and scrub; sl–2500m. Voice: very high hurried short strophes *weeterweet pjurrur - -*. Me.

14 BLACK-AND-YELLOW SILKY-FLYCATCHER *Phainoptila melanoxantha* (Capulinero Negro y Amarillo) L 20 cm. Nom (a) shown and race *parkeri* (b, ♀ of this race is striped below). Unmistakable. Rather thrush-like jizz. Habitat: montane forest. U,CRPa.

15 RUFOUS-BROWED PEPPERSHRIKE *Cyclarhis gujanensis* (Vireón Cejirrufo) L 14 cm. Unmistakable by rufous eye stripe. Habitat: forest edge, woodland, open areas with tree stands, bush, hedges, gardens; (sl)750–2500m. Voice: high fluting yodelling *fjuhfjúhfjeeóhfjuuer*. WSpr.

16 LOGGERHEAD SHRIKE *Lanius ludovicianus* (Lanio Americano) L 25 cm. Variable, pale individuals almost as grey as 16, but mask broader. Habitat: open country with scattered trees, bush, hedges. Voice: high swept-up *prrrwit* or jeering *wèèh wèèh*. MeGu.

17 NORTHERN SHRIKE *Lanius excubitor* (Lanio Norteño) L 25 cm. Pale grey mantle and crown, distinct eyebrow and buff wash over breast diagnostic. Habitat: open country. Voice: high nasal scolding *wehwewewekwek--*. Hyp,Me.

Plate 76

Plate 77

1 **DUSKY WARBLER** *Phylloscopus fuscatus* (Reinita Fusca) L 12 cm. Small, rather compact, round-headed. From 2 by darker, olive-tinged colour without any wing bar. Habitat: woodland edge, scrub at streams, thickets. Voice: sharp *zak*. V,NMe.

2 **ARCTIC WARBLER** *Phylloscopus borealis* (Reinita Artica) L 13 cm. Note greenish tinge, long eyebrow, wing bar. Habitat: woodland, bush, scrub. Voice: *dzic dzitdrutdrutdrutdrut*. V,NMe.

3 **GOLDEN-CROWNED KINGLET** *Regulus satrapa* (Reyezuelo Corona-dorada) L 10 cm. Unmistakable by face stripes and golden crest. Habitat: pine forest; >2000m. Voice: ultra high *seeseeseee-serererererere*. Me(Gu).

4 **RUBY-CROWNED KINGLET** *Regulus calendula* (Reyezuelo Sencillo) L 11 cm. Note large-eyed appearance without face stripes. Ruby crown normally concealed. Habitat: woodland; sl–3500m. Voice: ultra high *srèèk sreeh*; very high *fiwitjerretjerretjerre--*. MeGu.

5 **LONG-BILLED GNATWREN** *Ramphocaenus melanurus* (Soterillo Picudo) L 12 cm. Unmistakable by long bill and tail pattern. Habitat: forest interior and edge; <750m. Voice: e.g. very high shivering descending almost-trill *wiwiwifrufrufru--*. SMeCAm.

6 **TAWNY-FACED** (or Half-collared) **GNATWREN** *Microbates cinereiventris* (Soterillo Caricafé) L 10 cm. From 5 by short tail; note demarcation between breast and belly. Habitat: forest undergrowth. <1250m. Voice: *tjaptjup tjúuuw*. CAm.

7 **BLUE-GREY GNATCATCHER** *Polioptila caerulea* (Perlita Grisilla) L 11 cm. Shows more white in tail than 8 and 9 (tail mostly white below); bill shorter and slightly less white in wing than 10 (with more restricted range). Habitat: woodland, open areas with trees, scrub; sl–2500m. Voice: *tjèwtie*; high nasal *wuppertjèh-wuppertjèh*. WSpr.

8 **BLACK-TAILED GNATCATCHER** *Polioptila melanura* (Perlita Colinegra) L 11 cm. Narrow white margins to tail. Less white undertail coverts than 7. Habitat: dry open country with scattered scrub, riverine belts; sl–2000m. Voice: hoarse *chetchetchet tsjeeh-tsjeeh*. Me.

9 **CALIFORNIA GNATCATCHER** *Polioptila californica* (Perlita Californiana) L 11 cm. Not in range of 8. White margins to tail very narrow. Habitat: dry open areas with some scrub and bush, riverine belts; sl–1500m. Voice: high hoarse indignant *tsjèw-tsjèw-tsjèw*. NMe.

10 **BLACK-CAPPED GNATCATCHER** *Polioptila nigriceps* (Perlita Gorrinegra) L 11 cm. Lores black, not grey as 9, which has different range. Habitat: woodland, dry scrub; sl–1250m. E,Me.

11 **WHITE-LORED GNATCATCHER** *Polioptila albiloris* (Perlita Cejiblanca/Cabecinegra) L 11 cm. Shows much white on tertials and secondaries. ♀ and imm with white eyebrow. Habitat: dry scrub, open woodland, forest edge; sl–750(1750)m. Voice: very high inhaled sizzled *shreezupzup*. WSpr.

12 **TROPICAL GNATCATCHER** *Polioptila plumbea* (Perlita Tropical) L 11 cm. Face pattern diagnostic. Habitat: forest edge. Voice: ultra high sizzled trill. SMeCAm.

13 **SLATE-THROATED GNATCATCHER** *Polioptila schistaceigula* (Perlita Pechipizarrosa) L 10 cm. From 67.1 by different jizz and much more active behaviour. Habitat: forest canopy; <750m. U,Pa.

14 **TAWNY-CROWNED GREENLET** *Hylophilus ochraceiceps* (Verdillo Corona-leonada) L 11 cm. Distinctive whitish eye and tawny crown. Habitat: forest undergrowth; sl–1250m. Voice: high nasal *weehweehwitwit*. SMeCAm.

15 **LESSER GREENLET** *Hylophilus decurtatus* (Verdillo Menor/Menudo) L 9 cm. From warblers by large head and short tail. Habitat: upper and middle levels of forest, edge, tall second growth; sl–1500m. Voice: very high fast *swéehswéeh*; very high very short hurried *sisserit*. WSpr.

16 **SCRUB GREENLET** *Hylophilus flavipes* (Verdillo Matorralero) L 12 cm. Note pale eye and bill, large head. Heavier-billed and greener below than 14. Habitat: woodland, second growth, dry scrub; <1000m. Voice: very high rapid staccato *wikwikwik--* (5–8 x). CRPa.

17 **GOLDEN-FRONTED GREENLET** *Hylophilus aurantiifrons* (Verdillo Luisucho) L 11 cm. Dark eye diagnostic. Habitat: tall second growth, woodland. Voice: very high *swéeeh-it sweeswee*. Pa.

18 **CHESTNUT-SIDED SHRIKE VIREO** *Vireolanius melitophrys* (Vireón Pechicastaño) L 17 cm. Unmistakable by face pattern. Habitat: pine and mixed forest; 1250–3500m. Voice: mewing *pwîeeh*; drawn-up *piwueiúww*. MeGu.

Plate 77

Plate 77 continued

19 **GREEN SHRIKE VIREO** *Vireolanius pulchellus* (Vireón Esmeraldo/ino) L 14 cm. Heavy jizz, strong bill, grass-green above, yellow below. Note wing bars of imm. Habitat: forest canopy, woodland; sl–1750m. Voice: very high clear loud *twiwíwíwí*. SMeCAm.

20 **YELLOW-BROWED SHRIKE VIREO** *Vireolanius eximius* (Vireón Cejiamarillo) L 14 cm. From 19 by yellow eyebrow, from imm 19 by lack of wing bars and brighter colour. Habitat: forest canopy; <1000m. Voice: sustained *túuu - --*. U, Pa.

Plate78

1 **SLATY VIREO** *Vireo brevipennis* (Vireo Pizarra) L 12 cm. Unmistakable, but rather skulking. Habitat: forest edge, scrub, thickets; 1250–3000m. Voice: very high sharp decisive *titjústjúuiet titjúútsjúuiet*. E,Me. Note: vireos are less active and lively than warblers.

2 **WHITE-EYED VIREO** *Vireo griseus* (Vireo Ojiblanco) L 12 cm. Pale eye with white underparts diagnostic. Mexican races less yellow on flanks. Habitat: forest edge, brushy woodland, open areas with scattered scrub; sl–1250m. Voice: very high sharp *titjúúi-wiweet*. WSpr.

3 **MANGROVE VIREO** *Vireo pallens* (Vireo Manglero/de Manglar) L 12 cm. Eye colour and plumage may vary (a from Costa Rica, b from Mexico), but eye yellowish, not as white as 2, yellow more uniformly spread over underparts than 2, 5, 12 and white-chinned 13. Prefers (but not everywhere!) mangrove. Habitat: mangrove and adjacent scrub. Voice: high rattling *tjatjatjatjah*. WSpr.

4 **COZUMEL VIREO** *Vireo bairdi* (Vireo de Cozumel) L 12 cm. Restricted range. Habitat: scrubby woodland. Voice: high sharp rapid rhythmic *wietwietwiet--* (6–7 x). E,Me.

5 **BELL'S VIREO** *Vireo bellii* (Vireo de Bell) L 12 cm. Nom (a) and race *arizonae* (b) shown. Note white lores. Only one bright wing bar. Habitat: areas with scrub, thickets, hedges; sl–1500m. Voice: very high very rapid short twitters *tsjeedletsjeedletsjeeh*. WSpr.

6 **BLACK-CAPPED VIREO** *Vireo atricapillus* (Vireo Gorrinegro) L 11 cm. Unmistakable by black cap. Habitat: dry scrub, brushy woodland; sl(1000)–2000m. Voice: *tsièèh*; varied very high nasal short twitters interlaced with very short trills. Me.

7 **DWARF VIREO** *Vireo nelsoni* (Vireo Enano) L 11 cm. Note white ring, broken above eye, whiter wing bars than ♀ 6. Habitat: dry scrub; 1000–2500m. Voice: very high rapid loud twitters, each starting with nasal *èèh*. E,Me.

8 **GREY VIREO** *Vireo vicinior* (Vireo Gris) L 13 cm. Note long-tailed, plain appearance. From 11 by less distinct eye ring and wing bars. Habitat: dry scrub, sparse woodland; sl(1000)–1500m. Voice: very high rather hurried *wieweet-tjuw tireet- -*. NMe.

9 **BLUE-HEADED** (or Solitary) **VIREO** *Vireo solitarius* (Vireo Solitario) L 14 cm. Blue-grey head distinctive. Note yellow edges to flight feathers. Habitat: forest, woodland; sl–2500m. Voice: very high well-separated *tuéech tjèh tjeéweeh* or *weetjeweet tjuweh*. WSpr.

10 **CASSIN'S VIREO** *Vireo cassini* (Vireo de Cassin) L 13 cm. (?/9). As 9, but less bright, with little contrast between crown and back. Habitat: mixed forest, woodland; 500–2500m. Me.

11 **PLUMBEOUS VIREO** *Vireo plumbeus* (Vireo Plomizo) L 13 cm. (?/9). Most grey of all vireos. Rather indistinct wing bars. Habitat: pine and mixed forest, open woodland; sl–2500(3000)m. WSpr.

12 **YELLOW-THROATED VIREO** *Vireo flavifrons* (Vireo Gorjimarillo/Pechiamarillo) L 13 cm. Contrasting white belly distinctive. Habitat: forest canopy, woodland, plantations, gardens; sl–2000m. Voice: very high *tuwéeh*. WSpr.

13 **YELLOW-WINGED VIREO** *Vireo carmioli* (Vireo Aliamarillo) L 11 cm. Only vireo with yellow wing bars in its range. Habitat: montane forest canopy. Voice: very high thin *tjuwéeh tútjeeh* etc. CRPa.

14 **HUTTON'S VIREO** *Vireo huttoni* (Vireo de Hutton) L 12 cm. Note stocky, large-headed jizz. Large eyes with eye ring broken above eye. Easy to confuse with 77.4. Habitat: mixed forest and woodland; 1250–3500m. Voice: *srèèh srèèh*; ultra high swept-up sustained *pwéet - -*. MeGu.

▶

Plate 78

Plate 78 continued

15   GOLDEN VIREO *Vireo hypochryseus* (Vireo Dorado)   L 13 cm. From warblers by heavier bill. Habitat: forest edge, woodland, plantations, dry scrub thorn bush; <1000m. Voice: very high *wicwicwictst* ; very high fluted *tuweetwit-weetwit*. E,Me.

16   WARBLING VIREO *Vireo gilvus* (Vireo Gorjeador/Canoro)   L 12 cm. Greyish with striking eyebrow. Faint wing bars. Habitat: woodland, plantations; 750–2500m. Voice: *dzee*; very high warbling *weeweeohweetjuweewit*. WSpr.

17   BROWN-CAPPED VIREO *Vireo leucophrys* (Vireo Gorripardo/Montañero)   L 12 cm. (?/16). Brown-buff cap diagnostic. Habitat: montane forest, woodland; 1250–2000m. Voice: very high fluted *weeweeweetjuweehrer*. WSpr.

18   PHILADELPHIA VIREO *Vireo philadelphicus* (Vireo de Filadelfia/Amarillento)   L 13 cm. From 17 by grey cap and brighter yellow underparts (especially throat). Habitat: forest interior and edge, plantations; sl–2000m. Voice: nasal *rhet*; very high repeated *puwut - -*. U,WSpr.

19   YELLOW-GREEN VIREO *Vireo flavoviridis* (Vireo Amarillo-verdoso/Cabecigrís)   L 14 cm. (?/20). Distinct bright yellow flanks and undertail coverts. Little black above head. Habitat: forest, woodland, plantations, gardens, savanna; <1500m. Note long-headed, long-billed jizz of 19 – 22. Voice: very high *sreet tutweet teweet tuweet sréeh - -*. WSpr.

20   RED-EYED VIREO *Vireo olivaceus* (Vireo Ojirrojo)   L 15 cm. Note black line along white eyebrow. Habitat: any area with trees; 250–1500(2250)m. Voice: *tsjuw*; very high *wierroweet weeweet tutjuh - -*. WSpr.

21   BLACK-WHISKERED VIREO *Vireo altiloquus* (Vireo Bigotudo)   L 15 cm. From 19 and 20 by black malar stripe. Habitat: coastal woodland, scrub, mangrove. Voice: very high strong *tuh-tjuweh*. U,YMeBeCRPa.

22   YUCATAN VIREO *Vireo magister* (Vireo Yucateco)   L 15 cm. Overall dark and brownish, with black eyes, heavy bill, grey-green flanks. Habitat: scrubby woodland, mangrove. Voice: very high strong sharp *tjuwer titjuh wirwir--*. YMeBe.

Plate 79 continued

LE CONTE'S THRASHER *Toxostoma lecontei* (Cuitlacoche Pálido)   L 30 cm. Note overall pale colouring, black tail and malar stripe in otherwise weakly patterned face. Habitat: desert with some low bush and scrub. Voice: rather short streams of very high sharp fluted syllables and notes, each repeated 2–3 x. NMe.

Plate 79

1   **GREY CATBIRD** *Dumetella carolinensis* (Pájaro-gato Gris)   L 20 cm. Unmistakable by grey plumage and rufous undertail coverts. Habitat: forest interior and edge, second growth, shrubbery, coastal scrub; sl–(1500)2000m. Voice: mewing *wéeeh*; long sequences of independent short very high squeaky flutes as *weetwéettjher - -*. WSpr.

2   **BLACK CATBIRD** *Dumetella glabrirostris* (Pájaro-gato Negro)   L 20 cm. Other all-black birds are larger, with stout bills and less skulking. Habitat: forest edge, woodland, dense scrub. Voice: long sustained very high wailing flutes with many *wéet's* and *sjuut's*. YMeBe.

3   **BLUE MOCKINGBIRD** *Melanotis caerulescens* (Mulato Azul)   L 25 cm. Dark red eye in black mask diagnostic. Skulking, though sings exposed. Habitat: pine forest undergrowth, scrubby woodland; sl–3000m. Voice: series of well-separated rather short fluted strophes like *fúfishéetwushéetwee*. E,Me.

4   **BLUE-AND-WHITE MOCKINGBIRD** *Melanotis hypoleucus* (Mulato Pechiblanco)   L 25 cm. From 3 by white underparts. Habitat: dry scrub, woodland, forest edge; 1000–3000m. Voice: very high rattling *fjujiwéetwéetwéttjutju*. MeGuHoSa.

5   **NORTHERN MOCKINGBIRD** *Mimus polyglottos* (Cenzontle Norteño)   L 25 cm. Note pale eye and striking wing pattern. Habitat: dry open areas with scrub, bush, tree stands; sl–3000m. Voice: *tjiptjip--* (10 x) *--tuweetuwee--* (4 x) *--weh-rattle- -* etc, each well-accentuated. Me.

6   **TROPICAL MOCKINGBIRD** *Mimus gilvus* (Cenzontle Sureño)   L 25 cm. Less white in wing and more in tail than 5. Habitat: open areas with scrub, bush, tree stands; sl–500(2500)m. Voice: very high sharp staccato short phrases, each 3–7 x repeated in a constant stream. SMeCAm.I,Pa.

7   **SOCORRO MOCKINGBIRD** *Mimodes graysoni* (Cenzontle de Socorro)   L 25 cm. From 5 by pale stripes to flanks and no white in wing with faint bars. Habitat: wooded slopes. Voice: very high short sharp *wup wíppíp-wup* and other strophes. E,Me.

8   **SAGE THRASHER** *Oreoscoptes montanus* (Cuitlacoche de Artemisia)   L 20 cm. Note short thrush-like bill and striping on flanks. Habitat: dry open country with scattered bush, scrub, trees; sl–2500m. Me.

9   **BROWN THRASHER** *Toxostoma rufum* (Cuitlacoche Rojizo)   L 25 cm. See 10. Habitat: dry scrubby woodland. V,Me.

10   **LONG-BILLED THRASHER** *Toxostoma longirostre* (Cuitlacoche Piquilargo)   L 30 cm. Note streaked undertail coverts, brown, not rufous upperparts, pure white breast, all-black bill; stripes on underparts all black, not partly rufous. Habitat: dry woodland, scrub, hedges; sl–1500m. NMe.

11   **COZUMEL THRASHER** *Toxostoma guttatus* (Cuitlacoche de Cozumel)   L 25 cm. No other thrasher on Cozumel. Habitat: scrubby woodland. E,Me.

12   **GREY THRASHER** *Toxostoma cinereum* (Cuitlacoche Peninsular)   L 25 cm. Note arrow-shaped spots on white underparts. Habitat: dry areas with scrub, bush, trees, cacti. E,Me. Note: all thrashers have white tail corners.

13   **BENDIRE'S THRASHER** *Toxostoma bendirei* (Cuitlacoche de Bendire)   L 25 cm. From 14 by shorter bill, paler, more yellow iris, narrow streaks on breast. Habitat: dry scrub with cacti and grassy places; <750m. NMe.

14   **CURVE-BILLED THRASHER** *Toxostoma curvirostre* (Cuitlacoche Piquicurvo)   L 25 cm. See 13. Habitat: dry scrubby areas with cacti and some trees; 1000–3000m. Voice: *tsjuch*; very high melodious fluted strophes (10–15s), introduced by soft tinkling notes. Me.

15   **OCELLATED THRASHER** *Toxostoma ocellatum* (Cuitlacoche Manchado)   L 30 cm. Bold spotting on white underparts diagnostic. Habitat: dry scrubby open woodland; 1500–3000m. Voice: very long stream of very varied very high notes and strophes, sharp flutes, repetitions and mimics. E,Me.

16   **CALIFORNIA THRASHER** *Toxostoma redivivum* (Cuitlacoche Californiano)   L 30 cm. From 18 by more strongly patterned face, darker coloration and less contrasting undertail coverts. Habitat: dry open bush land; sl–2000m. Voice: rather slow stream of high *karrekeetpuweet--*. NMe.

17   **CRISSAL THRASHER** *Toxostoma crissale* (Cuitlacoche Crisal) L 30 cm. Greyer than 16 and 18, with dark rusty undertail coverts. Note pale eye. Habitat: dry scrubby areas; sl–2500m. Voice: series of hurried rather nasal twittering with *wehwehweet* etc. Me.

◀

Plate 79

Plate 80

1 **TOWNSEND'S SOLITAIRE** *Myadestes townsendi* (Clarín Norteño) L 20 cm. Wing pattern distinctive. Note upright posture, long-tailed jizz and typical eye ring of the solitaires. Habitat: dry montane woodland; 1750–3500 m. Voice: very high loud sustained warbling *wirrreweet--wir*. U,Me.

2 **BROWN-BACKED SOLITAIRE** *Myadestes occidentalis* (Clarín Jilguero) L 20 cm. Note brown-olive upperparts and white chin with black malar stripe. Habitat: forest, often along streams; 500–3500 m. Voice: very high rusty descending warbling. WSpr.

3 **SLATE-COLOURED SOLITAIRE** *Myadestes unicolor* (Clarín Unicolor) L 20 cm. From 4 by range, wing and face pattern. Habitat: forest; 1000–2750 m. Voice: very high mellow yet rusty *fjeehfjeeh-turruwwheeohwhee*. WSpr.

4 **BLACK-FACED SOLITAIRE** *Myadestes melanops* (Solitario Carinegro) L 17 cm. Only solitaire in its range. Note face, tail and wing pattern. Habitat: bamboo and undergrowth in montane forest. Voice: high well-separated *tjuuh fjóh fjeehohfjeehoh*, second part very high and shrill as badly oiled gate. CRPa.

5 **VARIED SOLITAIRE** *Myadestes coloratus* (Solitario Variado) L 18 cm. Distinctive. Only solitaire in its range. Habitat: forest; >750 m. Voice: *chuk*; short strophes like very high rusty *fjuwuheet*. Pa.

6 **ORANGE-BILLED NIGHTINGALE THRUSH** *Catharus aurantiirostris* (Zorzalito Piquinaranja; Zorzal Piquianaranjado) L 16 cm. Note bright eye ring; orange bill and legs distinctive. Habitat: dry woodland undergrowth, forest edge, gardens; 500–2500 m. Voice: very high *ftéewih tíh*; very high strong *tjuptjuptjeeohwrrr*. WSpr.

7 **RUSSET NIGHTINGALE THRUSH** *Catharus occidentalis* (Zorzalito Piquipardo) L 17 cm. Lower mandible with flesh base. Mantle more rufous russet and bill darker-tipped than 8. Habitat: open forest undergrowth; 1500–3500 m. Voice: very high short metallic whistle *sreeohweer*. E,Me.

8 **RUDDY-** (or Rufous-) **CAPPED NIGHTINGALE THRUSH** *Catharus frantzii* (Zorzalito de Frantzius; Zorzal Gorrirojizo) L 17 cm. Crown and nape contrasting russet. Habitat: montane forest undergrowth, tall second growth; 1500–2500(3500)m. Voice: high clear, sometimes rusty phrases as *wirohwirrwirr*. WSpr.

9 **BLACK-BILLED NIGHTINGALE THRUSH** *Catharus gracilirostris* (Zorzal Piquinegro) L 15 cm. Bill colour distinctive; note grey crown. Habitat: open places in montane forest; >2150 m. Voice: very high *uueeeh uueeeh* or drawn-up ultra high *sééésususwier*. CRPa.

10 **BLACK-HEADED NIGHTINGALE THRUSH** *Catharus mexicanus* (Zorzalito Coroninegro; Zorzal Cabecinegro) L 16 cm. Crown colour diagnostic; note orange bill, legs and eyelids. Habitat: forest undergrowth; 750–2000 m. Voice: very high often sizzled *sreesrowréesir*. WSpr.

11 **SLATY-BACKED NIGHTINGALE THRUSH** *Catharus fuscater* (Zorzal Sombrío) L 17 cm. Only thrush (except all-black 81.14) with pale eyes. Habitat: montane forest undergrowth. Voice: high penetrating *wuhooweehik*. CRPa.

12 **SPOTTED NIGHTINGALE THRUSH** *Catharus dryas* (Zorzalito Pechiamarillo) L 18 cm. Unmistakable by black hood. Habitat: forest undergrowth; 1250–3000 m. Voice: varied short melodious whistles like *vruh vrroh vruu-ih*. SMeGuHo.

13 **VEERY** *Catharus fuscescens* (Zorzalito Rojizo; Zorzal Dorsirrojizo) L 18 cm. Orange-buff above; weakly spotted breast. Habitat: forest and woodland floor. Voice: *pfeeuw*; very high sustained *vwérrywérrywérry*. WSpr.

14 **GREY-CHEEKED THRUSH** *Catharus minimus* (Zorzalito/Zorzal Carigrís) L 17 cm. From 15 by less distinct patterned face, indistinct lores, grey, not buff colouring of face sides. Habitat: woodland and plantations at streams. Voice: very high fluted *friohfriohweher*. U,SMeCAm.

15 **SWAINSON'S THRUSH** *Catharus ustulatus* (Zorzalito/Zorzal de Swainson) L 18 cm. Very much as 14, but with distinct buff lores. Habitat: any wooded area (winter). Voice: soft *djup*; very high *prupru féeohwéeh*. Thr.

16 **HERMIT THRUSH** *Catharus guttatus* (Zorzalito Colirrufo) L 17 cm. Note reddish tail and complete eye ring. Habitat: in and outside forest (winter period). Voice: slurred-up *nèèh*; very high slightly rusty *fjúuut towéehwih*. WSpr.

17 **WOOD THRUSH** *Catharus mustelinus* (Zorzalito Maculado; Zorzal del Bosque) L 19 cm. Unmistakable by colouring and spotting. Habitat: forest ground and undergrowth; <1750 m. Voice: high fast *weetwreetwéet* or *piuféeoh*. WSpr.

Plate 80

Plate 81

1   **NORTHERN WHEATEAR** *Oenanthe oenanthe* (Collalba Norteña) L 16 cm. Terrestrial bird; note upright stance. Habitat: coastal, open, grassy and scrubby areas. Voice: very high thin *wheet*. V,YMe.

2   **EASTERN BLUEBIRD** *Sialia sialis* (Azulejo Gorjicanelo) L 17 cm. From 3 by orange throat and blue mantle. Habitat: dry woodland, open areas with some trees and scattered bush; 500–2750 m. Voice: fast *tjirwirr*; high sweet yet slightly mewing *tjeeroweetweet*. WSpr.

3   **WESTERN BLUEBIRD** *Sialia mexicana* (Azulejo Gorjiazul) L 17 cm. Note brown mantle. Habitat: open pine woodland, open bush; 1500–3000 m. Voice: short sparrow-like chatter; high sweet clear *wheet wheetwitwheer*. Me.

4   **MOUNTAIN BLUEBIRD** *Sialia currucoides* (Azulejo Pálido) L 17 cm. No similar bird in the area. Note upright stance and white undertail coverts. Habitat: grassy areas with some trees and bush; 1000–2500 m. Voice: high *tjuh*; high *tjuuhtutjuwhur*. Me.

Note: in North America 5–14 are usually called Robins.

5   **MOUNTAIN THRUSH** *Turdus plebejus* (Zorzal Serrano; Mirlo Montañero) L 25 cm. Dark brown colouring with black bill distinctive. Habitat: montane forest interior and edge. Voice: *tjur*; very high rather hurried *tjow-tjew-tjow-tjeu-tjew- -*. SMeCAm.

6   **CLAY-COLOURED THRUSH** *Turdus grayi* (Zorzal/Mirlo Pardo) L 25 cm. Greenish bill; undertail coverts concolorous with rest of underparts. Habitat: areas with scattered tree stands, bush, hedges, gardens; sl–2000 m. Voice: high simple *prúweeh-puweeh-wéejoh-juju- -*. WSpr.

7   **PALE-VENTED THRUSH** *Turdus obsoletus* (Mirlo Vientriblanco) L 25 cm. White chin and belly diagnostic. Habitat: higher forest levels; 750–1500 m. Voice: high *tjuweeh-tjuweeh weeohweeh-reptrep*. CRPa.

8   **WHITE-THROATED THRUSH** *Turdus assimilis* (Zorzal/Mirlo Gorjiblanco) L 25 cm. Races *lygrus* (a) and *oblitus* (b) shown. Stripes on throat do not run into olive-grey breast. Habitat: forest, plantations, riverine belts; 750–1750(3000)m. Voice: very high varied *piupui wheewhee tuitje* (each syllable repeated twice). WSpr.

9   **RUFOUS-BACKED THRUSH** *Turdus rufopalliatus* (Zorzal Dorsirrufo) L 25 cm. From 10 by more uniform russet body. Habitat: woodland, plantations, gardens in dry areas; sl–1500 m. Voice: *fiutju weeh fiutju*. E,Me.

10   **GRAYSON'S THRUSH** *Turdus graysoni* (Zorzal de Grayson) L 25 cm. (?/9). Flanks paler than mantle. Habitat: forest interior and edge. E,Me.

11   **AMERICAN ROBIN** *Turdus migratorius* (Zorzal Petirrojo) L 25 cm. Nom (a) and race *confinis* (b) shown. Strong facial pattern with broken eye ring diagnostic. Habitat: forest, woodland; 1000–3500 m. Voice: *tjirre-tjirrep* or *dsjip*; high *wheewit-wheewit-tsjirrip-wheewit* etc. MeBeGu.

12   **RUFOUS-COLLARED THRUSH** *Turdus rufitorques* (Zorzal Cuellirrufo) L 25 cm. Unmistakable. Note dark hood and scapulars of ♀. Habitat: open woodland, settlement; 1000–3500 m. Voice: very high *tjurrup trur wih* (not very varied). SMeGuHoSa.

13   **BLACK THRUSH** *Turdus infuscatus* (Zorzal Negro) L 25 cm. ♂ distinctive; ♀ with uniform underparts, including unstriped or very faintly striped throat. Habitat: forest edge; 1250–3500 m. Voice: very high varied *sreek tujotujo wrrr sssi - -*. MeGuHoSa.

14   **SOOTY THRUSH** *Turdus nigrescens* (Mirlo Negruzco) L 25 cm. Eye, bill and leg colouring distinctive. Habitat: open montane areas. Voice: high simple *tjilping wit wit wit titjerrup*. CRPa.

15   **VARIED THRUSH** *Zoothera naevia* (Zorzal Pechicinchado) L 25 cm. Unmistakable. Habitat: lower storeys of woodland and forest; sl–2500 m. Voice: *tsjuh*; high hoarse drawn-out *sweeeeeh*. U,NMe.

16   **AZTEC THRUSH** *Zoothera pinicola* (Zorzal Azteca) L 25 cm. Unmistakable. Habitat: lower storeys of woodland and forest; 1750–3500 m. Voice: ultra high *sweehsweeh*; very high *prrrweet*. E,Me.

Plate 81

Plate 82

1 **WORM-EATING WARBLER** *Helmitheros vermivorus* (Chipe/Reinita Gusanero/a) L 13 cm. Head pattern with pale crown stripe diagnostic. Habitat: forest undergrowth, woodland, thickets; sl–1500 m. Voice: sharp *dz*. U,WSpr.

2 **SWAINSON'S WARBLER** *Limnothlypis swainsonii* (Chipe de Swainson) L 14 cm. Terrestrial bird. Distinctive russet-buff crown and long bill. Habitat: forest, swamps; <500 m. Voice: very high *tjeep*. U,MeBeGu.

3 **TENNESSEE WARBLER** *Vermivora peregrina* (Chipe Peregrino; Reinita Verdilla) L 12 cm. White undertail coverts and distinct eye stripe in all plumages diagnostic. Habitat: forest edge, open woodland, plantations, gardens; sl–3000 m. Voice: *tsih*; Winter Wren-like song. WSpr.

4 **ORANGE-CROWNED WARBLER** *Vermivora celata* (Chipe Corona-naranja; Reinita Olivada) L 11 cm. Contrasting yellow undertail coverts distinctive. Orange crown patch rarely visible. Habitat: dry woodland, neglected cultivation; sl–3000 m. Voice: very high sharp short canary-like trill. MeGu(CR).

5 **COLIMA WARBLER** *Vermivora crissalis* (Chipe Colimense) L 14 cm. Note large size, olive upperparts, striking eye ring. Habitat: dry open woodland; forest (winter); 1500–2500 m. Voice: very high *wrut writwrit* or rattling *witwitwit--* (7–10 x). Me.

6 **VIRGINIA'S WARBLER** *Vermivora virginiae* (Chipe de Virginia) L 12 cm. Note white eye ring. Yellow breast (♂) and yellow upper- and undertail coverts diagnostic. Habitat: dry scrub; 500–2500 m. Voice: *swit*. Me(BeGu).

7 **LUCY'S WARBLER** *Vermivora luciae* (Chipe de Lucy) L 11 cm. Predominantly grey. From 6 by russet uppertail and white undertail coverts. Habitat: dry scrub and bush, often along streams; <1500(1750)m. Voice: ultra high *tjih*; Winter Wren-like descending very rapid *trrrrrwutwutsreesree*. Me.

8 **NASHVILLE WARBLER** *Vermivora ruficapilla* (Chipe de Nashville; Reinita Cachetigrís) L 11 cm. From similar yellow-green warblers by striking eye ring and white in centre of belly. Habitat: woodland, scrub, plantations; sl–3000 m. Voice: sharp thin *tsjik*. WSpr.

9 **BLUE-WINGED WARBLER** *Vermivora pinus* (Chipe/Reinita Aliazul) L 12 cm. Note black stripe through yellow face and grey wings with distinct wing bars. Habitat: forest interior and edge; sl–2000 m. Note: 9 and 10 hybridise easily; shown are the most frequent hybrids 'Brewster's Warbler' (a) and less frequent 'Lawrence's Warbler' (b). Habitat: open woodland and forest. Voice: sharp *tsjik*. U,WSpr.

10 **GOLDEN-WINGED WARBLER** *Vermivora chrysoptera* (Chipe/Reinita Alidorado/a) L 12 cm. Unmistakable by yellow panel in wing. Habitat: forest interior and edge; sl–1750 m.Voice: sharp *tsjik*.U,WSpr.

11 **CRESCENT-CHESTED WARBLER** *Vermivora* (or *Parula*) *superciliosa* (Chipe Cejiblanco) L 11 cm. Eyebrow, lack of wing bars, red spot on breast diagnostic. Habitat: higher levels of pine and mixed forests; 1500–3500 m. Voice: ultra high dry trill *wrrrrrwrrri* or *srrrrrrreeh*. WSpr.

12 **NORTHERN PARULA** *Parula americana* (Parula Norteña) L 11 cm. Note yellowish lower mandible, broken eye ring without eyebrow, white belly contrasting with breast. ♂ from 13 by rufous-and-black breast band. Habitat: forest edge, open woodland, mangrove; sl–1000 m. Voice: high *tsjip*. WSpr.

13 **TROPICAL PARULA** *Parula pitiayumi* (Parula Tropical) L 11 cm. Note yellow lower mandible. Habitat: forest canopy, trees in adjacent areas; (250)2000–2500 m. Voice: high *tsjip*; ultra high short nasal warbling *fjeetwéetwéet* or Winter Wren-like *wiwiwiwitjitjitji*. WSpr.

14 **FLAME-THROATED WARBLER** *Parula gutturalis* (Reinita Garganta de Fuego) L 12 cm. Unmistakable by general colour pattern. Habitat: montane forest (canopy) and nearby trees: >1750 m. Voice: ultra high nasal *pssss*; very high *puWir-puWir-puWir*. CRPa.

15 **PROTHONOTARY WARBLER** *Protonotaria citrea* (Chipe Protonotario; Reinita Cabecidorada) L 13 cm. Large. Unmistakable. From other yellow warblers by grey wings. Habitat: swampy woodland, mangrove; <2000 m. Voice: high *sweet*. WSpr.

16 **YELLOW WARBLER** *Dendroica petechia* (Chipe/Reinita Amarillo/a) L 12 cm. Many races, which can be arranged in 3 groups: 'Yellow Warbler' (a, thr), 'Mangrove Warbler' (b, confined to mangrove; including *aureola* from Cocos Island) and 'Golden Warbler' (c, Cozumel). Unmistakable; 83.13 has different face pattern and indistinct wing bars. Habitat: woodland, semi-open areas with brush, hedges, fields, gardens, mangrove; 250–2000 m. Voice: very high *tsjik tsjik* or *tsjeeh*; very high rapid *sweetweetsweet-weeh-weeohweeh*.

17 **CAPE MAY WARBLER** *Dendroica tigrina* (Chipe Atigrado; Reinita Tigrina) L 12 cm. ♂ with much white in wing; ♀ from similar warblers by combination of eyebrow and distinct striping on underparts. Habitat: woodland, gardens; <500 m. Voice: *tseeh*. U,WSpr.

Plate 82

Plate 83

1   **PRAIRIE WARBLER** *Dendroica discolor* (Chipe Pradeño; Reinita Galana) L 12 cm. Well-marked yellow underparts and orange barring of mantle diagnostic. Habitat: open woodland, neglected cultivation. Voice: very high *tsss*. U,SMeCAm.

2   **CHESTNUT-SIDED WARBLER** *Dendroica pensylvanica* (Chipe Flanquicastaño; Reinita de Costillas Castañas) L 13 cm. Winter plumage (perching left) very different from summer. Note russet stripe over flanks. Habitat: forest, gardens; <1750 m. Voice: *tsjic*. WSpr.

3   **YELLOW-RUMPED WARBLER** *Dendroica coronata* (Chipe Rabadilla-amarilla; Reinita Lomiamarilla) L 13 cm. Three groups of races: 'Myrtle Warbler' (a, Thr), 'Audubon's Warbler' (b, Thr) and 'Goldman's Warbler' (c, SMeGu). Yellowish rump and patch to flanks diagnostic. Habitat: forest and edge, woodland, cultivations, fields; sl–1500 m. Voice: ultra high *tjip tjiptjip*.

4   **MAGNOLIA WARBLER** *Dendroica magnolia* (Chipe de Magnolia; Reinita Colifajeada) L 12 cm. White wing panel and black terminal tail band diagnostic. Habitat: forest, second growth, plantations, areas with thickets, hedges; sl–1500 m. Voice: nasal *sjeeh*. WSpr.

5   **HERMIT WARBLER** *Dendroica occidentalis* (Chipe Cabeciamarillo; Reinita Cabecigualda) L 12 cm. Yellow head with black nape (♂) and throat unique. Habitat: forest edge; 500–3500 m. Voice: dry *tsjip*. WSpr.

6   **BLACK-THROATED GREEN WARBLER** *Dendroica virens* (Chipe Dorsiverde; Reinita Cariamarilla) L 12 cm. Note differences in head pattern from 7. Habitat: forest, tall trees; sl–2000 m. Voice: dry *tusjip*. WSpr.

7   **TOWNSEND'S WARBLER** *Dendroica townsendi* (Chipe/Reinita de Townsend) L 12 cm. Note striped mantle. Habitat: forest, scrub; 500–3000 m. Voice: ultra high *tsjip*. WSpr.

8   **BLACKBURNIAN WARBLER** *Dendroica fusca* (Chipe/Reinita Gorjinaranja) L 12 cm. White V mark on mantle and large white area in wings distinctive. Habitat: forest canopy, tree stands, scrub, gardens; 750–1500(2000)m. Voice: *tsjip*. WSpr.

9   **YELLOW-THROATED WARBLER** *Dendroica dominica* (Chipe/Reinita Gorjiamarillo/a) L 14 cm. Black-bordered yellow throat patch diagnostic. Large-sized. Habitat: open woodland, gardens; sl–1500 m. Voice: very high *sjeet*. WSpr.

10   **GOLDEN-CHEEKED WARBLER** *Dendroica chrysoparia* (Chipe Caridorado) L 13 cm. Only warbler with yellow restricted to face sides. Habitat: mixed forest; 1500–3000 m. Voice: ultra high *thik thik*; very/ultra high *frúuh-fréeh-dufréehtji*. U,MeGuHoNi.

11   **GRACE'S WARBLER** *Dendroica graciae* (Chipe de Grace) L 13 cm. From larger 9 by striping on mantle and broader yellow eyebrow. Habitat: mixed forest. Voice: very high rapid *tjeedletjeedletjiijitji*. WSpr.

12   **KIRTLAND'S WARBLER** *Dendroica kirtlandii* (Chipe de Kirtland) L 15 cm. Two-toned plumage, grey above, yellow below, distinctive. Habitat: pine forest. Voice: high *dzz*. Hyp,NMe.

13   **PALM WARBLER** *Dendroica palmarum* (Chipe Playero; Reinita Coronicastaña) L 12 cm. Nom (a) and race *hypochrysea* (b) shown. Distinctive rufous cap and yellow vent; b from 82.16a by less pronounced yellow wing bars. Habitat: open areas at water; <750 m. Voice: metallic *tsjip*. U,WSpr.

14   **PINE WARBLER** *Dendroica pinus* (Chipe Pinero; Reinita de Pinos) L 13 cm. Note pale yellow patch behind dark cheek. Habitat: forest. Voice: high *tseep*. U,NMe.

15   **BAY-BREASTED WARBLER** *Dendroica castanea* (Chipe Pechicastaño; Reinita Castaña) L 13 cm. Winter plumage from similar side-striped 2 by head pattern. Habitat: any habitat (winter), but especially in forest; sl–1000 m. Voice: sharp *tsjic*. WSpr.

16   **BLACKPOLL WARBLER** *Dendroica striata* (Chipe Gorrinegro; Reinita Rayada) L 13 cm. Winter plumage siskin-like, but paler. Habitat: forest, tree stands. Voice: very high sharp *tsjik*. U,MeBe

17   **BLACK-AND-WHITE WARBLER** *Mniotilta varia* (Chipe Trepador; Reinita Trepadora) L 13 cm. Unmistakable. Note yellow feet. Habitat: tall scrub, woodland, gardens; sl–(2000) 2500 m. Voice: ultra high thin *tseeeh*. Thr.

18   **BLACK-THROATED GREY WARBLER** *Dendroica nigrescens* (Chipe Negrigrís) L 13 cm. Note yellow spot in front of eye. Habitat: woodland; 1500–3000 m. Voice: very high *tjutjutjutowhee*. Me(BeGu)

19   **CERULEAN WARBLER** *Dendroica cerulea* (Chipe/Reinita Cerúleo/a) L 11 cm. Unmistakable; ♀ bluish green. Habitat: forest; <750 m. Voice: high *tsip*. U,WSpr.

20   **BLACK-THROATED BLUE WARBLER** *Dendroica caerulescens* (Chipe Azuloso; Reinita Azul y Negro) L 11 cm. Unmistakable; ♀ with white wing patch as ♂. Habitat: forest edge, woodland; sl(500)–1250 m. Voice: very high *tic*. U,WSpr.

Plate 83

Plate 84

1   **CONNECTICUT WARBLER** *Oporornis agilis* (Chipe de Connecticut; Reinita Ojianillada) L 13 cm. Sharp demarcation between throat and breast distinctive. Note complete eye ring. Walks, does not hop. Habitat: forest, woodland. Voice: high *tzeek*. V,SMeCAm.

2   **MOURNING WARBLER** *Oporornis philadelphia* (Chipe Llorón; Reinita Enlutada) L 12 cm. Less pronounced eye ring than 1. Habitat: forest edge, second growth, thickets, neglected weedy cultivations. Voice: ultra high sharp *tsjirk*. WSpr.

3   **MACGILLIVRAY'S WARBLER** *Oporornis tolmiei* (Chipe de Tolmie; Reinita de Tupidero) L 12 cm. From 2 by white, broken eye ring. Habitat: forest interior and edge, second growth; sl–3000 m. Voice: very high *tuc tuc*; high rapid *sreesreereepuwurreweet*. WSpr.

4   **KENTUCKY WARBLER** *Oporornis formosus* (Chipe de Kentucky; Reinita Cachetinegra) L 13 cm. Note yellow throat, black lore, broken eye ring. Habitat: forest floor, thickets at edge, second growth. Voice: high *tsjuk*. WSpr.

5   **GREY-CROWNED YELLOWTHROAT** *Geothlypis poliocephala* (Mascarita Piquigruesa; Antifacito Coronigrís) L 14 cm. Paler race *poliocephala* not shown. Habitat: savanna, tall grass, hedges, bush, scrub; sl–1500 m. Voice: ultra high *tjéewur* or *tjéewurrur*; very high sharp warbling *tseetseeweetohweet*. WSpr.

6   **MASKED YELLOWTHROAT** *Geothlypis aequinoctialis* (Antifacito Sureño) L 14 cm. From 8 by grey crown, bordering black mask. Habitat: marsh, reed beds, flooded grassland, areas with tall weeds and some trees; 1000–1250 m. Voice: very high sibilant *sweet-sweey-sweeyohweeweeh*. CRPa.

7   **COMMON YELLOWTHROAT** *Geothlypis trichas* (Mascarita Común; Antifacito Norteño) L 12 cm. Several races, of these nom (a, Thr), *chapalensis* (b, Me) and yellow-bellied *chryseola* (c) shown. Distinctive, but see 10. Habitat: weedy and scrubby vegetation, marsh, flooded fields; sl–2500 m. Voice: ultra high hurried *weetjuurit - -* (3 x).

8   **OLIVE-CROWNED YELLOWTHROAT** *Geothlypis semiflava* (Antifacito Coroniolivo) L 13 cm. No grey on head. Not in range of 11. Habitat: tall grass and weeds in wet grassland; <1500 m. Voice: very high *tuweetjetuweetjietjutjuweeh*. CAm.

9   **ALTAMIRA** (or Yellow-crowned) **YELLOWTHROAT** *Geothlypis flavovelata* (Mascarita de Altamira) L 13 cm. Yellow peaked crown diagnostic. Habitat: marsh; <500 m. Voice: *tsjet*; very high hurried up and down *títsjíputi* - (2 x). E,Me.

10   **BELDING'S** (or Peninsular) **YELLOWTHROAT** *Geothlypis beldingi* (Mascarita de Belding) L 14 cm. Race *goldmani* (a) and nom (b) shown. From smaller 7 by stronger bill and brighter colours. Restricted range. Habitat: marsh. NMe.

11   **HOODED YELLOWTHROAT** *Geothlypis nelsoni* (Mascarita Matorralera) L 12 cm. From 7 by habitat, grey band at edge of mask. Habitat: dry scrub; 1250–3000 m. Voice: *tsjúchohtsjúchot*. E,Me.

12   **BLACK-POLLED YELLOWTHROAT** *Geothlypis speciosa* (Mascarita Transvolcanica) L 13 cm. Note saffron wash over underparts and black crown. Habitat: marsh, reeds at lakes; 1750–2500 m. Voice: *trits*; very high descending *weetweetjetjuotjuh* or rattling *weetweet-* (7 x). E,Me.

13   **WILSON'S WARBLER** *Wilsonia pusilla* (Chipe de Wilson; Reinita Gorrinegra) L 11 cm. Not unlike other unstriped yellow-bellied warblers, but no other one with black cap (♂) and yellow eyebrow. Habitat: forest, second growth, plantations, neglected fields; sl(1000)–3000 m. Voice: Winter Wren-like warble, very /ultra high *feefeefeetjutjuh*. Thr.

14   **CANADA WARBLER** *Wilsonia canadensis* (Chipe Collarejo; Reinita Pechirrayada) L 12 cm. From 83.12 by unmarked grey mantle; yellow throat isolated by band of breast striping. Habitat: tall second growth, plantations; sl–1750(2500)m. Voice: very high sharp *tsjup*. WSpr.

15   **HOODED WARBLER** *Wilsonia citrina* (Chipe/Reinita Encapuchado/a) L 13 cm. Unmistakable. Note unmarked cheeks of ♀. Habitat: forest interior and edge; sl–1250(1500)m. Voice: *sreet*; *weeteetohweeteet* (3 x) *weeteetsjrrr*. WSpr.

16   **COLLARED WHITESTART** *Myioborus torquatus* (Candelita Collareja) L 13 cm. Unmistakable. Habitat: montane forest and adjacent more open areas. Voice: ultra high *tsjip*; ultra high unstructured *tsjutsjurotjuwhotsjuh--*. CRPa.

▶

Plate 84

Plate 84 continued

17 **SLATE-THROATED WHITESTART** *Myioborus miniatus* (Pavito Gorjigrís; Candelita Pechinegra) L 13 cm. Several races occur, differing in colouring of underparts (from yellow to red) and barring of undertail coverts; of these nom (a) and *ballux* (b) shown. Rufous-russet crown and slate-black wings diagnostic. Habitat: middle levels of montane forest and woodland. Voice: very high *tritriwéehwéehwéeh*. WSpr.

18 **PAINTED WHITESTART** *Myioborus pictus* (Pavito Aliblanco) L 15 cm. Unmistakable. Habitat: woodland; 1000–3000 m. Voice: very high slurred-down *tjur*; very high fluted full meandering slightly descending *weetohweetohtjiptjiptjip*. WSpr.

19 **AMERICAN REDSTART** *Setophaga ruticilla* (Pavito Migratorio; Candelita Norteña) L 12 cm. Unmistakable. Habitat: forest interior and edge, scrubby woodland; sl–1500(2500)m. Voice: sharp *tsjic*. Thr.

Plate 85

1 **OLIVE WARBLER** *Peucedramus taeniatus* (Chipe Ocotero) L 13 cm. ♂ is unmistakable, ♀ shows distinct eyebrow and finely streaked ear patch. Habitat: pine forest, dry woodland; 1500–3500 m. Voice: high rapid *tjitu-tjitu-tjitu*. WSpr.

2 **RED-FACED WARBLER** *Cardellina rubrifrons* (Chipe Carirrojo) L 14 cm. Unmistakable. Habitat: woodland, forest (winter); 1500–3000 m. Voice: ultra high *tseet*; very high rapid warbling cheerful *wheetwheetsweetohsweet*. WSpr.

3 **RED WARBLER** *Ergaticus ruber* (Chipe Rojo) L 13 cm. Unmistakable. Habitat: forest, woodland; 1750–3500 m. Voice: very high rattling simple *wheetwheetsrrrrrrrohweet*. E,Me.

4 **PINK-HEADED WARBLER** *Ergaticus versicolor* (Chipe Rosado) L 13 cm. Unmistakable. Habitat: forest interior at edge; 1750–3500 m. Voice: ultra high slightly rattling *tjuhtjuhtítjítjít*. Gu.

5 **GREY-THROATED CHAT** *Granatellus sallaei* (Granatelo Yucateco) L 13 cm. Unmistakable. Habitat: thickets, woodland, forest; sl–1500 m. Voice: *tutrrrrr*; very high short descending *fifjiwijuwiweeh*. SMeGuBe.

6 **RED-BREASTED CHAT** *Granatellus venustus* (Granatelo Mexicano) L 15 cm. ♂ and ♀ darker and with more white in tail than 5. White throat of ♂ diagnostic. Habitat: woodland; sl–1250 m. Voice: *tsjt*; ultra high *tuwéetuwéesjeesjeeweeweeh*. E,Me.

7 **YELLOW-BREASTED CHAT** *Icteria virens* (Gritón Pechiamarillo; Reinita Grande) L 18 cm. Note large size, long tail, brilliant yellow throat, face pattern with distinct eye ring. Habitat: woodland, scrub, thickets; sl–1500(2500)m. Voice: high *tjaw tjuw wuw zutzutzut* or *tjawtjawtjaw*. Thr.

8 **FAN-TAILED WARBLER** *Basileuterus lachrymosa* (Chipe Roquero) L 15 cm. Habit of constant tail-fanning and tail-swinging distinctive. Habitat: woodland in rocky areas; <1750cm. Voice: very high up and down *seeohseeohseeohweet*. WSpr.

9 **GOLDEN-CROWNED WARBLER** *Basileuterus culicivorus* (Chipe/Reinita Corona-dorada) L 12 cm. Crown pattern (orange stripe, bordered black) distinctive. Habitat: forest understorey; <1500 m. Voice: very high *sreeh*; very high sharp calm *tutjututuwéetéeh*. WSpr.

10 **RUFOUS-CAPPED WARBLER** *Basileuterus rufifrons* (Chipe Gorirrufo; Reinita Cabecicastaña) L 13 cm. Several races occur, differing in extent of yellow on underparts, of these nom (a) and *salvini* (b) shown. Whitish belly and finely black-marked white streak under russet cheek diagnostic. Habitat: semi-open areas with trees, scrub, hedges, open woodland; sl–3000 m. Voice: ultra high Winter Wren-like warble (4s), ending in - -*wit weetweetweet*. MeGuBe.

11 **CHESTNUT-CAPPED WARBLER** *Basileuterus r. delattrii* (Chipe Gorricastaño) L 13 cm. Now race of 10. From 12 by white eye stripe. Habitat: dry woodland, thorn bush; sl–1500 m. Voice: very high *tit-trit-trit-triterit-trit trit-trit- -*. SMeCAm.

12 **GOLDEN-BROWED WARBLER** *Basileuterus belli* (Chipe Cejidorado) L 13 cm. No white in plumage. Habitat: forest interior and edge; 1250–3500 m. Voice: high *tjutjutitisfiweehweeh* (-*sfi-* ultra high). WSpr.

13 **PIRRE WARBLER** *Basileuterus ignotus* (Chipe del Pirre) L 13 cm. Eyebrow narrower than 9; face sides less black than greyer-breasted 14. Habitat: montane forest undergrowth. U,Pa.

Plate 85 continued

14 **BLACK-CHEEKED WARBLER** *Basileuterus melanogenys* (Reinita Carinegra) L 14 cm. Darker than 15 and not in same range. Habitat: montane forest (undergrowth) and adjacent areas; <1500 m. Voice: ultra high rapid tinkling (3–7s). CRPa.

15 **THREE-STRIPED WARBLER** *Basileuterus tristriatus* (Reinita Cabecilistada) L 13 cm. Distinct face pattern with central crown stripe grey, not rufous. Habitat: montane forest undergrowth. Voice: ultra high staccato *treetreetreetruwreet*. CRPa.

16 **BUFF-RUMPED WARBLER** *Basileuterus fulvicauda* (Reinita Guardaribera) L 13 cm. Unmistakable by rump and tail colouring. Habitat: at edges of shaded streams; 500–1500 m. Voice: very high short cheerful warbling. CAm.

17 **WRENTHRUSH** (or Zeledonia) *Zeledonia coronata* (Zeledonia) L 12 cm. Plump, long-legged, short-tailed, very dark. Note orange crown patch. Habitat: dense undergrowth of montane forest. Voice: very high drawn-up *pseeeér*; ultra high very fast *wseepuweeh*. CRPa.

18 **OVENBIRD** *Seiurus aurocapillus* (Chipe-suelero Coronado; Reinita Hornera) L 14 cm. Walks, does not hop. Unmistakable by white-rimmed eye and habits (walks quietly over forest ground). Habitat: forest floor, woodland, gardens. Voice: sustained *tsjip*; high short rapid *tjirrúpderrupderrup*. WSpr.

19 **NORTHERN WATERTHRUSH** *Seiurus noveboracensis* (Chipe-suelero Charquero; Reinita Acuática Norteña) L 14 cm. Note horizontal stance. From 20 by faint throat spotting, narrower and shorter eye stripe, greater contrast between buff flanks and bright white or pale grey underparts. Underparts less contrasting white than 20. Habitat: at quiet water bodies, also in mangrove. Voice: metallic *tsjuuk-tsjuuk*. Thr.

20 **LOUISIANA WATERTHRUSH** *Seiurus motacilla* (Chipe-suelero Arroyero; Reinita Acuatica Piquigrande) L 14 cm. See 19. Habitat: mainly at running water. Voice: strong *tsjirp*. WSpr.

Plate 86

1 **BANANAQUIT** *Coereba flaveola* (Platanero; Reinita Mielera) L 9 cm. Races *mexicana* (a) and *caboti* (b) shown. Unmistakable by fine, red-based bill. Habitat: forest edge, woodland, second growth, cultivations, gardens; sl–(1000)1500 m. Voice: ultra high weak *teetteeet-sreeuw* or *teeteeterreet-zweet*. SMeCAm.

2 **WHITE-EARED CONEBILL** *Conirostrum leucogenys* (Picocono Orejiblanco) L 9 cm. ♂ and ♀ with white rump. Habitat: forest canopy, woodland; <750 m. Voice: very high *tjirrup*; ultra high hurried unstructured twittering. U,Pa.

3 **VIRIDIAN DACNIS** *Dacnis viguieri* (Mielero Verde Azul) L 10 cm. Unmistakable. Note short, fine bill, yellow eyes. Habitat: forest canopy; <500 m. U,Pa.

4 **BLUE DACNIS** *Dacnis cayana* (Mielero Azulejo) L 14 cm. From 7 by shorter bill, blue edges to wing feathers, black bib. Habitat: forest canopy, also in clearings; <1000 m. Voice*: very high thin *tsweep tsweep* and squeaky *siup-sooee siup-sooee*. CAm.

5 **SHINING HONEYCREEPER** *Cyanerpes lucidus* (Mielero Luciente) L 10 cm. Black throat patch of ♂ larger than 6, ♀ without buff-ochre in face. Habitat: forest canopy; 250–1250 m. CAm.

6 **PURPLE HONEYCREEPER** *Cyanerpes caeruleus* (Mielero Purpúreo) L 10 cm. Note small bib of ♂ and warm-coloured face of ♀. Habitat: forest canopy; <500 m. Voice: high *tsree*. U,Pa.

7 **RED-LEGGED HONEYCREEPER** *Cyanerpes cyaneus* (Mielero Patirrojo) L 12 cm. Note green cap and black mantle of ♂. ♀ shows distinct eyebrow. Moulting birds may look blotchy with blue patches on green. Habitat: forest canopy and edge, plantations, adjacent areas with trees and hedges, gardens; <1500 m. Voice: very high dry *sreeeh*. WSpr.

8 **SCARLET-THIGHED DACNIS** *Dacnis venusta* (Mielero Celeste y Negro) L 12 cm. Unmistakable by red eye, short bill, black underparts. Habitat: forest (canopy) and adjacent areas; 250–1250(1500)m. CRPa.

9 **GREEN HONEYCREEPER** *Chlorophanes spiza* (Mielero Verde) L 13 cm. Unmistakable. Note long, curved, bi-coloured bill of ♀. Habitat: forest canopy, gardens; sl–1500 m. SMeCAm.

▶

Plate 86

Plate 86 continued

10   **BAY-HEADED TANAGER** *Tangara gyrola* (Tángara Cabecicastaña)   L 14 cm. From 11 by blue belly and all-green wing. Habitat: forest (upper levels) and nearby areas; 500–1500 m. Voice: very high thin *tzeeep*. CRPa.

11   **RUFOUS-WINGED TANAGER** *Tangara lavinia* (Tángara Alirrufa)   L 14 cm. Note rufous in wing. Habitat: forest canopy; 250–750 m. CAm.

12   **EMERALD TANAGER** *Tangara florida* (Tángara Orejinegra)   L 12 cm. Unmistakable. Habitat: forest canopy; 250–1000 m. CRPa.

13   **SILVER-THROATED TANAGER** *Tangara icterocephala* (Tángara Dorada)   L 13 cm. Unmistakable. Habitat: forest; sl–1500 m. Voice: ultra high inhaled *sfeeeh*. CRPa.

14   **SPECKLED TANAGER** *Tangara guttata* (Tángara Moteada)   L 13 cm. Note yellow tinge of upperparts. Habitat: upper forest levels; 250–1500 m. Voice: ultra high thin *tit tit - -*. CRPa

15   **AZURE-RUMPED** (or Cabanis's) **TANAGER** *Tangara cabanisi* (Tángara de Cabanis)   L 14 cm. Greenish-blue all over. Habitat: forest; 1000–1750 m. Voice*: very high sibilant *pfsweeeeo* and high trill *spspspnnnsp*. SMeGu.

16   **GREY-AND-GOLD TANAGER** *Tangara palmeri* (Tángara Doradigrís)   L 14 cm. From 15 by unmarked crown and different range. Habitat: upper forest levels; <1000 m. U,Pa.

17   **GOLDEN-HOODED TANAGER** *Tangara larvata* (Tángara Capucha-dorada)   L 13 cm. Unmistakable. Habitat: forest edge and clearings; <1000 m. Voice: ultra high accelerated trill *trrrrrrrr*. SMeCAm.

18   **GREEN-NAPED TANAGER** *Tangara fucosa* (Tángara de Nuca Verde)   L 13 cm. From 19 by colour of crown patch and different range. Habitat: forest interior and edge; <1350 m. U,Pa.

19   **SPANGLE-CHEEKED TANAGER** *Tangara dowii* (Tángara Vientricastaña)   L 13 cm. Distinctively coloured and patterned. Not in range of 18. Habitat: forest and nearby areas; 750–3000 m. CRPa.

20   **PLAIN-COLOURED TANAGER** *Tangara inornata* (Tángara Cenicienta)   L 12 cm. Grey overall with blue shoulder, lacking yellow rump of 88.4. Habitat: forest and nearby areas; <500 m. CRPa.

Plate 87

1   **BLUE-CROWNED CHLOROPHONIA** *Chlorophonia occipitalis* (Chlorofonia Coroniazul) L 13 cm. Not in range of 2 or 3. Habitat: forest; 1000–2500 m. Voice*: high descending pure whistled *plew* (2s), repeated frequently. WSpr.

2   **GOLDEN-BROWED CHLOROPHONIA** *Chlorophonia callophrys* (Chlorofonia Cejidorada) L 13 cm. Yellow neck and eyebrow (only ♂) diagnostic. Habitat: montane forest and adjacent more open areas. Voice: high unstructured *pfuuuh pruít - -*. CRPa.

3   **YELLOW-COLLARED CHLOROPHONIA** *Chlorophonia flavirostris* (Chlorofonia Cuellidorada)   L 10 cm. Pale eyes and red bill diagnostic. Habitat: forest. Voice: very high thin penetrating *fíjuuh fíjuuh - -*. U,Pa.

4   **OLIVE-BACKED EUPHONIA** *Euphonia gouldi* (Eufonia Olivácea)   L 10 cm. No similar bird in the area. Note dark-looking chestnut front of ♀. Habitat: forest; sl–1000 m. Voice: e.g. ultra high disyllabic low *piuuu-swirrr*. SMeCAm.

5   **YELLOW-THROATED EUPHONIA** *Euphonia hirundinacea* (Eufonia Gorjiamarilla)   L 11 cm. From 6 by thinner bill and mainly different range. ♀ whitish below in centre of underparts. Habitat: forest, second growth, gardens, semi-open areas with trees and edges, sl–1500 m. Voice: very high hurried warble (2s), with sharp *fjeet's* and nasal *njèèh's*. WSpr.

6   **THICK-BILLED EUPHONIA** *Euphonia laniirostris* (Eufonia Piquigruesa)   L 11 cm. Note thick bill. ♀ shows rather yellow underparts. Habitat: forest, second growth, gardens, semi-open areas with trees and edges, sl–1250 m. Voice: ultra high *weet weet weet* and high *tit tit - -*. CRPa.

7   **WHITE-VENTED EUPHONIA** *Euphonia minuta* (Eufonia Vientre-blanco/Menuda)   L 10 cm. White undertail coverts diagnostic. Not in same range as 10b. Habitat: forest and adjacent more open areas with hedges, orchards; sl–1000 m. Voice: very high thin *tsjip*. U,CAm.

▶

Plate 87

Plate 87 continued

8   YELLOW-CROWNED EUPHONIA *Euphonia luteicapilla* (Eufonia Coroniamarilla) L 10 cm. From other euphonias by extent of yellow on crown. Rich yellow ♀ difficult to separate from other ♀ euphonias. Habitat: forest edge, open woodland, open areas with scrub, hedges, tree stands; <1000 m. Voice: ultra high drawn-out *weeeet-weet*. NiCRPa.

9   SPOT-CROWNED EUPHONIA *Euphonia imitans* (Eufonia Vientrirrojiza) L 10 cm. Crown spots diagnostic, but difficult to see. Differs from other euphonias in its range by extent of yellow on crown. Only ♀ in range with buff underparts. Habitat: forest, second growth; <1500 m. Voice: very high well-separated *whít wirrrrr tjuwtjuwtjuw*. U, CRPa.

10   SCRUB EUPHONIA *Euphonia affinis* (Eufonia Gorjinegro/Gargantinegra) L 10 cm. Nom (a) and race *godmani* (b) shown. Note restricted yellow on forehead and small bill. See also 7. Habitat: forest, second growth, tree stands; sl–1250 m. Voice: very high sharp *deedeedee*; very fast canary-like twittering. WSpr.

11   ORANGE-BELLIED EUPHONIA *Euphonia xanthogaster* (Eufonia Vientrinaranja) L 11 cm. Not in range of 5, 8, 9 and 10. From 6 by smaller bill. Note grey collar of ♀. Habitat: undergrowth at forest edge; 450–1500 m. Voice: high short compressed phrases *tjrrrrrh-tutjuwtjut-trrrr*. U,Pa.

12   FULVOUS-VENTED EUPHONIA *Euphonia fulvicrissa* (Eufonia Vientrileonada) L 9 cm. Fulvous undertail coverts diagnostic. Not in range of similar buff-fronted ♀♀ of 4 and 9. Habitat: forest edge and clearings; <1000 m. Pa.

13   TAWNY-CAPPED EUPHONIA *Euphonia anneae* (Eufonia Gorricanela) L 11 cm. Tawny cap diagnostic; note greyish hind crown and breast of ♀. Habitat: forest; 500–2000 m. Voice: very high slightly nasal *tuweetwit*. CRPa.

14   BLUE-HOODED (or Blue-rumped or Elegant) EUPHONIA *Euphonia elegantissima* (Eufonia Capucha-azul/Capuchiceleste) L 11 cm. Unmistakable. Habitat: forest, tree stands; 500–3500 m. WSpr.

15   BLUE-AND-GOLD TANAGER *Bangsia arcaei* (Tángara de Costillas Negras) L 15 cm. No similar tanager in the area. Habitat: upper forest levels; 500–1250 m. Voice: very high sharp *tch-please teh-please*. U,CRPa.

16   YELLOW-WINGED TANAGER *Thraupis abbas* (Tángara Aliamarilla) L 17 cm. Unmistakable by wing pattern. Habitat: forest edge, plantations, areas with tree, hedges; sl–1750 m. WSpr.

17   BLUE-GREY TANAGER *Thraupis episcopus* (Tángara Azuligrís/Azuleja) L 15 cm. Unmistakable by bluish colour. Habitat: forest edge, semi-open areas with trees and hedges, plantations; sl–1500 m. Voice: very high rapid slightly mewing twittering (6s). WSpr.

18   PALM TANAGER *Thraupis palmarum* (Tángara Palmera) L 16 cm. Note dark flight feathers and greater wing coverts. Habitat: open country with trees (palms), hedges, woodland patches; sl–1250 m. Voice: very high rapid twittering (8s). (Ni)CRPa.

19   SWALLOW TANAGER *Tersina viridis* (Tersina) L 14 cm. No similar bird in the area. Gregarious, catches insects like a flycatcher. Habitat: open woodland. Voice: very high thin *fjit fjitfjit*. U,Pa.

Plate 88 continued

WESTERN TANAGER *Piranga ludoviciana* (Tángara Occidental/Carirroja)   L 17 cm.
Distinguished by wing pattern of winter plumage, striped dusky mantle, reddish glow to lores and chin. Habitat: woodland, forest, plantations; sl–3000 m. Voice: high fast chattering *ptwrrrirrrrirr.* Thr.

RED-HEADED TANAGER *Piranga erythrocephala* (Tángara Cabecirroja)   L 15 cm.
Unmistakable. Note white belly of ♀. Habitat: forest, plantations; 1000–3000 m. E,Me.

Plate 88

1   **STRIPE-HEADED TANAGER** *Spindalis zena* (Tángara Cabecirrayada)   L 14 cm. From similar birds like 91.16 by wing pattern and by golden mantle and breast. Habitat: forest interior and edge. E,Me.

2   **BLACK-THROATED SHRIKE TANAGER** *Lanio aurantius* (Tángara-lanio Gorjinegro) L 20 cm. From orioles (plate 97) by black head and yellow mantle. Habitat: middle levels of forest; sl–1250 m. Voice: high *pjéet-tut* or *faldereeh-falderah*. SMeBeGuHo.

3   **WHITE-THROATED SHRIKE TANAGER** *Lanio leucothorax* (Tángara Piquiganchuda) L 20 cm. As 2, but with white throat. ♀ by saffron-ochre throat. Habitat: middle forest levels; <1000 m. Voice: high lashing *wéetjuh wéetjuh - -* or very high *tjíeeuw*. U,CAm.

4   **SULPHUR-RUMPED TANAGER** *Heterospingus rubrifrons* (Tángara Lomiazufrada)   L 16 cm. Yellow rump and undertail coverts diagnostic. Habitat: forest (middle levels) and adjacent semi-open areas; <1000 m. CRPa.

5   **SCARLET-BROWED TANAGER** *Heterospingus xanthopygius* (Tángara Cejiescarlata)   L 17 cm. Unmistakable. Note white breast tufts and yellow rump of ♀. Habitat: forest; <1000 m. U,Pa.

6   **WHITE-SHOULDERED TANAGER** *Tachyphonus luctuosus* (Tángara Caponiblanca) L 14 cm. No similar white-shouldered bird in the area. Note grey head of ♀ paler on cheek and almost white on throat. Habitat: forest canopy, woodland; <750 m. Voice: toneless sharp rapid *tju-scratchscratchscratch*. U,CAm.

7   **TAWNY-CRESTED TANAGER** *Tachyphonus delatrii* (Tángara Coronidorada)   L 15 cm. Distinctive tawny-yellow crest. Habitat: lower forest levels; <1250 m. Voice: ultra high inhaled *fjeet-fjeet-fit trit-tutrit- -*. CAm.

8   **WHITE-LINED TANAGER** *Tachyphonus rufous* (Tángara Forriblanca)   L 17 cm. Note typical bi-toned tanager-bill. ♀ more rufous-brown than 7. Habitat: open woodland, cultivations; sl–1500 m. Voice: high dry *tjip tjip - -*. U,CRPa.

9   **RED-CROWNED ANT TANAGER** *Habia rubica* (Tángara-hormiguera Coronirroja)   L 18 cm. Dark red-brown overall. Narrow red crown bordered black. Habitat: forest, second growth; sl–1500 m. Voice: very high *peeteh-peeteh* or very high fluting *truhperritruhperritruh*, slightly crescendoing. WSpr.

10   **RED-THROATED ANT TANAGER** *Habia fuscicauda* (Tángara-hormiguera Gorjirroja) L 19 cm. Deeper red than 9 with more concealed red crown. ♀ from 9 by yellow chin and lack of yellow crown stripe. Habitat: undergrowth at forest edge; sl–500(1250)m. Voice: low *scratch*, continued in chattering mellow up and down *-tjuppoh tjuppoh tjupperoh*. WSpr.

11   **BLACK-CHEEKED ANT TANAGER** *Habia atrimaxillaris* (Tángara-hormiguera Carinegra) L 18 cm. Black cheeks diagnostic. Habitat: forest understorey. E,CR.

12   **ROSE-THROATED TANAGER** *Piranga roseogularis* (Tángara Yucateca)   L 16 cm. Red of crown, tail and wings sharply demarcated from greyish body. Note broken eye ring. Habitat: forest interior and edge; <250 m. Voice: mewing *tititihere*; *teet tjut tittjuut*. YMeBe.

13   **HEPATIC TANAGER** *Piranga flava* (Tángara Encinera/Bermeja)   L 18 cm. Shown is northern race. Southern race has less dusky back and cheek. Note long head with darker bill than 14. Habitat: pine and mixed forest; 500–3000 m. Voice: very high *u-whéetohwhéetjiohwheet*. WSpr.

14   **SUMMER TANAGER** *Piranga rubra* (Tángara Roja/Veranera)   L 17 cm. Unmistakable. ♀ overall more yellowish. Peaked crown. Habitat: woodland, forest edge; sl–1750 m. Voice: *tidderup*; unstructured sweet *pjur tseet tuweet - -*. Thr.

15   **SCARLET TANAGER** *Piranga olivacea* (Tángara Escarlata)   L 16 cm. Winter plumage as ♀, but with black wings. Habitat: forest, occasionally in bush land; sl–2500 m. U,WSpr.

16   **WHITE-WINGED TANAGER** *Piranga leucoptera* (Tángara Aliblanca) L 14 cm. From 15 by white wing bars and black lores. Habitat: montane forests; plantations. Voice: very high sandpiper-like *wéeweezweeh*. WSpr.

17   **FLAME-COLOURED TANAGER** *Piranga bidentata* (Tángara Dorsirrayada)   L 18 cm. Note striping on mantle and white corners to tail. Habitat: forest, plantations, 750–2750 m. WSpr.

◀

Plate 88

Plate 89

1   **CRIMSON-COLLARED TANAGER** *Ramphocelus sanguinolentus* (Tángara Cuellirroja/ Capuchirroja)   L 19 cm. Unmistakable. Habitat: forest, second growth; sl–1250 m. SMeCAm.

2   **CRIMSON-BACKED TANAGER** *Ramphocelus dimidiatus* (Tángara de Toro Encendido) L 16 cm. Crimson back and narrow white eye ring distinctive. Habitat: forest edge, thickets, scrub, suburban regions; <1300 m. Voice: high nasal *tsjuk tsjew tsik - -*. Pa.

3   **SCARLET-RUMPED TANAGER** *Ramphocelus passerinii* (Tángara Terciopelo/Lomiescarlata) L 16 cm. From 4 by red rump and different range. Habitat: forest edge, thickets, scrub, suburban regions; <1300 m. SMeCAm. Note: now split into two species: CHERRIE'S TANAGER *Ramphocelus costaricensis* (a, along Pacific coast) and PASSERINI'S TANAGER *Ramphocelus passerinii* (b, along Atlantic coast). ♂♂ similar, ♀♀ differing by colour of rump and upper breast.

4   **FLAME-** (or Yellow-)**RUMPED TANAGER** *Ramphocelus flammigerus* (Tángara de Espalda Rayada)   L 18 cm. No similar black bird with yellow rump in the area. Habitat: forest edge, thickets, scrub, suburban regions. Voice*: very high rattling staccato song consisting mainly of trills with whipping *swip* notes. Also sparrow-like *kep*. Pa.

5   **GREY-HEADED TANAGER** *Eucometis penicillata* (Tángara Cabecigrís)   L 16 cm. From ♀ 88.6 by slightly peaked crown, which is paler than face sides, and by brighter yellow-orange breast; also more confined to upper forest storeys. Habitat: forest, tall second growth; <1250 m. Voice: high nasal short fast twittering *fjeetfjeetfjeet weet weet*. U,SMeCAm.

6   **DUSKY-FACED TANAGER** *Mitrospingus cassini* (Tángara Carinegruzca)   L 19 cm. Striking pale eye in blackish mask diagnostic. Habitat: forest understorey and edge, woodland; <500 m. Voice: ultra high sharp *tsee-tuh what tseeterruh whatwhat - -*. CRPa.

7   **OLIVE TANAGER** *Chlorothraupis carmioli* (Tángara Aceitunada)   L 17 cm. Almost uniform dusky olive-green with brighter throat and lower belly. Note striking black bill. Habitat: lower forest storeys; <1500 m. Voice*: high pleasant musical thrush-like song, rising and falling *weoweeoweeoweeo-ps-wéeoo ps-wéeooo*. NiCRPa.

8   **LEMON-SPECTACLED TANAGER** *Chlorothraupis olivacea* (Tángara Ojeralimín)   L 17 cm. Lemon spectacles distinctive. Habitat: forest undergrowth. U,Pa.

9   **SOOTY-CAPPED BUSH TANAGER** *Chlorospingus pileatus* (Tángara de Monte Cejiblanca) L 14 cm. Black-capped (a) and brown-capped forms (b) shown. Larger than 86.1, with stubby bill, almost black upperparts. Habitat: montane forest. Voice: high *tjuk*; ultra high muttering. CRPa.

10   **COMMON BUSH TANAGER** *Chlorospingus ophthalmicus* (Chinchinero Común; Tángara de Monte Ojeruda)   L 14 cm. Nom (a) and race *punctulatus* (b) shown. White spot behind eye diagnostic. Habitat: forest interior and edge; sl–1500 m. Voice: ultra high hurried descending irregular *titi-tititru*. WSpr.

11   **ASHY-THROATED BUSH TANAGER** *Chlorospingus canigularis* (Tángara de Monte Gargantigrís)   L 13 cm. From 14 by greyish head and pale grey, not yellow throat. Habitat: forest; 500–1250 m. Voice: ultra high thin *tsjit tsjittitit tit - -*. U,CRPa.

12   **PIRRE BUSH TANAGER** *Chlorospingus inornatus* (Tángara de Monte del Pirre)   L 15 cm. Striking white eye in black mask, yellow underparts. Habitat: montane forest. E,Pa.

13   **TACARCUNA BUSH TANAGER** *Chlorospingus tacarcunae* (Tángara de Monte del Tacarcuna) L 13 cm. From 12 by uniform green-olive upperparts. Habitat: forest; 750–1500 m. Voice*: high initial note followed by harsh rattle *swip tsktsktsktsktsktsk*. U,Pa.

14   **YELLOW-THROATED BUSH TANAGER** *Chlorospingus flavigularis* (Tángara de Monte Goliamarillo)   L 15 cm. From 11 by yellow throat and greyish breast. Habitat: forest edge, second growth; <1000 m. Voice: ultra/very high *fjeet fjeet fjeet - -* or high nasal *djip djip*. Pa.

15   **YELLOW-BACKED TANAGER** *Hemithraupis flavicollis* (Tángara Lomiamarilla)   L 13 cm. Unmistakable. Note whitish belly of ♀. Habitat: forest canopy; <1000 m. U,Pa.

16   **BLACK-AND-YELLOW TANAGER** *Chrysothlypis chrysomelas* (Tángara Negro y Dorado) L 12 cm. ♂ distinctive. Note uniform yellow underparts of ♀. Habitat: forest canopy and edge; 500–1250 m. CRPa.

17   **ROSY THRUSH TANAGER** *Rhodinocichla rosea* (Tángara Huitlacoche/Pechirrosada) L 19 cm. Unmistakable. Terrestrial. Habitat: ground and undergrowth in woodland; sl–1000 m. Voice: high strong rapid *tjúw-to-tjúw*. MeCRPa.

Plate 89

Plate 90

1 **GREYISH SALTATOR** *Saltator coerulescens* (Saltador Grisáceo) L 20 cm. From larger 3 by bib, partly bordered grey, and by white crescent below eye. Habitat: forest edge, open woodland, second growth; sl–1500 m. Voice: high fluted *frèreh Jacqueh dormez-vóus*. WSpr.

2 **STREAKED SALTATOR** *Saltator albicollis* (Saltador Listado) L 18 cm. Heavily streaked below. Habitat: woodland, thickets, cultivations. Voice: ultra high *tzèh*; very high *tju-tjéw-to-tjéw*. CRPa.

3 **BLACK-HEADED SALTATOR** *Saltator atriceps* (Saltador Cabecinegro) L 25 cm. Blackish head with contrasting white chin and eye stripe distinctive. Buff-throated race *suffuscus* (Vera Cruz, not shown) from 4 by black nape. Imm in Laguna de Terminos region may show buff throat, but range of 4 is different. Isolated buff-rufous undertail coverts. Habitat: forest edge, second growth, scrub; sl–1750 m. Voice: cracking powerful nasal *tjih tjihtihwee-* with a dry rattle. WSpr.

4 **BUFF-THROATED SALTATOR** *Saltator maximus* (Saltador Gorjileonado/Gorgianteado) L 20 cm. Some races show only black malar stripe (a, restricted to East Panama), others have full black collar (of these *gigantoides* (b) shown). Yellow-buff on throat diagnostic. Habitat: forest edge, woodland, swamp; sl–1500 m. Voice: high fluted irregular *piuw pjiuw piuhweeh*. SMeCAm.

5 **SLATE-COLOURED GROSBEAK** *Pitylus grossus* (Picogrueso Piquirrojo) L 19 cm. Note red bill and white chin. Habitat: forest (canopy) and nearby more open areas; <1250 m. Voice: short fluted *tutjuteTJU-tutjuWéeh*. U,CAm.

6 **PYRRHULOXIA** *Cardinalis sinuatus* (Cardenal Desértico) L 20 cm. ♂ distinctly patterned. ♀ with pale bill, not pink as 7. Habitat: dry scrub, weedy fields, riverine thickets. Voice: long series of well-separated powerful 2–4 x repeated short phrases with *tuwéet towéet* and *tjuptjuptjup*. Me.

7 **NORTHERN CARDINAL** *Cardinalis cardinalis* (Cardenal Norteño) L 20 cm. ♂ unmistakable. Note red in wings and tail of ♀. Habitat: woodland, thickets, bush; sl–2000 m. Voice: ultra high *tsjik tsjik*; strong varied series full of repeated short syllables. MeBe.

8 **CRIMSON-COLLARED GROSBEAK** *Rhodothraupis celaeno* (Picogrueso Cuellirrojo) L 20 cm. Unmistakable. Habitat: woodland, second growth, scrub; sl–1250 m. E,Me.

9 **ROSE-BREASTED GROSBEAK** *Pheucticus ludovicianus* (Picogrueso Pechirrosado) L 19 cm. Unmistakable. Note white streak through crown of ♀. Habitat: forest, second growth, woodland, gardens; sl–1500 m. Voice: nasal *tjuk tiktik*. WSpr.

10 **BLACK-FACED GROSBEAK** *Caryothraustes poliogaster* (Picogrueso Carinegro) L 18 cm. From smaller 11 by grey upperparts and white belly. Habitat: forest interior and edge, semi-open growth; <1000(1250)m. Voice: very high decisive *tji-tjuw-tjuw-tjúw-tji- -*. SMeCAm.

11 **YELLOW-GREEN GROSBEAK** *Caryothraustes poliogaster* (Picogrueso Amarillo-verdoso) L 16 cm. No overlap in range with 10. Habitat: upper forest levels; 750–1250 m. Voice: very high staccato *tjew tjewtowee tjew - -*. U,Pa.

12 **BLACK-THIGHED GROSBEAK** *Pheucticus tibialis* (Picogrueso Vientriamarillo) L 20 cm. Large, heavy bill and small face mask distinctive. Habitat: forest and adjacent more open country; >(750)1000 m. Voice: high cheerful *wíe er méh gaat wéht ick nog níet*. CRPa.

13 **YELLOW GROSBEAK** *Pheucticus chrysopeplus* (Picogrueso Amarillo) L 24 cm. Unmistakable. Habitat: forest, woodland; sl–2500 m. MeGu.

14 **BLACK-HEADED GROSBEAK** *Pheucticus melanocephalus* (Picogrueso Tigrillo/Cabecinegro) L 20 cm. (?/9). Unmistakable. Note orange glow over breast of ♀. Habitat: dry woodland, thickets; 1500–3000 m. Voice: very high *tic*; very high sharp well-separated *urk irk tjutjuh tjiwee - -*. Me(CR).

15 **BLUE BUNTING** *Cyanocompsa parellina* (Colorín Azulinegro) L 14 cm. From 16 by facial pattern with black cheeks (circling blue spot); bill smaller and uniform dark grey; rump paler blue; Habitat: forest, woodland, scrub; sl–1750 m. Voice*: high *tsip* calls and quite thin and reedy robin-like song broken into phrases of 7 notes, e.g. *sioou-sioou-swipowip seeup-seeup-seeup*. WSpr.

16 **BLUE-BLACK GROSBEAK** *Cyanocompsa cyanoides* (Picogrueso Negro Azulado) L 18 cm. Uniform very dark blue with paler shoulder, cheek and front. Very heavy bill. Habitat: forest, second growth, thickets; sl–1000 m. Voice: very high well-separated fluted *wéet-weet-weetwéeturwéettuweet*. SMeCAm.

17 **GROSBEAK** *Guiraca caerulea* (Picogrueso Azul) L 17 cm. Rufous wing bars diagnostic. Habitat: forest edge, open woodland, cultivations, open areas with scattered trees and hedges; sl–1000(3000)m. Voice: very/ultra high loud rapid twittering (2s). Thr.

Plate 90

Plate 91

1   **INDIGO BUNTING** *Passerina cyanea* (Colorín Azul; Azulillo Norteño) L 13 cm. Less dark, more uniform blue than 90.16, with smaller, bi-coloured bill. See also 92.20 and 93.6 – 9. Habitat: open and semi-open areas with scattered scrub, bush, trees, cleared fields, weedy growth; <1500(2500)m. Voice: sharp *tjic tjic*; very high strong fluted *tsj-weetweetweet*. WSpr.

2   **ROSE-BELLIED** (or Rosita's) **BUNTING** *Passerina rositae* (Colorín de Rosito) L 14 cm. Unmistakable by colour of belly. Note narrow eye ring, in ♀ set in grey face side. Habitat: dry woodland, riverine belts. Voice: ultra high *tsiet*; very high descending *srietsriet--wuhsriet* (4s). E,Me.

3   **VARIED BUNTING** *Passerina versicolor* (Colorín Morado) L 12 cm. Unmistakable in good light; ♀ less well marked than ♀ 4. Habitat: thorn bush, dry woodland, arid scrub; sl–2000 m. Voice: very high sharp warbling strophes (2s). MeGu.

4   **LAZULI BUNTING** *Passerina amoena* (Colorín Lazulita) L 14 cm. Unmistakable; note strong wing bars; ♀ belly brighter than 3 and wing bars better defined. Habitat: woodland; sl–2500 m. Voice: very high sharp warbling strophes (3s). Me.

5   **ORANGE-BREASTED BUNTING** *Passerina leclancherii* (Colorín Pechinaranja) L 12 cm. Unmistakable. Note orange tone to breast of ♀. Habitat: thorn bush, dry woodland, arid scrub; sl–1250 m. Voice: high *wreetohwreetwitwetwit*. E,Me.

6   **PAINTED BUNTING** *Passerina ciris* (Colorín/Azulillo Sietecolores) L 13 cm. Unmistakable by bright red underparts. ♀ is yellow-green. Habitat: dry areas with tree stands, hedges, scrub, forest (winter); 500–1250 m. Voice: very high sharp fluted warbling strophes (2s). WSpr.

7   **DICKCISSEL** *Spiza americana* (Arrocero Americano; Sabanero Arrocero) L 15 cm. House Sparrow-like, but note black-bordered bib of ♂ and malar stripe of ♀. Habitat: open country, neglected fields; sl–1500 m. Voice: *tju-tjiEwtjEwtjEw*. Thr.

8   **WHITE-NAPED BRUSHFINCH** *Atlapetes albinucha* (Saltón Nuquiblanco) L 19 cm. From 9 by yellow belly, breast and range. Note white crown stripe through black hood. Habitat: forest, second growth; 750–2750 m. Voice: very high sustained *tsjeet-tjutsjeet-tjeet- -* (*tju* ultra high). E,Me.

9   **YELLOW-THROATED BRUSHFINCH** *Atlapetes gutturalis* (Saltón Gorjiamarillo/Gargantiamarilla) L 19 cm. Underparts grey, not yellow; no eyebrow. Habitat: weedy and brushy forest edge, plantations, cultivations, gardens; 750–2500(3000)m. Voice*: very high thin, reedy *tseep* notes, sometimes run together to *tseep-sip*. SMeCAm.

10   **RUFOUS-CAPPED BRUSHFINCH** *Atlapetes pileatus* (Saltón Gorrirrufo) L 16 cm. Unmistakable by rich yellow underparts and rufous crown. Habitat: weedy and brushy forest edge, plantations, cultivations; 750–3500 m. E,Me.

11   **CHESTNUT-CAPPED BRUSHFINCH** *Atlapetes brunneinucha* (Saltón Gorricastaño/Cabecicastaño) L 18 cm. Nom (a) and race *apertus* (b) shown. White chin and rufous crown distinctive. Habitat: forest understorey and brushy edge; 750–3500 m. Voice: ultra high weak sizzling (often including thin trills). WSpr.

12   **GREEN-STRIPED BRUSHFINCH** *Atlapetes virenticeps* (Saltón Verdirrayado) L 19 cm. From 13 by buff-green, not grey eye stripe and by different range. Habitat: weedy and brushy forest edge, cultivations; 1750–3500 m. E,Me.

13   **STRIPE-** (or Black-) **HEADED BRUSHFINCH** *Atlapetes atricapillus* (Saltón Cabecinegro) L 19 cm. Note dark grey eye stripe. Habitat: weedy and brushy forest edge; 250–1250 m. Voice*: ultra high notes ending in a short warble; like *pswe-psweer-tsipleswiple-psit*. U,CRPa.

14   **LARGE-FOOTED FINCH** *Pezopetes capitalis* (Saltón Patigrande) L 20 cm. Large size distinctive; very dark with large head. Habitat: montane areas with forest, second growth, overgrown clearings, bamboo. Voice: ultra high fluted *fjueet fijeh* (1/4s), each ultra short. CRPa.

15   **SOOTY-FACED FINCH** *Lysurus crassirostris* (Saltón Barranquero) L 16 cm. White chin and malar stripes distinctive. Habitat: dense undergrowth of steep montane forest. Voice: ultra high thin *tfuuh-tfjéehfjeeh*). CRPa.

16   **ORANGE-BILLED SPARROW** *Arremon aurantiirostris* (Rascador/Pinzón Piquinaranja) L 16 cm. Note orange bill, white, black-bordered throat, white eye stripe. Habitat: dense forest undergrowth; <750(1250)m. Voice: soft explosive *tsji*; ultra high thin warbling *tiktikkutak*. SMeCAm.

▶

Plate 91

Plate 91 continued

17 **WHITE-EARED GROUND SPARROW** *Melozone leucotis* (Rascador/Pinzón Orejiblanco) L 18 cm. Complicated head pattern with broken yellow collar diagnostic. Habitat: dense weedy vegetation at forest edge, thickets, tree stands; (500)1000–2000 m. Voice: ultra/very high thin *seeeweehtititititit*. SMeCAm.

18 **PREVOST'S** (or White-faced) **GROUND SPARROW** *Melozone biarcuatum* (Rascador Patilludo; Saltón Cafetalero) L 16 cm. Race *cabanisi* (a) and nom (b) shown. Note face pattern. Habitat: weedy and scrubby undergrowth, hedgerows, plantations; 100–3000 m. SMeCAm.

19 **RUSTY-CROWNED GROUND SPARROW** *Melozone kieneri* (Rascador Coronirrufo) L 16 cm. Not in range of 18. Habitat: dry woodland, thorn bush, semi-open areas; sl–2000 m. Voice: very high simple calm unstructured *tjitit-tjitit-tututut*. E,Me.

Plate 92

1 **OLIVE SPARROW** *Arremonops rufivirgatus* (Gorrión Oliváceo; Saltón Aceitunado) L 15 cm. From 2 and 3 by buff undertail coverts and brown, not black head stripes except in race *verticalis* (a, Yucatan). Habitat: dense scrub, dry woodland, thickets, riverine belts; <750(1000)m. Voice: very high fluted at the end bouncing-down *tseet tseet tjut tjewd tjeeterrrreweet*. MeBeGuCR.

2 **GREEN-BACKED SPARROW** *Arremonops chloronotus* (Gorrión Dorsiverde) L 16 cm. From 1a by overall brighter colouring with yellow undertail coverts. Habitat: forest edge, thorn bush, dry scrub; <750 m. SMeBeGuHo.

3 **BLACK-STRIPED SPARROW** *Arremonops conirostris* (Saltón Cabecilistado) L 16 cm. No yellow on underparts. Habitat: weedy vegetation, thickets, gardens, woodland; <1500 m. Voice: *wut* (high) --*weeh* (low); *wéet-wéet - - wéet*, accelerated to almost-rattle. CAm.

4 **GREEN-TAILED TOWHEE** *Pipilo chlorurus* (Rascador Coliverde) L 18 cm. Note green wings and tail. Habitat: dry open areas with some scrub and brush; sl–2500 m. Voice: very high varied *tjip drip threeeeh witwitwit--*, ending in fast rattle. Me.

5 **COLLARED TOWHEE** *Pipilo ocai* (Rascador Collarejo) L 20 cm. Dark above with rufous crown. Not in range of 91.16. Habitat: montane forest. Voice: ultra high descending sharp *fjieeeeeh* or strong *wrat-wrat*. E,Me.

6 **RUFOUS–SIDED** (Eastern, or Spotted) **TOWHEE** *Pipilo erythrophthalmus* (Rascador Ojirrojo) L 20 cm. Races *macronyx* (a) and *maculatus* (b) shown. Red eye and rufous flanks diagnostic. Habitat: open forest, areas with bush and scrub; 1000–3500 m. Voice*: high ringing upwardly inflected note *kwéep kwéee kwéeep*. Song includes *plew-plew-plew srréee-rrrr*, ending in rattle. MeGu.

7 **ABERT'S TOWHEE** *Pipilo aberti* (Rascador de Abert) L 20 cm. From 8, 9 and 10 mainly by face pattern, pale bill and black eye. Habitat: desert thickets and scrub, especially near streams. Voice: very high *tseet*'s with slow *tjuweetjuweetjuwee*. U,NMe.

8 **CALIFORNIA TOWHEE** *Pipilo crissalis* (Rascador Californiano) L 20 cm. Note face pattern, cinnamon on flanks, greyish breast. Habitat: scrub, brush, thickets, settlement; sl–2750 m. Voice: very high *tjinc*; ultra high *titjitjiturrrrrrtje*. NMe.

9 **CANYON TOWHEE** *Pipilo fuscus* (Rascador Arroyero) L 20 cm. Rufous stripe through crown distinctive. Habitat: scrub, brush, thickets, settlement; sl–3000 m. Voice: smacking *tjitjitjitjih*. Me.

10 **WHITE-THROATED TOWHEE** *Pipilo albicollis* (Rascador Oaxaqueño) L 20 cm. Note face pattern, narrow necklace and white breast. Habitat: dry scrub, woodland undergrowth; 1000–2500 m. Voice*: very high warbling song, strident in places, accelerating and rising in pitch in phrases. Includes - - *pirrup-pirrup-pirrup- -*. E,Me.

11 **RUDDY-BREASTED SEEDEATER** *Sporophila minuta* (Semillero Pechicanelo; Espiguero Menudo) L 10 cm. Note white wing spot. N-br ♂ as ♀. Habitat: neglected fields, savanna, marsh; sl–1000 m. Voice: high *tjuw*; very high slow warbling (3s). WSpr. Note: ♀♀ of seedeaters very difficult to separate, but normally always with ♂♂, which are easier to recognise.

12 **YELLOW-BELLIED SEEDEATER** *Sporophila nigricollis* (Espiguero Vientriamarillo) L 10 cm. Pale yellowish belly diagnostic. Note slaty bill of ♀. Habitat: open grassy areas. Voice: very high warbling *tidji--tjirip* (3s). CRPa.

▶

Plate 92

Plate 92 continued

13 WHITE-COLLARED SEEDEATER *Sporophila torqueola* (Semillero/Espiguero Collarejo) L 11 cm. Race *morelleti* (a) and nom (b) shown. White collar, narrowly broken at back, distinctive. Habitat: weedy and grassy areas, roadsides, cultivations, marsh; sl–1500 m. Voice: very/ultra high sharp slightly rattling *sweet shweetsritsreeh*. WSpr.

14 LESSON'S SEEDEATER *Sporophila bouvronides* (Espiguero de Lesson) L 11 cm. From 18 by all-black crown. Habitat: weedy and grassy areas, savanna, second growth, often near water. Voice: very high rapid rattled warbling *purrpúrrrrrtjatjatja*. V,Pa.

15 VARIABLE SEEDEATER *Sporophila americana* (Semillero/Espiguero Variable) L 11 cm. Races *corvina* (a) and *hicksii* (b) shown. From 17 by smaller bill. Note lack of wing bars. Habitat: grassy, weedy places, forest edge; <1000 m. Voice: very high cheerful warbling (3s). SMeCAm.

16 SLATE-COLOURED SEEDEATER *Sporophila schistacea* (Semillero Apizarrado; Espiguero Pizarroso) L 11 cm. Coloured slate-grey, not black, with yellow bill. Habitat: grassy areas near open woodland, forest edge; <1000 m. Voice*: very high scratchy sibilant song based around *sip sip-serreee psweeeo-psweeeoo*. U,CAm.

17 THICK-BILLED SEEDFINCH *Oryzoborus angolensis* (Semillero Piquigrueso/Picogrueso) L 12 cm. Thick bill diagnostic. Habitat: savanna, open woodland, forest edge; sl–1500 m. Voice: very high full fluted crescendoing strophes, often ending in nasal trills (6s). V,Pa.

18 LINED SEEDEATER *Sporophila lineola* (Semillero Lineado) L 11 cm. Note white stripe through crown. Habitat: savanna, open woodland, overgrown fields. SMeCAm.

19 NICARAGUAN (or Pink-billed) SEEDFINCH *Oryzoborus nuttingi* (Semillero Piquirrosado) L 15 cm. Massive bill diagnostic. Habitat: marshy, grassy and weedy areas. Voice: high irregular *petertjuwpetertjuwwuw*. U,NiCRPa.

20 BLUE-BLACK GRASSQUIT *Volatinia jacarina* (Semillero Brincador; Semillerito Negro Azulado) L 11 cm. Indigo-blue with fine pointed bill. Note striped underparts of ♀. Habitat: grassy and weedy areas, low scrub; <1750 m. Voice*: high warbling song of 3 strophes of musical warbles and rattles, slows to finish on 3 distinct notes *tu zieu zieu*. Also harsh 'fizzing' calls. WSpr.

Plate 93

1 SAFFRON FINCH *Sicalis flaveola* (Pinzón Sabanero Azafranado) L 14 cm. Unmistakable, no other uniform yellow bird in the area. Habitat: open woodland, savanna, suburban regions. Voice: very/ultra high unstructured warbling *tit-weertit- - tjitweet* (2s). I,Pa.

2 GRASSLAND YELLOWFINCH *Sicalis luteola* (Zacatero Amarillo; Chirigüe Sabanero) L 11 cm. No similar bird in its range. Habitat: grassland, fields. Voice: very high nasal hurried warbling (>10s). U,WSpr.

3 YELLOW-FACED GRASSQUIT *Tiaris olivacea* (Semillero/ito Oliváceo/Cariamarillo) L 11 cm. Unmistakable. Habitat: weedy and grassy areas, thickets, roadsides; sl–2000 m. Voice: ultra high short trill *srrrr*. WSpr.

4 YELLOW-GREEN FINCH *Pselliophorus luteoviridis* (Saltón Amarillo-verdoso) L 18 cm. From 5 by body colouring. Habitat: forest undergrowth, wet brush; 1250–1750 m. E,Pa.

5 YELLOW-THIGHED FINCH *Pselliophorus tibialis* (Saltón de Muslos Amarillos) L 18 cm. Unmistakable by yellow thighs. Habitat: undergrowth at forest edge; >1500 m. Voice*: very high staccato phrases of jangling sibilant notes and high trills. CRPa.

6 BLUE SEEDEATER *Amaurospiza concolor* (Semillero Azul/Azulado) L 13 cm. From 91.1 by uniform dull blue, not pure blue colouring; from 92.20 by blunt bill and different habitat; from 7 by different range. Habitat: forest edge, woodland, shrubbery, bamboo; 500–2000 m. U,CAm.

7 SLATE-BLUE SEEDEATER *Amaurospiza relicta* (Semillero Azuligrís) L 13 cm. (?/6). Paler than 6; no overlap in range. Habitat: forest undergrowth, bamboo, shrubbery; 1250–2500 m. E,Me.

8 SLATY FINCH *Haplospiza rustica* (Fringilo Plomizo) L 13 cm. Dark slate-grey coloured. Note faint breast striping running up to throat. Habitat: forest and adjacent areas, especially bamboo when seeding; 1250–3000 m. Voice: very/ultra high rapid nasal hurried *sréetosréetiweet*. U,WSpr.

▶

Plate 93

Plate 93 continued

9   **COCOS FINCH** *Pinaroloxias inornata* (Pinzón de la Isla del Coco)   L 12 cm. No similar bird on Cocos Island. Habitat: forest, woodland, open areas. E,CR.

10   **SLATY FLOWERPIERCER** *Diglossa plumbea* (Pinchaflor Plomizo)   L 10 cm. Bill shape diagnostic. Habitat: at flowering trees and shrub in or near montane forest. Voice: ultra high *sreesreesreeruhsreeh*. CRPa.

11   **CINNAMON-BELLIED FLOWERPIERCER** *Diglossa baritula* (Picaflor Vientre-canelo)   L 11 cm. Unmistakable. Habitat: flowering trees and shrub in montane forest, gardens; 1250–3500 m. Voice: very high short nasal fast twittering *witwitwitwitweetfjeetwhéet*. WSpr.

12   **PEG-BILLED FINCH** *Acanthidops bairdii* (Fringilo Piquiagudo)   L 14 cm. Very dark with distinctive bill shape and pale lower mandible. Variable (may be darker or paler than shown). Feeds on the ground. Note yellowish lore and moustache. Habitat: montane forest edge and clearings, bamboo. Voice*: very high buzzing and insect-like *spss spss spss*, unstructured, but mostly in twos and threes. Also ultra high single whistle. U,CRPa.

13   **SAVANNA SPARROW** *Passerculus sandwichensis* (Gorrión Sabanero; Sabanero Zanjero)   L 14 cm. Habitat: grassland, marsh; 1250–2500 m. Voice: ultra high thin *tsip*. WSpr.

14   **SEASIDE SPARROW** *Ammodramus maritimus* (Gorrión Marino)   L 14 cm. Note yellow over lore, dusky eye region, long bill. Habitat: coastal weedy marsh. V,NMe.

15   **SIERRA MADRE SPARROW** *Ammodramus baileyi* (Gorrión Serrano)   L 12 cm. Note notched tail, brown wings, tawny sides; yellow wing bend in flight. Habitat: localised in grassy, open pine woodland; 2250–3000 m. Voice: *pjíew*; simple partly inhaled partly nasal *tjiet-weeh-weh- -*. E,Me.

16   **BAIRD'S SPARROW** *Ammodramus bairdii* (Gorrión de Baird)   L 13 cm. Pale overall, grey streak through cheek. Habitat: grassland; 1250–2000 m. Voice: very high *tsji-tsji-terrrrrr*. U,NMe.

17   **LE CONTE'S SPARROW** *Ammodramus leconteii* (Gorrión de Le Conte)   L 12 cm. Note silvery lores and cheeks, patterned upperparts with white in mantle. Habitat: grassland, fields. V,Me.

18   **SHARP-TAILED SPARROW** *Ammodramus caudacutus* (Gorrión Coliagudo)   L 13 cm. Orange in face and rufous in wings diagnostic. Habitat: mainly in salt marshes. Voice*: high discordant hissing and jangling song including a distinctive nasal ringing phrase *--reeooreeoreeo*. Also very high insect-like *sip* calls. V,Me.

19   **GRASSHOPPER SPARROW** *Ammodramus savannarum* (Gorrión Chapulín; Sabanero Colicorto)   L 12 cm. Underparts unmarked except thin striping on breast sides. Habitat: grassland, fields; sl–2500 m. Voice: ultra high *tiitjt-srrrrrrrr* (grasshopper-like). Thr.

Plate 94

1   **STRIPED SPARROW** *Oriturus superciliosus* (Zacatonero Rayado)   L 17 cm. Note large size, thickset jizz, black bill, dark cheek, narrow white streak through brown crown. Habitat: grassland shrubby areas, open pine woodland; 1500–3500 m. Voice: ultra high rattle *tit-tjtjtjtjtj*. E,Me.

2   **FIELD SPARROW** *Spizella pusilla* (Gorrión Llanero)   L 14 cm. Long tail characteristic. Note pink bill, white eye ring. Habitat: dry grassland with scattered trees and brush; <500 m. Voice: sharp *tsjip*. U,NMe.

3   **WORTHEN'S SPARROW** *Spizella wortheni* (Gorrión de Worthen)   L 13 cm. Note unmarked face sides, which are grey as collar around neck, white eye ring. Habitat: dry grassland with scattered trees and brush; 1250–2500 m. Voice: cicada-like very high rattle *tjitji--* (1s). E,Me.

4   **BREWER'S SPARROW** *Spizella breweri* (Gorrión de Brewer)   L 13 cm. Small, dull-coloured, white eye ring. Habitat: dry grassland with scattered trees and brush; sl–2500 m. Voice: thin *tsjip*. NMe.

5   **BLACK-CHINNED SPARROW** *Spizella atrogularis* (Gorrión Barbinegro)   L 14 cm. Head all-grey with black mask in summer plumage. Habitat: dry open areas with some grass, brush, scrub; 250–2500 m. Voice: varied strophes as *tjeeh tjuw-tjeehweeterwirrrrr*, each ending in a trill. Me.

6   **CHIPPING SPARROW** *Spizella passerina* (Gorrión Cejiblanco; Chimbito Común)   L 13 cm. Note black lore, grey rump. Habitat: open grassy woodland, fields; 1000–3500 m. Voice: trills of varied pitch (3s). WSpr.

▶

Plate 94

Plate 94 continued

7 CLAY-COLOURED SPARROW *Spizella pallida* (Gorrión Pálido) L 13 cm. Less brightly coloured than 6 with slightly more contrasting grey neck, brown rump. Habitat: dry grassland with scattered trees and brush; sl–2750 m. Voice: thin *tsjirp*. MeGu.

8 SAGE SPARROW *Amphispiza belli* (Gorrión de Artemesia) L 15 cm. Note spot in front of eye, drab colouring, white outer tail feathers. Habitat: dry open areas with scattered bush and trees; sl–2000 m. Voice: very high hurried *tsittsoohtsitwurrrrtsittsit*. NMe.

9 BLACK-THROATED SPARROW *Amphispiza bilineata* (Gorrión Gorjinegro) L 14 cm. Unmistakable by clean black bib and unmarked body feathering. Habitat: open areas with scattered bush, cacti; sl–2500 m. Voice: hurried *tsitsiputsipurrrrr* (like an old fashioned alarm clock). NMe.

10 BLACK-CHESTED SPARROW *Aimophila humeralis* (Zacatonero Pechinegro) L 16 cm. Black breast distinctive. Habitat: dry scrub, woodland. Voice: ultra high *pwchit-tsíwíwíwí--*, developing into rattle. E,Me.

11 BRIDLED SPARROW *Aimophila mystacalis* (Zacatonero Bigote-blanco) L 16 cm. Resembling 10, but note black bib and different patterned back. Habitat: Voice: ultra high *ts-tsiet-tswi-twet*-rattle. E,Me.

12 FIVE-STRIPED SPARROW *Aimophila quinquestriata* (Zacatonero de Cinco-rayas) L 15 cm. From 9 by white throat, black spot on breast. Habitat: dry rocky areas with dense scrub. Voice: very high *titji* or *tjitjuw* or *tjewtjew* or similar rattles. Me.

13 STRIPE-HEADED SPARROW *Aimophila ruficauda* (Zacatonero Cabecirrayada; Sabanero Cabecilistado) L 17 cm. Head pattern with white stripe through black crown distinctive. Habitat: dry rock areas with patches of dry scrub. Voice: high hurried scratchy *petsútsjetsjúse wróng*. WSpr.

14 CASSIN'S SPARROW *Aimophila cassinii* (Zacatonero de Cassin) L 14cm. Note spotted mantle, narrow malar stripe, slightly peaked crown. As 13 with pale tail corners. Habitat: dry open areas with grass, scattered trees and brush; sl–2500 m. Voice: sharp *tsjeetutrrrweet* (metallic and varying in pitch). Me.

15 BOTTERI'S SPARROW *Aimophila botterii* (Zacatonero de Botteri; Sabanero Pechianteado) L 14 cm. Nom (a) and race *arizonae* (b) shown. From 14 by unmarked breast and flank sides and lack of malar stripe. Habitat: dry open woodland, savanna, fields; sl–2500 m. Voice: ultra high *tsjuh* or *fjuweet weet weetweetwerit* (as almost-rattle). WSpr.

16 CINNAMON-TAILED (or Sumichrast's) SPARROW *Aimophila sumichrasti* (Zacatonero de Sumichrast) L 16 cm. Cinnamon tail distinctive. Restricted range. Habitat: dry scrub; sl–1000 m. Voice: ultra high sharp hurried *tsjitsji--* or *tsitsitrrrrr*. E,Me.

17 RUFOUS-WINGED SPARROW *Aimophila carpalis* (Zacatonero Alirrufo) L 14 cm. Rufous shoulders diagnostic. From 18 - 20 by absence of white in face. Habitat: dry grassland with scattered trees and brush; sl–1250 m. Voice: very high rattling *tjut-wéetwetwetwetwet*. NMe.

18 RUFOUS-CROWNED SPARROW *Aimophila ruficeps* (Zacatonero Coronirrufo) L 14 cm. Note grey breast, grey in mantle and distinct eye ring. Habitat: dry rocky areas with scrub, bush, some grass; 750–3000 m. Voice: ultra high rapid slightly descending warbling *tseetseetseeweeewirwheer*. Me.

19 OAXACA SPARROW *Aimophila notosticta* (Zacatonero Oaxaqueño) L 16 cm. From 18 by warmer upperparts, from larger 20 by all-black bill. Habitat: dry scrub, open woodland; 1500–2000 m. Voice: ultra high sharp *tsjéeh-wehwehwehweehweeh*. E,Me.

20 RUSTY SPARROW *Aimophila rufescens* (Zacatonero/Sabanero Rojizo) L 18 cm. Nom (a) and race *discolor* (b) shown. Bolder face pattern than 19. Habitat: forest edge, dry woodland, scrubby areas, overgrown fields; 500–2750 m. Voice: varied, e.g. very high rapid *tsjech-tehtehtjuw*. WSpr.

Plate 95 continued

MCCOWN'S LONGSPUR *Calcarius mccownii* (Escribano de McCown)   L 15 cm. Note rufous shoulders. Tail mostly white except central tail feathers. Habitat: open areas with some short grass; 1000–2500 m. Voice: dry rattle *trrp*. U,NMe.

LAPLAND LONGSPUR *Calcarius lapponicus* (Escribano Artico)   L 16 cm. Extent of red in wing diagnostic. Outer two pairs of tail feathers white. Habitat: open grassland, fields. Voice: *tjrrut*. V,NMe.

CHESTNUT-COLLARED LONGSPUR *Calcarius ornatus* (Escribano Cuellicastaño)   L 14 cm. No red in wing; from 19 by distinct wing bars. Only outer pair of tail feathers and tips of second pair white. Habitat: open grassland and fields, often at lakes; 1000–2500 m. Voice: rapid *trrtrr*. Me.

Plate 95

1   **WEDGE-TAILED GRASS FINCH** *Emberizoides herbicola* (Sabanero Coludo)   L 18 cm. Very long pointed tail distinctive. Habitat: savanna, grassland, fields; sl–2000 m. Voice: very high fast short twitter *tut-tjerwih*. U,CRPa.

2   **LARK BUNTING** *Calamospiza melanocorys* (Gorrión Alipálido)   L 15 cm. Unmistakable in S plumage; note distinct white border of cheek and white in wings of other plumages. Habitat: open areas with grass and bush. Voice: nasal *èèh*; loud varied sustained *tjuwtjuwtjuwwuutwut--*. Me.

3   **VESPER SPARROW** *Pooecetes gramineus* (Gorrión Coliblanco)   L 15 cm. Note eye ring and pale centre to cheek, rufous shoulder. Bill smaller and crown less distinctly striped than 93.13. Habitat: dry brush, savanna, fields, open woodland; sl–2500 m. Voice: thin *tsjeet*. Me(Gu).

4   **LARK SPARROW** *Chondestes grammacus* (Gorrión Arlequín)   L 16 cm. Distinctly patterned. Note dark spot on breast. Habitat: open grass plains with some trees and bush; 1000–2000 m. Voice: ultra high *tsittsit*; stream of short very high strophes like *purrpurr* or *turrrrt* or *fjufju*. WSpr.

5   **FOX SPARROW** *Passerella iliaca* (Gorrión Rascador)   L 18 cm. Very variable, grey and red forms (a, b) shown. Note large size; eye stripe absent or weak. Habitat: forest undergrowth, woodland, scrub, thickets; sl–2750 m. Voice: ultra high *tsjek* or very high *tjic tjic*. U,NMe.

6   **SONG SPARROW** *Melospiza melodia* (Gorrión Cantor)   L 15 cm. Races *mexicana* (a) and *saltonis* (b) shown. From 5 by grey, pointed bill, prominent eye stripe, streaks on neck and mantle. Habitat: marsh, grassy areas near water, forest edge; sl–2500 m. Voice: high *wew wew*; very high *tjip*. Me.

7   **SWAMP SPARROW** *Melospiza georgiana* (Gorrión Pantanero)   L 14 cm. Note cinnamon cheeks, pure grey eyebrow and neck sides. Wings dark rufous. Habitat: fringing vegetation at water, wet grassland; sl–1750 m. Voice: sharp *tjeek*. Me.

8   **LINCOLN'S SPARROW** *Melospiza lincolnii* (Gorrión/Sabanero de Lincoln)   L 14 cm. Note buff around cheek patch extending down breast and flanks. Finely striped below. Habitat: weedy fields, brushy grassland, marsh, forest edge; sl–3000 m. Voice: very high *tsjeh*. WSpr.

9   **RUFOUS-COLLARED SPARROW** *Zonotrichia capensis* (Gorrión Chingolo; Chingolo) L 18 cm. Rufous collar distinctive. Habitat: cultivation, suburbs. Voice: very high *ih-witwitwitwitwit* as fast rattle. SMeCAm.

10   **WHITE-THROATED SPARROW** *Zonotrichia albicollis* (Gorrión Gorjiblanco)   L 16 cm. From 13 by white chin. Note spotted wing bars. Habitat: forest, open woodland, brush; sl–1250 m. Voice: ultra high metallic *tjirrup*. U,NMe.

11   **HARRIS'S SPARROW** *Zonotrichia querula* (Gorrión de Harris)   L 19 cm. No white on head except indistinct eye ring. Habitat: shrubby woodland. Hyp,NMe.

12   **GOLDEN-CROWNED SPARROW** *Zonotrichia atricapilla* (Gorrión Coronidorado)   L 17 cm. Note broad black eyebrow and partly golden crown. Habitat: bush land, scrubby areas, thickets; sl–2750 m. Voice: very high soft *tjerrup tjip-tjiptjip*. U,NMe.

13   **WHITE-CROWNED SPARROW** *Zonotrichia leucophrys* (Gorrión Coroniblanco)   L 17 cm. From smaller 10 by grey chin, pink bill, all-white eyebrow. Habitat: open woodland, brush, hedgerows; sl–2500 m. Voice: ultra high staccato *tjic tjic tjictjic - -* . Me.

14   **DARK-EYED JUNCO** *Junco hyemalis* (Junco Ojioscuro)   L 15 cm. Of several races nom (a), *oreganus* (b) and *caniceps* (c) shown. Unmistakable. Habitat: forest edge, open woodland, brushy areas; 1000–2500 m. Voice: smacking *tut-tut-tut*; very high sharp trill (2s). NMe.

15   **YELLOW-EYED JUNCO** *Junco phaeonotus* (Junco Ojilumbre)   L 16 cm. From 16 by different wing pattern, bi-coloured bill, different range. Habitat: open woodland, brush; 1250–3500 m. Voice: very high *tjutjutswrrrrrrrrohweehweeh*. MeGu.

16   **BAIRD'S JUNCO** *Junco bairdi* (Junco de Baird)   L 15 cm. (?/15). No similar bird in its range. Habitat: open woodland, savanna with scattered brush; 1250–2000 m. E,Me.

17   **GUADELUPE JUNCO** *Junco insularis* (Junco de Guadalupe)   L 15 cm. (?/14). No similar bird on Guadalupe. Habitat: steep woodland, scrub. E,Me (no map).

18   **VOLCANO JUNCO** *Junco vulcani* (Junco Paramero)   L 16 cm. No similar pale-eyed bird in its range and habitat. Habitat: open ground, low, dense bamboo; <2500 m. Voice*: very high short warbling phrase like *splipseewipseeklip* repeated. E,CRPa.

◀

Plate 95

Plate 96

1 **EASTERN MEADOWLARK** *Sturnella magna* (Pradero/Zacatero Común) L 25 cm. Very difficult to separate from 2, but generally brighter, especially crown and eye stripes; more white to tail sides. Best separated by song and calls. Habitat: savanna, grassland, fields; sl–2500 m. Voice: very high fluting *tjítjitwéeehohweer*. Thr.

2 **WESTERN MEADOWLARK** *Sturnella neglecta* (Pradero Occidental) L 25 cm. See 1. Habitat: savanna, grassland, fields; sl–2500 m. Voice: very high short hurried *fjífjuweeohweet*. Me.

3 **RED-BREASTED BLACKBIRD** *Sturnella militaris* (Tordo Pechirrojo) L 17 cm. Unmistakable. ♀ with some pink on breast. Habitat: savanna, grassland; <1000 m. Voice: very high inhaled disyllabic *sréwèèèh*. CRPa.

4 **MELODIOUS BLACKBIRD** *Dives dives* (Tordo Cantor) L 25 cm. Frequently flicks tail up. From similar all-black skulking 79.2 by different habitat. Habitat: open areas with scattered tree stands, bush, hedges; sl–2500 m. Voice: high melodious *whut whée-ut* or drawn-up *trrrr-uweeeét*. WSpr.

5 **RUSTY BLACKBIRD** *Euphagus carolinus* (Tordo Canadiense) L 20 cm. Only winter plumage (paler than similar 6) shown. Summer plumage as 6, but prefers different habitat. Habitat: open, swampy areas. Voice: very high rapid short drawn-up warbling ending ultra high *fjeeet*. V,NMe.

6 **BREWER'S BLACKBIRD** *Euphagus cyanocephalus* (Tordo de Brewer) L 25 cm. See 5. Habitat: open woodland, grassland, fields, brushy areas, cultivations; sl–1750(3000)m. Voice: ultra high *sisjeet* or very high *tjit* or *tjuw*. Me(Gu). Note: blackbirds have different summer and winter plumages, grackles and cowbirds do not.

7 **SLENDER-BILLED GRACKLE** *Quiscalus palustris* (Tordo Pantanero) L 35 cm. Thin bill distinctive. Habitat: marsh. E,Me, but probably extinct.

8 **GREAT-TAILED GRACKLE** *Quiscalus mexicanus* (Zanate Mayor; Clarinero Grande) L 40 cm. Large tail distinctive; flatter-headed than 10; ♀ colder brown. Habitat: grassland, fields, marsh, mangrove, suburban regions. Voice: very/ultra high shrill loud drawn-up *shreeét-weetweetweettit--*. Thr.

9 **COMMON GRACKLE** *Quiscalus quiscula* (Tordo Común) L 30 cm. Note greenish body gloss. Habitat: forest edge, open woodland, marsh, suburban regions. Voice: very high sharp twittering. Hyp,NMe.

10 **BOAT-TAILED GRACKLE** *Quiscalus major* (Tordo del Costa) L 40 cm. Note rounded head; ♀ is warm brown. Habitat: marsh and adjacent open areas. Voice: ultra high rasping *--shrshrishri--* with very high *--tjuptjup--*. Hyp,NMe.

11 **NICARAGUAN GRACKLE** *Quiscalus nicaraguensis* (Clarinero de Laguna) L 30 cm. Much shorter-tailed than 8; note grey in ♀ face. Habitat: wet grassland, fields, marsh. Voice: ultra/very high shrieks, shivers and drawn-up notes. NiCR.

12 **GIANT COWBIRD** *Scaphidura oryzivora* (Vaquero Gigante/Grande) L 35 cm. Large size and thick-necked jizz distinctive. Eye might be pale. Habitat: savanna, open woodland, fields; sl–750 m. Voice: very high dry short rattles, croaks and ultra high short *wreetteet*. U,SMeCAm.

13 **SHINY COWBIRD** *Molothrus bonariensis* (Vaquero Brilloso) L 20 cm. Overall shiny blue-violet; ♀ overall dark grey-brown (without gloss) and with dark eyes. Habitat: open woodland, fields, marsh, suburban regions; sl–2000 m. Voice: ultra high *fjeet*, rattles and very high warbled notes. YMePa.

14 **BRONZED** (or Red-eyed) **COWBIRD** *Molothrus aeneus* (Vaquero Ojirrojo) L 20 cm. Note ruff in neck, red eyes, shiny wings; ♀ overall very dark brown (without gloss) and with red eyes. Habitat: open woodlands, grasslands, fields, scrubland, suburban regions; sl–3000 m. Voice: ultra high inhaled flutes with dry rattles. Thr.

15 **BROWN-HEADED COWBIRD** *Molothrus ater* (Vaquero Cabecicafé) L 17 cm. Note greenish body, contrasting brown head. Paler below than 14 and with whitish chin; ♀ overall brown (without gloss) and with dark eyes and pale chin. Habitat: forest, woodland, savanna, areas with scattered trees. Voice: ultra high inhaled flutes with high *prittit*. Me.

16 **CRESTED OROPENDOLA** *Psarocolius decumanus* (Oropéndola Crestada) L 40 cm. From smaller 17 by different bill form and darker head. Habitat: forest clearings, tall second growth; <1000 m. Voice: very varied crackles, running-up bubbling, magpie-like chatters and sharp rattles. Pa.

▶

Plate 96

Plate 96 continued <DESIGNER: more text moved over>

17   CHESTNUT-HEADED (or Wagler's) OROPENDOLA *Psarocolius wagleri* (Oropéndola Cabecicastaña)   L 35 cm. See 16. Habitat: forest, tree stands; sl–1750 m. Voice: mellow barking, bubbling interlaced with sharp chatters and rattles. SMeCAm.

18   MONTEZUMA OROPENDOLA *Psarocolius montezuma* (Oropéndola de Moctezuma)   L 50 cm. From 19 by mainly rufous body. Ranges do not overlap. Habitat: forest, tall trees; sl–1500 m. Voice: low hurried bubbling *orreurreorre* together with nasal rhythmic hissing ending in *Whéw* flutes. SMeCAm.

19   BLACK OROPENDOLA *Psarocolius guatimozinus* (Oropéndola Negra)   L 45 cm. Blacker than 18. Habitat: forest canopy, tall trees. Voice: running-up bubbling together with unmelodious shrieks. U,Pa.

Plate 97

1   BLACK-COWLED ORIOLE *Icterus dominicensis* (Bolsero Capucha-negra)   L 20 cm. Black on breast further down than 2, with pure yellow underparts. Note black wings and mask of imm and ♀. Habitat: forest edge and clearings, semi-open areas with scattered trees; sl–500 m. Voice: very high sharp-fluted cautious *sweetohsweeterrohweeet*. SMeCAm.

2   BLACK-VENTED ORIOLE *Icterus wagleri* (Bolsero de Wagler)   L 20 cm. Black under- and uppertail coverts diagnostic. Habitat: dry scrub, areas with scattered trees and hedges; 500–2500 m. Voice: low *wèk*; high sharp strophes like *purowéet*. WSpr.

3   BAR-WINGED ORIOLE *Icterus maculialatus* (Bolsero Guatemalteco)   L 20 cm. From 4 by different range and deep yellow shoulder bar. Habitat: woodland, semi-open country with scattered trees; 750–1250 m. Voice: very high meandering fluting *fjeefjeewuweehwee*. SMeGuHoSa.

4   SCOTT'S ORIOLE *Icterus parisorum* (Bolsero Tunero)   L 20 cm. See 3; note yellow base to tail feathers. Habitat: dry woodland, desert scrub; sl–3000 m. Voice: very high sharp warbling *titjuwtjiwuwerwur*. Me.

5   AUDUBON'S (or Black-headed) ORIOLE *Icterus graduacauda* (Bolsero de Audubon)   L 25 cm. Nom (a) and race *dickeyae* (b) shown. Isolated black at head diagnostic. Habitat: forest edge and clearings, woodland; 500–2500 m. Voice: very high well-spaced *teetjouwtjaw-tjaw tjee - -*. Me.

6   YELLOW-TAILED ORIOLE *Icterus mesomelas* (Bolsero Coliamarillo)   L 20 cm. Note yellow wing bar, running from wing bend through secondaries. Habitat: forest edge, woodland, mangrove; <250 m. Voice: hurried fluted *wheetohréet* . WSpr.

7   YELLOW-BACKED ORIOLE *Icterus chrysater* (Bolsero Dorsidorado)   L 20 cm. Yellow back and all-black tail diagnostic. Habitat: woodland, areas with hedges and bush; 500–2500 m. Voice: very high fluted *tíeehtju-tjuítjéeh*. WSpr.

8   ORANGE-CROWNED ORIOLE *Icterus auricapillus* (Bolsero Real)   L 20 cm. From 9 –15 by all-black flight feathers. Habitat: forest edge, second growth; sl–2000 m. Voice: very high descending *whíeeh*. U,Pa.

9   SPOT-BREASTED ORIOLE *Icterus pectoralis* (Bolsero Pechimanchado)   L 25 cm. Spots to breast sides diagnostic, but these often difficult to see. From 13 by different wing pattern. Introduced on Cocos Island. Habitat: dry open woodland; <1500 m. Voice: high mellow robin-like flutes *whéepuweréet*. WSpr.

10   ORANGE ORIOLE *Icterus auratus* (Bolsero Yucateco)   L 19 cm. Orange mantle diagnostic. Habitat: dry open woodland. Voice: high *tíutju tjuh* or rattling staccato *titjutjutju--*. YMe.

11   STREAK-BACKED ORIOLE *Icterus pustulatus* (Bolsero Dorsirrayado/Dorsilistado)   L 20 cm. Races *microstictus* (a), *graysoni* (b) and *alticola* (c) shown. Wings patterned with grey, not with white. Note streaked/spotted mantle. Habitat: bush land, dry woodland, scrub; sl–1750 m. Voice: very high sharp-fluted *itchee-itchee-itch* or tit-like calls. WSpr.

12   HOODED ORIOLE *Icterus cucullatus* (Bolsero Cuculado)   L 19 cm. Races *nelsoni* (a) and *ignaeus* (b) shown. From similar double wing-banded 10 by black mantle and more extensive black on throat and breast. Habitat: woodland; open areas with scattered bush and trees; sl–1500 m. Voice: very high hurried fluted short twitters. MeBe.

▶

Plate 97

Plate 97 continued

13 **ALTAMIRA ORIOLE** *Icterus gularis* (Bolsero de Altamira) L 25 cm. Races *tamaulipensis* (a) and *flavescens* (b) shown. Note wing pattern with only one white bar. Habitat: open woodland; <1250 m. Voice: *shret-shret- -*; meandering fluted whistles *uh-wer-weeh-oh-wir-wee- -*. WSpr.

14 **BULLOCK'S ORIOLE** *Icterus bullockii* (Bolsero de Bullock) L 19 cm. Nom (a) and race *abeillei* (b) shown. (?/15). Head pattern and extensive white in wing distinctive. Habitat: forest, dry woodland, suburban regions; sl(1000)–3000 m. Voice: yelping and chirping *whetwhet-ictariteeteet*. MeGu.

15 **BALTIMORE** (or Northern) **ORIOLE** *Icterus galbula* (Bolsero de Baltimore/Norteño) L 19 cm. Dark summer plumage of ♂ unmistakable. Note olive-green mantle with double white wing bar of other plumages. Habitat: forest edge, woodland, suburban regions; sl–2500 m. Voice: high loud chirping *pirrepirre weet*-chatter. WSpr.

16 **ORCHARD ORIOLE** *Icterus spurius* (Bolsero Castaño) L 16 cm. Race *fuertesi* (Ochre Oriole, not shown) similar, but paler. Only black-headed oriole with chestnut/ochre, not yellow body Habitat: forest edge, orchards, suburban regions; sl–2000 m. Voice: very high fluted sometimes sharp *ictustweereweetwet--*. Thr.

17 **YELLOW-WINGED CACIQUE** *Cacicus melanicterus* (Cacique Mexicano) L 30 cm. Unmistakable. From 18 by thinner bill and black eye. Habitat: forest edge, open woodland, gardens. MeGu.

18 **YELLOW-RUMPED CACIQUE** *Cacicus cela* (Cacique Lomiamarillo) L 25 cm. Unmistakable. Habitat: forest canopy, scattered trees; <500 m. Voice: explosive *tsjew*; nasal shrieks like *wreetwitwitwit* or inhaled rattles or magpie-like chatters. Pa.

19 **SCARLET-RUMPED CACIQUE** *Cacicus uropygialis* (Cacique Lomiescarlata) L 25 cm. Unmistakable. Habitat: forest canopy, tall trees; <1250 m. Voice: very high hurried crescendoing *whiowhiowhiowheetor* starling-like strophes. CAm.

20 **YELLOW-BILLED CACIQUE** *Amblycercus holosericeus* (Cacique Piquiclaro/Picoplato) L 25 cm. Note long, yellowish bill and pale yellow, not blue eye. Habitat: dense undergrowth at forest edge; <3000 m. Voice: high *fiju-tjúw*. WSpr.

Plate 98

1 **BOBOLINK** *Dolichonyx oryzivorus* (Tordo Arrocero) L 16 cm. ♂ in br plumage unmistakable. Other plumages as sparrows but generally larger with pale nape and lores. Habitat: grassy areas with trees and scrub. Voice: very/ultra high nasal *wéetjurrewéetwéet--* or *wreeet tjurrewer-it*. U,WSpr.

2 **RED-WINGED BLACKBIRD** *Agelaius phoeniceus* (Tordo Sargento) L 25 cm. From 3 by buff, not white wing bar. Habitat: marsh, fields; sl–2500 m. Voice: very/ultra high scratchy *wutwutchéeeruw*. WSpr.

3 **TRICOLOURED BLACKBIRD** *Agelaius tricolor* (Tordo Tricolor) L 20 cm. Note contrasting white wing bar. ♀ from ♀ 2 by grey-brown plumage overall without rufous feather edges above and with less distinct streaking below. Habitat: marsh, fields. Voice: dry toneless croaking and chattering in chorus. NMe.

4 **YELLOW-HOODED BLACKBIRD** *Agelaius icterocephalus* (Tordo de Agua) L 25 cm. No white in wing and undertail coverts. Habitat: marsh, swamp. Voice: very high twittering interlaced with long inhaled notes. No map. Hyp, occurs in lowlands of northern South America.

5 **YELLOW-HEADED BLACKBIRD** *Xanthocephalus xanthocephalus* (Tordo Cabeciamarillo/ Cabecidorado) L 25 cm. Note white in wings and small yellow patch on undertail coverts. Habitat: marsh, fields; sl–2500 m. Voice: varied high hoarse hooting or toy-trumpet-like shrieking. WSpr.

6 **PURPLE FINCH** *Carpodacus purpureus* (Fringílido Purpureo) L 15 cm. ♂ extensively pink above and below; ♀ from ♀ 7 by distinct eyebrow. Habitat: forest interior and edge, woodland; sl–2500 m. Voice: *tjeet tjrrt*; very high rapid warbling round basic *-trrreeh-* sound. U,NMe.

7 **CASSIN'S FINCH** *Carpodacus cassinii* (Fringílido de Cassin) L 15 cm. From 6 by contrasting red forehead, ♀ by indistinct eyebrow. Habitat: dry woodland; 2000–3500 m. Voice: very high sharp hurried warbling U,Me.

▶

Plate 98

Plate 98 continued

8   **HOUSE FINCH** *Carpodacus mexicanus* (Fringílido Mexicano)   L 15 cm. Slender jizz, short bill, striped flanks. Habitat: open woodland, savanna, dry scrub, towns. Voice: *wurk*; e.g. descending *witwitwitwittefjeetohfjeet*. Me.

9   **RED CROSSBILL** *Loxia curvirostra* (Picotuerto Rojo)   L 15 cm. Unmistakable bill. Habitat: pine and mixed forest; 1000–3500 m. Voice: *jip-jip-jip* or *tjurp tjurp*; *pjtrSítSítSít djurp*. U,WSpr.

10   **PINE SISKIN** *Carduelis pinus* (Dominico Pinero)   L 12 cm. Striping to flanks and yellow in wings and tail variable, but note greyish head and mantle. Habitat: pine forest, woodland, open areas with scattered trees; 1750–3500 m. Voice: drawn-out *shrée*. Me(Gu).

11   **LAWRENCE'S GOLDFINCH** *Carduelis lawrencei* (Dominico de Lawrence)   L 12 cm. Unmistakable by grey colouring with yellow restricted to wings and green to breast and rump. Habitat: dry open woodland, bush land; sl–2500 m. Voice: *tihóoh*; very high nasal twittering. U,NMe.

12   **BLACK-CAPPED SISKIN** *Carduelis atriceps* (Dominico Coroninegro)   L 12 cm. Unmistakable. Habitat: humid montane woodland, open areas with scattered trees; 2000–3500 m. Voice*: very high fast slurred song, typical of genus. SMeGu.

13   **AMERICAN GOLDFINCH** *Carduelis tristis* (Dominico Americano)   L 12 cm. Unmistakable. Note yellow lesser coverts of ♀. Habitat: forest edge, open woodland; sl–2000 m. Voice: very high *sree-sree*; very high warbling with short rattles. Me.

14   **BLACK-HEADED SISKIN** *Carduelis notata* (Dominico Cabecinegro)   L 11 cm. Black mask sharply contrasting with yellow collar and underparts. Habitat: woodland, open areas with scattered pines; 500–3000 m. WSpr.

15   **LESSER GOLDFINCH** *Carduelis psaltria* (Dominico Dorsioscuro; Jilguero Menor)   L 11 cm. Races *colombiana* (a) and *hesperophila* (b) shown. Unmistakable. Habitat: open woodland, fields; sl–3000 m. Voice: toy-trumpet-like *to you* or *tjeer*; very high nasal warbling. WSpr.

16   **HOODED GROSBEAK** *Coccothraustes abeillei* (Pepitero Encapuchado)   L 18 cm. Black head diagnostic. Habitat: forest interior and edge; 1000–3500 m. U,MeGuSa.

17   **YELLOW-BELLIED SISKIN** *Carduelis xanthogastra* (Jilguero Vientriamarillo)   L 11 cm. From 15 by yellow in tail and wings and by black throat. Habitat: montane forest and adjacent more open areas. Voice: in flight, high hoarse warbling with low and ultra high notes. CRPa.

18   **EVENING GROSBEAK** *Coccothraustes vespertinus* (Pepitero Norteño)   L 17 cm. From 16 by different head pattern and colouring. Habitat: montane woodland; 1500–3000 m. Voice: very/ultra high rasping *cree-it* or *threw*. U,Me.

19   **HOUSE SPARROW** *Passer domesticus* (Gorrión Domestico/Común)   L 18 cm. Grey cap of ♂ and buff eyebrow of ♀ diagnostic. ♂ shows horn-coloured bill in n-br plumage. Habitat: settlement, towns. Voice: *tjup tjup tjurp*. Thr.

DISTRIBUTION MAPS

The first and most important step when trying to identify an unknown species is to compare it with the plates. Confirmation of an identification is possible when the bird is seen in its habitat as described in the captions opposite the plates.

Abundance, as indicated in the key below, is a relative concept. An attempt has been made to express it in terms of the likelihood of seeing or hearing a species within its range and habitat. This is a rather rough method, however, because the likelihood of detecting a species depends also upon such factors as size, colouring, behaviour or lifestyle, so that the true abundance, understood as the numerical strength of a species, can be much higher or lower than the number of individuals heard or seen in a given area at a given moment.

The information about range and status provided in the distribution can support or weaken your identification. Look, for instance, at map 50.19, which gives the range of the Bumblebee Hummingbird. According to the distribution map, it is highly unlikely if not impossible to see it in Guatemala, because it is restricted to central Mexico, so the very small hummingbird with purple whiskers you have seen in Guatemala is probably the Wine-throated Hummingbird, whose distribution is given in map 50.20.

The status is indicated by the intensity of the shading, an asterisk or a thin cross. An asterisk in a map indicates the place of a small permanent or migrating population, cut off from its main range by the border of the area with the USA or Columbia (e.g. see map 87.11, Orange-bellied Euphonia; the main range of the species is further south), or points to a small isolated population of a species (e.g. 50.4, Mexican Sheartail, which has a small population in central Veracruz, while it is common in northern coastal Yucatan).

The English bird names are given below the maps; each map is further referenced to its species by the plate number and species number (e.g. species number 4 on plate 20 is 20.4).

The shaded areas on the maps give an impression of the known range of species. The scale of the maps, however, prevents very detailed information; in a few cases there might for instance be pockets of breeding inside migration areas.

Distribution is given within the checklist area except for some seabirds.

Races within the range of a species are indicated by letters (a, b, c) on the maps as mentioned in the plate captions. See for instance map 17.1 (White Hawk).

A small cross refers to the place where only incidentally a species has been sighted.

KEY TO SYMBOLS AND STATUS	Resident	Transient	Present in northern winter	Present in northern summer	Likelihood of detecting species in its range and habitat
Common to frequent					60–100 %
Frequent to uncommon					10–60 %
Uncommon to rare					very small

Small isolated pocket	✳	<10 % chance of detecting species
Rare or vagrant	⊕	<1 % chance of detecting species
Hypothetical, extinct or unsubstantiated sighting	?	

Note: in some maps (where distribution is restricted to the beach with adjacent strips of sea and land) resident, transient and wintering status are indicated by **R R R R**, **T T T T** and **W W W W**. The boundary between breeding and other parts of a species' range is often indicated by ----.

EXAMPLE

7.12 AMERICAN COOT

This is the distribution map of the American Coot, number 12 on plate 7, which is common from Mexico to Honduras and frequent in the rest of the area. In most of Mexico it is a resident, while in the rest of the area it is only present in the (northern) winter. It has also been seen as a vagrant on the Isla Clarión. (See also Introduction, under occurrence, page 16.)

Note: Cocos Island (Isla del Coco, Costa Rica) is situated much farther offshore than indicated on the maps.

1.1 SHORT-TAILED ALBATROSS

1.2 BLACK-FOOTED ALBATROSS

1.3 WANDERING ALBATROSS

1.4 WAVED ALBATROSS

1.5 GREY-HEADED ALBATROSS

1.6 LAYSAN ALBATROSS

1.7 NORTHERN FULMAR

1.8 SOUTHERN FULMAR

1.9 BLACK PETREL

1.10 CORY'S SHEARWATER

2.1 JUAN FERNANDEZ PETREL

2.2 WHITE-NECKED PETREL

2.3 DARK-RUMPED PETREL

2.4 KERMADEC PETREL

2.5 HERALD PETREL

2.6 MURPHY'S PETREL

2.7 TAHITI PETREL

2.8 COOK'S PETREL

2.9 BLACK-WINGED PETREL

2.10 MOTTLED PETREL

2.11 STEJNEGER'S PETREL

233

Maps for species 2.12 to 4.4

2.12 WHITE-WINGED PETREL

2.13 BLACK-CAPPED PETREL

2.14 BULWER'S PETREL

3.1 PINK-FOOTED SHEARWATER

3.2 FLESH-FOOTED SHEARWATER

3.3 GREAT SHEARWATER

3.4 WEDGE-TAILED SHEARWATER

3.5 BULLER'S SHEARWATER

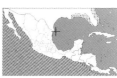

3.6 SOOTY SHEARWATER

3.7 SHORT-TAILED SHEARWATER

3.8 CHRISTMAS SHEARWATER

3.9 BLACK-VENTED SHEARWATER

3.10 MANX SHEARWATER

3.11 LITTLE SHEARWATER

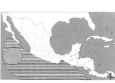

3.12 TOWNSEND'S SHEARWATER

3.13 AUDUBON'S SHEARWATER

3.14 CAPE PETREL

4.1 WILSON'S STORM-PETREL

4.2 WHITE-VENTED STORM-PETREL

4.3 FORK-TAILED STORM-PETREL

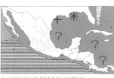

4.4 LEACH'S STORM-PETREL

4.5 GUADALUPE STORM-PETREL

4.6 BAND-RUMPED STORM-PETREL

4.7 WEDGE-RUMPED STORM-PETREL

4.8 ASHY STORM-PETREL

4.9 BLACK STORM-PETREL

4.10 MARKHAM'S STORM-PETREL

4.11 LEAST STORM-PETREL

4.12 WHITE-FACED STORM-PETREL

5.1 WHITE-TAILED TROPICBIRD

5.2 RED-BILLED TROPICBIRD

5.3 RED-TAILED TROPICBIRD

5.4 MASKED BOOBY

5.5 BLUE-FOOTED BOOBY

5.6 BROWN BOOBY

5.7 RED-FOOTED BOOBY

5.8 PERUVIAN BOOBY

5.9 NORTHERN GANNET

5.10 MAGNIFICENT FRIGATEBIRD

5.11 GREAT FRIGATEBIRD

6.1 COMMON MURRE

6.2 PIGEON GUILLEMOT

235

Maps for species 6.3 to 7.7

6.3 XANTUS'S MURRELET

6.4 CRAVERI'S MURRELET

6.5 ANCIENT MURRELET

6.6 CASSIN'S AUKLET

6.7 CRESTED AUKLET

6.8 RHINOCEROS AUKLET

6.9 PARAKEET AUKLET

6.10 TUFTED PUFFIN

6.11 HORNED PUFFIN

6.12 RED-THROATED LOON

6.13 PACIFIC LOON

6.14 COMMON LOON

6.15 YELLOW-BILLED LOON

6.16 GALAPAGOS PENGUIN

7.1 LEAST GREBE

7.2 PIED-BILLED GREBE

7.3 ATITLAN GREBE

7.4 HORNED GREBE

7.5 RED-NECKED GREBE

7.6 EARED GREBE

7.7 WESTERN GREBE

236

7.8 CLARK'S GREBE

7.9 PURPLE GALLINULE

7.10 PURPLE SWAMPHEN

7.11 COMMON MOORHEN

7.12 AMERICAN COOT

7.13 SUNGREBE

7,14 SUNBITTERN

8.1 AMERICAN WHITE PELICAN

8.2 BROWN PELICAN

8.3 DOUBLE-CRESTED CORMORANT

8.4 GREAT CORMORANT

8.5 NEOTROPIC CORMORANT

8.6 BRANDT'S CORMORANT

8.7 PELAGIC CORMORANT

8.8 GUANAY CORMORANT

8.9 ANHINGA

9.1 PINNATED BITTERN

9.2 AMERICAN BITTERN

9.3 LEAST BITTERN

9.4 BARE-THROATED TIGER HERON

9.5 RUFESCENT TIGER HERON

237

Maps for species 9.6 to 10.8

9.6 FASCIATED TIGER HERON

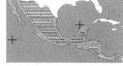

9.7 SNOWY EGRET

9.8 LITTLE BLUE HERON

9.9 TRICOLOURED HERON

9.10 REDDISH EGRET

9.11 LITTLE EGRET

9.12 CATTLE EGRET

9.13 CHESTNUT-BELLIED HERON

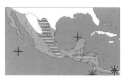

9.14 GREEN HERON

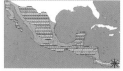

9.15 BLACK-CROWNED NIGHT HERON

9.16 YELLOW-CROWNED NIGHT HERON

9.17 BOAT-BILLED HERON

9.18 CAPPED HERON

10.1 GREAT BLUE HERON

10.2 GREAT EGRET

10.3 COCOI HERON

10.4 WHITE IBIS

10.5 SCARLET IBIS

10.6 GLOSSY IBIS

10.7 WHITE-FACED IBIS

10.8 GREEN IBIS

10.9 BUFF-NECKED IBIS

10.10 LIMPKIN

10.11 ROSEATE SPOONBILL

10.12 JABIRU

10.13 WOOD STORK

10.14 GREATER FLAMINGO

10.15 WHOOPING CRANE

10.16 SANDHILL CRANE

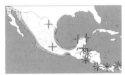

11.1 FULVOUS WHISTLING DUCK

11.2 WHITE-FACED WHISTLING DUCK

11.3 BLACK-BELLIED WHISTLING DUCK

11.4 TUNDRA SWAN

11.5 TRUMPETER SWAN

11.6 GREATER WHITE-FRONTED GOOSE

11.7 SNOW GOOSE

11.8 ROSS'S GOOSE

11.9 BRANT

11.10 CANADA GOOSE

11.11 COMB DUCK

11.12 MUSCOVY DUCK

11.13 HOODED MERGANSER

11.14 COMMON MERGANSER

11.15 RED-BREASTED MERGANSER

12.1 WOOD DUCK

12.2 GREEN-WINGED TEAL

12.3 MALLARD

12.4 HAWAIIAN DUCK

12.5 MEXICAN DUCK

12.6 MOTTLED DUCK

12.7 AMERICAN BLACK DUCK

12.8 NORTHERN PINTAIL

12.9 BLUE-WINGED TEAL

12.10 GARGANEY

12.11 CINNAMON TEAL

12.12 NORTHERN SHOVELER

12.13 GADWALL

12.14 EURASIAN WIGEON

12.15 AMERICAN WIGEON

12.16 WHITE-CHEEKED PINTAIL

13.1 CANVASBACK

13.2 REDHEAD

13.3 RING-NECKED DUCK

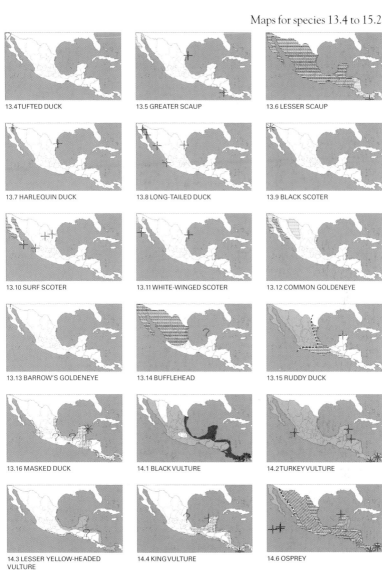

13.4 TUFTED DUCK

13.5 GREATER SCAUP

13.6 LESSER SCAUP

13.7 HARLEQUIN DUCK

13.8 LONG-TAILED DUCK

13.9 BLACK SCOTER

13.10 SURF SCOTER

13.11 WHITE-WINGED SCOTER

13.12 COMMON GOLDENEYE

13.13 BARROW'S GOLDENEYE

13.14 BUFFLEHEAD

13.15 RUDDY DUCK

13.16 MASKED DUCK

14.1 BLACK VULTURE

14.2 TURKEY VULTURE

14.3 LESSER YELLOW-HEADED
VULTURE

14.4 KING VULTURE

14.6 OSPREY

14.7 BALD EAGLE

15.1 GREY-HEADED KITE

15.2 HOOK-BILLED KITE

Maps for species 15.3 to 17.4

15.3 SHARP-SHINNED HAWK

15.4 WHITE-BREASTED HAWK

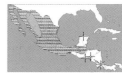

15.5 COOPER'S HAWK

15.6 NORTHERN GOSHAWK

15.7 BICOLOURED HAWK

15.8 TINY HAWK

15.9 CRANE HAWK

16.1 SWALLOW-TAILED KITE

16.2 WHITE-TAILED KITE

16.3 MISSISSIPPI KITE

16.4 PLUMBEOUS KITE

16.5 PEARL KITE

16.6 DOUBLE-TOOTHED KITE

16.7 SNAIL KITE

16.8 SLENDER-BILLED KITE

16.9 NORTHERN HARRIER

16.10 LONG-WINGED HARRIER

17.1 WHITE HAWK

17.2 SEMIPLUMBEOUS HAWK

17.3 PLUMBEOUS HAWK

17.4 BARRED HAWK

242

17.5 BLACK-COLLARED HAWK

17.6 HARRIS'S HAWK

17.7 WHITE-TAILED HAWK

18.1 SOLITARY EAGLE

18.2 COMMON BLACK HAWK

18.3 GREAT BLACK HAWK

18.4 MANGROVE BLACK HAWK

18.5 ZONE-TAILED HAWK

18.6 SHORT-TAILED HAWK

18.7 GREY HAWK

18.8 ROADSIDE HAWK

19.1 SAVANNA HAWK

19.2 RED-SHOULDERED HAWK

19.3 BROAD-WINGED HAWK

19.4 SWAINSON'S HAWK

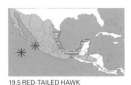

19.5 RED-TAILED HAWK

19.6 FERRUGINOUS HAWK

19.7 ROUGH-LEGGED BUZZARD

20.1 GOLDEN EAGLE

20.2 CRESTED EAGLE

20.3 HARPY EAGLE

243

Maps for species 20.4 to 23.3

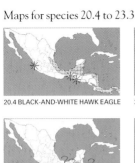

20.4 BLACK-AND-WHITE HAWK EAGLE   20.5 BLACK HAWK EAGLE   20.6 ORNATE HAWK EAGLE

21.1 RED-THROATED CARACARA   21.2 CRESTED CARACARA   21.3 YELLOW-HEADED CARACARA

21.4 LAUGHING FALCON   21.5 BARRED FOREST FALCON   21.6 COLLARED FOREST FALCON

21.7 SLATY-BACKED FOREST FALCON   22.1 AMERICAN KESTREL   22.2 APLOMADO FALCON

22.3 BAT FALCON   22.4 ORANGE-BREASTED FALCON   22.5 MERLIN

22.6 PEREGRINE FALCON   22.7 PRAIRIE FALCON   22.8 GYRFALCON

23.1 PLAIN CHACHALACA   23.2 WAGLER'S CHACHALACA   23.3 WEST MEXICAN CHACHALACA

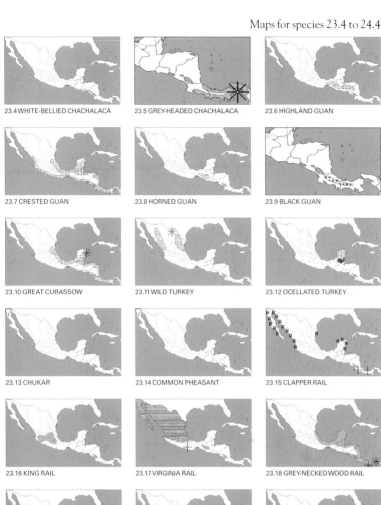

23.4 WHITE-BELLIED CHACHALACA

23.5 GREY-HEADED CHACHALACA

23.6 HIGHLAND GUAN

23.7 CRESTED GUAN

23.8 HORNED GUAN

23.9 BLACK GUAN

23.10 GREAT CURASSOW

23.11 WILD TURKEY

23.12 OCELLATED TURKEY

23.13 CHUKAR

23.14 COMMON PHEASANT

23.15 CLAPPER RAIL

23.16 KING RAIL

23.17 VIRGINIA RAIL

23.18 GREY-NECKED WOOD RAIL

23.19 RUFOUS-NECKED WOOD RAIL

23.20 SPOTTED RAIL

24.1 YELLOW RAIL

24.2 RUDDY CRAKE

24.3 GREY-BREASTED CRAKE

24.4 BLACK RAIL

245

Maps for species 24.5 to 25.6

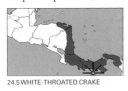

24.5 WHITE-THROATED CRAKE

24.6 UNIFORM CRAKE

24.7 SORA

24.8 YELLOW-BREASTED CRAKE

24.9 COLOMBIAN CRAKE

24.10 PAINT-BILLED CRAKE

24.11 OCELLATED CRAKE

24.12 LONG-TAILED WOOD PARTRIDGE

24.13 BEARDED WOOD PARTRIDGE

24.14 BUFFY-CROWNED WOOD PARTRIDGE

24.15 SPOTTED WOOD QUAIL

24.16 BLACK-EARED WOOD QUAIL

24.17 MARBLED WOOD QUAIL

24.18 BLACK-BREASTED WOOD QUAIL

24.19 TACARCUNA WOOD QUAIL

25.1 TAWNY-FACED QUAIL

25.2 SINGING QUAIL

25.3 BANDED QUAIL

25.4 SCALED QUAIL

25.5 ELEGANT QUAIL

25.6 GAMBEL'S QUAIL

25.7 CALIFORNIA QUAIL

25.8 MOUNTAIN QUAIL

25.9 MONTEZUMA QUAIL

25.10 OCELLATED QUAIL

25.11 NORTHERN BOBWHITE

25.12 BLACK-THROATED BOBWHITE

25.13 CRESTED BOBWHITE

25.14 SPOT-BELLIED BOBWHITE

25.15 GREAT TINAMOU

25.16 HIGHLAND TINAMOU

25.17 LITTLE TINAMOU

25.18 CHOCO TINAMOU

25.19 THICKET TINAMOU

25.20 SLATY-BREASTED TINAMOU

26.1 DOUBLE-STRIPED THICK-KNEE

26.2 SOUTHERN LAPWING

26.3 GREY PLOVER

26.4 AMERICAN GOLDEN PLOVER

26.5 PACIFIC GOLDEN PLOVER

26.6 AMERICAN OYSTERCATCHER

26.7 BLACK OYSTERCATCHER

247

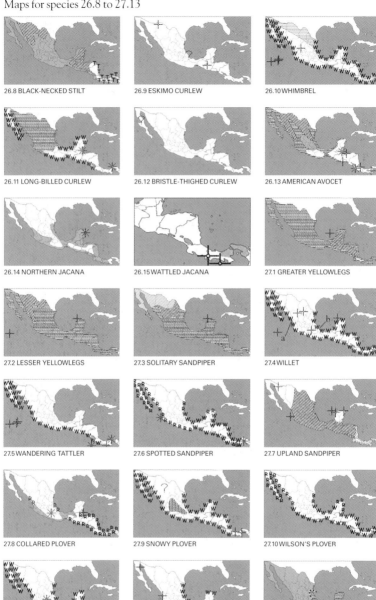

26.8 BLACK-NECKED STILT

26.9 ESKIMO CURLEW

26.10 WHIMBREL

26.11 LONG-BILLED CURLEW

26.12 BRISTLE-THIGHED CURLEW

26.13 AMERICAN AVOCET

26.14 NORTHERN JACANA

26.15 WATTLED JACANA

27.1 GREATER YELLOWLEGS

27.2 LESSER YELLOWLEGS

27.3 SOLITARY SANDPIPER

27.4 WILLET

27.5 WANDERING TATTLER

27.6 SPOTTED SANDPIPER

27.7 UPLAND SANDPIPER

27.8 COLLARED PLOVER

27.9 SNOWY PLOVER

27.10 WILSON'S PLOVER

27.11 SEMIPALMATED PLOVER

27.12 PIPING PLOVER

27.13 KILLDEER

27.14 MOUNTAIN PLOVER

27.15 EURASIAN DOTTEREL

28.1 HUDSONIAN GODWIT

28.2 BAR-TAILED GODWIT

28.3 MARBLED GODWIT

28.4 BUFF-BREASTED SANDPIPER

28.5 RUFF

28.6 SHORT-BILLED DOWITCHER

28.7 LONG-BILLED DOWITCHER

28.8 WILSON'S SNIPE

28.9 AMERICAN WOODCOCK

28.10 WILSON'S PHALAROPE

28.11 RED-NECKED PHALAROPE

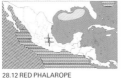

28.12 RED PHALAROPE

28.13 RUDDY TURNSTONE

28.14 BLACK TURNSTONE

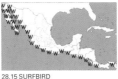

28.15 SURFBIRD

29.1 RED KNOT

29.2 SANDERLING

29.3 SEMIPALMATED SANDPIPER

29.4 WESTERN SANDPIPER

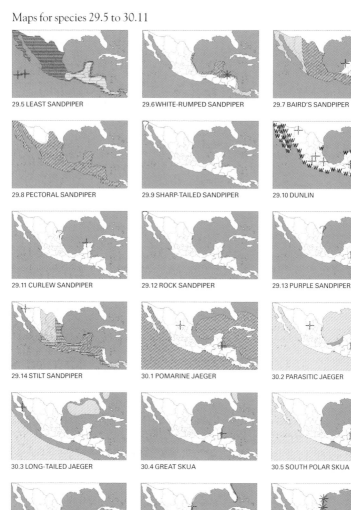

29.5 LEAST SANDPIPER

29.6 WHITE-RUMPED SANDPIPER

29.7 BAIRD'S SANDPIPER

29.8 PECTORAL SANDPIPER

29.9 SHARP-TAILED SANDPIPER

29.10 DUNLIN

29.11 CURLEW SANDPIPER

29.12 ROCK SANDPIPER

29.13 PURPLE SANDPIPER

29.14 STILT SANDPIPER

30.1 POMARINE JAEGER

30.2 PARASITIC JAEGER

30.3 LONG-TAILED JAEGER

30.4 GREAT SKUA

30.5 SOUTH POLAR SKUA

30.6 CHILEAN SKUA

30.7 GREAT BLACK-BACKED GULL

30.8 LESSER BLACK-BACKED GULL

30.9 KELP GULL

30.10 OLROG'S GULL

30.11 YELLOW-FOOTED GULL

30.12 BAND-TAILED GULL

31.1 BLACK-TAILED GULL

31.2 SLATY-BACKED GULL

31.3 WESTERN GULL

31.4 HERRING GULL

31.5 CALIFORNIA GULL

31.6 GLAUCOUS-WINGED GULL

31.7 GLAUCOUS GULL

31.8 THAYER'S GULL

31.9 GREY-HEADED GULL

31.10 SWALLOW-TAILED GULL

31.11 GREY GULL

32.1 HEERMANN'S GULL

32.2 MEW GULL

32.3 RING-BILLED GULL

32.4 BLACK-HEADED GULL

32.5 LAUGHING GULL

32.6 FRANKLIN'S GULL

32.7 BLACK-LEGGED KITTIWAKE

32.8 BONAPARTE'S GULL

32.9 SABINE'S GULL

Maps for species 32.10 to 34.10

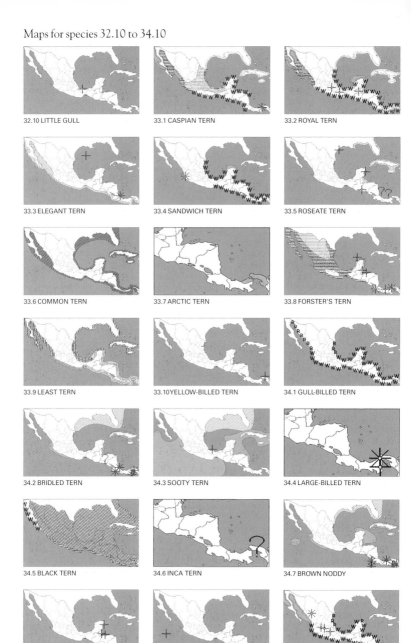

32.10 LITTLE GULL

33.1 CASPIAN TERN

33.2 ROYAL TERN

33.3 ELEGANT TERN

33.4 SANDWICH TERN

33.5 ROSEATE TERN

33.6 COMMON TERN

33.7 ARCTIC TERN

33.8 FORSTER'S TERN

33.9 LEAST TERN

33.10 YELLOW-BILLED TERN

34.1 GULL-BILLED TERN

34.2 BRIDLED TERN

34.3 SOOTY TERN

34.4 LARGE-BILLED TERN

34.5 BLACK TERN

34.6 INCA TERN

34.7 BROWN NODDY

34.8 BLACK NODDY

34.9 WHITE TERN

34.10 BLACK SKIMMER

35.2 SCALED PIGEON

35.3 PALE-VENTED PIGEON

35.4 PLUMBEOUS PIGEON

35.5 WHITE-CROWNED PIGEON

35.6 RED-BILLED PIGEON

35.7 BAND-TAILED PIGEON

35.8 SHORT-BILLED PIGEON

35.9 RUDDY PIGEON

35.10 DUSKY PIGEON

35.11 PURPLISH-BACKED QUAIL DOVE

35.12 TUXTLA QUAIL DOVE

35.13 BUFF-FRONTED QUAIL DOVE

35.14 RUSSET-CROWNED QUAIL DOVE

35.15 RUFOUS-BREASTED QUAIL DOVE

35.16 OLIVE-BACKED QUAIL DOVE

35.17 RUDDY QUAIL DOVE

35.18 VIOLACEOUS QUAIL DOVE

35.19 WHITE-FACED QUAIL DOVE

36.1 WHITE-WINGED DOVE

36.2 ZENAIDA DOVE

36.3 MOURNING DOVE

Maps for species 36.4 to 37.6

36.4 SOCORRO DOVE

36.5 EARED DOVE

36.6 SPOTTED DOVE

36.7 EURASIAN COLLARED DOVE

36.8 INCA DOVE

36.9 COMMON GROUND DOVE

36.10 PLAIN-BREASTED GROUND DOVE

36.11 RUDDY GROUND DOVE

36.12 BLUE GROUND DOVE

36.13 MAROON-CHESTED GROUND DOVE

36.14 WHITE-TIPPED DOVE

36.15 GREY-HEADED DOVE

36.16 BROWN-BACKED DOVE

36.17 CARIBBEAN DOVE

36.18 GREY-CHESTED DOVE

37.1 GREEN PARAKEET

37.2 PACIFIC PARAKEET

37.3 RED-THROATED PARAKEET

37.4 SOCORRO PARAKEET

37.5 ORANGE-FRONTED PARAKEET

37.6 CRIMSON-FRONTED PARAKEET

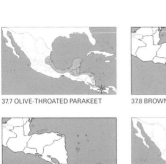

37.7 OLIVE-THROATED PARAKEET

37.8 BROWN-THROATED PARAKEET

37.9 SULPHUR-WINGED PARAKEET

37.10 PAINTED PARAKEET

37.11 BARRED PARAKEET

37.12 MEXICAN PARROTLET

37.13 SPECTACLED PARROTLET

37.14 ORANGE-CHINNED PARAKEET

37.15 RED-FRONTED PARROTLET

37.16 BLUE-FRONTED PARROTLET

37.17 WHITE-CROWNED PARROT

37.18 BLUE-HEADED PARROT

38.1 BLUE-AND-YELLOW MACAW

38.2 MILITARY MACAW

38.3 SCARLET MACAW

38.4 GREAT GREEN MACAW

38.5 RED-AND-GREEN MACAW

38.6 CHESTNUT-FRONTED MACAW

38.7 THICK-BILLED PARROT

38.8 MAROON-FRONTED PARROT

38.9 BROWN-HOODED PARROT

38.10 SAFFRON-HEADED PARROT

38.11 WHITE-FRONTED PARROT

38.12 YELLOW-LORED PARROT

38.13 RED-CROWNED PARROT

38.14 LILAC-CROWNED PARROT

38.15 RED-LORED PARROT

38.16 YELLOW-CROWNED PARROT

38.17 MEALY PARROT

38.18 YELLOW-HEADED PARROT

39.1 DWARF CUCKOO

39.2 BLACK-BILLED CUCKOO

39.3 YELLOW-BILLED CUCKOO

39.4 MANGROVE CUCKOO

39.5 GREY-CAPPED CUCKOO

39.6 COCOS CUCKOO

39.7 SQUIRREL CUCKOO

39.8 LITTLE CUCKOO

39.9 STRIPED CUCKOO

39.10 PHEASANT CUKOO

39.11 LESSER GROUND CUCKOO

39.12 RUFOUS-VENTED GROUND CUCKOO

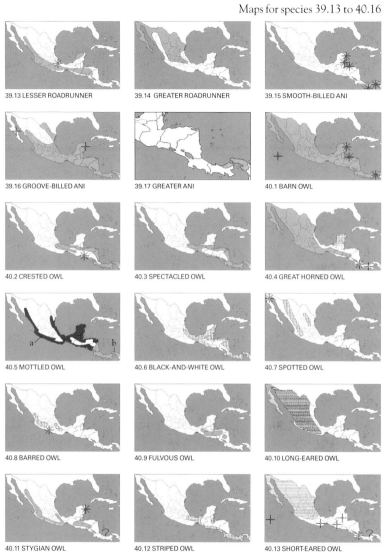

39.13 LESSER ROADRUNNER

39.14 GREATER ROADRUNNER

39.15 SMOOTH-BILLED ANI

39.16 GROOVE-BILLED ANI

39.17 GREATER ANI

40.1 BARN OWL

40.2 CRESTED OWL

40.3 SPECTACLED OWL

40.4 GREAT HORNED OWL

40.5 MOTTLED OWL

40.6 BLACK-AND-WHITE OWL

40.7 SPOTTED OWL

40.8 BARRED OWL

40.9 FULVOUS OWL

40.10 LONG-EARED OWL

40.11 STYGIAN OWL

40.12 STRIPED OWL

40.13 SHORT-EARED OWL

40.14 NORTHERN SAW-WHET OWL

40.15 UNSPOTTED SAW-WHET OWL

40.16 BURROWING OWL

Maps for species 41.1 to 42.1

41.1 FLAMMULATED OWL

41.2 EASTERN SCREECH OWL

41.3 WESTERN SCREECH OWL

41.4 TROPICAL SCREECH OWL

41.5 BARE-SHANKED SCREECH OWL

41.6 BALSAS SCREECH OWL

41.7 PACIFIC SCREECH OWL

41.8 WHISKERED SCREECH OWL

41.9 VERMICULATED SCREECH OWL

41.10 BRIDLED SCREECH OWL

41.11 MOUNTAIN PYGMY OWL

41.12 NORTHERN PYGMY OWL

41.13 COSTA RICAN PYGMY OWL

41.14 CAPE PYGMY OWL

41.15 LEAST PYGMY OWL

41.16 COLIMA PYGMY OWL

41.17 TAMAULIPAS PYGMY OWL

41.18 CENTRAL AMERICAN PYGMY OWL

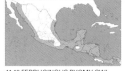

41.19 FERRUGINOUS PYGMY OWL

41.20 ELF OWL

42.1 GREAT POTOO

42.2 GREY POTOO

42.3 NORTHERN POTOO

42.4 OILBIRD

42.5 SHORT-TAILED NIGHTJAR

42.6 LESSER NIGHTHAWK

42.7 COMMON NIGHTHAWK

42.8 ANTILLEAN NIGHTHAWK

42.9 PAURAQUE

42.10 OCELLATED POORWILL

42.11 EARED POORWILL

42.12 YUCATAN POORWILL

43.1 COMMON POORWILL

43.2 WHIP-POOR-WILL

43.3 STEPHEN'S WHIP-POOR-WILL

43.4 CHUCK-WILL'S-WIDOW

43.5 TAWNY-COLLARED NIGHTJAR

43.6 YUCATAN NIGHTJAR

43.7 BUFF-COLLARED NIGHTJAR

43.8 SPOT-TAILED NIGHTJAR

43.9 RUFOUS NIGHTJAR

43.10 DUSKY NIGHTJAR

259

Maps for species 43.11 to 45.3

43.11 WHITE-TAILED NIGHTJAR

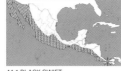

44.1 BLACK SWIFT

44.2 WHITE-CHINNED SWIFT

44.3 CHESTNUT-COLLARED SWIFT

44.4 SPOT-FRONTED SWIFT

44.5 WHITE-FRONTED SWIFT

44.6 WHITE-COLLARED SWIFT

44.7 WHITE-NAPED SWIFT

44.8 CHIMNEY SWIFT

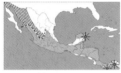

44.9 VAUX'S SWIFT

44.10 CHAPMAN'S SWIFT

44.11 SHORT-TAILED SWIFT

44.12 ASHY-TAILED SWIFT

44.13 BAND-RUMPED SWIFT

44.14 GREY-RUMPED SWIFT

44.15 WHITE-THROATED SWIFT

44.16 LESSER SWALLOW-TAILED SWIFT

44.17 GREAT SWALLOW-TAILED SWIFT

45.1 BRONZY HERMIT

45.2 RUFOUS-BREASTED HERMIT

45.3 BAND-TAILED BARBTHROAT

45.4 LONG-BILLED HERMIT

45.5 MEXICAN HERMIT

45.6 GREEN HERMIT

45.7 PALE-BELLIED HERMIT

45.8 WHITE-WHISKERED HERMIT

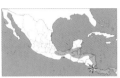

45.9 STRIPE-THROATED HERMIT

45.10 WHITE-TIPPED SICKLEBILL

45.11 TOOTH-BILLED HUMMINGBIRD

45.12 WEDGE-TAILED SABREWING

45.13 LONG-TAILED SABREWING

45.14 RUFOUS SABREWING

45.15 SCALY-BREASTED HUMMINGBIRD

45.16 VIOLET SABREWING

45.17 WHITE-NECKED JACOBIN

45.18 GREEN-BREASTED MANGO

45.19 BLACK-THROATED MANGO

45.20 VERAGUAS MANGO

46.1 RUBY TOPAZ

46.2 EMERALD-CHINNED HUMMINGBIRD

46.3 VIOLET-HEADED HUMMINGBIRD

46.4 SHORT-CRESTED COQUETTE

261

46.5 BLACK-CRESTED COQUETTE

46.6 RUFOUS-CRESTED COQUETTE

46.7 WHITE-CRESTED COQUETTE

46.8 GREEN THORNTAIL

46.9 CANIVET'S EMERALD

46.10 SALVIN'S EMERALD

46.11 GOLDEN-CROWNED EMERALD

46.12 COZUMEL EMERALD

46.13 GARDEN EMERALD

46.14 DUSKY HUMMINGBIRD

46.15 BROAD-BILLED HUMMINGBIRD

46.16 DOUBLEDAY'S HUMMINGBIRD

46.17 GREEN-FRONTED LANCEBILL

47.1 MEXICAN WOODNYMPH

47.2 CROWNED WOODNYMPH

47.3 FIERY-THROATED HUMMINGBIRD

47.4 VIOLET-BELLIED HUMMINGBIRD

47.5 SAPPHIRE-THROATED
HUMMINGBIRD

47.6 BLUE-HEADED SAPPHIRE

47.7 BLUE-THROATED GOLDENTAIL

47.8 WHITE-EARED HUMMINGBIRD

47.9 XANTHUS'S HUMMINGBIRD

47.10 VIOLET-CAPPED HUMMINGBIRD

47.11 STRIPE-TAILED HUMMINGBIRD

47.12 WHITE-TAILED HUMMINGBIRD

47.13 BLACK-BELLIED HUMMINGBIRD

47.14 BLUE-CAPPED HUMMINGBIRD

47.15 WHITE-TAILED EMERALD

47.16 COPPERY-HEADED EMERALD

47.17 RUFOUS-CHEEKED HUMMINGBIRD

47.18 SNOWCAP

48.1 WHITE-BELLIED EMERALD

48.2 HONDURAN EMERALD

48.3 AZURE-CROWNED HUMMINGBIRD

48.4 MANGROVE HUMMINGBIRD

48.5 INDIGO-CAPPED HUMMINGBIRD

48.6 STEELY-VENTED HUMMINGBIRD

48.7 BLUE-TAILED HUMMINGBIRD

48.8 SNOWY-BELLIED HUMMINGBIRD

48.9 BERYLLINE HUMMINGBIRD

48.10 BLUE-CHESTED HUMMINGBIRD

48.11 CHARMING HUMMINGBIRD

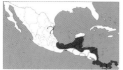

48.12 RUFOUS-TAILED HUMMINGBIRD

48.13 BUFF-BELLIED HUMMINGBIRD

48.14 CINNAMON HUMMINGBIRD

48.15 VIOLET-CROWNED HUMMINGBIRD

48.16 GREEN-FRONTED HUMMINGBIRD

48.17 CINNAMON-SIDED HUMMINGBIRD

49.1 GREEN-CROWNED BRILLIANT

49.2 BROWN VIOLET-EAR

49.3 GREEN VIOLET-EAR

49.4 BRONZE-TAILED PLUMELETEER

49.5 WHITE-VENTED PLUMELETEER

49.6 WHITE-BELLIED MOUNTAIN GEM

49.7 GREY-TAILED MOUNTAIN GEM

49.8 WHITE-THROATED MOUNTAIN GEM

49.9 PURPLE-THROATED MOUNTAIN GEM

49.10 GREEN-THROATED MOUNTAIN GEM

49.11 GREEN-BREASTED MOUNTAIN GEM

49.12 AMETHYST-THROATED HUMMINGBIRD

49.13 BLUE-THROATED HUMMINGBIRD

49.14 GARNET-THROATED HUMMINGBIRD

49.15 MAGNIFICENT HUMMINGBIRD

49.16 GREENISH PUFFLEG

49.17 PURPLE-CROWNED FAIRY

49.18 LONG-BILLED STARTHROAT

49.19 PLAIN-CAPPPED STARTHROAT

50.1 SPARKLING-TAILED WOODSTAR

50.2 MAGENTA-THROATED WOODSTAR

50.3 PURPLE-THROATED WOODSTAR

50.4 MEXICAN SHEARTAIL

50.5 SLENDER SHEARTAIL

50.6 LUCIFER HUMMINGBIRD

50.7 BEAUTIFUL HUMMINGBIRD

50.8 RUBY-THROATED HUMMINGBIRD

50.9 BLACK-CHINNED HUMMINGBIRD

50.10 ANNA'S HUMMINGBIRD

50.11 COSTA'S HUMMINGBIRD

50.12 CALLIOPE HUMMINGBIRD

50.13 VOLCANO HUMMINGBIRD

50.14 GLOW-THROATED HUMMINGBIRD

50.15 SCINTILLANT HUMMINGBIRD

50.16 BROAD-TAILED HUMMINGBIRD

50.17 RUFOUS HUMMINGBIRD

50.18 ALLEN'S HUMMINGBIRD

50.19 BUMBLEBEE HUMMINGBIRD

50.20 WINE-THROATED HUMMINGBIRD

51.1 BLACK-THROATED TROGON

51.2 WHITE-TAILED TROGON

51.3 BLACK-HEADED TROGON

51.4 CITREOLINE TROGON

51.5 VIOLACEOUS TROGON

51.6 ORANGE-BELLIED TROGON

51.7 BLACK-TAILED TROGON

51.8 MOUNTAIN TROGON

51.9 ELEGANT TROGON

51.10 COLLARED TROGON

51.11 BAIRD'S TROGON

51.12 SLATY-TAILED TROGON

51.13 LATTICE-TAILED TROGON

51.14 EARED QUETZAL

51.15 RESPLENDENT QUETZAL

51.16 GOLDEN-HEADED QUETZAL

51.17 DUSKY-BACKED JACAMAR

51.18 RUFOUS-TAILED JACAMAR

51.19 GREAT JACAMAR

52.1 TODY MOTMOT

52.2 BLUE-THROATED MOTMOT

52.3 RUSSET-CROWNED MOTMOT

52.4 BROAD-BILLED MOTMOT

52.5 RUFOUS MOTMOT

52.6 KEEL-BILLED MOTMOT

52.7 BLUE-CROWNED MOTMOT

52.8 TURQUOISE-BROWED MOTMOT

52.9 RINGED KINGFISHER

52.10 BELTED KINGFISHER

52.11 GREEN-AND-RUFOUS KINGFISHER

52.12 AMAZON KINGFISHER

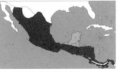

52.13 GREEN KINGFISHER

52.14 AMERICAN PYGMY KINGFISHER

52.15 PIED PUFFBIRD

52.16 WHITE-NECKED PUFFBIRD

52.17 BLACK-BREASTED PUFFBIRD

52.18 WHITE-WHISKERED PUFFBIRD

52.19 BARRED PUFFBIRD

53.1 SPOT-CROWNED BARBET

267

53.2 RED-HEADED BARBET

53.3 PRONG-BILLED BARBET

53.4 WHITE-FRONTED NUNBIRD

53.5 LANCEOLATED MONKLET

53.6 GREY-CHEEKED NUNLET

53.7 EMERALD TOUCANET

53.8 YELLOW-EARED TOUCANET

53.9 COLLARED ARACARI

53.10 FIERY-BILLED ARACARI

53.11 KEEL-BILLED TOUCAN

53.12 CHESTNUT-MANDIBLED
TOUCAN

53.13 CHOCÓ TOUCAN

53.14 PALE-BILLED WOODPECKER

53.15 CRIMSON-BELLIED
WOODPECKER

53.16 CRIMSON-CRESTED
WOODPECKER

53.17 IMPERIAL WOODPECKER

54.1 LEWIS'S WOODPECKER

54.2 ACORN WOODPECKER

54.3 GOLDEN-NAPED WOODPECKER

54.4 RED-HEADED WOODPECKER

54.5 YUCATAN WOODPECKER

54.6 RED-BELLIED WOODPECKER

54.7 GILA WOODPECKER

54.8 BLACK-CHEEKED WOODPECKER

54.9 GOLDEN-CHEEKED WOODPECKER

54.10 GREY-BREASTED WOODPECKER

54.11 HOFFMANN'S WOODPECKER

54.12 GOLDEN-FRONTED WOODPECKER

54.13 RED-CROWNED WOODPECKER

55.1 LADDER-BACKED WOODPECKER

55.2 NUTTALL'S WOODPECKER

55.3 HAIRY WOODPECKER

55.4 DOWNY WOODPECKER

55.5 STRICKLAND'S WOODPECKER

55.6 ARIZONA WOODPECKER

55.7 BRONZE-WINGED WOODPECKER

55.8 GOLDEN-OLIVE WOODPECKER

55.9 GREY-CROWNED WOODPECKER

55.10 RUFOUS-WINGED WOODPECKER

55.11 STRIPE-CHEEKED WOODPECKER

55.12 GOLDEN-GREEN WOODPECKER

55.13 SPOT-BREASTED WOODPECKER

Maps for species 56.1 to 57.9

56.1 NORTHERN FLICKER

56.2 GILDED FLICKER

56.3 SMOKY-BROWN WOODPECKER

56.4 RED-RUMPED WOODPECKER

56.5 YELLOW-BELLIED SAPSUCKER

56.6 RED-NAPED SAPSUCKER

56.7 RED-BREASTED SAPSUCKER

56.8 WILLIAMSON'S SAPSUCKER

56.9 CINNAMON WOODPECKER

56.10 CHESTNUT-COLOURED
WOODPECKER

56.11 LINEATED WOODPECKER

56.12 PILEATED WOODPECKER

57.1 TAWNY-WINGED WOODCREEPER

57.2 PLAIN-BROWN WOODCREEPER

57.3 RUDDY WOODCREEPER

57.4 LONG-TAILED WOODCREEPER

57.5 STRONG-BILLED WOODCREEPER

57.6 BARRED WOODCREEPER

57.7 BLACK-BANDED WOODCREEPER

57.8 STRAIGHT-BILLED WOODCREEPER

57.9 COCOA WOODCREEPER

270

57.10 IVORY-BILLED WOODCREEPER

57.11 SPOTTED WOODCREEPER

57.12 BLACK-STRIPED WOODCREEPER

57.13 WHITE-STRIPED WOODCREEPER

57.14 STREAK-HEADED WOODCREEPER

57.15 SPOT-CROWNED WOODCREEPER

57.16 RED-BILLED SCYTHEBILL

57.17 BROWN-BILLED SCYTHEBILL

58.1 OLIVACEOUS PICULET

58.2 PLAIN XENOPS

58.3 STREAKED XENOPS

58.4 SPOTTED BARBTAIL

58.5 WEDGE-BILLED WOODCREEPER

58.6 OLIVACEOUS WOODCREEPER

58.7 BUFFY TUFTEDCHEEK

58.8 STREAK-BREASTED TREEHUNTER

58.9 BEAUTIFUL TREERUNNER

58.10 RUDDY TREERUNNER

58.11 TAWNY-THROATED LEAFTOSSER

58.12 SCALY-THROATED LEAFTOSSER

58.13 GREY-THROATED LEAFTOSSER

58.14 SHARP-TAILED STREAMCREEPER

59.1 RUFOUS-BREASTED SPINETAIL

59.2 SLATY SPINETAIL

59.3 PALE-BREASTED SPINETAIL

59.4 RED-FACED SPINETAIL

59.5 COIBA SPINETAIL

59.6 LINEATED FOLIAGE GLEANER

59.7 STRIPED FOLIAGE GLEANER

59.8 SCALY-THROATED FOLIAGE GLEANER

59.9 SLATY-WINGED FOLIAGE GLEANER

59.10 BUFF-FRONTED FOLIAGE GLEANER

59.11 BUFF-THROATED FOLIAGE GLEANER

59.12 RUDDY FOLIAGE GLEANER

59.13 DOUBLE-BANDED GREYTAIL

59.14 PLAIN ANTVIREO

59.15 SPOT-CROWNED ANTVIREO

59.16 STREAK-CROWNED ANTVIREO

59.17 TACARCUNA TAPACULO

59.18 SILVERY-FRONTED TAPACULO

59.19 NARIÑO TAPACULO

60.1 GREAT ANTSHRIKE

60.2 BARRED ANTSHRIKE

60.3 FASCIATED ANTSHRIKE

60.4 SPECKLED ANTSHRIKE

60.5 BLACK ANTSHRIKE

60.6 BLACK-HOODED ANTSHRIKE

60.7 RUSSET ANTSHRIKE

60.8 SLATY ANTSHRIKE

60.9 SLATY ANTWREN

60.10 CHECKER-THROATED ANTWREN

60.11 WHITE-FLANKED ANTWREN

60.12 DOT-WINGED ANTWREN

60.13 STREAKED ANTWREN

60.14 PYGMY ANTWREN

60.15 WHITE-FRINGED ANTWREN

60.16 RUFOUS-WINGED ANTWREN

60.17 RUFOUS-RUMPED ANTWREN

61.1 DUSKY ANTBIRD

61.2 JET ANTBIRD

61.3 BARE-CROWNED ANTBIRD

61.4 IMMACULATE ANTBIRD

61.5 CHESTNUT-BACKED ANTBIRD

273

Maps for species 61.6 to 62.6

61.6 DULL-MANTLED ANTBIRD

61.7 WHITE-BELLIED ANTBIRD

61.8 BICOLOURED ANTBIRD

61.9 WING-BANDED ANTBIRD

61.10 SPOTTED ANTBIRD

61.11 OCELLATED ANTBIRD

61.12 BLACK-HEADED ANTTHRUSH

61.13 MEXICAN ANTTHRUSH

61.14 BLACK-FACED ANTTHRUSH

61.15 RUFOUS-BREASTED ANTTHRUSH

61.16 SPECTACLED ANTPITTA

61.17 OCHRE-BREASTED ANTPITTA

61.18 FULVOUS-BELLIED ANTPITTA

61.19 SCALED ANTPITTA

61.20 BLACK-CROWNED ANTPITTA

62.1 GREAT KISKADEE

62.2 LESSER KISKADEE

62.3 BOAT-BILLED FLYCATCHER

62.4 SOCIAL FLYCATCHER

62.5 RUSTY-MARGINED FLYCATCHER

62.6 WHITE-RINGED FLYCATCHER

62.7 GOLDEN-BELLIED FLYCATCHER

62.8 GOLDEN-CROWNED FLYCATCHER

62.9 STREAKED FLYCATCHER

62.10 SULPHUR-BELLIED FLYCATCHER

62.11 PIRATIC FLYCATCHER

62.12 GREY-CAPPED FLYCATCHER

62.13 TROPICAL KINGBIRD

62.14 COUCH'S KINGBIRD

62.15 CASSIN'S KINGBIRD

62.16 THICK-BILLED KINGBIRD

62.17 WESTERN KINGBIRD

62.18 CATTLE TYRANT

63.1 OLIVE-SIDED FLYCATCHER

63.2 DARK PEWEE

63.3 WESTERN WOOD PEWEE

63.4 EASTERN WOOD PEWEE

63.5 GREATER PEWEE

63.6 TROPICAL PEWEE

63.7 OCHRACEOUS PEWEE

63.8 PANAMA FLYCATCHER

63.9 DUSKY-CAPPED FLYCATCHER

275

63.10 YUCATAN FLYCATCHER

63.11 ASH-THROATED FLYCATCHER

63.12 NUTTING'S FLYCATCHER

63.13 GREAT CRESTED FLYCATCHER

63.14 BROWN-CRESTED FLYCATCHER

63.15 FLAMMULATED FLYCATCHER

63.16 SCRUB FLYCATCHER

63.17 TAWNY-BREASTED FLYCATCHER

63.18 SULPHUR-RUMPED FLYCATCHER

63.19 BLACK-TAILED FLYCATCHER

63.20 BRIGHT-RUMPED ATTILA

64.1 WHITE-FRONTED TYRANNULET

64.2 SOOTY-HEADED TYRANNULET

64.3 PALTRY TYRANNULET

64.4 YELLOW-BELLIED TYRANNULET

64.5 BROWN-CAPPED TYRANNULET

64.6 NORTHERN BEARDLESS TYRANNULET

64.7 SOUTHERN BEARDLESS TYRANNULET

64.8 MOUSE-COLOURED TYRANNULET

64.9 YELLOW-CROWNED TYRANNULET

64.10 YELLOW TYRANNULET

64.11 YELLOW-GREEN TYRANNULET

64.12 RUFOUS-BROWED TYRANNULET

64.13 BRAN-COLOURED FLYCATCHER

64.14 YELLOW-OLIVE FLYCATCHER

64.15 YELLOW-MARGINED FLYCATCHER

64.16 BLACK-BILLED FLYCATCHER

64.17 TAWNY-CHESTED FLYCATCHER

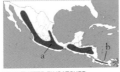

64.18 TUFTED FLYCATCHER

64.19 BELTED FLYCATCHER

64.20 PILEATED FLYCATCHER

65.1 GREENISH ELAENIA

65.2 FOREST ELAENIA

65.3 GREY ELAENIA

65.4 CARIBBEAN ELAENIA

65.5 YELLOW-BELLIED ELAENIA

65.6 MOUNTAIN ELAENIA

65.7 LESSER ELAENIA

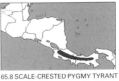

65.8 SCALE-CRESTED PYGMY TYRANT

65.9 PALE-EYED PYGMY TYRANT

65.10 BLACK-CAPPED PYGMY TYRANT

65.11 BRONZE-OLIVE PYGMY TYRANT

277

Maps for species 65.12 to 66.12

65.12 RUDDY-TAILED FLYCATCHER

65.13 NORTHERN BENTBILL

65.14 SOUTHERN BENTBILL

65.15 SLATE-HEADED TODY FLYCATCHER

65.16 COMMON TODY FLYCATCHER

65.17 BLACKHEADED TODY FLYCATCHER

65.18 STUB-TAILED SPADEBILL

65.19 WHITE-THROATED SPADEBILL

65.20 GOLDEN-CROWNED SPADEBILL

66.1 COCOS FLYCATCHER

66.2 YELLOW-BELLIED FLYCATCHER

66.3 ACADIAN FLYCATCHER

66.4 ALDER FLYCATCHER

66.5 WILLOW FLYCATCHER

66.6 WHITE-THROATED FLYCATCHER

66.7 LEAST FLYCATCHER

66.8 HAMMOND'S FLYCATCHER

66.9 DUSKY FLYCATCHER

66.10 GREY FLYCATCHER

66.11 PINE FLYCATCHER

66.12 PACIFIC SLOPE FLYCATCHER

66.13 CORDILLERAN FLYCATCHER

66.14 BUFF-BREASTED FLYCATCHER

66.15 OCHRE-BELLIED FLYCATCHER

66.16 YELLOWISH FLYCATCHER

66.17 BLACK-CAPPED FLYCATCHER

66.18 OLIVE-STRIPED FLYCATCHER

66.19 SLATY-CAPPED FLYCATCHER

66.20 SEPIA-CAPPED FLYCATCHER

67.1 BLACK PHOEBE

67.2 EASTERN PHOEBE

67.3 SAY'S PHOEBE

67.4 VERMILION FLYCATCHER

67.5 GREY KINGBIRD

67.6 EASTERN KINGBIRD

67.7 GIANT KINGBIRD

67.8 SIRYSTES

67.9 FORK-TAILED FLYCATCHER

67.10 SCISSOR-TAILED FLYCATCHER

67.11 LONG-TAILED TYRANT

67.12 EYE-RINGED FLATBILL

67.13 OLIVACEOUS FLATBILL

279

67.14 ROYAL FLYCATCHER

67.15 BROWNISH TWISTWING

67.16 PIED WATER TYRANT

67.17 TORRENT TYRANNULET

67.18 SHARPBILL

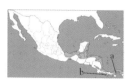

68.1 THRUSHLIKE SCHIFFORNIS

68.2 RUFOUS PIHA

68.3 RUFOUS MOURNER

68.4 SPECKLED MOURNER

68.5 BROAD-BILLED SAPAYOA

68.6 GREY-HEADED PIPRITES

68.7 GOLDEN-COLLARED MANAKIN

68.8 WHITE-COLLARED MANAKIN

68.9 ORANGE-COLLARED MANAKIN

68.10 GREEN MANAKIN

68.11 GOLDEN-HEADED MANAKIN

68.12 RED-CAPPED MANAKIN

68.13 WHITE-RUFFED MANAKIN

68.14 LONG-TAILED MANAKIN

68.15 LANCE-TAILED MANAKIN

68.16 WHITE-CROWNED MANAKIN

68.17 BLUE-CROWNED MANAKIN

69.1 ONE-COLOURED BECARD

69.2 ROSE-THROATED BECARD

69.3 GREY-COLLARED BECARD

69.4 CINNAMON BECARD

69.5 WHITE-WINGED BECARD

69.6 BLACK-AND-WHITE BECARD

69.7 BARRED BECARD

69.8 CINEREOUS BECARD

69.9 LOVELY COTINGA

69.10 TURQUOISE COTINGA

69.11 BLUE COTINGA

69.12 MASKED TITYRA

69.13 BLACK-CROWNED TITYRA

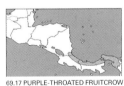

69.14 SNOWY COTINGA

69.15 BLACK-TIPPED COTINGA

69.16 YELLOW-BILLED COTINGA

69.17 PURPLE-THROATED FRUITCROW

69.18 BARE-NECKED UMBRELLABIRD

69.19 THREE-WATTLED BELLBIRD

70.1 BROWN-CHESTED MARTIN

281

70.2 PURPLE MARTIN

70.3 GREY-BREASTED MARTIN

70.4 SINALOA MARTIN

70.5 CARIBBEAN MARTIN

70.6 SOUTHERN MARTIN

70.7 TREE SWALLOW

70.8 MANGROVE SWALLOW

70.9 VIOLET-GREEN SWALLOW

70.10 WHITE-WINGED SWALLOW

70.11 BLUE-AND-WHITE SWALLOW

70.12 BLACK-CAPPED SWALLOW

70.13 WHITE-THIGHED SWALLOW

70.14 BANK SWALLOW

70.15 RIDGWAY'S ROUGH-WINGED
SWALLOW

70.16 NORTHERN ROUGH-WINGED
SWALLOW

70.17 SOUTHERN ROUGH-WINGED
SWALLOW

70.18 CAVE SWALLOW

70.19 CLIFF SWALLOW

70.20 BARN SWALLOW

71.1 STELLER'S JAY

71.2 BLUE JAY

71.3 PINYON JAY

71.4 SCRUB JAY

71.5 MEXICAN JAY

71.6 AZURE-HOODED JAY

71.7 BLACK-THROATED JAY

71.8 DWARF JAY

71.9 WHITE-THROATED JAY

71.10 SILVERY-THROATED JAY

71.11 BUSHY-CRESTED JAY

71.12 SAN BLAS JAY

71.13 YUCATAN JAY

71.14 PURPLISH-BACKED JAY

72.1 BLACK-CHESTED JAY

72.2 GREEN JAY

72.3 UNICOLOURED JAY

72.4 BROWN JAY

72.5 BLACK-THROATED MAGPIE JAY

72.6 WHITE-THROATED MAGPIE JAY

72.7 TUFTED JAY

72.8 CLARK'S NUTCRACKER

72.9 AMERICAN CROW

72.10 TAMAULIPAS CROW

72.11 SINALOA CROW

72.12 CHIHUAHUAN CROW

72.13 COMMON RAVEN

72.14 HOUSE CROW

73.1 MEXICAN CHICKADEE

73.2 MOUNTAIN CHICKADEE

73.3 BRIDLED TITMOUSE

73.4 BLACK-CRESTED TITMOUSE

73.5 PLAIN TITMOUSE

73.6 VERDIN

73.7 BUSHTIT

73.8 WRENTIT

73.9 RED-BREASTED NUTHATCH

73.10 WHITE-BREASTED NUTHATCH

73.11 PYGMY NUTHATCH

73.12 BROWN CREEPER

73.13 HORNED LARK

73.14 WHITE WAGTAIL

73.15 YELLOW WAGTAIL

73.16 BLACK-BACKED WAGTAIL

73.17 RED-THROATED PIPIT

73.18 AMERICAN PIPIT

73.19 SPRAGUE'S PIPIT

73.20 YELLOWISH PIPIT

74.1 STRIPE-BREASTED WREN

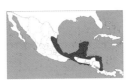

74.2 SPOT-BREASTED WREN

74.3 HAPPY WREN

74.4 RUFOUS-AND-WHITE WREN

74.5 SINALOA WREN

74.6 BANDED WREN

74.7 CAROLINA WREN

74.8 PLAIN WREN

74.9 SOOTY-HEADED WREN

74.10 BLACK-THROATED WREN

74.11 BLACK-BELLIED WREN

74.12 BAY WREN

74.13 RIVERSIDE WREN

74.14 STRIPE-THROATED WREN

74.15 RUFOUS-BREASTED WREN

74.16 BUFF-BREASTED WREN

74.17 CANYON WREN

Maps for species 74.18 to 76.1

74.18 NAVA'S WREN

74.19 SLENDER-BILLED WREN

75.1 WHITE-BELLIED WREN

75.2 BEWICK'S WREN

75.3 HOUSE WREN

75.4 OCHRACEUS WREN

75.5 COZUMEL WREN

75.6 CLARION WREN

75.7 SOCORRO WREN

75.8 WINTER WREN

75.9 RUFOUS-BROWED WREN

75.10 MARSH WREN

75.11 SEDGE WREN

75.12 TIMBERLINE WREN

75.13 WHITE-BREASTED WOOD WREN

75.14 GREY-BREASTED WOOD WREN

75.15 NORTHERN NIGHTINGALE WREN

75.16 SOUTHERN NIGHTINGALE WREN

75.17 SONG WREN

75.18 ROCK WREN

76.1 WHITE-HEADED WREN

286

76.2 GIANT WREN

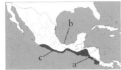

76.3 RUFOUS-NAPED WREN

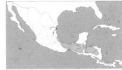

76.4 BAND-BACKED WREN

76.5 GREY-BARRED WREN

76.6 SPOTTED WREN

76.7 BOUCARD'S WREN

76.8 YUCATAN WREN

76.9 CACTUS WREN

76.10 CEDAR WAXWING

76.11 GREY SILKY-FLYCATCHER

76.12 LONG-TAILED SILKY-FLYCATCHER

76.13 PHAINOPEPLA

76.14 BLACK-AND-YELLOW SILKY-FLYCATCHER

76.15 RUFOUS-BROWED PEPPERSHRIKE

76.16 LOGGERHEAD SHRIKE

76.17 NORTHERN SHRIKE

76.18 BLACK-CAPPED DONACOBIUS

76.19 EUROPEAN STARLING

76.20 AMERICAN DIPPER

77.1 DUSKY WARBLER

77.2 ARCTIC WARBLER

77.3 GOLDEN-CROWNED KINGLET

77.4 RUBY-CROWNED KINGLET

77.5 LONG-BILLED GNAT WREN

77.6 TAWNY-FACED GNAT WREN

77.7 BLUE-GREY GNATCATCHER

77.8 BLACK-TAILED GNATCATCHER

77.9 CALIFORNIA GNATCATCHER

77.10 BLACK-CAPPED GNATCATCHER

77.11 WHITE-LORED GNATCATCHER

77.12 TROPICAL GNATCATCHER

77.13 SLATE-THROATED GNATCATCHER

77.14 TAWNY-CROWNED GREENLET

77.15 LESSER GREENLET

77.16 SCRUB GREENLET

77.17 GOLDEN-FRONTED GREENLET

77.18 CHESTNUT-SIDED SHRIKE VIREO

77.19 GREEN SHRIKE VIREO

77.20 YELLOW-BROWED SHRIKE VIREO

78.1 SLATY VIREO

78.2 WHITE-EYED VIREO

78.3 MANGROVE VIREO

78.4 COZUMEL VIREO

78.5 BELL'S VIREO

78.6 BLACK-CAPPED VIREO

78.7 DWARF VIREO

78.8 GREY VIREO

78.9 BLUE-HEADED VIREO

78.10 CASSIN'S VIREO

78.11 PLUMBEOUS VIREO

78.12 YELLOW-THROATED VIREO

78.13 YELLOW-WINGED VIREO

78.14 HUTTON'S VIREO

78.15 GOLDEN VIREO

78.16 WARBLING VIREO

78.17 BROWN-CAPPED VIREO

78.18 PHILADELPHIA VIREO

78.19 YELLOW-GREEN VIREO

78.20 RED-EYED VIREO

78.21 BLACK-WHISKERED VIREO

78.22 YUCATAN VIREO

79.1 GREY CATBIRD

79.2 BLACK CATBIRD

289

Maps for species 79.3 to 80.5

79.3 BLUE MOCKINGBIRD

79.4 BLUE-AND-WHITE MOCKINGBIRD

79.5 NORTHERN MOCKINGBIRD

79.6 TROPICAL MOCKINGBIRD

79.7 SOCORRO MOCKINGBIRD

79.8 SAGE THRASHER

79.9 BROWN THRASHER

79.10 LONG-BILLED THRASHER

79.11 COZUMEL THRASHER

79.12 GREY THRASHER

79.13 BENDIRE'S THRASHER

79.14 CURVE-BILLED THRASHER

79.15 OCELLATED THRASHER

79.16 CALIFORNIA THRASHER

79.17 CRISSAL THRASHER

79.18 LE CONTE'S THRASHER

80.1 TOWNSEND'S SOLITAIRE

80.2 BROWN-BACKED SOLITAIRE

80.3 SLATE-COLOURED SOLITAIRE

80.4 BLACK-FACED SOLITAIRE

80.5 VARIED SOLITAIRE

290

80.6 ORANGE-BILLED NIGHTINGALE THRUSH

80.7 RUSSET NIGHTINGALE THRUSH

80.8 RUDDY-CAPPED NIGHTINGALE THRUSH

80.9 BLACK-BILLED NIGHTINGALE THRUSH

80.10 BLACK-HEADED NIGHTINGALE THRUSH

80.11 SLATY-BACKED NIGHTINGALE THRUSH

80.12 SPOTTED NIGHTINGALE THRUSH

80.13 VEERY

80.14 GREY-CHEEKED THRUSH

80.15 SWAINSON'S THRUSH

80.16 HERMIT THRUSH

80.17 WOOD THRUSH

81.1 NORTHERN WHEATEAR

81.2 EASTERN BLUEBIRD

81.3 WESTERN BLUEBIRD

81.4 MOUNTAIN BLUEBIRD

81.5 MOUNTAIN THRUSH

81.6 CLAY-COLOURED THRUSH

81.7 PALE-VENTED THRUSH

81.8 WHITE-THROATED THRUSH

81.9 RUFOUS-BACKED THRUSH

81.10 GRAYSON'S THRUSH

81.11 AMERICAN ROBIN

81.12 RUFOUS-COLLARED THRUSH

81.13 BLACK THRUSH

81.14 SOOTY THRUSH

81.15 VARIED THRUSH

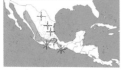

81.16 AZTEC THRUSH

82.1 WORM-EATING WARBLER

82.2 SWAINSON'S WARBLER

82.3 TENNESSEE WARBLER

82.4 ORANGE-CROWNED WARBLER

82.5 COLIMA WARBLER

82.6 VIRGINIA'S WARBLER

82.7 LUCY'S WARBLER

82.8 NASHVILLE WARBLER

82.9 BLUE-WINGED WARBLER

82.10 GOLDEN-WINGED WARBLER

82.11 CRESCENT-CHESTED WARBLER

82.12 NORTHERN PARULA

82.13 TROPICAL PARULA

82.14 FLAME-THROATED WARBLER

82.15 PROTHONOTARY WARBLER

82.16 YELLOW WARBLER

82.17 CAPE MAY WARBLER

83.1 PRAIRIE WARBLER

83.2 CHESTNUT-SIDED WARBLER

83.3 YELLOW-RUMPED WARBLER

83.4 MAGNOLIA WARBLER

83.5 HERMIT WARBLER

83.6 BLACK-THROATED GREEN WARBLER

83.7 TOWNSEND'S WARBLER

83.8 BLACKBURNIAN WARBLER

83.9 YELLOW-THROATED WARBLER

83.10 GOLDEN-CHEEKED WARBLER

83.11 GRACE'S WARBLER

83.12 KIRTLAND'S WARBLER

83.13 PALM WARBLER

83.14 PINE WARBLER

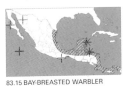

83.15 BAY-BREASTED WARBLER

83.16 BLACKPOLL WARBLER

83.17 BLACK-AND-WHITE WARBLER

83.18 BLACK-THROATED GREY WARBLER

293

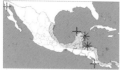

83.19 CERULEAN WARBLER

83.20 BLACK-THROATED BLUE WARBLER

84.1 CONNECTICUT WARBLER

84.2 MOURNING WARBLER

84.3 MACGILLIVRAY'S WARBLER

84.4 KENTUCKY WARBLER

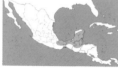

84.5 GREY-CROWNED YELLOWTHROAT

84.6 MASKED YELLOWTHROAT

84.7 COMMON YELLOWTHROAT

84.8 OLIVE-CROWNED YELLOWTHROAT

84.9 ALTAMIRA YELLOWTHROAT

84.10 BELDING'S YELLOWTHROAT

84.11 HOODED YELLOWTHROAT

84.12 BLACK-POLLED YELLOWTHROAT

84.13 WILSON'S WARBLER

84.14 CANADA WARBLER

84.15 HOODED WARBLER

84.16 COLLARED WHITESTART

84.17 SLATE-THROATED WHITESTART

84.18 PAINTED WHITESTART

84.19 AMERICAN REDSTART

85.1 OLIVE WARBLER

85.2 RED-FACED WARBLER

85.3 RED WARBLER

85.4 PINK-HEADED WARBLER

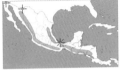

85.5 GREY-THROATED CHAT

85.6 RED-BREASTED CHAT

85.7 YELLOW-BREASTED CHAT

85.8 FAN-TAILED WARBLER

85.9 GOLDEN-CROWNED WARBLER

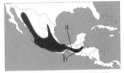

85.10 RUFOUS-CAPPED WARBLER

85.11 CHESTNUT-CAPPED WARBLER

85.12 GOLDEN-BROWED WARBLER

85.13 PIRRE WARBLER

85.14 BLACK-CHEEKED WARBLER

85.15 THREE-STRIPED WARBLER

85.16 BUFF-RUMPED WARBLER

85.17 WREN THRUSH

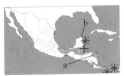

85.18 OVENBIRD

85.19 NORTHERN WATERTHRUSH

85.20 LOUISIANA WATERTHRUSH

86.1 BANANAQUIT

295

86.2 WHITE-EARED CONEBILL

86.3 VIRIDIAN DACNIS

86.4 BLUE DACNIS

86.5 SHINING HONEYCREEPER

86.6 PURPLE HONEYCREEPER

86.7 RED-LEGGED HONEYCREEPER

86.8 SCARLET-THIGHED DACNIS

86.9 GREEN HONEYCREEPER

86.10 BAY-HEADED TANAGER

86.11 RUFOUS-WINGED TANAGER

86.12 EMERALD TANAGER

86.13 SILVER-THROATED TANAGER

86.14 SPECKLED TANAGER

86.15 AZURE-RUMPED TANAGER

86.16 GREY-AND-GOLD TANAGER

86.17 GOLDEN-HOODED TANAGER

86.18 GREEN-NAPED TANAGER

86.19 SPANGLE-CHEEKED TANAGER

86.20 PLAIN-COLOURED TANAGER

87.1 BLUE-CROWNED
CHLOROPHONIA

87.2 GOLDEN-BROWED
CHLOROPHONIA

87.3 YELLOW-COLLARED CHLOROPHONIA

87.4 OLIVE-BACKED EUPHONIA

87.5 YELLOW-THROATED EUPHONIA

87.6 THICK-BILLED EUPHONIA

87.7 WHITE-VENTED EUPHONIA

87.8 YELLOW-CROWNED EUPHONIA

87.9 SPOT-CROWNED EUPHONIA

87.10 SCRUB EUPHONIA

87.11 ORANGE-BELLIED EUPHONIA

87.12 FULVOUS-VENTED EUPHONIA

87.13 TAWNY-CAPPED EUPHONIA

87.14 BLUE-HOODED EUPHONIA

87.15 BLUE-AND-GOLD TANAGER

87.16 YELLOW-WINGED TANAGER

87.17 BLUE-GREY TANAGER

87.18 PALM TANAGER

87.19 SWALLOW TANAGER

88.1 STRIPE-HEADED TANAGER

88.2 BLACK-THROATED SHRIKE TANAGER

88.3 WHITE-THROATED SHRIKE TANAGER

88.4 SULPHUR-RUMPED TANAGER

297

Maps for species 88.5 to 89.6

88.5 SCARLET-BROWED TANAGER

88.6 WHITE-SHOULDERED TANAGER

88.7 TAWNY-CRESTED TANAGER

88.8 WHITE-LINED TANAGER

88.9 RED-CROWNED ANT TANAGER

88.10 RED-THROATED ANT TANAGER

88.11 BLACK-CHEEKED ANT TANAGER

88.12 ROSE-THROATED TANAGER

88.13 HEPATIC TANAGER

88.14 SUMMER TANAGER

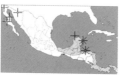

88.15 SCARLET TANAGER

88.16 WHITE-WINGED TANAGER

88.17 FLAME-COLOURED TANAGER

88.18 WESTERN TANAGER

88.19 RED-HEADED TANAGER

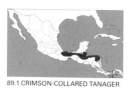

89.1 CRIMSON-COLLARED TANAGER

89.2 CRIMSON-BACKED TANAGER

89.3 SCARLET-RUMPED TANAGER

89.4 FLAME-RUMPED TANAGER

89.5 GREY-HEADED TANAGER

89.6 DUSKY-FACED TANAGER

89.7 OLIVE TANAGER

89.8 LEMON-SPECTACLED TANAGER

89.9 SOOTY-CAPPED BUSH TANAGER

89.10 COMMON BUSH TANAGER

89.11 ASHY-THROATED BUSH TANAGER

89.12 PIRRE BUSH TANAGER

89.13 TACARCUNA BUSH TANAGER

89.14 YELLOW-THROATED BUSH TANAGER

89.15 YELLOW-BACKED TANAGER

89.16 BLACK-AND-YELLOW TANAGER

89.17 ROSY THRUSH TANAGER

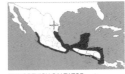

90.1 GREYISH SALTATOR

90.2 STREAKED SALTATOR

90.3 BLACK-HEADED SALTATOR

90.4 BUFF-THROATED SALTATOR

90.5 SLATE-COLOURED GROSBEAK

90.6 PYRRHULOXIA

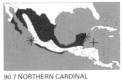

90.7 NORTHERN CARDINAL

90.8 CRIMSON-COLLARED GROSBEAK

90.9 ROSE-BREASTED GROSBEAK

90.10 BLACK-FACED GROSBEAK

90.11 YELLOW-GREEN GROSBEAK

90.12 BLACK-THIGHED GROSBEAK

90.13 YELLOW GROSBEAK

90.14 BLACK-HEADED GROSBEAK

90.15 BLUE BUNTING

90.16 BLUE-BLACK GROSBEAK

90.17 BLUE GROSBEAK

91.1 INDIGO BUNTING

91.2 ROSE-BELLIED BUNTING

91.3 VARIED BUNTING

91.4 LAZULI BUNTING

91.5 ORANGE-BREASTED BUNTING

91.6 PAINTED BUNTING

91.7 DICKCISSEL

91.8 WHITE-NAPED BRUSHFINCH

91.9 YELLOW-THROATED BRUSHFINCH

91.10 RUFOUS-CAPPED BRUSHFINCH

91.11 CHESTNUT-CAPPED BRUSHFINCH

91.12 GREEN-STRIPED BRUSHFINCH

91.13 STRIPE-HEADED BRUSHFINCH

91.14 LARGE-FOOTED FINCH

91.15 SOOTY-FACED FINCH

91.16 ORANGE-BILLED SPARROW

91.17 WHITE-EARED GROUND SPARROW

91.18 PREVOST'S GROUND SPARROW

91.19 RUSTY-CROWNED GROUND SPARROW

92.1 OLIVE SPARROW

92.2 GREEN-BACKED SPARROW

92.3 BLACK-STRIPED SPARROW

92.4 GREEN-TAILED TOWHEE

92.5 COLLARED TOWHEE

92.6 RUFOUS–SIDED TOWHEE

92.7 ABERT'S TOWHEE

92.8 CALIFORNIA TOWHEE

92.9 CANYON TOWHEE

92.10 WHITE-THROATED TOWHEE

92.11 RUDDY-BREASTED SEEDEATER

92.12 YELLOW-BELLIED SEEDEATER

92.13 WHITE-COLLARED SEEDEATER

92.14 LESSON'S SEEDEATER

92.15 VARIABLE SEEDEATER

92.16 SLATE-COLOURED SEEDEATER

301

92.17 THICK-BILLED SEEDFINCH

92.18 LINED SEEDEATER

92.19 NICARAGUAN SEEDFINCH

92.20 BLUE-BLACK GRASSQUIT

93.1 SAFFRON FINCH

93.2 GRASSLAND YELLOWFINCH

93.3 YELLOW-FACED GRASSQUIT

93.4 YELLOW-GREEN FINCH

93.5 YELLOW-THIGHED FINCH

93.6 BLUE SEEDEATER

93.7 SLATE-BLUE SEEDEATER

93.8 SLATY FINCH

93.9 COCOS FINCH

93.10 SLATY FLOWERPIERCER

93.11 CINNAMON-BELLIED
FLOWERPIERCER

93.12 PEG-BILLED FINCH

93.13 SAVANNA SPARROW

93.14 SEASIDE SPARROW

93.15 SIERRA MADRE SPARROW

93.16 BAIRD'S SPARROW

93.17 LE CONTE'S SPARROW

93.18 SHARP-TAILED SPARROW

93.19 GRASSHOPPER SPARROW

94.1 STRIPED SPARROW

94.2 FIELD SPARROW

94.3 WORTHEN'S SPARROW

94.4 BREWER'S SPARROW

94.5 BLACK-CHINNED SPARROW

94.6 CHIPPING SPARROW

94.7 CLAY-COLOURED SPARROW

94.8 SAGE SPARROW

94.9 BLACK-THROATED SPARROW

94.10 BLACK-CHESTED SPARROW

94.11 BRIDLED SPARROW

94.12 FIVE-STRIPED SPARROW

94.13 STRIPE-HEADED SPARROW

94.14 CASSIN'S SPARROW

94.15 BOTTERI'S SPARROW

94.16 CINNAMON-TAILED SPARROW

94.17 RUFOUS-WINGED SPARROW

94.18 RUFOUS-CROWNED SPARROW

94.19 OAXACA SPARROW

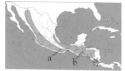

94.20 RUSTY SPARROW

95.1 WEDGE-TAILED GRASS FINCH

95.2 LARK BUNTING

95.3 VESPER SPARROW

95.4 LARK SPARROW

95.5 FOX SPARROW

95.6 SONG SPARROW

95.7 SWAMP SPARROW

95.8 LINCOLN'S SPARROW

95.9 RUFOUS-COLLARED SPARROW

95.10 WHITE-THROATED SPARROW

95.11 HARRIS'S SPARROW

95.12 GOLDEN-CROWNED SPARROW

95.13 WHITE-CROWNED SPARROW

95.14 DARK-EYED JUNCO

95.15 YELLOW-EYED JUNCO

95.16 BAIRD'S JUNCO

95.18 VOLCANO JUNCO

95.19 MCCOWN'S LONGSPUR

95.20 LAPLAND LONGSPUR

95.21 CHESTNUT-COLLARED LONGSPUR

96.1 EASTERN MEADOWLARK

96.2 WESTERN MEADOWLARK

96.3 RED-BREASTED BLACKBIRD

96.4 MELODIOUS BLACKBIRD

96.5 RUSTY BLACKBIRD

96.6 BREWER'S BLACKBIRD

96.7 SLENDER-BILLED GRACKLE

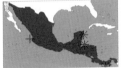

96.8 GREAT-TAILED GRACKLE

96.9 COMMON GRACKLE

96.10 BOAT-TAILED GRACKLE

96.11 NICARAGUAN GRACKLE

96.12 GIANT COWBIRD

96.13 SHINY COWBIRD

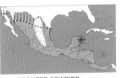

96.14 BRONZED COWBIRD

96.15 BROWN-HEADED COWBIRD

96.16 CRESTED OROPENDOLA

96.17 CHESTNUT-HEADED OROPENDOLA

96.18 MONTEZUMA OROPENDOLA

96.19 BLACK OROPENDOLA

97.1 BLACK-COWLED ORIOLE

97.2 BLACK-VENTED ORIOLE

305

97.3 BAR-WINGED ORIOLE

97.4 SCOTT'S ORIOLE

97.5 AUDUBON'S ORIOLE

97.6 YELLOW-TAILED ORIOLE

97.7 YELLOW-BACKED ORIOLE

97.8 ORANGE-CROWNED ORIOLE

97.9 SPOT-BREASTED ORIOLE

97.10 ORANGE ORIOLE

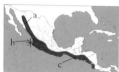

97.11 STREAK-BACKED ORIOLE

97.12 HOODED ORIOLE

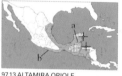

97.13 ALTAMIRA ORIOLE

97.14 BULLOCK'S ORIOLE

97.15 BALTIMORE ORIOLE

97.16 ORCHARD ORIOLE

97.17 YELLOW-WINGED CACIQUE

97.18 YELLOW-RUMPED CACIQUE

97.19 SCARLET-RUMPED CACIQUE

97.20 YELLOW-BILLED CACIQUE

98.1 BOBOLINK

98.2 RED-WINGED BLACKBIRD

98.3 TRICOLOURED BLACKBIRD

306

98.5 YELLOW-HEADED BLACKBIRD

96.6 PURPLE FINCH

98.7 CASSIN'S FINCH

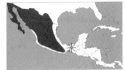

98.8 HOUSE FINCH

98.9 RED CROSSBILL

98.10 PINE SISKIN

98.11 LAWRENCE'S GOLDFINCH

98.12 BLACK-CAPPED SISKIN

98.13 AMERICAN GOLDFINCH

98.14 BLACK-HEADED SISKIN

98.15 LESSER GOLDFINCH

98.16 HOODED GROSBEAK

98.17 YELLOW-BELLIED SISKIN

98.18 EVENING GROSBEAK

98.19 HOUSE SPARROW

307

BIBLIOGRAPHY AND LIST OF FURTHER READING

OTHER FIELD GUIDES

S. N, G. Howell, S. Webb,
A Guide to the Birds of Mexico and Northern Central America
(Oxford University Press, 1995)

F. G. Stiles, A. F. Skutch, D. Gardner,
A Guide to the Birds of Costa Rica
(Cornell University Press, 1989)

R. S. Ridgely, J. A. Gwynne, *A Guide to the Birds of Panama with Costa Rica, Nicaragua and Honduras* (Princeton University Press, 1989)

Field guides for adjacent regions:

D. Sibley, *The North American Bird Guide* (Pica Press, 2000)

S. L. Hilty, W. L. Brown, G. Tudor,
A Guide to the Birds of Colombia
(Princeton University Press, 1986)

BASIC LITERATURE

J. del Hoyo, A. Elliott and
J. Sargatal, *Handbook of the Birds of the World* (Lynx, Barcelona)

(v.I)	*Ostrich – Ducks* (1992)
(v.II)	*New World Vultures – Guineafowl* (1994)
(v.III)	*Hoatzin – Auks* (1996)
(v.IV)	*Barn-owls – Hummingbirds* (1997)
(v.V)	*Sandgrouse – Cuckoos* (1999)
(v.VI)	*Mousebirds – Hornbills* (2001)
(v.VII)	*Jacamars – Woodpeckers* (2002)

Other volumes yet to be published.

American Ornithologists' Union,
Check-list of North American Birds
7th ed (AOU, 1998)

C. G. Sibley and B. L. Monroe,
Distribution and Taxonomy of Birds of the World (Yale University Press, 1990; supplement 1993)

BOOKS ON BIRD GROUPS

K. Baker, *Warblers of Europe, Asia and North Africa* (Helm, 1997)

D. Brewer and B. K. MacKay, *Wrens, Dippers and Thrashers* (Helm, 2001)

C. Byers, U. Olsson and J. Curson, *Buntings and Sparrows* (Pica Press, 1995)

P. Chantler and G. Driessens, *Swifts* 2nd ed (Pica Press, 2000)

N. Cleere and D. Nurney, *Nightjars* (Pica Press, 1998)

P. Clement, A. Harris and J. Davis, *Finches and Sparrows* (Helm, 1993)

P. Clement and R. Hathway, *Thrushes* (Helm, 2000)

J. Curson, D. Quinn and D. Beadle, *New World Warblers* (Helm, 1994)

J. Ferguson-Lees and D. A. Christie, *Raptors of the World* (Helm, 2001)

C. H. Fry, K. Fry and A. Harris, *Kingfishers, Bee-eaters and Rollers* (Helm, 1992)

D. Gibbs, E. Barnes and J. Cox, *Pigeons and Doves* (Pica Press, 2001)

J. Hancock and J. Kushlan, *The Herons Handbook* (Croom Helm, 1984)

S. Harrop and D. Quinn, *Tits, Nuthatches and Treecreepers* (Helm, 1996)

P. Harrison, *Seabirds* (Croom Helm, 1983)

P. Hayman, J. Marchant and T. Prater, *Shorebirds* (Houghton Mifflin, 1986)

M. L. Isler and P. R. Isler, *Tanagers* (Helm, 1999)

A. Jaramillo and P. Burke, *New World Blackbirds* (Helm, 1999)

C. König, F. Weick and J.-H. Becking, *Owls* (Pica Press, 1999)

S. Madge and H. Burn, *Wildfowl* (Helm, 1987)

S. Madge and H. Burn, *Crows and Jays* (Helm, 1999)

K. M. Olsen and H. Larsson, *Skuas and Jaegers* (Pica Press, 1997)

B. Taylor and B. van Perlo, *Rails* (Pica Press, 1998)

A. Turner and C. Rose, *Swallows and Martins* (Helm, 1989)

H. Winkler, D. A. Christie and D. Nurney, *Woodpeckers* (Pica Press, 1995)

BIRD SOUNDS

Many commercial recordings of bird sounds exist on cassette and on CD. Alternatively, search for 'neotropical bird sounds' on the internet.

INTERNET

Many things you want to know about birds can be found on the internet. If you type in the common or scientific name of a bird species in the dialogue window of a large search engine, you can be overwhelmed with information. Several search engines even offer the possibility of searching for pictures e.g. of bird species. A rich source of information is e.g. **www.bsc-eoc.org**. This site is maintained by Bird Studies Canada, which is recognised as a leading and respected not-for-profit conservation organisation dedicated to advancing the understanding, appreciation and conservation of wild birds and their habitats, in Canada and elsewhere, through studies that engage the skills, enthusiasm and support of its members, volunteers, staff and the interested public.

NEOTROPICAL BIRD CLUB

Special mention should be made of the Neotropical Bird Club (NBC) and its biannual journal *Cotinga*. The NBC aims to:

- foster an interest in the birds of the Neotropics amongst birdwatchers throughout the world
- increase awareness of the importance of support for conservation in the area
- mobilise the increasing number of enthusiastic birdwatchers active in the region to contribute to the conservation of Neotropical birds
- provide a forum for the publication of articles and notes about Neotropical birds, their identification and conservation and thus enhance information exchange in this subject area
- channel efforts towards priority species and sites, drawing attention to conservation needs
- publicise the activities of local groups and individuals, and improve liaison and collaboration between these same people and other birdwatchers.

The journal *Cotinga* features articles with news, notices, recent publications, expedition results, reviews and preliminary or interim publication of studies on Neotropical birds by contributors from all parts of the world in English, Spanish and Portuguese.

The NBC is open to all and the Club welcomes new members.
Further details can be obtained from the membership secretary,
Neotropical Bird Club,
c/o The Lodge, Sandy, Beds.
SG19 2DL, UK or
c/o American Birding Association,
PO Box 6599, Colorado Springs,
CO 80934, USA.

Also the website can be visited:
www.neotropicalbirdclub.org.

Index of scientific names

Numbers refer to the relevant plate, followed by the number of the bird on that plate.

Abeillia abeillei, 46.2
Acanthidops bairdii, 93.12
Accipiter bicolor, 15.7
  chionogaster, 15.4
  cooperii, 15.5
  gentilis, 15.6
  striatus, 15.3
  superciliosus, 15.8
Actitis macularia, 27.6
Aechmophorus clarki, 7.8
  occidentalis, 7.7
Aegolius acadicus, 40.14
  ridgwayi, 40.15
Aeronautes saxatilis, 44.15
Aethia cristatella, 6.7
Agamia agami, 9.13
Agelaius icterocephalus, 98.4
  phoeniceus, 98.2
  tricolor, 98.3
Agriocharis gallopavo, 23.11
Aimophila botterii, 94.15
  carpalis, 94.17
  cassinii, 94.14
  humeralis, 94.10
  mystacalis, 94.11
  notosticta, 94.19
  quinquestriata, 94.12
  rufescens, 94.20
  ruficauda, 94.13
  ruficeps, 94.18
  sumichrasti, 94.16
Aix sponsa, 12.1
Ajaia ajaja, 10.11
Alectoris chukar, 23.13
Amaurolimnas concolor, 24.6
Amaurospiza concolor, 93.6
  relicta, 93.7
Amazilia amabilis, 48.10
  beryllina, 48.9
  boucardi, 48.4
  candida, 48.1
  cyanifrons, 48.5
  cyanocephala, 48.3
  cyanura, 48.7
  decora, 48.11
  edward, 48.8
  luciae, 48.2
  rutila, 48.14
  saucerottei, 48.6
  tzacatl, 48.12
  violiceps, 48.15
  viridifrons, 48.16
  v. wagneri L, 48.17
  yucatanensis, 48.13
Amazona albifrons, 38.11
  autumnalis, 38.15
  farinosa, 38.17
  finschi, 38.14
  ochrocephala, 38.16

  oratrix, 38.18
  viridigenalis, 38.13
  xantholora 38.12
Amblycercus holosericeus,
  97.20
Ammodramus baileyi, 93.15
  bairdii, 93.16
  caudacutus, 93.18
  leconteii, 93.17
  maritimus, 93.14
  savannarum, 93.19
Amphispiza belli, 94.8
  bilineata, 94.9
Anabacerthia variegaticeps,
  59.8
Anas acuta, 12.8
  americana, 12.15
  bahamensis, 12.16
  clypeata, 12.12
  crecca, 12.2
  cyanoptera, 12.11
  diazi, 12.5
  discors, 12.9
  fulvigula, 12.6
  penelope, 12.14
  platyrhynchos, 12.3
  querquedula, 12.10
  rubripes, 12.7
  strepera, 12.13
  wyvilliana, 12.4
Androdon aequatorialis,
  45.11
Anhinga anhinga, 8.9
Anous minutus, 34.8
  stolidus, 34.7
Anser albifrons, 11.6
  caerulescens, 11.7
  rossii, 11.8
Anthracothorax nigricollis,
  45.19
  prevostii, 45.18
  veraguensis, 45.20
Anthus cervinus, 73.17
  lutescens, 73.20
  rubescens, 73.18
  spragueii, 73.19
Aphanotriccus audax, 64.16
  capitalis, 64.17
Aphelocoma californica, 71.4
  ultramarina, 71.5
  unicolor, 72.3
Aphriza virgata, 28.15
Aquila chrysaetos, 20.1
Ara ambigua, 38.4
  ararauna, 38.1
  chloroptera, 38.5
  macao, 38.3
  militaris, 38.2
  severa, 38.6

Aramides axillaris, 23.19
  cajanea, 23.18
Aramus guarauna, 10.10
Aratinga brevipes, 37.4
  canicularis, 37.5
  finschi, 37.6
  holochlora, 37.1
  nana, 37.7
  pertinax, 37.8
  rubritorquis, 37.3
  strenua, 37.2
Archilochus alexandri, 50.9
  colubris, 50.8
Ardea cocoi, 10.3
  herodias, 10.1
Arenaria interpres, 28.13
  melanocephala, 28.14
Arremon aurantiirostris, 91.16
Arremonops chloronotus, 92.2
  conirostris, 92.3
  rufivirgatus, 92.1
Asio clamator, 40.12
  flammeus, 40.13
  otus, 40.10
  stygius, 40.11
Aspatha gularis, 52.2
Asturina nitida, 18.7
Atalotriccus pilaris, 65.9
Athene cunicularia, 40.16
Atlapetes albinucha, 91.8
  atricapillus, 91.13
  brunneinucha, 91.11
  gutturalis, 91.9
  pileatus, 91.10
  virenticeps, 91.12
Attila spadiceus, 63.20
Aulacorhynchus prasinus, 53.7
Auriparus flaviceps, 73.6
Automolus ochrolaemus, 59.11
  rubiginosus, 59.12
Aythya affinis, 13.6
  americana, 13.2
  collaris, 13.3
  fuligula, 13.4
  marila, 13.5
  valisineria, 13.1

Bangsia arcaei, 87.15
Bartramia longicauda, 27.7
Baryphthengus martii, 52.5
Basileuterus belli, 85.12
  culicivorus, 85.9
  fulvicauda, 85.16
  ignotus, 85.13
  lachrymosa, 85.8
  melanogenys, 85.14
  rufifrons, 85.10
  r. delattrii, 85.11
  tristriatus, 85.15

Bolborhynchus lineola, 37.11
Bombycilla cedrorum, 76.10
Botaurus lentiginosus, 9.2
  pinnatus, 9.1
Brachygalba salmoni, 51.17
Branta bernicla, 11.9
  canadensis, 11.10
Brotogeris jugularis, 37.14
Bubo virginianus, 40.4
Bubulcus ibis, 9.12
Bucephala albeola, 13.14
  clangula, 13.12
  islandica, 13.13
Bulweria bulwerii, 2.14
Burhinus bistriatus, 26.1
Busarellus nigricollis, 17.5
Buteo albicaudatus, 17.7
  albonotatus, 18.5
  brachyurus, 18.6
  jamaicensis, 19.5
  lagopus, 19.7
  lineatus, 19.2
  magnirostris, 18.8
  platypterus, 19.3
  regalis, 19.6
  swainsoni, 19.4
Buteogallus anthracinus, 18.2
  meridionalis, 19.1
  subtilis, 18.4
  urubitinga, 18.3
Butorides striatus, 9.14
  virescens, 9.14

Cacicus cela, 97.18
  melanicterus, 97.17
  uropygialis, 97.19
Cairina moschata, 11.12
Calamospiza melanocorys, 95.2
Calcarius lapponicus, 95.20
  mccownii, 95.19
  ornatus, 95.21
Calidris acuminata, 29.9
  alba, 29.2
  alpina, 29.10
  bairdii, 29.7
  canutus, 29.1
  ferruginea, 29.11
  fuscicollis, 29.6
  maritima, 29.13
  mauri, 29.4
  melanotos, 29.8
  minutilla, 29.5
  ptilocnemis, 29.12
  pusilla, 29.3
Callipepla californica, 25.7
  douglasii, 25.5
  gambelii, 25.6
  squamata, 25.4
Calliphlox bryantae, 50.2
  mitchellii, 50.3
Calocitta colliei, 72.5
  formosa, 72.6
Calonectris diomedea, 1.10
Calothorax lucifer, 50.6

pulcher, 50.7
Calypte anna, 50.10
  costae, 50.11
Campephilus guatemalensis, 53.14
  haematogaster, 53.15
  imperialis, 53.17
  melanoleucos, 53.16
Camptostoma imberbe, 64.6
  obsoletum, 64.7
Campylopterus curvipennis, 45.12
  excellens, 45.13
  hemileucurus, 45.16
  rufus, 45.14
Campylorhamphus pusillus, 57.17
  trochilirostris, 57.16
Campylorhynchus
  albobrunneus, 76.1
  brunneicapillus, 76.9
  chiapensis, 76.2
  gularis, 76.6
  jocosus, 76.7
  megalopterus, 76.5
  rufinucha, 76.3
  yucatanicus, 76.8
  zonatus, 76.4
Capito maculicoronatus, 53.1
Caprimulgus arizonae, 43.3
  badius, 43.6
  carolinensis, 43.4
  cayannensis, 43.11
  maculicaudus, 43.8
  ridgwayi, 43.7
  rufus, 43.9
  salvini, 43.5
  saturatus, 43.10
  vociferus, 43.2
Capsiempis flaveola, 64.10
Cardellina rubrifrons, 85.2
Cardinalis cardinalis, 90.7
  sinuatus, 90.6
Carduelis atriceps, 98.12
  lawrencei, 98.11
  notata, 98.14
  pinus, 98.10
  psaltria, 98.15
  tristis, 98.13
  xanthogastra, 98.17
Carpodacus cassinii, 98.7
  mexicanus, 98.8
  purpureus, 98.6
Carpodectes antoniae, 69.16
  hopkei, 69.15
  nitidus, 69.14
Caryothraustes poliogaster, 90.11
  poliogaster, 90.10
Casmerodius albus, 10.2
Catharacta chilensis, 30.6
  maccormicki, 30.5
  skua, 30.4
Cathartes aura, 14.2

burrovianus, 14.3
Catharus aurantiirostris, 80.6
  dryas, 80.12
  frantzii, 80.8
  fuscater, 80.11
  fuscescens, 80.13
  gracilirostris, 80.9
  guttatus, 80.16
  mexicanus, 80.10
  minimus, 80.14
  mustelinus, 80.17
  occidentalis, 80.7
  ustulatus, 80.15
Catherpes mexicanus, 74.17
  navai, 74.18
  sumichrasti, 74.19
Catoptrophorus semipalmatus, 27.4
Celeus castaneus, 56.10
  loricatus, 56.9
Cephalopterus glabricollis, 69.18
Cepphus columba, 6.2
Cercomacra nigricans, 61.2
  tyrannina, 61.1
Cerorhinca monocerata, 6.8
Certhia americana, 73.12
Ceryle alcyon, 52.10
  torquata, 52.9
Chaetura andrei, 44.12
  brachyura, 44.11
  chapmani, 44.10
  cinereiventris, 44.14
  fumosa, 44.13
  pelagica, 44.8
  spinicauda, 44.13
  vauxi, 44.9
Chalybura buffoni, 49.5
  urochrysia, 49.4
Chamaea fasciata, 73.8
Chamaepetes unicolor, 23.9
Charadrius alexandrinus, 27.9
  collaris, 27.8
  melodus, 27.12
  montanus, 27.14
  morinellus, 27.15
  semipalmatus, 27.11
  vociferus, 27.13
  wilsonia, 27.10
Chiroxiphia lanceolata, 68.15
  linearis, 68.14
Chlidonias niger, 34.5
Chloroceryle aenea, 52.14
  amazona, 52.12
  americana, 52.13
  inda, 52.11
Chlorophanes spiza, 86.9
Chlorophonia callophrys, 87.2
  flavirostris, 87.3
  occipitalis, 87.1
Chloropipo holochlora, 68.11
Chlorospingus canigularis, 89.11
  flavigularis, 89.14
  inornatus, 89.12
310

ophthalmicus, 89.10
  pileatus, 89.9
  tacarcunae, 89.13
Chlorostilbon assimilis, 46.13
  auriceps, 46.11
  canivettii, 46.9
  c. salvini, 46.10
  forficatus, 46.12
Chlorothraupis carmioli, 89.7
  olivacea, 89.8
Chondestes grammacus, 95.4
Chondrohierax uncinatus, 15.2
Chordeiles acutipennis, 42.6
  gundlachii, 42.8
  minor, 42.7
Chrysolampis mosquitus, 46.1
Chrysothlypis chrysomelas,
  89.16
Cinclus mexicanus, 76.20
Circus buffoni, 16.10
  cyaneus, 16.9
Cistothorus palustris, 75.10
  platensis, 75.11
Clangula hyemalis, 13.8
Claravis mondetoura, 36.13
  pretiosa, 36.12
Cnipodectes subbrunneus, 67.15
Coccothraustes abeillei, 98.16
  vespertinus, 98.18
Coccyzus americanus, 39.3
  erythropthalmus, 39.2
  ferrugineus, 39.6
  lansbergi, 39.5
  minor, 39.4
  pumilus, 39.1
Cochlearius cochlearius, 9.17
Coereba flaveola, 86.1
Colaptes auratus, 56.1
  chrysoides, 56.2
Colibri delphinae, 49.2
  thalassinus, 49.3
Colinus cristatus, 25.13
  leucopogon, 25.14
  nigrogularis, 25.12
  virginianus, 25.11
Colonia colonus, 67.12
Columba cayennensis, 35.3
  fasciata, 35.7
  flavirostris, 35.6
  goodsoni, 35.10
  leucocephala, 35.5
  livia, 35.1
  nigrirostris, 35.8
  plumbea, 35.4
  speciosa, 35.2
  subvinacea, 35.9
Columbina inca, 36.8
  minuta, 36.10
  passerina, 36.9
  talpacoti, 36.11
Conirostrum leucogenys, 86.2
Conopias albovittata, 62.6
Contopus borealis, 63.1
  cinereus, 63.6

lugubris, 63.2
  ochraceus, 63.7
  pertinax, 63.5
  sordidulus, 63.3
  virens, 63.4
Coragyps atratus, 14.1
Corapipo leucorrhoa, 68.13
Corvus brachyrhynchos, 72.9
  corax, 72.13
  cryptoleucus, 72.12
  imparatus, 72.10
  sinaloae, 72.11
  splendens, 72.14
Cotinga amabilis, 69.9
  nattereri, 69.11
  ridgwayi, 69.10
Coturnicops noveboracensis, 24.1
Cranioleuca dissita, 59.5
  erythrops, 59.4
Crax rubra, 23.10
Creagrus furcatus, 31.10
Crotophaga ani, 39.15
  major, 39.17
  sulcirostris, 39.16
Crypturellus boucardi, 25.20
  cinnamomeus, 25.19
  kerriae, 25.18
  soui, 25.17
Cyanerpes caeruleus, 86.6
  cyaneus, 86.7
  lucidus, 86.5
Cyanocitta cristata, 71.2
  stelleri, 71.1
Cyanocompsa cyanoides, 90.16
  parellina, 90.15
Cyanocorax affinis, 72.1
  beecheii, 71.14
  dickeyi, 72.7
  melanocyaneus 71.11
  morio, 72.4
  sanblasianus, 71.12
  yncas, 72.2
  yucatanicus, 71.13
Cyanolyca argentigula, 71.10
  cucullata, 71.6
  mirabilis, 71.9
  nana, 71.8
  pumilo, 71.7
Cyclarhis gujanensis, 76.15
Cyclorrhynchus psittacula, 6.9
Cygnus buccinator, 11.5
  columbianus, 11.4
Cymbilaimus lineatus, 60.3
Cynanthus latirostris, 46.15
  l. doubledayi, 46.16
  sordidus, 46.14
Cyphorhinus phaeocephalus, 75.17
Cypseloides cherriei, 44.4
  cryptus, 44.2
  niger, 44.1
  rutilus, 44.3
  storeri, 44.5
Cyrtonyx montezumae, 25.9
  ocellatus, 25.10

Dacnis cayana, 86.4
  venusta, 86.8
  viguieri, 86.3
Dactylortyx thoracicus, 25.2
Damophila julie, 47.4
Daption capense, 3.14
Daptrius americanus, 21.1
Deconychura longicauda, 57.4
Deltarhynchus flammulatus,
  63.15
Dendrocincla anabatina, 57.1
  fuliginosa, 57.2
  homochroa, 57.3
  homochroa, 58.7
Dendrocolaptes certhia, 57.6
  picumnus, 57.7
Dendrocygna autumnalis, 11.3
  bicolor, 11.1
  viduata, 11.2
Dendroica caerulescens, 83.20
  castanea, 83.15
  cerulea, 83.19
  chrysoparia, 83.10
  coronata, 83.3
  discolor, 83.1
  dominica, 83.9
  fusca, 83.8
  graciae, 83.11
  kirtlandii, 83.12
  magnolia, 83.4
  nigrescens, 83.18
  occidentalis, 83.5
  palmarum, 83.13
  pensylvanica, 83.2
  petechia, 82.16
  pinus, 83.14
  striata, 83.16
  tigrina, 82.17
  townsendi, 83.7
  virens, 83.6
Dendrortyx barbatus, 24.13
  leucophrys, 24.14
  macroura, 24.12
Diglossa baritula, 93.11
  plumbea, 93.10
Diomedea albatrus, 1.1
  chrysostema, 1.5
  exulans, 1.3
  immutabilis, 1.6
  irrorata, 1.4
  nigripes, 1.2
Discosura conversii, 46.8
Dives dives, 96.4
Dolichonyx oryzivorus, 98.1
Donacobius atricapillus, 76.17
Doricha eliza, 50.4
  enicura, 50.5
Doryfera ludoviciae, 46.17
Dromococcyx phasianellus,
  39.10
Dryocopus lineatus, 56.11
  pileatus, 56.12
Dumetella carolinensis, 79.1
  glabrirostris, 79.2

311

Dysithamnus mentalis, 59.14
  puncticeps, 59.15
  striaticeps, 59.16

Egretta caerulea, 9.8
  garzetta, 9.11
  rufescens, 9.10
  thula, 9.7
  tricolor, 9.9
Elaenia chiriquensis, 65.7
  flavogaster, 65.5
  frantzii, 65.6
  martinica, 65.4
Elanoides forficatus, 16.1
Elanus leucurus, 16.2
Electron carinatum, 52.6
  platyrhynchum, 52.4
Elvira chionura, 47.15
  cupreiceps, 47.16
Emberizoides herbicola, 95.1
Empidonax affinis, 66.11
  albigularis, 66.6
  alnorum, 66.4
  atriceps, 66.17
  difficilis, 66.12
  flavescens, 66.16
  flaviventris, 66.2
  fulvifrons, 66.14
  hammondii, 66.8
  mimimus, 66.7
  oberholseri, 66.9
  occidentalis, 66.13
  traillii, 66.5
  virescens, 66.3
  wrightii, 66.10
Eremophila alpestris, 73.13
Ergaticus ruber, 85.3
  versicolor, 85.4
Eubucco bourcierii, 53.2
Eucometis penicillata, 89.5
Eudocimus albus, 10.4
  ruber, 10.5
Eugenes fulgens, 49.15
Eumomota superciliosa, 52.8
Euphagus carolinus, 96.5
  cyanocephalus, 96.6
Eupherusa cyanophrys, 47.14
  eximia, 47.11
  nigriventris, 47.13
  poliocerca, 47.12
Euphonia affinis, 87.10
  anneae, 87.13
  elegantissima, 87.14
  fulvicrissa, 87.12
  gouldi, 87.4
  hirundinacea, 87.5
  imitans, 87.9
  laniirostris, 87.6
  luteicapilla, 87.8
  minuta, 87.7
  xanthogaster, 87.11
Euptilotis neoxenus, 51.14
Eurypyga helias, 7.14
Eutoxeres aquila, 45.10

Falco columbarius, 22.5
  deiroleucus, 22.4
  femoralis, 22.2
  mexicanus, 22.7
  peregrinus, 22.6
  rufigularis, 22.3
  rusticolus, 22.8
  sparverius, 22.1
Florisuga mellivora, 45.17
Fluvicola pica, 67.16
Formicarius analis, 61.14
  monileger, 61.13
  nigricapillus, 61.12
  rufipectus, 61.15
Formicifora grisea, 60.15
Forpus conspicillatus, 37.13
  cyanopygius, 37.12
Fratercula cirrhata, 6.10
  corniculata, 6.11
Fregata magnificens, 5.10
  minor, 5.11
Fulica americana, 7.12
Fulmarus glacialis, 1.7
  glacialoides, 1.8

Galbula ruficauda, 51.18
Gallinago delicata, 28.8
Gallinula chloropus, 7.11
Gampsonyx swainsonii, 16.5
Gavia adamsii, 6.15
  arctica, 6.13
  immer, 6.14
  stellata, 6.12
Geococcyx californianus, 39.14
  velox, 39.15
Geothlypis aequinoctialis, 84.6
  beldingi, 84.10
  flavovelata, 84.9
  nelsoni, 84.11
  poliocephala, 84.5
  semiflava, 84.8
  speciosa, 84.12
  trichas, 84.7
Geotrygon albifacies, 35.19
  carrikeri, 35.12
  chiriquensis, 35.15
  costaricensis, 35.13
  goldmani, 35.14
  lawrencii, 35.11
  montana, 35.17
  veraguensis, 35.15
  violacea, 35.18
Geranospiza caerulescens, 15.9
Glaucidium brasilianum, 41.19
  californicum, 41.12
  gnoma, 41.11
  griseiceps, 41.18
  hoskinsii, 41.14
  costaricanum, 41.13
  minutissimum, 41.15
  palmarum, 41.16
  sanchezi, 41.17
Glaucis aenea, 45.1
  hirsuta, 45.2

Glyphorhynchus spirurus, 58.5
Goethalsia bella, 47.17
Goldmania violiceps, 47.10
Grallaria guatimalensis, 61.19
Grallaricula flavirostris, 61.17
Granatellus sallaei, 85.5
  venustus, 85.6
Grus americana, 10.15
  canadensis, 10.16
Guiraca caerulea, 90.17
Gygis alba, 34.9
Gymnocichla nudiceps, 61.3
Gymnogyps californianus, 14.5
Gymnopithys leucaspis, 61.8
Gymnorhinus cyanocephalus, 71.3

Habia atrimaxillaris, 88.11
  fuscicauda, 88.10
  rubica, 88.9
Haematopus bachmani, 26.7
  palliatus, 26.6
Haliaeetus leucocephalus, 14.7
Haplophaedia aureliae, 49.16
Haplospiza rustica, 93.8
Harpagus bidentatus, 16.6
Harpia harpyja, 20.3
Harpyhaliaetus solitarius, 18.1
Heliodoxa jacula, 49.1
Heliomaster constantii, 49.19
  longirostris, 49.18
Heliornis fulica, 7.13
Heliothryx barroti, 49.17
Helmitheros vermivorus, 82.1
Hemithraupis flavicollis, 89.15
Henicorhina leucophrys, 75.14
  leucosticta, 75.13
Herpetotheres cachinnans, 21.4
Herpsilochmus rufimarginatus, 60.16
Heteroscelus incanus, 27.5
Heterospingus rubrifrons, 88.4
  xanthopygius, 88.5
Himantopus mexicanus, 26.8
Hirundo fulva, 70.18
  pyrrhonota, 70.19
  rustica, 70.20
Histrionicus histrionicus, 13.7
Hylocharis eliciae, 47.7
  grayi, 47.6
  leucotis, 47.8
  xantusii, 47.9
Hyloctistes subulatus, 59.7
Hylomanes momotula, 52.1
Hylopezus dives, 61.18
  perspicillatus, 61.16
Hylophilus aurantiifrons, 77.17
  decurtatus, 77.15
  flavipes, 77.16
  ochraceiceps, 77.14
Hylophylax naevioides, 61.10

Icteria virens, 85.7
Icterus auratus, 97.10

auricapillus, 97.8
  bullockii, 97.14
  chrysater, 97.7
  cucullatus, 97.12
  dominicensis, 97.1
  galbula, 97.15
  graduacauda, 97.5
  gularis, 97.13
  maculialatus, 97.3
  mesomelas, 97.6
  parisorum, 97.4
  pectoralis, 97.9
  pustulatus, 97.11
  spurius, 97.16
  wagleri, 97.2
Ictinia mississippiensis, 16.3
  plumbea, 16.4
Ixobrychus exilis, 9.3

Jabiru mycteria, 10.12
Jacamerops aurea, 51.19
Jacana jacana, 26.15
  spinosa, 26.14
Junco bairdi, 95.16
  hyemalis, 95.14
  insularis, 95.17
  phaeonotus, 95.15
  vulcani, 95.18

Klais guimeti, 46.3

Lampornis amethystinus, 49.12
  calolaema, 49.9
  castaneoventris, 49.8
  c. cinereicauda, 49.7
  clemenciae, 49.13
  hemileucus, 49.6
  sybillae, 49.11
  viridipallens, 49.10
Lamprolaima rhami, 49.14
Lanio aurantius, 88.2
  leucothorax, 88.3
Laniocera rufescens, 68.4
Lanius excubitor, 76.18
  ludovicianus, 76.16
Larosterna inca, 34.6
Larus argentatus, 31.4
  atlanticus, 30.10
  atricilla, 32.5
  belcheri, 30.12
  californicus, 31.5
  canus, 32.2
  cirrocephalus, 31.9
  crassirostris, 31.1
  delawarensis, 32.3
  dominicanus, 30.9
  fuscus, 30.8
  glaucescens, 31.6
  heermanni, 32.1
  hyperboreus, 31.7
  livens, 30.11
  marinus, 30.7
  minutus, 32.10
  modestus, 31.11

  occidentalis, 31.3
  philadelphia, 32.8
  pipixcan, 32.6
  ridibundus, 32.4
  schistisagus, 31.2
  thayeri, 31.8
Laterallus albigularis, 24.5
  exilis, 24.3
  jamaicensis, 24.4
  ruber, 24.2
Legatus leucophaius, 62.11
Lepidocolaptes affinis, 57.15
  leucogaster, 57.13
  souleyetii, 57.14
Lepidopyga coeruleogularis, 47.5
Leptodon cayanensis, 15.1
Leptopogon amaurocephalus, 66.20
  superciliaris, 66.19
Leptotila battyi, 36.16
  cassinii, 36.18
  jamaicensis, 36.17
  plumbeiceps, 36.15
  verreauxi, 36.14
Leucopternis albicollis, 17.1
  plumbea, 17.3
  princeps, 17.4
  semiplumbea, 17.2
Limnodromus griseus, 28.6
  scolopaceus, 28.7
Limnothlypis swainsonii, 82.2
Limosa fedoa, 28.3
  haemastica, 28.1
  lapponica, 28.2
Lipaugus unirufus, 68.2
Lochmias nematura, 58.14
Lophodytes cucullatus, 11.13
Lophornis adorabilis, 46.7
  brachylophus, 46.4
  delattrei, 46.6
  helenae, 46.5
Lophostrix cristata, 40.2
Lophotriccus pileatus, 65.8
Loxia curvirostra, 98.9
Lurocalis semitorquatus, 42.5
Lysurus crassirostris, 91.15

Machetornis rixosus, 62.18
Malacoptila panamensis, 52.18
Manacus aurantiacus, 68.9
  candei, 68.8
  vitellinus, 68.7
Margarornis bellulus, 58.9
  rubiginosus, 58.10
Megarynchus pitangua, 62.3
Melanerpes aurifrons, 54.12
  carolinus, 54.6
  chrysauchen, 54.3
  chrysogenys, 54.9
  erythrogaster, 54.4
  formicivorus, 54.2
  hoffmannii, 54.11
  hypopolius, 54.10
  lewis, 54.1

  pucherani, 54.8
  pygmaeus, 54.5
  rubricapillus, 54.13
  uropygialis, 54.7
Melanitta fusca, 13.11
  nigra, 13.9
  perspicillata, 13.10
Melanotis caerulescens, 79.3
  hypoleucus, 79.4
Meleagris ocellata, 23.12
Melospiza georgiana, 95.7
  lincolnii, 95.8
  melodia, 95.6
Melozone biarcuatum, 91.18
  kieneri, 91.19
  leucotis, 91.17
Mergus merganser, 11.14
  serrator, 11.15
Mesembrinibis cayennensis, 10.8
Micrastur mirandollei, 21.7
  ruficollis, 21.5
  semitorquatus, 21.6
Micrathene whitneyi, 41.20
Microbates cinereiventris, 77.6
Microcerculus marginatus, 75.16
  philomela, 75.15
Microchera albocoronata, 47.18
Micromonacha lanceolata, 53.5
Micropalama himantopus, 29.14
Micropygia schomburgkii, 24.11
Microrhopias quixensis, 60.12
Milvago chimachima, 21.3
Mimodes graysoni, 79.7
Mimus gilvus, 79.6
  polyglottos, 79.5
Mionectes oleagineus, 66.15
  olivaceus, 66.18
Mitrephanes phaeocercus, 64.18
Mitrospingus cassinii, 89.6
Mniotilta varia, 83.17
Molothrus aeneus, 96.14
  ater, 96.15
  bonariensis, 96.13
Momotus mexicanus, 52.3
  momota, 52.7
Monasa morphoeus, 53.4
Morococcyx erythropygus, 39.11
Morphnus guianensis, 20.2
Morus bassanus, 5.9
Motacilla alba, 73.14
  flava, 73.15
  lugens, 73.16
Myadestes coloratus, 80.5
  melanops, 80.4
  occidentalis, 80.2
  townsendi, 80.1
  unicolor, 80.3
Mycteria americana, 10.13
Myiarchus cinerascens, 63.11
  crinitus, 63.13
  nuttigi, 63.12
  panamensis, 63.8
  tuberculifer, 63.9

tyrannulus, 63.14
Myiobius atricaudus, 63.19
  barbatus, 63.18
  villosus, 63.17
Myioborus miniatus, 84.17
  pictus, 84.18
  torquatus, 84.16
Myiodynastes chrysocephalus, 62.8
  hemichrysus, 62.7
  luteiventris, 62.10
  maculatus, 62.9
Myiopagis caniceps, 65.3
  gaimardii, 65.2
  viridicata, 65.1
Myiophobus fasciatus, 64.13
Myiornis atricapillus, 65.10
Myiozetetes cayanensis, 62.5
  granadensis, 62.12
  similis, 62.4
Myrmeciza exsul, 61.5
  immaculata, 61.4
  laemosticta, 61.6
  longipes, 61.7
Myrmornis torquata, 61.9
Myrmotherula axillaris, 60.11
  brachyura, 60.14
  fulviventris, 60.10
  schisticolor, 60.9
  surinamensis, 60.13

Neochelidon tibialis, 70.13
Neocrex columbianus, 24.9
  erythrops, 24.10
Neomorphus geoffroyi, 39.12
Nesotriccus ridgwayi, 66.1
Nonnula ruficapilla, 53.6
Notharchus macrorhynchos,
    52.16
  pectoralis, 52.17
  tectus, 52.15
Nothocercus bonapartei, 25.16
Notiochelidon cyanoleuca,
    70.11
  pileata, 70.12
Nucifraga columbiana, 72.8
Numenius americanus, 26.11
  borealis, 26.9
  phaeopus, 26.10
  tahitiensis, 26.12
Nyctanassa violacea, 9.16
Nyctibius grandis, 42.1
  griseus, 42.2
  jamaicensis, 42.3
Nycticorax nycticorax, 9.15
Nyctidromus albicollis, 42.9
Nyctiphrynus mcleodii, 42.11
  ocellatus, 42.10
  yucatanicus, 42.12
Nystalus radiatus, 52.19

Oceanites gracilis, 4.2
  oceanicus, 4.1
Oceanodroma castro 4.6
  furcata 4.3

homochroa, 4.8
leucorhoa, 4.4
macrodactyla, 4.5
markhami, 4.10
melania, 4.9
microsoma, 4.11
tethys, 4.7
Odontophorus dialeucos, 24.19
  gujanensis, 24.17
  guttatus, 24.15
  leucolaemus, 24.18
  melanotis (erythrops),
    24.16
Oenanthe oenanthe, 81.1
Oncostoma cinereigulare, 65.13
  olivaceum, 65.14
Onychorhynchus coronatus,
    67.14
Oporornis agilis, 84.1
  formosus, 84.4
  philadelphia, 84.2
  tolmiei, 84.3
Oreophasis derbianus, 23.8
Oreortyx pictus, 25.8
Oreoscoptes montanus, 79.8
Oriturus superciliosus, 94.1
Ornithion brunneicapillum,
    64.5
  semiflavum, 64.4
Ortalis cinereiceps, 23.5
  leucogastra, 23.4
  poliocephala, 23.3
  vetula, 23.1
  wagleri, 23.2
Oryzoborus angolensis, 92.17
  nuttingi, 92.19
Otus asio, 41.2
  barbarus, 41.10
  choliba, 41.4
  clarkii, 41.5
  cooperi, 41.7
  flammeolus, 41.1
  guatemalae, 41.9
  kennicottii, 41.3
  seductus, 41.6
  trichopsis, 41.8
Oxyruncus cristatus, 67.18
Oxyura dominica, 13.16
  jamaicensis, 13.15

Pachyramphus aglaiae, 69.2
  albogriseus, 69.6
  cinnamomeus, 69.4
  homochrous, 69.1
  major, 69.3
  polychopterus, 69.5
  rufus, 69.8
  versicolor, 69.7
Pandion haliaetus, 14.6
Panterpe insignis, 47.3
Panyptila cayennensis, 44.16
  sanctihieronymi, 44.17
Parabuteo unicinctus, 17.6
Pardirallus maculatus, 23.20

Parula americana, 82.12
  gutturalis, 82.14
  pitiayumi, 82.13
Parus atricristatus, 73.4
  gambeli, 73.2
  inornatus, 73.5
  ridgwayi, 73.5
  sclateri, 73.1
  wollweberi, 73.3
Passer domesticus, 98.19
Passerculus sandwichensis,
    93.13
Passerella iliaca, 95.5
Passerina amoena, 91.4
  ciris, 91.6
  cyanea, 91.1
  leclancherii, 91.5
  rositae, 91.2
  versicolor, 91.3
Pelagodroma marina, 4.12
Pelecanus erythrorhynchos, 8.1
  occidentalis, 8.2
Penelope purpurascens, 23.7
Penelopina nigra, 23.6
Peucedramus taeniatus, 85.1
Pezopetes capitalis, 91.14
Phaenostictus mcleannani,
    61.11
Phaeochroa cuvierii, 45.15
Phaeomyias murina, 64.8
Phaeoprogne tapera, 70.1
Phaethon aethereus, 5.2
  lepturus, 5.3
  rubricauda, 5.3
Phaethornis anthophilus, 45.7
  guy, 45.6
  longirostris, 45.4
  l. mexicanus, 45.5
  striigularis, 45.9
  yaruqui, 45.8
Phaetusa simplex, 34.4
Phainopepla nitens, 76.13
Phainoptila melanoxantha,
    76.14
Phalacrocorax auritus, 8.3
  bougainvillii, 8.8
  brasilianus, 8.5
  carbo, 8.4
  pelagicus, 8.7
  penicillatus, 8.6
Phalaenoptilus nuttallii, 43.1
Phalaropus fulicarius, 28.12
  lobatus, 28.11
Pharomachrus auriceps, 51.16
  mocinno, 51.15
Phasianus colchicus, 23.14
Pheucticus chrysopeplus, 90.13
  ludovicianus, 90.9
  melanocephalus, 90.14
  tibialis, 90.12
Philohydor lictor, 62.2
Philomachus pugnax, 28.5
Philortyx fasciatus, 25.3
Philydor fuscipennis, 59.9

rufus, 59.10
Phoenicopterus ruber, 10.14
Phyllomyias griseiceps, 64.2
  zeledoni, 64.1
Phylloscartes flavovirens, 64.11
  superciliaris, 64.12
Phylloscopus borealis, 77.2
  fuscatus, 77.1
Piaya cayana, 39.7
  minuta, 39.8
Picoides arizonae, 55.6
  nuttallii, 55.2
  pubescens, 55.4
  scalaris, 55.1
  stricklandi, 55.5
  villosus, 55.3
Piculus auricularis, 55.9
  callopterus, 55.11
  chrysochloros, 55.12
  punctigula, 55.13
  rubiginosus, 55.8
  r. aeruginosus, 55.7
  simplex, 55.10
Picumnus olivaceus, 58.1
Pilherodius pileatus, 9.18
Pinaroloxias inornata, 93.9
Pionopsitta haematotis, 38.9
  pyrilia, 38.10
Pionus menstruus, 37.18
  senilis, 37.17
Pipilo aberti, 92.7
  albicollis, 92.10
  chlorurus, 92.4
  crissalis, 92.8
  erythrophthalmus, 92.6
  fuscus, 92.9
  ocai, 92.5
Pipra coronata, 68.17
  erythrocephala, 68.11
  mentalis, 68.12
  pipra, 68.16
Piprites griseiceps, 68.6
Piranga bidentata, 88.17
  erythrocephala, 88.19
  flava, 88.13
  leucoptera, 88.16
  ludoviciana, 88.18
  olivacea, 88.15
  roseogularis, 88.12
  rubra, 88.14
Pitangus sulphuratus, 62.1
Pittasoma michleri, 61.20
Pitylus grossus, 90.5
Platyrhinchus cancrominus,
  65.18
  coronatus, 65.20
  mystaceus, 65.19
Plegadis chihi, 10.7
  falcinellus, 10.6
Pluvialis dominica, 26.4
  fulva, 26.5
  squatarola, 26.3
Podiceps auritus, 7.4
  grisegena, 7.5

nigricollis, 7.6
Podilymbus gigas, 7.3
  podiceps, 7.2
Polioptila albiloris, 77.11
  caerulea, 77.7
  californica, 77.9
  melanura, 77.8
  nigriceps, 77.10
  plumbea, 77.12
  schistaceigula, 77.13
Polyborus plancus, 21.2
Pooecetes gramineus, 95.3
Porphyrio martinica, 7.9
  porphyrio, 7.10
Porzana carolina, 24.7
  flaviventer, 24.8
Premnoplex brunnescens, 58.4
Procellaria parkinsoni, 1.9
Procnias tricarunculata, 69.19
Progne chalybea, 70.3
  dominicensis, 70.5
  modesta, 70.6
  sinaloae, 70.4
  subis, 70.2
Protonotaria citrea, 82.15
Psaltriparus minimus, 73.7
Psarocolius decumanus, 96.16
  guatimozinus, 96.19
  montezuma, 96.18
  wagleri, 96.17
Pselliophorus luteoviridis, 93.4
  tibialis, 93.5
Pseudocolaptes lawrencii, 58.7
Pseudotriccus pelzelni, 65.11
Pterodroma arminjoniana, 2.5
  cervicalis, 2.2
  cookii, 2.8
  externa, 2.1
  hasitata, 2.13
  inexpectata, 2.10
  leucoptera, 2.12
  longirostris, 2.11
  neglecta, 2.4
  nigripennis, 2.9
  phaeopygia, 2.3
  rostrata, 2.7
  ultima, 2.6
Pteroglossus frantzii, 53.10
  torquatus, 53.9
Ptilogonys caudatus, 76.12
  cinereus, 76.11
Ptychoramphus aleuticus, 6.6
Puffinus assimilis, 3.11
  auricularis, 3.12
  bulleri, 3.5
  carneipes, 3.2
  creatopus, 3.1
  gravis, 3.3
  griseus, 3.6
  lherminieri, 3.13
  nativitatus, 3.8
  opisthomelas, 3.9
  pacificus, 3.4
  puffinus, 3.10

tenuirostris, 3.7
Pulsatrix perspicillata, 40.3
Pygmornis longuemareus
  (*striigularis*), 45.9
Pyrocephalus rubinus, 67.4
Pyrrhura hoffmannzi, 37.9
  picta, 37.10

Querula purpurata, 69.17
Quiscalus major, 96.10
  mexicanus, 96.8
  nicaraguensis, 96.11
  palustris, 96.7
  quiscula, 96.9

Rallus elegans, 23.16
  limicola, 23.17
  longirostris, 23.15
Ramphastos sulfuratus, 53.11
  swainsonii, 53.12
Ramphocaenus melanurus, 77.5
Ramphocelus costaricensis, 89.3
  dimidiatus, 89.2
  flammigerus, 89.4
  passerinii, 89.3
  sanguinolentus, 89.1
Ramphostos brevis, 53.13
Recurvirostra americana, 26.13
Regulus calendula, 77.4
  satrapa, 77.3
Rhodinocichla rosea, 89.17
Rhodothraupis celaeno, 90.8
Rhynchocyclus brevirostris,
  67.12
  olivaceus, 67.13
Rhynchopsitta pachyrhyncha,
  38.7
  terrisi, 38.8
Rhynchortyx cinctus, 25.1
Rhytipterna holerythra, 68.3
Riparia riparia, 70.14
Rissa tridactyla, 32.7
Rostrhamus hamatus, 16.8
  sociabilis, 16.7
Rynchops niger, 34.10

Salpinctes obsoletus, 75.18
Saltator albicollis, 90.2
  atriceps, 90.3
  coerulescens, 90.1
  maximus, 90.4
Sapayoa aenigma, 68.5
Sarcoramphus papa, 14.4
Sarkidiornis melanotos, 11.11
Sayornis nigricans, 67.1
  phoebe, 67.2
  saya, 67.3
Scaphidura oryzivora, 96.12
Schiffornis turdinus, 68.1
Sclerurus albigularis, 58.13
  guatemalensis, 58.12
  mexicanus, 58.11
Scolopax minor, 28.9
Scytalopus argentifrons, 59.18

panamensis, 59.17
vicinior, 59.19
Seiurus aurocapillus, 85.18
motacilla, 85.20
noveboracensis, 85.19
Selasphorus ardens, 50.14
ellioti, 50.20
flammula, 50.13
heloisa, 50.19
platycercus, 50.16
rufus, 50.17
sasin, 50.18
scintilla, 50.15
Selenidera spectabilis, 53.8
Semnornis frantzii, 53.3
Serpophaga cinerea, 67.17
Setophaga ruticilla, 84.19
Sialia currucoides, 81.4
mexicana, 81.3
sialis, 81.2
Sicalis flaveola, 93.1
luteola, 93.2
Sirystes sibilator, 67.8
Sitta canadensis, 73.9
carolensis, 73.10
pygmaea, 73.11
Sittasomus griseicapillus,
58.6
Spheniscus mendiculus, 6.16
Sphyrapicus nuchalis, 56.6
ruber, 56.7
thyroideus, 56.8
varius, 56.5
Spindalis zena, 88.1
Spiza americana, 91.7
Spizaetus ornatus, 20.6
tyrannus, 20.5
Spizaster melanoleucus, 20.4
Spizella atrogularis, 94.5
breweri, 94.4
pallida, 94.7
passerina, 94.6
pusilla, 94.2
wortheni, 94.3
Sporophila americana, 92.15
bouvronides, 92.14
lineola, 92.18
minuta, 92.11
nigricollis, 92.12
schistacea, 92.16
torqueola, 92.13
Steatornis caripensis, 42.4
Steganopus tricolor, 28.10
Stelgidopteryx ridgwayi, 70.15
ruficollis, 70.17
serripennis, 70.16
Stellula calliope, 50.12
Stercorarius longicaudus, 30.3
parasiticus, 30.2
pomarinus, 30.1
Sterna anaethetus, 34.2
antillarum, 33.9
caspia, 33.1
dougallii, 33.5

elegans, 33.3
forsteri, 33.8
fuscata, 34.3
hirundo, 33.6
maxima, 33.2
nilotica, 34.1
paradisaea, 33.7
sandvicensis, 33.4
superciliaris, 33.10
Streptopelia chinensis, 36.6
decaocto, 36.7
Streptoprocne semicollaris, 44.7
zonaris, 44.6
Strix fulvescens, 40.9
nigrolineata, 40.6
occidentalis, 40.7
varia, 40.8
virgata L 35 cm., 40.5
Sturnella magna, 96.1
militaris, 96.3
neglecta, 96.2
Sturnus vulgaris, 76.19
Sublegatus arenarum, 63.16
Sula dactylatra, 5.4
leucogaster, 5.6
nebouxii, 5.5
sula, 5.7
variegata, 5.8
Synallaxis albescens, 59.3
brachyura, 59.2
erythrothorax, 59.1
Syndactyla subalaris, 59.6
Synthliboramphus antiquus, 6.5
craveri, 6.4
hypoleucus, 6.3

Tachybaptus dominicus, 7.1
Tachycineta albilinea, 70.8
albiventer, 70.10
bicolor, 70.7
thalassina, 70.9
Tachyphonus delatrii, 88.7
luctuosus, 88.6
rufus, 88.8
Tangara cabanisi, 86.15
dowii, 86.19
florida, 86.12
fucosa, 86.18
guttata, 86.14
gyrola, 86.10
icterocephala, 86.13
inornata, 86.20
larvata, 86.17
lavinia, 86.11
palmeri, 86.16
Tapera naevia, 39.9
Taraba major, 60.1
Terenotriccus erythrurus, 65.12
Terenura callinota, 60.17
Tersina viridis, 87.19
Thalurania colombica, 47.2
fannyi, 47.2
ridgwayi, 47.1
Thamnistes anabatinus, 60.7

Thamnophilus atrinucha, 60.8
bridgesi, 60.6
doliatus, 60.2
nigriceps, 60.5
Theristicus caudatus, 10.9
Thraupis abbas, 87.16
episcopus, 87.17
palmarum, 87.18
Threnetes ruckeri, 45.3
Thripadectes rufobrunneus, 58.8
Thryomanes bewickii, 75.2
Thryorchilus browni, 75.12
Thryothorus atrogularis, 74.10
fasciatoventris, 74.11
felix, 74.3
leucopogon, 74.14
leucotis, 74.16
ludovicianus, 74.7
maculipectus, 74.2
modestus, 74.8
nigricapillus, 74.12
pleurostictus, 74.6
rufalbus, 74.4
rutilus, 74.15
semibadius, 74.13
sinaloa, 74.5
spadix, 74.9
thoracicus, 74.1
Tiaris olivacea, 93.3
Tigrisoma fasciatum, 9.6
lineatum, 9.5
mexicanum, 9.4
Tilmatura dupontii, 50.1
Tinamus major, 25.15
Tityra inquisitor, 69.13
semifasciata, 69.12
Todirostrum cinereum, 65.16
nigriceps, 65.17
sylvia, 65.15
Tolmomyias assimilis, 64.15
sulphurescens, 64.14
Touit costaricensis, 37.15
dilectissima, 37.16
Toxostoma bendirei, 79.13
cinereum, 79.12
crissale, 79.17
curvirostre, 79.14
guttatus, 79.11
lecontei, 79.18
longirostre, 79.10
ocellatum, 79.15
redivivum, 79.16
rufum, 79.9
Tringa flavipes, 27.2
melanoleuca, 27.1
solitaria, 27.3
Troglodytes aedon, 75.3
beani, 75.5
ochraceus, 75.4
rufociliatus, 75.9
sissonii, 75.7
tanneri, 75.6
troglodytes, 75.8
Trogon aurantiiventris, 51.6

bairdii, 51.11
citreolus, 51.4
clathratus, 51.13
collaris, 51.10
elegans, 51.9
massena, 51.12
melanocephalus, 51.3
melanurus, 51.7
mexicanus, 51.8
rufus, 51.1
violaceus, 51.5
viridis, 51.2
Tryngites subruficollis, 28.4
Turdus assimilis, 81.8
grayi, 81.6
graysoni, 81.10
infuscatus, 81.13
migratorius, 81.11
nigrescens, 81.14
obsoletus, 81.7
plebejus, 81.5
rufitorques, 81.12
rufopalliatus, 81.9
Tyrannulus elatus, 64.9
Tyrannus couchii, 62.14
crassirostris, 62.16
cubebsis, 67.7
dominicensis, 67.5
forficatus, 67.10
melancholicus, 62.13
savana, 67.9
tyrannus, 67.6
verticalis, 62.17
vociferans, 62.15
Tyto alba, 40.1

Uria aalge, 6.1
Uropsila leucogastra, 75.1

Vanellus chilensis, 26.2
Veniliornis fumigatus, 56.3
kirkii, 56.4
Vermivora celata, 82.4
chrysoptera, 82.10
crissalis, 82.5
luciae, 82.7
peregrina, 82.3
pinus, 82.9
ruficapilla, 82.8
superciliosa, 82.11
virginiae, 82.6
Vireo altiloquus, 78.21
atricapillus, 78.6
bairdi, 78.4
bellii, 78.5
brevipennis, 78.1
carmioli, 78.13
cassini, 78.10
flavifrons, 78.12
flavoviridis, 78.19
gilvus, 78.16
griseus, 78.2
huttoni, 78.14
hypochryseus, 78.15
leucophrys, 78.17
magister, 78.22
nelsoni, 78.7
olivaceus, 78.20
pallens, 78.3
philadelphicus, 78.18
plumbeus, 78.11
solitarius, 78.9
vicinior, 78.8
Vireolanius eximius, 77.20
melitophrys, 77.18
pulchellus, 77.19
Volatinia jacarina, 92.20

Wilsonia canadensis, 84.14
citrina, 84.15
pusilla, 84.13

Xanthocephalus
xanthocephalus, 98.5
Xema sabini, 32.9
Xenerpestes minlosi, 59.13
Xenops minutus, 58.2
rutilans, 58.3
Xenornis setifrons, 60.4
Xenotriccus callizonus, 64.19
mexicanus, 64.20
Xiphocolaptes promeropirhynchus, 57.5
Xiphorhynchus erythropygius, 57.11
flavigaster, 57.10
lachrymosus, 57.12
picus, 57.8
susurrans, 57.9

Zeledonia coronata, 85.17
Zenaida asiatica, 36.1
auriculata, 36.5
aurita, 36.2
graysoni, 36.4
macroura, 36.3
Zimmerius vilissimus, 64.3
Zonotrichia albicollis, 95.10
atricapilla, 95.12
capensis, 95.9
leucophrys, 95.13
querula, 95.11
Zoothera naevia, 81.15
pinicola, 81.16

Index of Spanish names

Numbers refer to the relevant plate, followed by the number of the bird on that plate.

Achichilique Piquiamarillo, 7.7
Piquinaranja, 7.8
Agachona Común, 28.8
Aguila Arpía, 20.3
Blanquinegra, 20.4
Cabeciblanca, 14.7
Crestada, 20.2
Elegante, 20.6
Pescador, 14.6
Real, 20.1
Solitaria, 18.1
Tirana, 20.5
Aguililla Aluda, 19.3
Artica, 19.7
Aura, 18.5
Blanca, 17.1
Caminera, 18.8
Canela, 17.5
Coliblanca, 17.7
Colicorta, 18.6
Colirroja, 19.5

de Harris, 17.6
de Swainson, 19.4
Gris, 18.7
Negra Mayor, 18.3
Negra Menor, 18.2
Pechirroja, 19.2
Real, 19.6
Aguilucho de Azara, 16.10
Norteño, 16.9
Aguja Canela, 28.3
Lomiblanca, 28.1
Agujeta Común, 28.6
Piquilarga, 28.7
Ala de Sable Violácea, 45.16
Albatros Cabecigrís, 1.5
de las Galápagos, 1.4
de Laysan, 1.6
Patinegro, 1.2
Rabón, 1.1
Viajero, 1.3
Alcaraván Americano, 26.1

Alcita Crestada, 6.7
de Cassin, 6.6
Rinoceronte, 6.8
Alitorcido Pardo, 67.15
Alondra Cornuda, 73.13
Amazilia Canela, 48.14
Coliazul, 48.7
Corona de Berilo, 48.11
Culiazul, 48.6
Gorriazul, 48.5
Manglera, 48.4
Pechiazul, 48.10
Pechiblanca, 48.1
Rabirrufa, 48.12
Vientriblanca, 48.8
Ampelis Americano, 76.10
Añapero Colicorto, 42.5
Menor, 42.6
Querequeté, 42.8
Zumbón, 42.7
Andarríos Maculado, 27.6

Solitario, 27.3
Anhinga Americana, 8.9
Antifacito Coronigrís, 84.5
  Coroniolivo, 84.8
  Norteño, 84.7
  Sureño, 84.6
Apizarrada Plomizo, 60.8
Aquilillo Blanco y Negro, 20.4
  Negro, 20.5
  Penachudo, 20.6
Arao Común, 6.1
  Paloma, 6.2
Arquitecto Güitío, 59.3
  Plomizo, 59.2
Arrocero Americano, 91.7
Atila Lomiamarilla, 63.20
  Rabadilla-brillante, 63.20
Atrapamoscas Jinete, 62.18
  de Rabadilla Blanca, 67.8
Aura Cabecirrojo, 14.2
  Sabanera, 14.3
Avefría Sureña, 26.2
Avetorito/illo Americano, 9.3
  Pantanero, 9.3
Avetoro Americano, 9.2
  Neotropical, 9.1
  Norteño, 9.2
Avoceta Americana, 26.13
Azulejo Gorjiazul, 81.3
  Gorjicanelo, 81.2
  Pálido, 81.4
Azulillo Norteño, 91.1
  Sietecolores, 91.6

Baloncillo, 73.6
Barbudo Cabecirroja, 53.2
  Cocora, 53.3
  Coronipunteado, 53.1
Batará Barrada, 60.2
  Barreteado, 60.2
  Café, 60.7
  Grande, 60.1
  Lineado, 60.3
  Mayor, 60.1
  Moteado, 60.4
  Negro, 60.5
  Negruzco, 60.6
  Plomizo, 60.8
Batarito Cabecigrís, 59.14
  Cabecipunteado, 59.15
  Pechirrayado, 59.16
  Sencillo, 59.14
Becacina Común, 28.8
Biemparado Grande, 42.1
  Norteño, 42.3
Bienteveo Grande, 62.1
  Menor, 62.2
Bisbita Americana, 73.18
  Caminero, 73.20
  de Sprague, 73.19
  Dorsiolivo 73.21
  Gorrirufa, 73.17
Bobo Blanco, 5.4
  Enmascarado, 5.4

Moreno, 5.6
  Norteño, 5.9
  Patiazul, 5.5
  Patirrojo, 5.7
  Peruano, 5.8
  Vientre-blanco, 5.6
Bolsero Capucha-negra, 97.1
  Castaño, 97.16
  Coliamarillo, 97.6
  Cuculado, 97.12
  de Altamira, 97.13
  de Audubon, 97.5
  de Baltimore, 97.15
  de Bullock, 97.14
  de Wagler, 97.2
  Dorsidorado, 97.7
  Dorsilistado, 97.11
  Dorsirrayado, 97.11
  Guatemalteco, 97.3
  Norteño, 97.15
  Pechimanchado, 97.9
  Real, 97.8
  Tunero, 97.4
  Yucateco, 97.10
Branta, 11.9
Breñero Gorgipallido, 59.11
  Rojizo, 59.12
Brillante Frentiverde, 49.1
Buco Barbón, 52.18
  Barreteado, 52.19
  Collarejo, 52.16
  Pechinegro, 52.17
  Pinto, 52.15
Búho Barrado, 40.8
  Blanquinegro, 40.6
  Café, 40.5
  Cornialbanco, 40.2
  Cornudo, 40.4
  de Anteojos, 40.3
  Fulvo, 40.9
  Grande, 40.4
  Listado, 40.12
  Llanero, 40.16
  Manchado, 40.7
  Orejicorto, 40.13
  Penachudo, 40.2
Búho-cornudo Cariblanco,
  40.12
  Caricafé, 40.10
  Oscuro, 40.11

Cabezón Aliblanco, 69.5
  Canelo, 69.4
  Cejiblanco, 69.6
  Cuelligrís, 69.3
  Ondeado, 69.7
  Rufo, 69.8
  Unicolor, 69.1
Cacique Lomiamarillo, 97.18
  Lomiescarlata, 97.19
  Mexicano, 97.17
  Picoplato, 97.20
  Piquiclaro, 97.20
Calamón Común, 7.10

Calzadito Verdoso Norteño, 49.1◀
Camea, 73.8
Campanero Tricarunculado,
  69.19
Candelero Americano, 26.8
Candelita Collareja, 84.16
  Norteña, 84.19
  Pechinegra, 84.17
Capulinero Colilargo, 76.12
  Gris, 76.11
  Negro, 76.13
  Negro y Amarillo, 76.14
Caracara Avispera, 21.1
  Cabecigualdo, 21.3
  Cargahuesos, 21.2
  Comecacao, 21.1
  Común, 21.2
Carao, 10.10
Cardenal Desértico, 90.6
  Norteño, 90.7
Carpinterito Oliváceo, 58.1
Carpintero Alibronceado, 55.7
  Alirrufo, 55.10
  Arlequín, 54.2
  Bebedor, 56.5
  Cabecirrojo, 54.4
  Cachetidorado, 54.9
  Cachetinegro, 54.8
  Café, 56.3
  Canelo, 56.9
  Careto, 54.2
  Carinegro, 54.8
  Carminoso, 53.15
  Castaño, 56.10
  Collarejo, 56.1
  Coronigrís, 55.9
  Crestirrojo, 53.16
  de Arizona, 55.6
  de California, 56.12
  de Gila, 54.7
  de Hoffmann, 54.11
  de Lewis, 54.1
  de Nuttall, 55.2
  de Strickland, 55.5
  Frentidorado, 54.12
  Imperial, 53.17
  Lineado, 56.11
  Listado, 55.1
  Lomirrojo, 56.4
  Norteamericano, 56.2
  Nuquidorado, 54.3
  Nuquirrojo, 54.13
  Oliváceo, 55.8
  Panameño, 55.11
  Pardo, 56.3
  Pechigrís, 54.10
  Pechipunteado, 55.13
  Picoplata, 53.14
  Piquiclaro, 53.14
  Plumonado, 55.4
  Serranero, 55.3
  Verde Dorado, 55.8
  Verdidorado, 55.12
  Vientrirrojo, 54.6

Yucatero, 54.5
Carpintero-velloso Mayor, 55.3
Cascanueces Americano, 72.8
Cenzontle de Socorro, 79.7
  Norteño, 79.5
  Sureño, 79.6
Cerceta Aliazul, 12.9
  Aliverde, 12.2
  Castaña, 12.11
  Cejiblanca, 12.10
Cernícalo Americano, 22.1
Chachalaca Cabecigrís, 23.5
  Común, 23.1
  Mexicana, 23.3
  Olivácea, 23.1
  Vientre-blanco, 23.4
  Vientre-castaña, 23.2
Chara Azuleja, 71.4
  Centroamericana, 71.11
  Crestada, 71.2
  de Beechy, 71.14
  de Niebla, 71.7
  de Omiltemi, 71.9
  de San Blas, 71.12
  de Steller, 71.1
  Enana, 71.8
  Gorriazul, 71.6
  Papán, 72.4
  Pechigrís, 71.5
  Pinta, 72.7
  Piñonera, 71.3
  Unicolor, 72.3
  Verde, 72.2
  Yucateca, 71.13
Charrán Blanco, 34.9
  Chico, 33.9
  Común, 33.6
  de Forster, 33.8
  Embridado, 34.2
  Inca, 34.6
  Pecudo, 34.4
  Piquinegro, 34.1
  Sombrío, 34.3
Chimbito Común, 94.6
Chinchinero Común, 89.10
Chingolo, 95.9
Chipe Aliazul, 82.9
  Alidorado, 82.10
  Amarillo, 82.16
  Atigrado, 82.17
  Azuloso, 83.20
  Cabeciamarillo, 83.5
  Caridorado, 83.10
  Carirrojo, 85.2
  Cejiblanco, 82.11
  Cejidorado, 85.12
  Cerúleo, 83.19
  Colimense, 82.5
  Collarejo, 84.14
  Corona-naranja, 85.9
  Corona-naranja, 82.4
  de Connecticut, 84.1
  de Grace, 83.11
  de Kentucky, 84.4

de Kirtland*, 83.12
de Lucy, 82.7
de Magnolia, 83.4
de Nashville, 82.8
de Swainson, 82.2
de Tolmie, 84.3
de Townsend, 83.7
de Virginia, 82.6
de Wilson, 84.13
del Pirre, 85.13
Dorsiverde, 83.6
Encapuchado, 84.15
Flanquicastaño, 83.2
Gorirrufo, 85.10
Gorjiamarillo, 83.9
Gorjinaranja, 83.8
Gorricastaño, 85.11
Gorrinegro, 83.16
Gusanero, 82.1
Llorón, 84.2
Negrigrís, 83.18
Ocotero, 85.1
Pechicastaño, 83.15
Peregrino, 82.3
Pinero, 83.14
Playero, 83.13
Pradeño, 83.1
Protonotario, 82.15
Rabadilla-amarilla, 83.3
Rojo, 85.3
Roquero, 85.8
Rosado, 85.4
Trepador, 83.17
Chipe-suelero Arroyero, 85.20
  Charquero, 85.19
  Coronado, 85.18
Chirigüe Sabanero, 93.2
Chispita Gorginaranja, 50.15
  Volcanera, 50.13
Chlorofonia Cejidorada, 87.2
  Coroniazul, 87.1
  Cuellidorada, 87.3
Chocha Americana, 28.9
Chorlitejo Collarejo, 27.8
  Patinegro, 27.9
  Picudo, 27.10
  Semipalmado, 27.11
  Tildío, 27.13
Chorlito Carambolo, 27.15
  Chiflador, 27.12
  Collarejo, 27.8
  de Rompientes, 28.15
  Dorado Menor, 26.4
  Gris, 26.3
  Llanero, 27.14
  Níveo, 27.9
  Piquigrueso, 27.10
  Semipalmado, 27.11
  Tildío, 27.13
Chorlo Gris, 26.3
Chorlo-dorado Americano, 26.4
  Asiático, 26.5
Chotacabras Coliblanco, 43.11
  Colicorta, 42.5

de Paso, 43.4
Gritón, 43.2
Mayor, 42.7
Menor, 42.6
Ocelado, 42.10
Rojizo, 43.9
Sombrío, 43.10
Chupasavia de Williamson, 56.8
  Nuquirroja, 56.6
  Pechirroja, 56.7
  Vientre-amarillo, 56.5
Cigüeña Americana, 10.13
Cigüeñón, 10.13
Cigüeñuela Cuellinegro, 26.8
Cisne de Tundra, 11.4
  Trompetero, 11.5
Clarín Jilguero, 80.2
  Norteño, 80.1
  Unicolor, 80.3
Clarinero de Laguna, 96.11
  Grande, 96.8
Codorniz Barrada, 25.3
  Bolanchaco, 24.15
  Californiana, 25.7
  Carirroja, 24.17
  Carirrufa, 25.1
  Crestada, 25.13
  de Gambel, 25.6
  de Moctezuma, 25.9
  de Montaña, 25.8
  del Tacarcuna, 24.19
  Elegante, 25.5
  Escamosa, 25.4
  Moteada, 24.15
  Ocelada, 25.10
  Pechicastaña, 24.16
  Pechinegra, 24.18
  Silbadora, 25.2
  Vientrimanchada, 25.14
Codorniz-cotui,
  Centroamericana, 25.14
  Norteña, 25.11
  Yucateca, 25.12
Colaespina Carirroja, 59.4
  De Coiba, 59.5
Colagrís Alibandeado, 59.13
Colibrí Alicastaño, 49.14
  Barbiesmeralda, 46.2
  Barbinegro, 50.9
  Cabeciazul, 46.3
  Canelo, 48.14
  Coliazul, 48.7
  Colidorado, 47.7
  Colipinto, 50.1
  Colirrayado, 47.11
  Colirrufo, 48.12
  Corona-verde, 48.16
  Corona-violeta, 48.15
  Coroniazul, 48.3
  de Anna, 50.10
  de Berilo, 48.9
  de Buffon, 49.5
  de Caliope, 50.12
  de Costa, 50.11

de Doubleday, 46.16
de Goldman, 47.10
de Julia, 47.4
de Xantus, 47.9
del Pirre, 47.17
Flanquicanelo, 48.17
Garganta de Fuego, 47.3
Garganta de Rubí, 50.8
Garganta de Zafiro, 47.5
Gorjirrubi, 50.8
Guerrerense, 47.12
Magnífico, 49.15
Montañés Coligrís, 49.7
Montañés Gorgimorado, 49.9
Montañés Variable, 49.8
Montañés Vientriblanco, 49.6
Oaxaqueño, 47.14
Orejiblanco, 47.8
Orejivioláceo Pardo, 49.2
Orejivioláceo Verde, 49.3
Patirrojo, 49.4
Pechiescamado, 45.15
Pechinegro, 47.13
Picopunzón, 49.17
Piquiancho, 46.15
Piquidentado, 45.11
Piquilargo, 49.18
Pochotero, 49.19
Prieto, 46.14
Rubí, 46.1
Vientre-canelo, 48.13
Colibrí-serrano Gorjiamatisto,
49.12
Gorjiazul, 49.13
Gorjiverde, 49.10
Pechiverde, 49.11
Colicerda Verde, 46.8
Colimbo Artico, 6.13
Común, 6.14
Gorjirrojo, 6.12
Piquiamarillo, 6.15
Collalba Norteña, 81.1
Colorín Azul, 91.1
Azulinegro, 90.15
de Rosito, 91.2
Lazulita, 91.4
Morado, 91.3
Pechinaranja, 91.5
Sietecolores, 91.6
Combatiente, 28.5
Cóndor Californiano, 14.5
Copete de Nieve, 47.18
Copetón Colipardo, 63.8
Crestioscuro, 63.9
Crestipardo, 63.14
de Nutting, 63.12
Garganticeniza, 63.11
Gorjicenizo, 63.11
Piquiplano, 63.15
Tirano, 63.14
Triste, 63.9
Viajero, 63.13
Coqueta Crestiblanca, 46.7
Cresticorta, 46.4

Crestinegra, 46.5
Crestirrojiza, 46.6
Cormorán Bicrestado, 8.3
de Brandt, 8.6
Grande, 8.4
Guanay, 8.8
Neotropical, 8.5
Pelágico, 8.7
Correcaminos Mayor, 39.14
Menor, 39.13
Correlimos Acuminado, 29.9
de Baird, 29.7
Grande, 29.1
Lomiblanco, 29.6
Menudo, 29.5
Occidental, 29.4
Oscuro, 29.13
Patilargo, 29.14
Pectoral, 29.8
Roquero, 29.12
Semipalmado, 29.3
Vagamundo, 27.5
Zarapitín, 29.11
Costurero Piquicorto, 28.6
Piquilargo, 28.7
Cotinga Azul, 69.11
Azuleja, 69.9
Blanca, 69.15
Linda, 69.9
Nivosa, 69.14
Piquiamarillo, 69.16
Turquesa, 69.10
Cotorra-serrana Occidental, 38.7
Oriental, 38.8
Cuclillo Cabecigrís, 39.5
Enano, 39.1
de Antifaz, 39.4
de la Isla Coco, 39.6
Faisán, 39.10
Listado, 39.9
Piquigualdo, 39.3
Piquinegro, 39.2
Sabanero, 39.11
Cuco Ardilla, 39.7
Faisán, 39.10
Hormiguero, 39.12
Manglero, 39.4
Menor, 39.8
Piquiamarillo, 39.3
Piquinegro, 39.2
Rayado, 39.9
Cuco-terrestre Menor, 39.11
Cuervo Americano, 72.9
Domestico, 72.14
Grande, 72.13
Llanero, 72.12
Sinaloense, 72.11
Tamaulipeco, 72.10
Cuevero de Sumichrast, 74.19
Cuitlacoche Californiano, 79.16
Crisal, 79.17
de Artemesia, 79.8
de Bendire, 79.13
de Cozumel, 79.11

Manchado, 79.15
Peninsular, 79.12
Piquicurvo, 79.14
Piquilargo, 79.10
Pálido, 79.18
Rojizo, 79.9

Dominico Americano, 98.13
Cabecinegro, 98.14
Coroninegro, 98.12
de Lawrence, 98.11
Dorsioscuro, 98.15
Pinero, 98.10
Donacobio, 76.17

Elainia Copetona, 65.5
Gris, 65.3
Montañera, 65.6
Sabanera, 65.7
Selvática, 65.2
Verdosa, 65.1
Elanio Caracolero, 16.7
Coliblanco, 16.2
Colinegro, 16.3
Enano, 16.5
Plomizo, 16.8
Plomizo, 16.4
Tijereta, 16.1
Elenia, 65.1
Caribeña, 65.4
Serrana, 65.6
Viente-amarillo, 65.5
Ermitaño Barbudo, 45.3
Bronceado, 45.1
Chico, 45.9
Colilargo, 45.4
de Yaruqui, 45.8
Enano, 45.9
Hirsuto, 45.2
Mexicano, 45.5
Verde, 45.6
Vientripálido, 45.7
Escribano Artico, 95.20
Cuellicastaño, 95.21
de McCown, 95.19
Esmeralda Coliblanca, 47.15
de Canivet, 46.9
de Coronilla Cobriza, 47.16
de Cozumel, 46.12
de Salvin, 46.10
Hondureña, 48.2
Mexicana, 46.11
Piquinegro, 46.13
Rabihorcada, 46.9
Vientre-blanco, 48.1
Esmerejón, 22.5
Espátula Rosada, 10.11
Espatulilla Cabecigrís, 65.15
Cabecinegra, 65.17
Común, 65.16
Espiguero Collarejo, 92.13
de Lesson, 92.14
Menudo, 92.11
Pizarroso, 92.16

Variable, 92.15
Vientriamarillo, 92.12
Estornino Europeo, 76.19
Estrellita de Mitchell, 50.3
    Gorgimorada, 50.2
Eufonia Capucha-azul, 87.14
    Capuchiceleste, 87.14
    Coroniamarilla, 87.8
    Gargantinegra, 87.10
    Gorjiamarilla, 87.5
    Gorjinegro, 87.10
    Gorricanela, 87.13
    Menuda, 87.7
    Olivácea, 87.4
    Piquigruesa, 87.6
    Vientre-blanco, 87.7
    Vientrileonada, 87.12
    Vientrinaranja, 87.11
    Vientrirrojiza, 87.9

Faisán Vulgar, 23.14
Falárapo Cuellirrojo, 28.11
    de Wilson, 28.10
    Piquigrueso, 28.12
Falaropo de Wilson, 28.10
    Picofino, 28.11
    Rojo, 28.12
Fandangero Colicuña, 45.12
    Colilargo, 45.13
    Morado, 45.16
    Pechiescamoso, 45.15
    Rufo, 45.14
Flamenco Americano, 10.14
Focha Americana, 7.12
Fragata Magnífica, 5.10
    Pelágica, 5.11
Frailecillo Coletudo, 6.10
    Corniculado, 6.11
Fringílido de Cassin, 98.7
    Mexicano, 98.8
    Purpureo, 98.6
Fringilo Piquiagudo, 93.12
    Plomizo, 93.8
Fulmar Austral, 1.8
    Norteño, 1.7
Fumarel Negro, 34.5

Gallareta Americana, 7.12
    Frentirroja, 7.11
    Morada, 7.9
Gallina-de-monte,
    Centroamericana, 24.14
    Coluda, 24.12
    Veracruzana, 24.13
Gallineta Común, 7.11
    Morada, 7.9
Gallito Hormiguero
    Cabecinegro, 61.12
    Hormiguero Carinegro, 61.14
    Hormiguero Pechicastaño,
    61.15
Ganso Blanco, 11.7
    Canadiense, 11.10
    Careto Mayor, 11.6

de Ross, 11.8
Garcella Verde, 9.14
Garceta Azul, 9.8
    Común, 9.11
    Grande, 10.2
    Nivosa, 9.7
    Rojiza, 9.10
    Tricolor, 9.9
Garcilla Buyerera, 9.12
Garrapatero Mayor, 39.17
    Asurcado, 39.16
    Piquiliso, 39.15
Garza Agami, 9.13
    Azul, 9.8
    Capirotada, 9.18
    Cuca, 10.3
    Cucharón, 9.17
    del Sol, 7.14
    Ganadera, 9.12
    Grande, 10.2
    Nivea, 9.7
    Pechicastaña, 9.13
    Rojiza, 9.10
    Tricolor, 9.9
    Verde, 9.14
Garza-nocturna Coroniclara,
    9.16
    Coroninegra, 9.15
Garza-tigre Cuellinuda, 9.4
    de Río, 9.6
    de Selva, 9.5
    Gorjinuda, 9.4
Garzón Azulado, 10.1
    Cenizo, 10.1
Gavilán Alicastaño, 17.6
    Aludo, 19.3
    Azor, 15.6
    Bicolor, 15.7
    Blanco, 17.1
    Cabecigrís, 15.1
    Cangrejero, 18.2
    Chapulinero, 18.8
    Coliblanco, 17.7
    Colicorto, 18.6
    Colifajeado, 18.5
    Colirrojo, 19.5
    de Ciénega, 17.5
    de Cooper, 15.5
    de Swainson, 19.4
    del Pacífico, 18.4
    Dorsiplomizo, 17.2
    Enano, 15.8
    Gorgirrayado, 16.6
    Gris, 18.7
    Negra Mayor, 18.3
    Pajarero, 15.3
    Pechiblanco, 15.4
    Pechinegro, 17.4
    Pescador, 14.6
    Piquiganchudo, 15.2
    Plomizo, 17.3
    Ranero, 15.9
    Rastrero, 16.9
    Sabanero, 19.1

Zancudo, 15.9
Gaviota Aliglauca, 31.6
    Argéntea, 31.4
    Blanca, 31.7
    Cabecigrís, 31.9
    Californiana, 31.5
    Cangrejera, 30.10
    Colifajeada, 30.12
    Colinegra, 31.1
    de Bonaparte, 32.8
    de Franklin, 32.6
    de Heermann, 32.1
    de Kamchatka, 31.2
    de Sabine, 32.9
    de Thayer, 31.8
    Dorsinegra Mayor, 30.7
    Dorsinegra Menor, 30.8
    Dorsinegra Sureña, 30.9
    Encapuchada, 32.4
    Mínima, 32.10
    Occidental, 31.3
    Patamarilla, 30.11
    Patinegra, 32.7
    Piquiamarilla, 32.2
    Piquianillada, 32.3
    Plateada, 31.4
    Reidora, 32.5
    Tijereta, 31.10
Golondrina Aliblanca, 70.10
    Arbolera, 70.7
    Azuliblanca, 70.11
    Bicolor, 70.7
    Cariblanca, 70.9
    Gorrinegra, 70.12
    Lomiblanca, 70.8
    Manglera, 70.8
    Musliblanca, 70.13
    Pueblera, 70.18
    Ranchera, 70.20
    Ribereña, 70.14
    Risquera, 70.19
    Tijereta, 70.20
    Verde Violácea, 70.9
Golondrina-alirrasposa Sureña,
    70.17
Golondrina-aliserrada Norteña,
    70.16
    Yucateca, 70.15
Golondrina-boba Blanca, 34.9
    Café, 34.7
    Negra, 34.8
Golondrina-marina Amazónica,
    33.10
    Ártica, 33.7
    Caspica, 33.1
    Común, 33.6
    de Forster, 33.8
    de Sandwich, 33.4
    Elegante, 33.3
    Embridada, 34.2
    Mínima, 33.9
    Negra, 34.5
    Oscura, 34.3
    Piquigruesa, 34.1

Real, 33.2
Rosada, 33.5
Gorrión Alipálido, 95.2
 Arlequín, 95.4
 Barbinegro, 94.5
 Cantor, 95.6
 Cejiblanco, 94.6
 Chapulín, 93.19
 Chingolo, 95.9
 Coliagudo, 93.18
 Coliblanco, 95.3
 Común, 98.19
 Coroniblanco, 95.13
 Coronidorado, 95.12
 de Artemesia, 94.8
 de Baird, 93.16
 de Brewer, 94.4
 de Harris, 95.11
 de Le Conte, 93.17
 de Lincoln, 95.8
 de Worthen, 94.3
 Domestico, 98.19
 Dorsiverde, 92.2
 Gorjiblanco, 95.10
 Gorjinegro, 94.9
 Llanero, 94.2
 Marino, 93.14
 Oliváceo, 92.1
 Pantanero, 95.7
 Pálido, 94.7
 Rascador, 95.5
 Sabanero, 93.13
 Serrano, 93.15
Granatelo Mexicano, 85.6
 Yucateco, 85.5
Gritón Pechiamarillo, 85.7
Grulla Americana, 10.15
 Canadiense, 10.16
Guacamaya Roja, 38.3
 Verde, 38.2
 Verde Mayor, 38.4
Guacamayo Aliverde, 38.5
 Azulamarillo, 38.1
 Rojo, 38.3
 Severo, 38.6
 Verde Mayor, 38.4
Guáchero, 42.4
Guajalote Ocelado, 23.12
 Silvestre, 23.11
Guitio Pechirrufo, 59.1

Hada Coronimorada, 49.17
Halcón Aplomado, 22.2
 Cuelliblanco, 22.3
 de Monte Barreteado, 21.5
 de Monte Collarejo, 21.6
 de Monte Dorsigrís, 21.7
 Gerifalte, 22.8
 Guaco, 21.4
 Murcielaguero, 22.3
 Pechirrufo, 22.4
 Peregrino, 22.6
 Pradeño, 22.7
Halcón-selvático Barrado, 21.5

 de Monte Collarejo, 21.6
Hocofaisán, 23.10
Hojarrasquero Gorgianteado,
 59.11
 Rojizo, 59.12
Hormiguerito Alifranjeado,
 61.9
 Alipunteado, 60.12
 Alirrufo, 60.16
 Apizarrado, 60.9
 Blancibordado, 60.15
 Café, 60.10
 Flanquiblanco, 60.11
 Lomirrufo, 60.17
 Pigmeo, 60.14
 Pizarroso, 60.9
 Rayado, 60.13
 Vientriblanco, 61.7
Hormiguero Alimaculado, 61.6
 Azabache, 61.2
 Bicolor, 61.8
 Calvo, 61.3
 Dorsicastaño, 61.5
 Immaculado, 61.4
 Moteado, 61.10
 Negruzco, 61.1
 Ocelado, 61.11
Hormiguero-cholino Escamoso,
 61.19
Hormiguero-gallito Mexicano,
 61.13

Ibis Blanco, 10.4
 Caríblanco, 10.7
 Común, 10.9
 Lustroso, 10.6
 Morito, 10.6
 Rojo, 10.5
 Verde, 10.8

Jabirú, 10.12
Jacamar Colirrufo, 51.18
 Dorsioscuro, 51.17
 Grande, 51.19
 Rabirrufo, 51.18
Jacana Centroamericana, 26.14
 Mesoamericana, 26.14
 Sureña, 26.15
Jacobino Nuquiblanco, 45.17
Jilguero Menor, 98.15
 Vientriamarillo, 98.17
Junco Ojilumbre,
 de Baird, 95.16
 de Guadalupe, 95.1795.15
 Ojioscuro, 95.14
 Paramero, 95.18

Lanio Americano, 76.16
 Norteño, 76.18
Lavandera Amarilla, 73.15
 Blanca, 73.14
 Dorsinegra, 73.16
Lechucita Neotropical, 41.4
 Parda, 40.15

 Serranera, 41.5
 Vermiculada, 41.9
Lechuza Blanco y Negro, 40.6
 Café, 40.5
 Campestre, 40.13
 de Campanario, 40.1
 Llanero, 40.16
 Ratonera, 40.1
Llorón Café, 68.1
 Degollado, 69.2
 Moteado, 68.4
 Plomizo, 69.2
 Rojiso, 68.3
Lomiamarillo, 63.18
Loro Cabeciamarillo, 38.16
 Cabeciamarillo, 38.18
 Cabeciazul, 37.18
 Cabecigualdo, 38.10
 Cabecipardo, 38.9
 Cachete-amarillo, 38.15
 Corona-violeta, 38.14
 Coroniblanco, 37.17
 Frentiblanco, 38.11
 Frentirrojo, 38.15
 Orejirrojo, 38.9
 Tamaulipeco, 38.13
 Verde, 38.17
 Yucateco, 38.12
Luis Grande, 62.1
 Gregario, 62.4
 Piquigrueso, 62.3

Mango de Veragua, 45.20
 Gorginegro, 45.19
 Pechiverde, 45.18
Manguito Pechiverde, 45.18
Martín Azul, 70.2
 de Ríos, 70.1
 Grande, 70.5
 Pechigrís, 70.3
 Purpúrea, 70.2
 Sinaloense, 70.4
 Sureño, 70.6
Martin-pescador Amazona,
 52.12
 Amazónico, 52.12
 Collarejo, 52.9
 Enano, 52.14
 Norteño, 52.10
 Verde, 52.13
 Vientrirrufo, 52.11
Martinete Cabecipinto, 9.16
 Coroninegra, 9.15
Mascarita Común, 84.7
 de Altamira, 84.9
 de Belding, 84.10
 Matorralera, 84.11
 Piquigruesa, 84.5
 Transvolcanica, 84.12
Matraca Chiapaneca, 76.2
 de Nava, 74.18
 del Balsas, 76.7
 Desértica, 76.9
 Manchada, 76.6

Nuquirrufa, 76.3
Yucateca, 76.8
Matraca-barrada Serrana, 76.5
Tropical, 76.4
Mergo Copetón, 11.15
de Caperuza, 11.13
Mayor, 11.14
Mérgulo Antiguo, 6.5
de Craveri, 6.4
de Xantus, 6.3
Lorito, 6.9
Mielero Azulejo, 86.4
Celeste y Negro, 86.8
Luciente, 86.5
Patirrojo, 86.7
Purpúreo, 86.6
Verde, 86.9
Verde Azul, 86.3
Milano Bidentado, 16.6
Cabecigrís, 15.1
Caracolero, 16.7
Coliblanco, 16.2
de Misisipi, 16.3
Piquiganchudo, 15.2
Plomizo, 16.4
Tijereta, 16.1
Mirlo Gorjiblanco, 81.8
Montañero, 81.5
Negruzco, 81.14
Pardo, 81.6
Vientriblanco, 81.7
Mirlo-acuático Americano, 76.20
Plomizo, 76.20
Mochuelo Común, 41.19
Enano, 41.15
Montañero, 41.13
Momoto Canelo Mayor, 52.5
Cejiceleste, 52.8
Cejiturquesa, 52.8
Común, 52.7
Coroniazul, 52.7
Coronicafé, 52.3
Enano, 52.1
Gorjiazul, 52.2
Pico Quilla, 52.6
Piquiancho, 52.4
Piquianillado, 52.6
Monja Frentiblanca, 53.4
Monjito Rayado, 53.5
Mosquerito Amarillo, 64.10
Amarillento, 66.16
Amarillo-verdoso, 64.11
Bronceado, 65.11
Cabecinegro, 66.17
Cabecipardo, 66.20
Cejiblanco, 66.4
Cejiblanco, 64.3
Cejigrís, 64.3
Cejirrufo, 64.12
Chebec, 66.7
Chillón, 64.6
Colicorto, 66.18
Colicorto, 65.10

Colirrufo, 65.12
Colinegro, 63.19
Coroniamarillo, 64.9
Coronitiznado, 64.2
de Charral, 66.4
de Traill, 66.5
de Yelmo, 65.8
Frentiblanco, 64.1
Gargantiblanco, 66.6
Gorricafé, 64.5
Guardarríos, 67.17
Lampino Norteño, 64.6
Moñudo, 64.18
Murino, 64.8
Ojiblanco, 65.9
Ojimanchado, 66.18
Orejinegro, 66.19
Pechileonado, 63.17
Pechirrayado, 64.13
Penachudo, 64.18
Silbador, 64.7
Verdoso, 66.3
Vientre-amarillo, 66.2
Vientre-amarillo, 64.4
Mosquero Aceitunado, 66.15
Ailero, 66.4
Alicastaño, 62.5
Amarillento, 66.16
Barranqueño, 66.13
Cabecianillado, 62.6
Cabecigrís, 62.12
Cabecinegro, 66.17
Cardenal, 67.4
Cejiblanco, 62.4
Colinegro, 63.19
Coludo, 67.12
Coronidorado, 62.8
de Agua, 67.1
de Hammond, 66.8
de la Isla del Coco, 66.1
del Balsas, 64.20
Fajado, 64.19
Fibí, 67.2
Gorgigrís, 63.16
Gorjiblanco, 66.6
Gorripardo, 66.20
Gris, 66.10
Listado, 62.9
Llanero, 67.3
Mínimo, 66.7
Moñudo, 64.18
Negro, 67.1
Occidental, 66.12
Oscuro, 66.9
Pechicanelo, 66.14
Pechileonado, 64.17
Pechirrayado, 64.13
Penachudo, 64.18
Pinero, 66.11
Piquinegro, 64.16
Pirata, 62.11
Real, 67.14
Saucero, 66.5
Verdoso, 66.3

Vientre-amarillo, 66.2
Vientre-ocre, 66.15
Vientriazufrado, 62.10
Vientridorado, 62.7
Mosquerón Picudo, 62.3
Mulato Azul, 79.3
Pechiblanco, 79.4

Negreta Aliblanca, 13.11
de Marejada, 13.10
Negra, 13.9
Nictibio Común, 42.3
Grande, 42.1
Urutaú, 42.2
Ninfa Coronada, 47.2
Mexicana, 47.1
Violeta y Verde, 47.2
Nonula Carigrís, 53.6

Ojodorado Común, 13.12
Islándico, 13.13
Orejavioleta Café, 49.2
Verde, 49.3
Oropéndola Cabecicastaña, 96.17
Crestada, 96.16
de Moctezuma, 96.18
Negra, 96.19
Ostrero Americano, 26.6
Negro, 26.7

Pachacua Norteña, 43.1
Prío, 42.11
Yucateca, 42.12
Págalo Chileno, 30.6
Colilargo, 30.3
Grande, 30.4
Parásito, 30.2
Pomarino, 30.1
Sureño, 30.5
Pagaza Elegante, 33.3
Mayor, 33.1
Puntiamarilla, 33.4
Real, 33.2
Paíño Cenizo, 4.8
Colirrojo, 5.3
Danzarín, 4.7
de Elliot, 4.2
de Galápagos, 4.7
de Guadelupe, 4.5
de Harcourt, 4.6
de Leach, 4.4
de Markham, 4.10
de Wilson, 4.1
Menudo, 4.11
Minimo, 4.11
Negro, 4.9
Pechialbo, 4.12
Rabifajeado, 4.6
Rabihorcado, 4.3
Pájara-sombrilla Cuellinudo, 69.18
Pájaro-cantil, 7.13
Pájaro-gato Gris, 79.1

Negro, 79.2
Pajuil, 23.6
Paloma Aliblanca, 36.1
  Arroyera, 36.14
  Cabecigrís, 36.15
  Caribeña, 36.17
  Coliblanca, 36.14
  Collareja, 35.7
  Colorada, 35.3
  Coroniblanca, 35.5
  Coronigrís, 36.15
  de Socorro, 36.4
  de Zenaida, 36.2
  Doméstica, 35.1
  Encinera, 35.7
  Escamosa, 35.2
  Huilota, 36.3
  Montaraz de Coiba, 36.16
  Morada, 35.6
  Oscura, 35.10
  Pechigrís, 36.18
  Piquicorta, 35.8
  Piquinegra, 35.8
  Piquirroja, 35.6
  Plomiza, 35.4
  Rabuda, 36.3
  Rojiza, 35.9
  Torcaza, 36.5
  Vientre-claro, 35.3
Paloma-perdiz Bigotiblanca,
  35.15
  Cariblanca, 35.19
  Costarriqueña, 35.13
  de Goldman, 35.14
  de Veracruz, 35.12
  Morena, 35.11
  Pechicanela, 35.15
  Rojiza, 35.17
  Sombría, 35.11
  Violácea, 35.18
Papamoscas Pirata, 62.11
  Rayado, 62.9
  Vientre-amarillo, 62.10
Pardela Blanca Común, 3.1
  Chica, 3.11
  Colicorta, 3.7
  Colicuña, 3.4
  de Audubon, 3.13
  de Buller, 3.5
  de Cory, 1.10
  de Townsend, 3.12
  Gris, 3.6
  Manx, 3.10
  Mayor, 3.3
  Mexicana, 3.9
  Pardo, 3.8
  Patipalida, 3.2
  Patirrosada, 3.1
  Sombría, 3.6
Paro Cejiblanco, 73.2
  Crestinegro, 73.4
  Embridado, 73.3
  Mexicano, 73.1
  Sencillo, 73.5

Parula Norteña, 82.12
  Tropical, 82.13
Patamarilla Mayor, 27.1
  Menor, 27.2
Patiamarillo Mayor, 27.1
  Menor, 27.2
Pato Aguja, 8.9
  Arcoíris, 12.1
  Arlequín, 13.7
  Cabecirrojo, 13.2
  Cabeciverde, 12.3
  Calvo, 12.15
  Cantil, 7.13
  Chalcuán, 12.15
  Coacoxtle, 13.1
  Colilargo, 13.8
  Crestudo, 11.11
  Cuchara, 12.12
  Cucharón Norteño, 12.12
  de Collar, 12.3
  de Hawai, 12.4
  Enmascarado, 13.16
  Gargantillo, 12.16
  Golondrino Norteño, 12.8
  Mexicano, 12.5
  Monja, 13.14
  Pinto, 12.13
  Piquianillado, 13.3
  Rabudo, 12.8
  Real, 11.12
  Silbón, 12.14
  Sombrío, 12.7
  Tejano, 12.6
  Tepalcate, 13.15
Pato-boludo Mayor, 13.5
  Menor, 13.6
  Moñudo, 13.4
Pava Crestada, 23.7
  Negra, 23.9
Pavito Aliblanco, 84.18
  Gorjigrís, 84.17
  Migratorio, 84.19
Pavo Cojolito, 23.7
Pavón Cornudo, 23.8
  Grande, 23.10
Pelícano Blanco Americano, 8.1
  Café, 8.2
  Pardo, 8.2
Pepitero Encapuchado, 98.16
  Norteño, 98.18
Perdiz Chucar, 23.13
  Montañera, 24.14
Perico Aliazufrado, 37.9
  Azteco, 37.7
  de Socorro, 37.4
  Frentinaranja, 37.5
  Frentirrojo, 37.6
  Gorjirrojo, 37.3
  Pechisucio, 37.7
  Pertinax, 37.8
  Pintado, 37.10
  Verde Centroamericano, 37.2
  Verde Mexicano, 37.1
Periquito Alirroja, 37.15

Barbinaranja, 37.14
Barrado, 37.11
Cariazul, 37.16
de Anteojos, 37.13
Listado, 37.11
Mexicano, 37.12
Perlita Cabecinegra, 77.11
  Californiana, 77.9
  Cejiblanca, 77.11
  Colinegra, 77.8
  Gorrinegra, 77.10
  Grisilla, 77.7
  Pechipizarrosa, 77.13
  Tropical, 77.12
Petrel Alinegro, 2.9
  Cuelliblanco, 2.2
  Damero, 3.14
  de Bulwer, 2.14
  de Cook, 2.8
  de Galápagos, 2.3
  de Gould, 2.12
  de Juan Fernandez, 2.1
  de Kermadic, 2.4
  de Murphy, 2.6
  de Parkinson, 1.9
  de Stejneger, 2.11
  de Tahiti, 2.7
  Gorrinegro, 2.13
  Heráldico, 2.5
  Lomioscuro, 2.3
  Moteado, 2.10
Pibí Boreal, 63.1
  Mayor, 63.5
  Occidental, 63.3
  Ocráceo, 63.7
  Oriental, 63.4
  Sombrío, 63.2
  Tropical, 63.6
Picaflor Vientre-canelo, 93.11
Pico de Hoz, 45.10
  de Lanza Frentiverde, 46.17
Pico-Cichura, 9.17
Picoagudo, 67.18
Picochato Rabón, 65.18
Picocono Orejiblanco, 86.2
Picocurvo Norteño, 65.13
Picogrueso Amarillo, 90.13
  Amarillo-verdoso, 90.11
  Azul, 90.17
  Cabecinegro, 90.14
  Carinegro, 90.10
  Cuellirrojo, 90.8
  Negro Azulado, 90.16
  Pechirrosado, 90.9
  Piquirrojo, 90.5
  Tigrillo, 90.14
  Vientriamarillo, 90.12
Picolargo Coroniazul, 49.18
  Coronioscuro, 49.19
Picolezna Sencillo, 58.2
Picopando Canelo, 28.3
  Colibarrado, 28.2
  Ornemantado, 28.1
Picoplano de Anteojos, 67.12

Ojiblanco, 64.14
Picotuerto Rojo, 98.9
Pigüilo, 27.4
Piha Rojiza, 68.2
Rufa, 68.2
Pijiji Aliblanco, 11.3
Canelo, 11.1
Cariblanco, 11.2
Común, 11.3
Pinchaflor Plomizo, 93.10
Pingüino de las Galápagos, 6.16
Pinzón de la Isla del Coco, 93.9
Orejiblanco, 91.17
Piquinaranja, 91.16
Sabanero Azafranado, 93.1
Piquichato Coronirrufo, 65.20
Gargantiblanco, 65.19
Norteño, 65.18
Piquiplano Aliamarillo, 64.15
Azufrado, 64.14
de Anteojos, 67.12
Oliváceo, 67.13
Piquitorcido Norteño, 65.13
Surteño, 65.14
Plañidera Moteada, 68.4
Rojiza, 68.3
Platanero, 86.1
Playerito de Baird, 29.7
Mínimo, 29.5
Occidental, 29.4
Rabadilla-blanca, 29.6
Semipalmado, 29.3
Playero Alzacolita, 27.6
Arenero, 29.2
Blanco, 29.2
Correlimos Pechinegro, 29.10
de Marejada, 28.15
Dorsirrojo, 29.10
Gordo, 29.1
Pectoral, 29.8
Pihuihui, 27.4
Pradero, 28.4
Solitario, 27.3
Vagabundo, 27.5
Zancudo, 29.14
Polluela Amarilla, 24.1
Café, 24.6
Colombiana, 24.9
Colorada, 24.2
Gargantiblanca, 24.5
Negra, 24.4
Ocelada, 24.11
Pechiamarilla, 24.8
Pechigrís, 24.3
Piquirroja, 24.10
Rojiza, 24.2
Sora, 24.7
Porrón Collarejo, 13.3
Mayor, 13.5
Menor, 13.6
Praderito Pechianteado, 28.4
Pradero, 27.7
Común, 96.1
Occidental, 96.2

Quérula Gorgimorada, 69.17
Quetzal Cabecidorado, 51.16
Centroamericano, 51.15
Mexicano, 51.14

Rabadilla-amarilla, 63.18
Rabihorcado Grande, 5.11
Magno, 5.10
Rabijunco Coliblanco, 5.1
Piquirrojo, 5.2
Rascador Arroyero, 92.9
Californiano, 92.8
Coliverde, 92.4
Collarejo, 92.5
Coronirrufo, 91.19
de Abert, 92.7
Oaxaqueño, 92.10
Ojirrojo, 92.6
Orejiblanco, 91.17
Patilludo, 91.18
Piquinaranja, 91.16
Rascón Café, 24.6
Cuelligrís, 23.18
Cuellirrufo, 23.19
de Virginia, 23.17
Moteado, 23.20
Picudo, 23.15
Pinto, 23.20
Real, 23.16
Rayador Americano, 34.10
Negro, 34.10
Reinita Acuatica Piquigrande,
85.20
Acuática Norteña, 85.19
Aliazul, 82.9
Alidorada, 82.10
Amarilla, 82.16
Artica, 77.2
Azul y Negro, 83.20
Cabecicastaña, 85.10
Cabecidorada, 82.15
Cabecigualda, 83.5
Cabecilistada, 85.15
Cachetigrís, 82.8
Cachetinegra, 84.4
Cariamarilla, 83.6
Carinegra, 85.14
Castaña, 83.15
Cerúlea, 83.19
Colifajeada, 83.4
Corona-dorada, 85.9
Coronicastaña, 83.13
de Costillas Castañas, 83.2
de Pinos, 83.14
de Townsend, 83.7
de Tupidero, 84.3
Encapuchada, 84.15
Enlutada, 84.2
Fusca, 77.1
Galana, 83.1
Garganta de Fuego, 82.14
Gorjiamarilla, 83.9
Gorjinaranja, 83.8
Gorrinegra, 84.13

Grande, 85.7
Guardaribera, 85.16
Gusanera, 82.1
Hornera, 85.18
Lomiamarilla, 83.3
Mielera, 86.1
Ojianillada, 84.1
Olivada, 82.4
Pechirrayada, 84.14
Rayada, 83.16
Tigrina, 82.17
Trepadora, 83.17
Verdilla, 82.3
Reyezuelo Corona-dorada, 77.3
Sencillo, 77.4
Riachuelero, 58.14

Sabanera, 41.7
Sabanero Arrocero, 91.7
Cabecilistado, 94.13
Colicorto, 93.19
Coludo, 95.1
de Lincoln, 95.8
Pechianteado, 94.15
Rojizo, 94.20
Zanjero, 93.13
Saltador Cabecinegro, 90.3
Gorjianteado, 90.4
Gorjileonado, 90.4
Grisáceo, 90.1
Listado, 90.2
Saltapalos Canadiense, 73.9
Enano, 73.11
Pechiblanco, 73.10
Saltapared Barranquero, 74.17
Cejirrufo, 75.9
de Bewick, 75.2
de Carolina, 74.7
de Clarión, 75.6
de Cozumel, 75.5
de Socorro, 75.7
Feliz, 74.3
Invernal, 75.8
Pantanero, 75.10
Pechimanchado, 74.2
Roquero, 75.18
Rufiblanco, 74.4
Ruiseñor, 75.15
Sabanero, 75.11
Sencillo, 74.8
Sinaloense, 74.5
Vientre-barrado, 74.6
Vientre-blanco, 75.1
Saltapared-continental,
Norteño, 75.3
Saltapared-selvatico,
Pechiblanco, 75.13
Pechigrís, 75.14
Saltarín Cabecigrís, 68.6
Cabecirrojo, 68.12
Capuchidorado, 68.11
Colilargo, 68.14
Coludo, 68.15
Coroniblanco, 68.16

Coroniceleste, 68.17
Cuelliblanco, 68.8
Cuellidorada, 68.7
Cuellinaranja, 68.9
Gorgiblanco, 68.13
Toledo, 68.14
Verde, 68.10
Salteador Colilargo, 30.3
Parásito, 30.2
Polar, 30.5
Pomarino, 30.1
Saltón Aceitunado, 92.1
Amarillo-verdoso, 93.4
Barranquero, 91.15
Cabecicastaño, 91.11
Cabecilistado, 92.3
Cabecinegro, 91.13
Cafetalero, 91.18
de Muslos Amarillos, 93.5
Gargantiamarilla, 91.9
Gorjiamarillo, 91.9
Gorricastaño, 91.11
Gorrirrufo, 91.10
Nuquiblanco, 91.8
Patigrande, 91.14
Verdirrayado, 91.12
Sapayoa, 68.5
Sastrecillo, 73.7
Semiller/ito Cariamarillo, 93.3
Negro Azulado, 92.20
OlivÁceo, 93.3
Semillero Apizarrado, 92.16
Azul, 93.6
Azulado, 93.6
Azuligrís, 93.7
Brincador, 92.20
Cariamarillo, 93.3
Collarejo, 92.13
Lineado, 92.18
Oliváceo, 93.3
Pechicanelo, 92.11
Picogrueso, 92.17
Piquigrueso, 92.17
Piquirrosado, 92.19
Variable, 92.15
Solitario Carinegro, 80.4
Variado, 80.5
Soterillo Caricafé, 77.6
Picudo, 77.5
Soterrey Cabeciblanco, 76.1
Cabecisombrio, 74.9
Canoro, 75.17
Cantarino, 75.1
Carimoteado, 74.15
Castaño, 74.12
Chinchirigüí, 74.8
Cholincillo, 75.16
Cucarachero, 75.3
de Costillas Barreteada, 74.6
del Bambú, 75.12
Golirrayado, 74.14
Gorginegro, 74.10
Matraquero, 76.4
Nuquirrufo, 76.3

Ocroso, 75.4
Pechianteado, 74.16
Pechibarreteado, 74.13
Pechiblanco, 75.13
Pechigrís, 75.14
Pechimoteado, 74.2
Pechirrayado, 74.1
Roquero, 75.18
Rufiblanco, 74.4
Ruiseñor, 75.15
Sabanero, 75.11
Vientrinegro, 74.11
Subepalo Bello, 58.09
Moteado, 58.4
Rojizo, 58.10

Tángara Aceitunada, 89.7
Aliamarilla, 87.16
Aliblanca, 88.16
Alirrufa, 86.11
Azuleja, 87.17
Azuligrís, 87.17
Bermeja, 88.13
Cabecicastaña, 86.10
Cabecigrís, 89.5
Cabecirrayada, 88.1
Cabecirroja, 88.19
Caponiblanca, 88.6
Capucha-dorada, 86.17
Capuchirroja, 89.1
Carinegruzca, 89.6
Carirroja, 88.18
Cejiescarlata, 88.5
Cenicienta, 86.20
Coronidorada, 88.7
Cuellirroja, 89.1
de Cabanis, 86.15
de Costillas Negras, 87.15
de Monte del Pirre, 89.12
de Monte Cejiblanca, 89.9
de Monte del Tacarcuna, 89.13
de Monte Goliamarillo, 89.14
de Monte Gargantagrís , 89.11
de Monte Ojeruda, 89.10
de Toro Encendido, 89.2
de Espalda Rayada, 89.4
de Nuca Verde, 86.18
Dorada, 86.13
Doradigrís, 86.16
Dorsirrayada, 88.17
Encinera, 88.13
Escarlata, 88.15
Forriblanca, 88.8
Huitlacoche, 89.17
Lomiamarilla, 89.15
Lomiazufrada, 88.4
Lomiescarlata, 89.3
Moteada, 86.14
Negro y Dorado, 89.16
Occidental, 88.18
Ojeralimín, 89.1
Orejinegra, 86.12
Palmera, 87.18
Pechirrosada, 89.17

Piquiganchuda, 88.3
Roja, 88.14
Terciopelo, 89.3
Veranera, 88.14
Vientricastaña, 86.19
Yucateca, 88.12
Tángara-hormiguera Carinegra,
88.11
Coronirroja, 88.9
Gorjirroja, 88.10
Tángara-lanio Gorjinegro, 88.2
Tapacaminos Carolinense, 43.4
Colimanchado, 43.8
Común, 42.9
Cuerporruin, 43.3
Cuerprihuiu, 43.2
Picuyo, 42.9
Préstame-tu-cuchillo, 43.7
Ti-cuer, 43.5
Yucateco, 43.6
Tapacuelo de Nariño, 59.19
de Tacarcuna, 59.17
Frentiplateado, 59.18
Tecolote Barbudo, 41.10
Bigotudo, 41.8
de Cooper, 41.7
del Balsas, 41.6
Flameado, 41.1
Occidental, 41.3
Oriental, 41.2
Vermiculado, 41.9
Tecolote-abetero Norteño,
40.14
Sureño, 40.15
Tecolotito Centroamericano,
Colimense, 41.16
Común, 41.19
del Cabo, 41.14
Enano, 41.20
Norteño, 41.12
Serrano, 41.11
Tamaulipeco, 41.17
Tersina, 87.19
Tijereta Centroamericana, 50.5
Norteña, 50.6
Oaxaqueña, 50.7
Rosada, 67.10
Sabanera, 67.9
Yucateca, 50.4
Tinamú Canelo, 25.19
Chico, 25.17
del Chocó, 25.18
Grande, 25.15
Jamuey, 25.20
Mayor, 25.15
Menor, 25.17
Pizarroso, 25.20
Serrano, 25.16
Tirahojas Barbiescamado, 58.12
Gargantigrís, 58.13
Pechirrufo, 58.11
Tirano de Agua Pinto, 67.16
de Cassin, 62.15
de Couch, 62.14

Gris, 67.5
Norteño, 67.6
Occidental, 62.17
Piquigrueso, 62.16
Real, 67.7
Tropical, 62.13
Viajero, 67.6
Tirano-tijereta Rosado, 67.10
Sabanero, 67.9
Tityra Carirroja, 69.12
Coroninegra, 69.13
Enmascarada, 69.12
Piquinegra, 69.13
Tiñosa Común, 34.7
Negra, 34.8
Tordo Arrocero, 98.1
Cabeciamarillo, 98.5
Cabecidorado, 98.5
Canadiense, 96.5
Cantor, 96.4
Común, 96.9
de Agua, 98.4
de Brewer, 96.6
del Costa, 96.10
Pantanero, 96.7
Pechirrojo, 96.3
Sargento, 98.2
Tricolor, 98.3
Tordo-saltarín, 68.1
Torero, 31.11
Tororoi Dorsiescamado, 61.19
Pechicanelo, 61.18
Pechiescamoso, 61.20
Pechilistado, 61.16
Piquigualdo, 61.17
Tórtola Moteada, 36.6
Turca, 36.7
Tórtola/ita Azul, 36.12
Azulada, 36.12
Colilarga, 36.8
Común, 36.9
Menuda, 36.10
Pechilisa, 36.10
Pechimorada, 36.13
Rojiza, 36.11
Serranera, 36.13
Trepador Alirrubio, 57.1
Americano, 73.12
Barreteado, 57.6
Cabecipunteado, 57.15
Cabecirrayado, 57.14
Delgado, 57.4
Gigante, 57.5
Gorjianteado, 57.9
Manchado, 57.11
Pardo, 57.2
Pico de Hoz, 57.17
Pinto, 57.12
Piquiclaro, 57.10
Rojizo, 57.3
Vientribarreteado, 57.7
Trepadorcito Aceitunado, 58.6
Pico de Cuña, 58.5
Trepamusgo Alipizarrosa, 59.9

Cachetón, 58.7
Cuellirojizo, 58.8
de Anteojos, 59.8
Lineado, 59.6
Rayado, 59.7
Rojizo, 59.10
Trepatroncos Alileonado, 57.1
Barrado, 57.6
Blanquirrayado, 57.13
Corona-punteada, 57.15
Corona-rayada, 57.14
Gigante, 57.5
Gorjipálido, 57.9
Manchado, 57.11
Oliváceo, 58.6
Piquiclaro, 57.10
Piquicuña, 58.5
Piquirrecto, 57.8
Piquirrojo, 57.16
Rojizo, 57.3
Vientre-barrado, 57.7
Trogón Cabecinegro, 51.3
Cabeciverde, 51.1
Citrino, 51.4
Coliblanco, 51.2
Colinegro, 51.7
Colioscuro, 51.12
Coliplomizo, 51.12
Collarejo, 51.10
Elegante, 51.9
Mexicano, 51.8
Ojiblanco, 51.13
Vientrianaranjado, 51.6
Vientribermejo, 51.11
Violáceo, 51.5
Tucan de Swainson, 53.12
del Chocó, 53.13
Pico Iris, 53.11
Pico-multicolor, 53.11
Tucancillo Collarejo, 53.9
Orejiamarillo, 53.8
Piquianaranjado, 53.10
Verde, 53.7
Tucaneta Verde, 53.7

Urraca de Toca Celeste, 71.6
Gorgiplateada, 71.10
Parda, 72.4
Pechinegra, 72.1
Urraca-hermosa Cariblanca, 72.6
Carinegra, 72.5
Copetona, 72.6

Vaquero Brilloso, 96.13
Cabecicafé, 96.15
Gigante, 96.12
Grande, 96.12
Ojirrojo, 96.14
Vencejo Barbiblanco, 44.2
Collarejo, 44.6
Común, 44.9
Cuelliblanco, 44.6
Cuellicastaño, 44.3
de Chapman, 44.10

de Cherrie, 44.4
de Chimenea, 44.8
de Paso, 44.8
de Rabadilla Clara, 44.13
de Tormenta, 44.12
de Vaux, 44.9
Frentiblanco, 44.5
Gorjiblanco, 44.15
Lomigrís, 44.14
Negro, 44.1
Nuquiblanco, 44.7
Rabón, 44.11
Sombrío, 44.2
Vencejo-tijereta Mayor, 44.17
Menor, 44.16
Verdillo Corona-leonada, 77.14
Luisucho, 77.17
Matorralero, 77.16
Menor, 77.15
Menudo, 77.15
Vireo Aliamarillo, 78.13
Amarillento, 78.18
Amarillo-verdoso, 78.19
Bigotudo, 78.21
Cabecigrís, 78.19
Canoro, 78.16
de Bell, 78.5
de Cassin, 78.10
de Cozumel, 78.4
de Filadelfia, 78.18
de Hutton, 78.14
de Manglar, 78.3
Dorado, 78.15
Enano, 78.7
Gorjeador, 78.16
Gorjimarillo, 78.12
Gorrinegro, 78.6
Gorripardo, 78.17
Gris, 78.8
Manglero, 78.3
Montañero, 78.17
Ojiblanco, 78.2
Ojirrojo, 78.20
Pechiamarillo, 78.12
Pizarra, 78.1
Plomizo, 78.11
Solitario, 78.9
Yucateco, 78.22
Vireón Cejiamarillo, 77.20
Cejirrufo, 76.15
Esmeraldo, 77.19
Pechicastaño, 77.18
Vuelvepiedras Negro, 28.14
Rojizo, 28.13

Xenops Común, 58.2
Rayado, 58.3

Zacatero Amarillo, 93.2
Común, 96.1
Zacatonero Alirrufo, 94.17
Bigote-blanco, 94.11
Cabecirrayada, 94.13
Coronirrufo, 94.18

327

de Botteri, 94.15
de Cassin, 94.14
de Cinco-rayas, 94.12
de Sumichrast, 94.16
Oaxaqueño, 94.19
Pechinegro, 94.10
Rayado, 94.1
Rojizo, 94.20
Zafiro Cabeciazul, 47.6
Gorjiazul, 47.7
Zambullidor Cornudo, 7.4
Cuellirroja, 7.5
de Atitlán, 7.3
Enano, 7.1
Mediano, 7.6
Menor, 7.1
Orejudo, 7.6
Piquipinto, 7.2
Zanate Mayor, 96.8
Zarapito Boreal, 26.9
del Pacífico, 26.12
Ganga, 27.7

Piquilargo, 26.11
Trinador, 26.10
Zeledonia, 85.17
Zopilote Cabecigualdo, 14.3
Cabecirrojo, 14.2
Negro, 14.1
Rey, 14.4
Zorzal Azteca, 81.16
Cabecinegro, 80.10
Carigrís, 80.14
Cuellirrufo, 81.12
de Grayson, 81.10
de Swainson, 80.15
del Bosque, 80.17
Dorsirrojizo, 80.13
Dorsirrufo, 81.9
Gorjiblanco, 81.8
Gorrirojizo, 80.8
Negro, 81.13
Pardo, 81.6
Pechicinchado, 81.15
Petirrojo, 81.11

Piquianaranjado, 80.6
Piquinegro, 80.9
Serrano, 81.5
Sombrío, 80.11
Zorzalito Carigrís, 80.14
Colirrufo, 80.16
Coroninegro, 80.10
de Frantzius, 80.8
de Swainson, 80.15
Maculado, 80.17
Pechiamarillo, 80.12
Piquinaranja, 80.6
Piquipardo, 80.7
Rojizo, 80.13
Zumbador Ardiente, 50.14
Centroamericano, 50.20
Coliancho, 50.16
de Allen, 50.18
Mexicano, 50.19
Rufo, 50.17

Index of English names

Numbers refer to the relevant plate, followed by the number of the bird on that plate.

Albatross, Black-footed, 1.2
Grey-headed, 1.5
Laysan, 1.6
Short-tailed, 1.1
Wandering, 1.3
Waved, 1.4
Anhinga, 8.9
Ani, Greater, 39.17
Groove-billed, 39.16
Smooth-billed, 39.15
Antbird, Bare-crowned, 61.3
Bicoloured, 61.8
Chestnut-backed, 61.5
Dull-mantled, 61.6
Dusky, 61.1
Immaculate, 61.4
Jet, 61.2
Ocellated, 61.11
Spotted, 61.10
White-bellied, 61.7
Wing-banded, 61.9
Antpitta, Black-crowned, 61.20
Fulvous-bellied, 61.18
Ochre-breasted, 61.17
Scaled, 61.19
Spectacled, 61.16
Antshrike, Barred, 60.2
Black, 60.5
Black-hooded, 60.6
Fasciated, 60.3
Great, 60.1
Russet, 60.7
Slaty, 60.8
Speckled, 60.4
Antthrush, Black-faced, 61.14
Black-headed, 61.12
Mexican, 61.13

Rufous-breasted, 61.15
Antvireo, Plain, 59.14
Spot-crowned, 59.15
Streak-crowned, 59.16
Antwren, Checker-throated, 60.10
Dot-winged, 60.12
Pygmy, 60.14
Rufous-rumped, 60.17
Rufous-winged, 60.16
Slaty, 60.9
Streaked, 60.13
White-flanked, 60.11
White-fringed, 60.15
Aracari, Collared, 53.9
Fiery-billed, 53.10
Attila, Bright-rumped, 63.20
Auklet, Cassin's, 6.6
Crested, 6.7
Parakeet, 6.9
Rhinoceros, 6.8
Avocet, American, 26.13

Bananaquit, 86.1
Barbet, Prong-billed, 53.3
Red-headed, 53.2
Spot-crowned, 53.1
Barbtail, Spotted, 58.4
Barbthroat, Band-tailed, 45.3
Becard, Barred, 69.7
Black-and-white, 69.6
Cinereous, 69.8
Cinnamon, 69.4
Grey-collared, 69.3
One-coloured, 69.1
Rose-throated, 69.2
White-winged, 69.5

Bellbird, Three-wattled, 69.19
Bentbill, Northern, 65.13
Southern, 65.14
Bittern, American, 9.2
Least, 9.3
Pinnated, 9.1
Blackbird, Brewer's, 96.6
Melodious, 96.4
Red-breasted, 96.3
Red-winged, 98.2
Rusty, 96.5
Tricoloured, 98.3
Yellow-headed, 98.5
Yellow-hooded, 98.4
Bluebird, Eastern, 81.2
Mountain, 81.4
Western, 81.3
Bobolink, 98.1
Bobwhite, Black-throated, 25.12
Crested, 25.13
Northern, 25.11
Spot-bellied, 25.14
Booby, Blue-footed, 5.5
Brown, 5.6
Masked, 5.4
Peruvian, 5.8
Red-footed, 5.7
Brant, 11.9
Brilliant, Green-crowned, 49.1
Brushfinch, Chestnut-capped, 91.11
Green-striped, 91.12
Rufous-capped, 91.10
Stripe-headed, 91.11
White-naped, 91.8
Yellow-throated, 91.9
Bufflehead, 13.14

328

Bunting, Blue, 90.15
  Indigo, 91.1
  Lark, 95.2
  Lazuli, 91.4
  Orange-breasted, 91.5
  Painted, 91.6
  Rose-bellied, 91.2
  Varied, 91.3
Bushtit, 73.7
Buzzard, Rough-legged, 19.7

Cacique, Scarlet-rumped, 97.19
  Yellow-billed, 97.20
  Yellow-rumped, 97.18
  Yellow-winged, 97.17
Canvasback, 13.1
Caracara, Crested, 21.2
  Red-throated, 21.1
  Yellow-headed, 21.3
Cardinal, Northern, 90.7
Catbird, Black, 79.2
  Grey, 79.1
Chachalaca, Grey-headed, 23.5
  Plain, 23.1
  Wagler's, 23.2
  West Mexican, 23.3
  White-bellied, 23.4
Chat, Grey-throated, 85.5
  Red-breasted, 85.6
  Yellow-breasted, 85.7
Chickadee, Mexican, 73.1
  Mountain, 73.2
Chlorophonia, Blue-crowned,
  87.1
  Golden-browed, 87.2
  Yellow-collared, 87.3
Chuck-will's-widow, 43.4
Chukar, 23.13
Condor, California, 14.5
Conebill, White-eared, 86.2
Coot, American, 7.12
Coquette, Black-crested, 46.5
  Rufous-crested, 46.6
  Short-crested, 46.4
  White-crested, 46.7
Cormorant, Brandt's, 8.6
  Double-crested, 8.3
  Great, 8.4
  Guanay, 8.8
  Neotropic, 8.5
  Pelagic, 8.7
Cotinga, Black-tipped, 69.15
  Blue, 69.11
  Lovely, 69.9
  Snowy, 69.14
  Turquoise, 69.10
  Yellow-billed, 69.16
Cowbird, Bronzed, 96.14
  Brown-headed, 96.15
  Giant, 96.12
  Shiny, 96.13
Crake, Colombian, 24.9
  Grey-breasted, 24.3
  Ocellated, 24.11

Paint-billed, 24.10
  Ruddy, 24.2
  Uniform, 24.6
  White-throated, 24.5
  Yellow-breasted, 24.8
Crane, Sandhill, 10.16
  Whooping, 10.15
Creeper, Brown, 73.12
Crossbill, Red, 98.9
Crow, American, 72.9
  Chihuahuan, 72.12
  House, 72.14
  Sinaloa, 72.11
  Tamaulipas, 72.10
Cuckoo, Black-billed, 39.2
  Cocos, 39.6
  Dwarf, 39.1
  Grey-capped, 39.5
  Lesser ground, 39.11
  Little, 39.8
  Mangrove, 39.4
  Rufous-vented ground, 39.12
  Squirrel, 39.7
  Striped, 39.9
  Yellow-billed, 39.3
Cukoo, Pheasant, 39.10
Curassow, Great, 23.10
Curlew, Bristle-thighed, 26.12
  Eskimo, 26.9
  Long-billed, 26.11

Dacnis, Blue, 86.4
  Scarlet-thighed, 86.8
  Viridian, 86.3
Dickcissel, 91.7
Dipper, American, 76.20
Donacobius, Black-capped,
  76.17
Dotterel, Eurasian, 27.15
Dove, Ground, 36.12
  Brown-backed, 36.16
  Buff-fronted quail, 35.13
  Caribbean, 36.17
  Common Ground, 36.9
  Eared, 36.5
  Eurasian Collared, 36.7
  Grey-chested, 36.18
  Grey-headed, 36.15
  Inca, 36.8
  Maroon-chested Ground, 36.13
  Mourning, 36.3
  Olive-backed Quail, 35.15
  Plain-breasted Ground, 36.10
  Purplish-backed Quail, 35.11
  Ruddy Ground, 36.11
  Ruddy Quail, 35.17
  Rufous-breasted Quail, 35.15
  Russet-crowned Quail, 35.14
  Socorro, 36.4
  Spotted, 36.6
  Tuxtla Quail, 35.12
  Violaceous Quail, 35.18
  White-faced Quail, 35.19
  White-tipped, 36.14

White-winged, 36.1
  Zenaida, 36.2
Dowitcher, Long-billed, 28.7
  Short-billed, 28.6
Duck, American Black, 12.7
  Black-bellied Whistling, 11.3
  Comb, 11.11
  Fulvous Whistling, 11.1
  Harlequin, 13.7
  Hawaiian, 12.4
  Long-tailed, 13.8
  Masked, 13.16
  Mexican, 12.5
  Mottled, 12.6
  Muscovy, 11.12
  Ring-necked, 13.3
  Ruddy, 13.15
  Tufted, 13.4
  White-faced Whistling, 11.2
  Wood, 12.1
Dunlin, 29.10

Eagle, Bald, 14.7
  Black Hawk, 20.5
  Black-and-white Hawk,
  20.4
  Crested, 20.2
  Golden, 20.1
  Harpy, 20.3
  Ornate Hawk, 20.6
  Solitary, 18.1
Egret, Cattle, 9.12
  Great, 10.2
  Little, 9.11
  Reddish, 9.10
  Snowy, 9.7
Elaenia, Caribbean, 65.4
  Forest, 65.2
  Greenish, 65.1
  Grey, 65.3
  Lesser, 65.7
  Mountain, 65.6
  Yellow-bellied, 65.5
Emerald, Canivet's, 46.12
  Coppery-headed, 47.16
  Cozumel, 46.12
  Garden, 46.13
  Golden-crowned, 46.11
  Honduran, 48.2
  Salvin's, 46.10
  White-bellied, 48.1
  White-tailed, 47.15
Euphonia, Blue-hooded,
  87.14
  Fulvous-vented, 87.12
  Olive-backed, 87.4
  Orange-bellied, 87.11
  Scrub, 87.10
  Spot-crowned, 87.9
  Tawny-capped, 87.13
  Thick-billed, 87.6
  White-vented, 87.7
  Yellow-crowned, 87.8
  Yellow-throated, 87.5

Fairy, Purple-crowned, 49.17
Falcon, Aplomado, 22.2
  Barred Forest, 21.5
  Bat, 22.3
  Collared Forest, 21.6
  Laughing, 21.4
  Orange-breasted, 22.4
  Peregrine, 22.6
  Prairie, 22.7
  Slaty-backed Forest, 21.7
Finch, Cassin's, 98.7
  Cocos, 93.9
  House, 98.8
  Large-footed, 91.14
  Peg-billed, 93.12
  Purple, 98.6
  Saffron, 93.1
  Slaty, 93.8
  Sooty-faced, 91.15
  Wedge-tailed Grass, 95.1
  Yellow-green, 93.4
  Yellow-thighed, 93.5
Flamingo, Greater, 10.14
Flatbill, Eye-ringed, 67.12
  Olivaceous, 67.13
Flicker, Gilded, 56.2
  Northern, 56.1
Flowerpiercer, Cinnamon-
  bellied, 93.11
  Slaty, 93.10
Flycatcher, Acadian, 66.3
  Alder, 66.4
  Ash-throated, 63.11
  Belted, 64.19
  Black-billed, 64.16
  Black-capped, 66.17
  Black-headed Tody, 65.17
  Black-tailed, 63.19
  Boat-billed, 62.3
  Bran-coloured, 64.13
  Brown-crested, 63.14
  Buff-breasted, 66.14
  Cocos, 66.1
  Common Tody, 65.16
  Cordilleran, 66.13
  Dusky, 66.9
  Dusky-capped, 63.9
  Flammulated, 63.15
  Fork-tailed, 67.9
  Golden-bellied, 62.7
  Golden-crowned, 62.8
  Great Crested, 63.13
  Grey, 66.10
  Grey-capped, 62.12
  Hammond's, 66.8
  Least, 66.7
  Nutting's, 63.12
  Ochre-bellied, 66.15
  Olive-sided, 63.1
  Olive-striped, 66.18
  Pacific Slope, 66.12
  Panama, 63.8
  Pileated, 64.20
  Pine, 66.11

Piratic, 62.11
  Royal, 67.14
  Ruddy-tailed, 65.12
  Rusty-margined, 62.5
  Scissor-tailed, 67.10
  Scrub, 63.16
  Sepia-capped, 66.20
  Slate-headed Tody, 65.15
  Slaty-capped, 66.19
  Social, 62.4
  Streaked, 62.9
  Sulphur-bellied, 62.10
  Sulphur-rumped, 63.18
  Tawny-breasted, 63.17
  Tawny-chested, 64.17
  Tufted, 64.18
  Vermilion, 67.4
  White-ringed, 62.6
  White-throated, 66.6
  Willow, 66.5
  Yellow-bellied, 66.2
  Yellow-margined, 64.15
  Yellow-olive, 64.14
  Yellowish, 66.16
Foliage Gleaner, Buff-fronted,
  59.10
  Buff-throated, 59.11
  Lineated, 59.6
  Ruddy, 59.12
  Scaly-throated, 59.8
  Slaty-winged, 59.9
  Striped, 59.7
Frigatebird, Great, 5.11
  Magnificent, 5.10
Fruitcrow, Purple-throated, 69.17
Fulmar, Northern, 1.7
  Southern, 1.8

Gadwall, 12.13
Gallinule, Purple, 7.9
Gannet, Northern, 5.9
Garganey, 12.10
Gnatcatcher, Black-capped,
  77.10
  Black-tailed, 77.8
  Blue-grey, 77.7
  California, 77.9
  Slate-throated, 77.13
  Tropical, 77.12
  White-lored, 77.11
Gnatwren, Long-billed, 77.5
  Tawny-faced, 77.6
Godwit, Bar-tailed, 28.2
  Hudsonian, 28.1
  Marbled, 28.3
Goldeneye, Barrow's, 13.13
  Common, 13.12
Goldentail, Blue-throated, 47.7
Goldfinch, American, 98.13
  Lawrence's, 98.11
  Lesser, 98.15
Goose, Canada, 11.10
  Greater White-fronted, 11.6
  Ross's, 11.8

Snow, 11.7
Goshawk, Northern, 15.6
Grackle, Boat-tailed, 96.10
  Common, 96.9
  Great-tailed, 96.8
  Nicaraguan, 96.11
  Slender-billed, 96.7
Grassquit, Blue-black, 92.20
  Yellow-faced, 93.3
Grebe, Atitlan, 7.3
  Clark's, 7.8
  Eared, 7.6
  Horned, 7.4
  Least, 7.1
  Pied-billed, 7.2
  Red-necked, 7.5
  Western, 7.7
Greenlet, Golden-fronted, 77.17
  Lesser, 77.15
  Scrub, 77.16
  Tawny-crowned, 77.14
Greytail, Double-banded, 59.13
Grosbeak, Black-faced, 90.10
  Black-headed, 90.14
  Black-thighed, 90.12
  Blue, 90.17
  Blue-black, 90.16
  Crimson-collared, 90.8
  Evening, 98.18
  Hooded, 98.16
  Rose-breasted, 90.9
  Slate-coloured, 90.5
  Yellow, 90.13
  Yellow-green, 90.11
Guan, Black, 23.9
  Crested, 23.7
  Highland, 23.6
  Horned, 23.8
Guillemot, Pigeon, 6.2
Gull, Band-tailed, 30.12
  Black-headed, 32.4
  Black-tailed, 31.1
  Bonaparte's, 32.8
  California, 31.5
  Franklin's, 32.6
  Glaucous, 31.7
  Glaucous-winged, 31.6
  Great Black-backed, 30.7
  Grey, 31.11
  Grey-headed, 31.9
  Heermann's, 32.1
  Herring, 31.4
  Kelp, 30.9
  Laughing, 32.5
  Lesser Black-backed, 30.8
  Little, 32.10
  Mew, 32.2
  Olrog's, 30.10
  Ring-billed, 32.3
  Sabine's, 32.9
  Slaty-backed, 31.2
  Swallow-tailed, 31.10
  Thayer's, 31.8
  Western, 31.3

Yellow-footed, 30.11
Gyrfalcon, 22.8

Harrier, Long-winged, 16.10
  Northern, 16.9
Hawk, Barred, 17.4
  Bicoloured, 15.7
  Black-collared, 17.5
  Broad-winged, 19.3
  Common Black, 18.2
  Cooper's, 15.5
  Crane, 15.9
  Ferruginous, 19.6
  Great black, 18.3
  Grey, 18.7
  Harris's, 17.6
  Mangrove Black, 18.4
  Plumbeous, 17.3
  Red-shouldered, 19.2
  Red-tailed, 19.5
  Roadside, 18.8
  Savanna, 19.1
  Semiplumbeous, 17.2
  Sharp-shinned, 15.3
  Short-tailed, 18.6
  Swainson's, 19.4
  Tiny, 15.8
  White, 17.1
  White-breasted, 15.4
  White-tailed, 17.7
  Zone-tailed, 18.5
Hawk Eagle, Black, 20.5
  Black-and-white, 20.4
  Ornate, 20.6
Hermit, Bronzy, 45.1
  Green, 45.6
  Stripe-throated, 45.9
  Long-billed, 45.4
  Mexican, 45.5
  Pale-bellied, 45.7
  Rufous-breasted, 45.2
  White-whiskered, 45.8
Heron, Bare-throated Tiger, 9.4
  Black-crowned Night, 9.15
  Boat-billed, 9.17
  Capped, 9.18
  Chestnut-bellied, 9.13
  Cocoi, 10.3
  Fasciated Tiger, 9.6
  Great Blue, 10.1
  Green, 9.14
  Little Blue, 9.8
  Rufescent Tiger, 9.5
  Striated, 9.14
  Tricoloured, 9.9
  Yellow-crowned Night, 9.16
Honeycreeper, Green, 86.9
  Purple, 86.6
  Red-legged, 86.7
  Shining, 86.5
Hummingbird, Allen's, 50.18
  Amethyst-throated, 49.12
  Anna's, 50.10
  Azure-crowned, 48.3

Beautiful, 50.7
Berylline, 48.9
Black-bellied, 47.13
Black-chinned, 50.9
Blue-capped, 47.14
Blue-chested, 48.10
Blue-tailed, 48.7
Blue-throated, 49.13
Broad-billed, 46.15
Broad-tailed, 50.16
Buff-bellied, 48.13
Bumblebee, 50.19
Calliope, 50.12
Charming, 48.11
Cinnamon, 48.14
Cinnamon-sided, 48.17
Costa's, 50.11
Doubleday's, 46.16
Dusky, 46.14
Emerald-chinned, 46.2
Fiery-throated, 47.3
Garnet-throated, 49.14
Glow-throated, 50.14
Green-fronted, 48.16
Indigo-capped, 48.5
Lucifer, 50.6
Magnificent, 49.15
Mangrove, 48.4
Ruby-throated, 50.8
Rufous, 50.17
Rufous-cheeked, 47.17
Rufous-tailed, 48.12
Sapphire-throated, 47.5
Scaly-breasted, 45.15
Scintillant, 50.15
Snowy-bellied, 48.8
Steely-vented, 48.6
Stripe-tailed, 47.11
Tooth-billed, 45.11
Violet-bellied, 47.4
Violet-capped, 47.10
Violet-crowned, 48.15
Violet-headed, 46.3
Volcano, 50.13
White-eared, 47.8
White-tailed, 47.12
Wine-throated, 50.20
Xanthus's, 47.9

Ibis, Buff-necked, 10.9
  Glossy, 10.6
  Green, 10.8
  Scarlet, 10.5
  White, 10.4
  White-faced, 10.7

Jabiru, 10.12
Jacamar, Dusky-backed, 51.17
  Great, 51.19
  Rufous-tailed, 51.18
Jacana, Northern, 26.14
  Wattled, 26.15
Jacobin, White-necked, 45.17
Jaeger, Long-tailed, 30.3

Parasitic, 30.2
Pomarine, 30.1
Jay, Azure-hooded, 71.6
  Black-chested, 72.1
  Black-throated, 71.7
  Black-throated Magpie, 72.5
  Blue, 71.2
  Brown, 72.4
  Bushy-crested, 71.11
  Dwarf, 71.8
  Green, 72.2
  Mexican, 71.5
  Pinyon, 71.3
  Purplish-backed, 71.14
  San Blas, 71.12
  Scrub, 71.4
  Silvery-throated, 71.10
  Steller's, 71.1
  Tufted, 72.7
  Unicoloured, 72.3
  White-throated, 71.9
  White-throated Magpie, 72.6
  Yucatan, 71.13
Junco, Baird's, 95.16
  Dark-eyed, 95.14
  Guadelupe, 95.17
  Volcano, 95.18
  Yellow-eyed, 95.15

Kestrel, American, 22.1
Killdeer, 27.13
Kingbird, Cassin's, 62.15
  Couch's, 62.14
  Eastern, 67.6
  Giant, 67.7
  Grey, 67.5
  Thick-billed, 62.16
  Tropical, 62.13
  Western, 62.17
Kingfisher, Amazon, 52.12
  American Pygmy, 52.14
  Belted, 52.10
  Green, 52.13
  Green-and-rufous, 52.11
  Ringed, 52.9
Kinglet, Golden-crowned, 77.3
  Ruby-crowned, 77.4
Kiskadee, Great, 62.1
  Lesser, 62.2
Kite, Double-toothed, 16.6
  Grey-headed, 15.1
  Hook-billed, 15.2
  Mississippi, 16.3
  Pearl, 16.5
  Plumbeous, 16.4
  Slender-billed, 16.8
  Snail, 16.7
  Swallow-tailed, 16.1
  White-tailed, 16.2
Kittiwake, Black-legged, 32.7
Knot, Red, 29.1

Lancebill, Green-fronted, 46.17
Lapwing, Southern, 26.2

Lark, Horned, 73.13
Leaftosser, Grey-throated, 58.14
  Scaly-throated, 58.13
  Tawny-throated, 58.12
Limpkin, 10.10
Longspur, Chestnut-collared, 95.21
  Lapland, 95.20
  McCown's, 95.19
Loon, Common, 6.14
  Pacific, 6.13
  Red-throated, 6.12
  Yellow-billed, 6.15

Macaw, Blue-and-yellow, 38.1
  Chestnut-fronted, 38.6
  Great Green, 38.4
  Military, 38.2
  Red-and-green, 38.5
  Scarlet, 38.3
Mallard, 12.3
Manakin, Blue-crowned, 68.17
  Golden-collared, 68.7
  Golden-headed, 68.11
  Green, 68.10
  Lance-tailed, 68.15
  Long-tailed, 68.14
  Orange-collared, 68.9
  Red-capped, 68.12
  White-collared, 68.8
  White-crowned, 68.16
  White-ruffed, 68.13
Mango, Black-throated, 45.19
  Green-breasted, 45.18
  Veraguas, 45.20
Martin, Brown-chested, 70.1
  Caribbean, 70.5
  Grey-breasted, 70.3
  Purple, 70.2
  Sinaloa, 70.4
  Southern, 70.6
Meadowlark, Eastern, 96.1
  Western, 96.2
Merganser, Common, 11.14
  Hooded, 11.13
  Red-breasted, 11.15
Merlin, 22.5
Mockingbird, Blue, 79.3
  Blue-and-white, 79.4
  Northern, 79.5
  Socorro, 79.7
  Tropical, 79.6
Monklet, Lanceolated, 53.5
Moorhen, Common, 7.11
Motmot, Blue-crowned, 52.7
  Blue-throated, 52.2
  Broad-billed, 52.4
  Keel-billed, 52.6
  Rufous, 52.5
  Russet-crowned, 52.3
  Tody, 52.1
  Turquoise-browed, 52.8
Mountain Gem, Green-breasted, 49.11

Green-throated, 49.10
  Grey-tailed, 49.7
  Purple-throated, 49.9
  White-bellied, 49.6
  White-throated, 49.8
Mourner, Rufous, 68.3
  Speckled, 68.4
Murre, Common, 6.1
Murrelet, Ancient, 6.5
  Craveri's, 6.4
  Xantus's, 6.3

Nighthawk, Antillean, 42.8
  Common, 42.7
  Lesser, 42.6
  Short-tailed, 42.5
Nightjar, Buff-collared, 43.7
  Dusky, 43.10
  Rufous, 43.9
  Spot-tailed, 43.8
  Tawny-collared, 43.5
  White-tailed, 43.11
  Yucatan, 43.6
Noddy, Black, 34.8
  Brown, 34.7
Nunbird, White-fronted, 53.4
Nunlet, Grey-cheeked, 53.6
Nutcracker, Clark's, 72.8
Nuthatch, Pygmy, 73.11
  Red-breasted, 73.9
  White-breasted, 73.10

Oilbird, 42.4
Oriole, Altamira, 97.13
  Audubon's, 97.5
  Baltimore, 97.15
  Bar-winged, 97.3
  Black-cowled, 97.1
  Black-vented, 97.2
  Bullock's, 97.14
  Hooded, 97.12
  Orange, 97.10
  Orange-crowned, 97.8
  Orchard, 97.16
  Scott's, 97.4
  Spot-breasted, 97.9
  Streak-backed, 97.11
  Yellow-backed, 97.7
  Yellow-tailed, 97.6
Oropendola, Black, 96.19
  Chestnut-headed, 96.17
  Crested, 96.16
  Montezuma, 96.18
Osprey, 14.6
Ovenbird, 85.18
Owl, Balsas Screech, 41.6
  Bare-shanked Screech, 41.5
  Barn, 40.1
  Barred, 40.8
  Black-and-white, 40.6
  Bridled Screech, 41.10
  Burrowing, 40.16
  Cape Pygmy, 41.14

Central American Pygmy, 41.18
  Colima Pygmy, 41.16
  Costa Rican Pygmy, 41.13
  Crested, 40.2
  Eastern Screech, 41.2
  Elf, 41.20
  Ferruginous Pygmy, 41.19
  Flammulated, 41.1
  Fulvous, 40.9
  Great Horned, 40.4
  Least Pygmy, 41.15
  Long-eared, 40.10
  Mottled, 40.5
  Mountain Pygmy, 41.11
  Northern Pygmy, 41.12
  Northern Saw-whet, 40.14
  PacificScreech, 41.7
  Short-eared, 40.13
  Spectacled, 40.3
  Spotted, 40.7
  Striped, 40.12
  Stygian, 40.11
  Tamaulipas Pygmy, 41.17
  Tropical Screech, 41.4
  Unspotted Saw-whet, 40.15
  Vermiculated Screech, 41.9
  Western Screech, 41.3
  Whiskered Screech, 41.8
Oystercatcher, American, 26.6
  Black, 26.7

Parakeet, Barred, 37.11
  Brown-throated, 37.8
  Crimson-fronted, 37.6
  Green, 37.1
  Olive-throated, 37.7
  Orange-chinned, 37.14
  Orange-fronted, 37.5
  Pacific, 37.2
  Painted, 37.10
  Red-throated, 37.3
  Socorro, 37.4
  Sulphur-winged, 37.9
Parrot, Blue-headed, 37.18
  Brown-hooded, 38.9
  Lilac-crowned, 38.14
  Maroon-fronted, 38.8
  Mealy, 38.17
  Red-crowned, 38.13
  Red-lored, 38.15
  Saffron-headed, 38.10
  Thick-billed, 38.7
  White-crowned, 37.17
  White-fronted, 38.11
  Yellow-crowned, 38.16
  Yellow-headed, 38.18
  Yellow-lored, 38.12
Parrotlet, Blue-fronted, 37.16
  Mexican, 37.12
  Red-fronted, 37.15
  Spectacled, 37.13
Partridge, Bearded Wood, 24.13
  Buffy-crowned Wood, 24.14

Long-tailed Wood, 24.12
Parula, Northern, 82.12
    Tropical, 82.13
Pauraque, 42.9
Pelican, American White, 8.1
    Brown, 8.2
Penguin, Galapagos, 6.16
Peppershrike, Rufous-browed,
    76.15
Petrel, Black, 1.9
    Black-capped, 2.13
    Black-winged, 2.9
    Bulwer's, 2.14
    Cape, 3.14
    Cook's, 2.8
    Dark-rumped, 2.3
    Herald, 2.5
    Juan Fernandez, 2.1
    Kermadec, 2.4
    Mottled, 2.10
    Murphy's, 2.6
    Stejneger's, 2.11
    Tahiti, 2.7
    White-necked, 2.2
    White-winged, 2.12
Pewee, Boreal, 63.1
    Dark, 63.2
    Eastern Wood, 63.4
    Greater, 63.5
    Ochraceous, 63.7
    Tropical, 63.6
    Western Wood, 63.3
Phainopepla, 76.13
Phalarope, Red, 28.12
    Red-necked, 28.11
    Wilson's, 28.10
Pheasant, Common, 23.14
Phoebe, Black, 67.1
    Eastern, 67.2
    Say's, 67.3
Piculet, Olivaceous, 58.1
Pigeon, Band-tailed, 35.7
    Dusky, 35.10
    Feral, 35.1
    Pale-vented, 35.3
    Plumbeous, 35.4
    Red-billed, 35.6
    Ruddy, 35.9
    Scaled, 35.2
    Short-billed, 35.8
    White-crowned, 35.5
Piha, Rufous, 68.2
Pintail, Northern, 12.8
    White-cheeked, 12.16
Pipit, American, 73.18
    Red-throated, 73.17
    Sprague's, 73.19
    Yellowish, 73.20
Piprites, Grey-headed, 68.6
Plover, American Golden, 26.4
    Collared, 27.8
    Grey, 26.3
    Mountain, 27.14
    Pacific Golden, 26.5

Piping, 27.12
    Semipalmated, 27.11
    Snowy, 27.9
    Wilson's, 27.10
Plumeleteer, Bronze-tailed, 49.4
    White-vented, 49.5
Poorwill, Common, 43.1
    Eared, 42.11
    Ocellated, 42.10
    Yucatan, 42.12
Potoo, Common, 42.3
    Great, 42.1
    Grey, 42.2
Puffbird, Barred, 52.19
    Black-breasted, 52.17
    Pied, 52.15
    White-necked, 52.16
    White-whiskered, 52.18
Puffin, Horned, 6.11
    Tufted, 6.10
Puffleg, Greenish, 49.16
Pyrrhuloxia, 90.6

Quail, Banded, 25.3
    Black-breasted Wood, 24.18
    Black-eared Wood, 24.16
    California, 25.7
    Elegant, 25.5
    Gambel's, 25.6
    Marbled Wood, 24.17
    Montezuma, 25.9
    Mountain, 25.8
    Ocellated, 25.10
    Scaled, 25.4
    Singing, 25.2
    Spotted Wood, 24.15
    Tacarcuna Wood, 24.19
    Tawny-faced, 25.1
Quetzal, Eared, 51.14
    Golden-headed, 51.16
    Resplendent, 51.15

Rail, Black, 24.4
    Clapper, 23.15
    Grey-necked Wood, 23.18
    King, 23.16
    Rufous-necked Wood, 23.19
    Spotted, 23.20
    Virginia, 23.17
    Yellow, 24.1
Raven, Common, 72.13
Redhead, 13.2
Redstart, American, 84.19
Roadrunner, Greater, 39.14
    Lesser, 39.13
Robin, American, 81.11
Ruff, 28.5

Sabrewing, Long-tailed, 45.13
    Rufous, 45.14
    Violet, 45.16
    Wedge-tailed, 45.12
Saltator, Black-headed, 90.3
    Buff-throated, 90.4

    Greyish, 90.1
    Streaked, 90.2
Sanderling, 29.2
Sandpiper, Baird's, 29.7
    Buff-breasted, 28.4
    Curlew, 29.11
    Least, 29.5
    Pectoral, 29.8
    Purple, 29.13
    Rock, 29.12
    Semipalmated, 29.3
    Sharp-tailed, 29.9
    Solitary, 27.3
    Spotted, 27.6
    Stilt, 29.14
    Upland, 27.7
    Western, 29.4
    White-rumped, 29.6
Sapaoya, Broad-billed, 68.5
Sapphire, Blue-headed, 47.6
Sapsucker, Red-breasted, 56.7
    Red-naped, 56.6
    Williamson's, 56.8
    Yellow-bellied, 56.5
Scaup, Greater, 13.5
    Lesser, 13.6
Schiffornis, Thrushlike, 68.1
Scoter, Black, 13.9
    Surf, 13.10
    White-winged, 13.11
Scythebill, Brown-billed, 57.17
    Red-billed, 57.16
Seedeater, Blue, 93.6
    Lesson's, 92.14
    Lined, 92.18
    Ruddy-breasted, 92.11
    Slate-blue, 93.7
    Slate-coloured, 92.16
    Variable, 92.15
    White-collared, 92.13
    Yellow-bellied, 92.12
Seedfinch, Nicaraguan, 92.19
    Thick-billed, 92.17
Sharpbill, 67.18
Sheartail, Mexican, 50.4
    Slender, 50.5
Shearwater, Audubon's, 3.13
    Black-vented, 3.9
    Buller's, 3.5
    Christmas, 3.8
    Cory's, 1.10
    Flesh-footed, 3.2
    Grea, 3.3
    Little, 3.11
    Manx, 3.10
    Pink-footed, 3.1
    Short-tailed, 3.7
    Sooty, 3.6
    Townsend's, 3.12
    Wedge-tailed, 3.4
Shoveler, Northern, 12.12
Shrike, Loggerhead, 76.16
    Northern, 76.18
Sicklebill, White-tipped, 45.10

Silky-flycatcher, Black-and-
  yellow, 76.14
  Grey, 76.11
  Long-tailed, 76.12
Sirystes, 67.8
Siskin, Black-capped, 98.12
  Black-headed, 98.14
  Pine, 98.10
  Yellow-bellied, 98.17
Skimmer, Black, 34.10
Skua, Chilean, 30.6
  Great, 30.4
  South Polar, 30.5
Snipe, Wilson's, 28.8
Snowcap, 47.18
Solitaire, Black-faced, 80.4
  Brown-backed, 80.2
  Slate-coloured, 80.3
  Townsend's, 80.1
  Varied, 80.5
Sora, 24.7
Spadebill, Golden-crowned,
  65.20
  Stub-tailed, 65.18
  White-throated, 65.19
Sparrow, Baird's, 93.16
  Black-chested, 94.10
  Black-chinned, 94.5
  Black-striped, 92.3
  Black-throated, 94.9
  Botteri's, 94.15
  Brewer's, 94.4
  Bridled, 94.11
  Cassin's, 94.14
  Chipping, 94.6
  Cinnamon-tailed, 94.16
  Clay-coloured, 94.7
  Field, 94.2
  Five-striped, 94.12
  Fox, 95.5
  Golden-crowned, 95.12
  Grasshopper, 93.19
  Green-backed, 92.2
  Harris's, 95.11
  House, 98.19
  Lark, 95.4
  Le Conte's, 93.17
  Lincoln's, 95.8
  Oaxaca, 94.19
  Olive, 92.1
  Orange-billed, 91.16
  Prevost's Ground, 91.18
  Rufous-collared, 95.9
  Rufous-crowned, 94.18
  Rufous-winged, 94.17
  Rusty, 94.20
  Rusty-crowned Ground, 91.19
  Sage, 94.8
  Savannah, 93.13
  Seaside, 93.14
  Sharp-tailed, 93.18
  Sierra Madre, 93.15
  Song, 95.6
  Stripe-headed, 94.13

Striped, 94.1
Swamp, 95.7
Vesper, 95.3
White-crowned, 95.13
White-eared Ground, 91.17
White-throated, 95.10
Worthen's, 94.3
Spinetail, Coiba, 59.5
  Pale-breasted, 59.3
  Red-faced, 59.4
  Rufous-breasted, 59.1
  Slaty, 59.2
Spoonbill, Roseate, 10.11
Starling, European, 76.19
Starthroat, Long-billed, 49.18
  Plain-cappped, 49.19
Stilt, Black-necked, 26.8
Stork, Wood, 10.13
Storm-petrel, Ashy, 4.8
  Band-rumped, 4.6
  Black, 4.9
  Fork-tailed, 4.3
  Guadalupe, 4.5
  Leach's, 4.4
  Least, 4.11
  Markham's, 4.10
  Wedge-rumped, 4.7
  White-faced, 4.12
  White-vented, 4.2
  Wilson's, 4.1
Streamcreeper, Sharp-tailed,
  58.15
Sunbittern, 7.14
Sungrebe, 7.13
Surfbird, 28.15
Swallow, Bank, 70.14
  Barn, 70.20
  Black-capped, 70.12
  Blue-and-white, 70.11
  Cave, 70.18
  Cliff, 70.19
  Mangrove, 70.8
  Northern Rough-winged, 70.16
  Ridgway's Rough-winged, 70.15
  Southern Rough-winged, 70.17
  Tree, 70.7
  Violet-green, 70.9
  White-thighed, 70.13
  White-winged, 70.10
Swamphen, Purple, 7.10
Swan, Trumpeter, 11.5
  Tundra, 11.4
Swift, Ashy-tailed, 44.12
  Band-rumped, 44.13
  Black, 44.1
  Chapman's, 44.10
  Chestnut-collared, 44.3
  Chimney, 44.8
  Costa Rican, 44.13
  Great Swallow-tailed,
  44.17
  Grey-rumped, 44.14
  Lesser Swallow-tailed,
  44.16

Short-tailed, 44.11
Spot-fronted, 44.4
Vaux's, 44.9
White-chinned, 44.2
White-collared, 44.6
White-fronted, 44.5
White-naped, 44.7
White-throated, 44.15

Tanager, Ashy-throated Bush,
  89.11
  Azure-rumped, 86.15
  Bay-headed, 86.10
  Black-and-yellow, 89.16
  Black-cheeked Ant, 88.11
  Black-throated Shrike, 88.2
  Blue-and-gold, 87.15
  Blue-grey, 87.17
  Cherrie's, 89.3
  Common Bush, 89.10
  Crimson-backed, 89.2
  Crimson-collared, 89.1
  Dusky-faced, 89.6
  Emerald, 86.12
  Flame-coloured, 88.17
  Flame-rumped, 89.4
  Golden-hooded, 86.17
  Green-naped, 86.18
  Grey-and-gold, 86.16
  Grey-headed, 89.5
  Hepatic, 88.13
  Lemon-spectacled, 89.8
  Olive, 89.7
  Palm, 87.18
  Passerini's, 89.3
  Pirre Bush, 89.12
  Plain-coloured, 86.20
  Red-crowned Ant, 88.9
  Red-headed, 88.19
  Red-throated Ant, 88.10
  Rose-throated, 88.12
  Rosy Thrush, 89.17
  Rufous-winged, 86.11
  Scarlet, 88.15
  Scarlet-browed, 88.5
  Scarlet-rumped, 89.3
  Silver-throated, 86.13
  Sooty-capped Bush, 89.9
  Spangle-cheeked, 86.19
  Speckled, 86.14
  Stripe-headed, 88.1
  Sulphur-rumped, 88.4
  Summer, 88.14
  Swallow, 87.19
  Tacarcuna Bush, 89.13
  Tawny-crested, 88.7
  Western, 88.18
  White-lined, 88.8
  White-shouldered, 88.6
  White-throated Shrike, 88.3
  White-winged, 88.16
  Yellow-backed, 89.15
  Yellow-throated Bush, 89.14
  Yellow-winged, 87.16
334

Tapaculo, Nariño, 59.19
  Silvery-fronted, 59.18
  Tacarcuna, 59.17
Tattler, Wandering, 27.5
Teal, Blue-winged, 12.9
  Cinnamon, 12.11
  Green-winged, 12.2
Tern, White, 34.9
  Arctic, 33.7
  Black, 34.5
  Bridled, 34.2
  Caspian, 33.1
  Common, 33.6
  Elegant, 33.3
  Forster's, 33.8
  Gull-billed, 34.1
  Inca, 34.6
  Large-billed, 34.4
  Least, 33.9
  Roseate, 33.5
  Royal, 33.2
  Sandwich, 33.4
  Sooty, 34.3
  Yellow-billed, 33.10
Thick-knee, Double-striped,
  26.1
Thorntail, Green, 46.8
Thrasher, Bendire's, 79.13
  Brown, 79.9
  California, 79.16
  Cozumel, 79.11
  Crissal, 79.17
  Curve-billed, 79.14
  Grey, 79.12
  Le Conte's, 79.18
  Long-billed, 79.10
  Ocellated, 79.15
  Sage, 79.8
Thrush, Aztec, 81.16
  Black, 81.13
  Black-billed Nightingale, 80.9
  Black-headed Nightingale,
  80.10
  Clay-coloured, 81.6
  Grayson's, 81.10
  Grey-cheeked, 80.14
  Hermit, 80.16
  Mountain, 81.5
  Orange-billed Nightingale,
  80.6
  Pale-vented, 81.7
  Ruddy-capped Nightingale,
  80.8
  Rufous-backed, 81.9
  Rufous-collared, 81.12
  Russet Nightingale, 80.7
  Slaty-backed Nightingale,
  80.11
  Sooty, 81.14
  Spotted Nightingale, 80.12
  Swainson's, 80.15
  Varied, 81.15
  White-throated, 81.8
  Wood, 80.17

Tinamou, Choco, 25.18
  Great, 25.15
  Highland, 25.16
  Little, 25.17
  Slaty-breasted, 25.20
  Thicket, 25.19
Titmouse, Black-crested, 73.4
  Bridled, 73.3
  Juniper, 73.5
  Oak, 73.5
  Plain, 73.5
Tityra, Black-crowned, 69.13
  Masked, 69.12
Topaz, Ruby, 46.1
Toucan, Chestnut-mandibled,
  53.12
  Chocó, 53.13
  Keel-billed, 53.11
Toucanet, Emerald, 53.7
  Yellow-eared, 53.8
Towhee, Abert's, 92.7
  California, 92.8
  Canyon, 92.9
  Collared, 92.5
  Green-tailed, 92.4
  Rufous-sided, 92.6
  White-throated, 92.10
Treehunter, Streak-breasted,
  58.9
Treerunner, Beautiful, 58.10
  Ruddy, 58.11
Trogon, Baird's, 51.11
  Black-headed, 51.3
  Black-tailed, 51.7
  Black-throated, 51.1
  Citreoline, 51.4
  Collared, 51.10
  Elegant, 51.9
  Lattice-tailed, 51.13
  Mountain, 51.8
  Orange-bellied, 51.6
  Slaty-tailed, 51.12
  Violaceous, 51.5
  White-tailed, 51.2
Tropicbird, Red-billed, 5.2
  Red-tailed, 5.3
  White-tailed, 5.1
Tuftedcheek, Buffy, 58.8
Turkey, Ocellated, 23.12
  Wild, 23.11
Turnstone, Black, 28.14
  Ruddy, 28.13
Twistwing, Brownish, 67.15
Tyrannulet, Brown-capped, 64.5
  Mouse-coloured, 64.8
  Northern Beardless, 64.6
  Paltry, 64.3
  Rufous-browed, 64.12
  Sooty-headed, 64.2
  Southern Beardless, 64.7
  Torrent, 67.17
  White-fronted, 64.1
  Yellow, 64.10
  Yellow-bellied, 64.4

Yellow-crowned, 64.9
  Yellow-green, 64.11
Tyrant, Black-capped Pygmy,
  65.10
  Bronze-olive Pygmy, 65.11
  Cattle, 62.18
  Long-tailed, 67.12
  Pale-eyed Pygmy, 65.9
  Pied water, 67.16
  Scale-crested Pygmy, 65.8

Umbrellabird, Bare-necked,
  69.18

Veery, 80.13
Verdin, 73.6
Violet-ear, Brown, 49.2
  Green, 49.3
Vireo, Bell's, 78.5
  Black-capped, 78.6
  Blue-headed, 78.9
  Black-whiskered, 78.21
  Brown-capped, 78.17
  Cassin's, 78.10
  Chestnut-sided Shrike, 78.18
  Cozumel, 78.4
  Dwarf, 78.7
  Golden, 78.15
  Green Shrike, 78.19
  Grey, 78.8
  Hutton's, 78.14
  Mangrove, 78.3
  Philadelphia, 78.18
  Plumbeous, 78.11
  Red-eyed, 78.20
  Slaty, 78.1
  Warbling, 78.16
  White-eyed, 78.2
  Yellow-browed Shrike, 78.20
  Yellow-green, 78.19
  Yellow-throated, 78.12
  Yellow-winged, 78.13
  Yucatan, 78.22
Vulture, Black, 14.1
  King, 14.4
  Lesser Yellow-headed, 14.3
  Turkey, 14.2

Wagtail, Black-backed, 73.16
  White, 73.14
  Yellow, 73.15
Warbler, Arctic, 77.2
  Bay-breasted, 83.15
  Black-and-white, 83.17
  Black-cheeked, 85.14
  Black-throated blue, 83.20
  Black-throated green, 83.6
  Black-throated grey, 83.18
  Blackburnian, 83.8
  Blackpoll, 83.16
  Blue-winged, 82.9
  Buff-rumped, 85.16
  Canada, 84.14
  Cape May, 82.17

Cerulean, 83.19
Chestnut-capped, 85.11
Chestnut-sided, 83.2
Colima, 82.5
Connecticut, 84.1
Crescent-chested, 82.11
Dusky, 77.1
Fan-tailed, 85.8
Flame-throated, 82.14
Golden-browed, 85.12
Golden-cheeked, 83.10
Golden-crowned, 85.9
Golden-winged, 82.10
Grace's, 83.11
Hermit, 83.5
Hooded, 84.15
Kentucky, 84.4
Kirtland's, 83.12
Lucy's, 82.7
Macgillivray's, 84.3
Magnolia, 83.4
Mourning, 84.2
Nashville, 82.8
Olive, 85.1
Orange-crowned, 82.4
Palm, 83.13
Pine, 83.14
Pink-headed, 85.4
Pirre, 85.13
Prairie, 83.1
Prothonotary, 82.15
Red, 85.3
Red-faced, 85.2
Rufous-capped, 85.10
Swainson's, 82.2
Tennessee, 82.3
Three-striped, 85.15
Townsend's, 83.7
Virginia's, 82.6
Wilson's, 84.13
Worm-eating, 82.1
Yellow, 82.16
Yellow-rumped, 83.3
Yellow-throated, 83.9
Waterthrush, Louisiana, 85.20
    Northern, 85.19
Waxwing, Cedar, 76.10
Wheatear, Northern, 81.1
Whimbrel, 26.10
Whip-poor-will, 43.2
    Stephen's, 43.3
Whitestart, Collared, 84.16
    Painted, 84.18
    Slate-throated, 84.17
Wigeon, American, 12.15
    Eurasian, 12.14
Willet, 27.4
Woodcock, American, 28.9
Woodcreeper, Barred, 57.6
    Black-banded, 57.7
    Black-striped, 57.12
    Cocoa, 57.9
    Ivory-billed, 57.10
    Long-tailed, 57.4

Olivaceous, 58.6
Plain-brown, 57.2
Ruddy, 57.3
Ruddy, 58.7
Spot-crowned, 57.15
Spotted, 57.11
Straight-billed, 57.8
Streak-headed, 57.14
Strong-billed, 57.5
Tawny-winged, 57.1
Wedge-billed, 58.5
White-striped, 57.13
Woodnymph, Crowned, 47.2
    Green-crowned, 47.2
    Mexican, 47.1
    Violet-crowned, 47.2
Woodpecker, Acorn, 54.2
    Arizona, 55.6
    Black-cheeked, 54.8
    Bronze-winged, 55.7
    Chestnut-coloured, 56.10
    Cinnamon, 56.9
    Crimson-bellied, 53.15
    Crimson-crested, 53.16
    Downy, 55.4
    Gila, 54.7
    Golden-cheeked, 54.9
    Golden-fronted, 54.12
    Golden-green, 55.12
    Golden-naped, 54.3
    Golden-olive, 55.8
    Grey-breasted, 54.10
    Grey-crowned, 55.9
    Hairy, 55.3
    Hoffmann's, 54.11
    Imperial, 53.17
    Ladder-backed, 55.1
    Lewis's, 54.1
    Lineated, 56.11
    Nuttall's, 55.2
    Pale-billed, 53.14
    Pileated, 56.12
    Red-bellied, 54.6
    Red-crowned, 54.13
    Red-headed, 54.4
    Red-rumped, 56.4
    Rufous-winged, 55.10
    Smoky-brown, 56.3
    Spot-breasted, 55.13
    Strickland's, 55.5
    Stripe-cheeked, 55.11
    Yucatan, 54.5
Woodstar, Magenta-throated, 50.2
    Purple-throated, 50.3
    Sparkling-tailed, 50.1
Wren, Band-backed, 76.4
    Banded, 74.6
    Bay, 74.12
    Bewick's, 75.2
    Black-bellied, 74.11
    Black-throated, 74.10
    Boucard's, 76.7
    Buff-breasted, 74.16

Cactus, 76.9
Canyon, 74.17
Carolina, 74.7
Clarion, 75.6
Cozumel, 75.5
Giant, 76.2
Grey-barred, 76.5
Grey-breasted Wood, 75.14
Happy, 74.3
House, 75.3
Marsh, 75.10
Nava's, 74.18
Northern Nightingale, 75.15
Ochraceus, 75.4
Plain, 74.8
Riverside, 74.13
Rock, 75.18
Rufous-and-white, 74.4
Rufous-breasted, 74.15
Rufous-browed, 75.9
Rufous-naped, 76.3
Sedge, 75.11
Sinaloa, 74.5
Slender-billed, 74.19
Socorro, 75.7
Song, 75.17
Sooty-headed, 74.9
Southern Nightingale, 75.16
Spot-breasted, 74.2
Spotted, 76.6
Stripe-breasted, 74.1
Stripe-throated, 74.14
Timberline, 75.12
White-bellied, 75.1
White-breasted Wood, 75.13
White-headed, 76.1
Winter, 75.8
Yucatan, 76.8
Wrenthrush, 85.17
Wrentit, 73.8

Xenops, Plain, 58.2
    Streaked, 58.3

Yellowfinch, Grassland, 93.2
Yellowlegs, Greater, 27.1
    Lesser, 27.2
Yellowthroat, Altamira, 84.9
    Belding's, 84.10
    Black-polled, 84.12
    Common, 84.7
    Grey-crowned, 84.5
    Hooded, 84.11
    Masked, 84.6
    Olive-crowned, 84.8